THE
TROUBLES

THE TROUBLES

A JAUNDICED GLANCE BACK AT THE MOVEMENT OF THE SIXTIES

by
JOSEPH
CONLIN

FRANKLIN
WATTS

*New York • London
Toronto • Sydney*

1982

FOR D.M.C.

Library of Congress Cataloging in Publication Data

Conlin, Joseph Robert.
The troubles, a jaundiced glance back
at the movement of the sixties.

Bibliography: p.
Includes index.

1. Radicalism—United States. 2. Right and
left (Political science) 3. United States—
Social conditions—1960-   I. Title.
HN90.R3C66   303.4'84   81-22001
ISBN 0-531-09856-7   AACR2

CONTENTS

THE
TROUBLES

PREFACE

This book had its beginnings about ten years ago when I thought I might write a history of the American left in the twentieth century. I began to research that project, since abandoned without perceptibly disconsoling the American Historical Association, at both ends of the period. The idea was to sketch out unifying themes at the outset.

But I soon found myself preoccupied with the Movement of the 1960s, then lately deceased, and with rather more to say on the subject than would gracefully fit into the final chapter of a book of reasonable size. Moreover, rather than discovering the unifying themes, I realized that the various organizations of the New Left, not to mention the antiorganizational Counterculture, did not belong in a book that was also about the Socialist and Communist parties and the interests and attitudes they represented. That is, they did not all belong together unless I was also going to include some of my mother's favorite recipes, a little physics, and foldout street plans of the major towns of Lombardy. Old Left and New Left had scarcely more in common.

I was not, of course, quite the first to observe a break in the history of American dissent. The New Left was self-consciously new from the day in 1960 that sociologist C. Wright Mills called for its creation, in "A Letter to the New Left." Movement activists never doubted that they were novel—unique in history!—and a good many thoughtful writers have agreed at least in part. Kirkpatrick Sale, the author of an excellent narrative history of SDS (Students for a Democratic Society) published about the time I was fiddling with my own research, played this theme when he wrote that the New Left was "the first really *homegrown* left in America, taking its impulses not from European ideologies and practices (at least not until the end), but from dissatisfactions and distortions in the American experience."

My distinction is somewhat different. Homegrown? Yes. But, as I see it, the New Left was not at all "new" as human

high jinks go, or, by my definition, very "left." Rather than
something in which, implicitly, would-be American radicals
ought to exult, like the inhabitants of the county that produces
the biggest pumpkins, the lesson of the sixties for such people
would seem to be that they should give up backyard ideological gardening and buy their political provisions somewhere
else, just as they buy their remarkable sound systems and the
paprika they sprinkle on fund-raising party hors d'oeuvres.
For, among other things, it seems to me that it was the
Movement of the sixties, and particularly the response of the
American intelligentsia to it, that killed what there was of a
radical political tradition in this country, killed it cold dead as
avowed enemies of radicalism were never quite able to do.

But I leave lessons for readers to take for themselves. A
few paragraphs below I shall formally abjure any contemporary purposes in writing this book. On the other hand, there
is no sense denying that I was moved to write it because of
contemporary experiences. Increasingly since about 1980, in
conversation with young people—people born in the sixties—
one hears wistful characterizations of the era of the New Left
and Counterculture as a time of welling humanism, selfless
social conscience, and political idealism practiced by a remarkable generation of altruistic crusaders. It would seem that in
our fad-sensitive society, the sixties are "coming back into
style."

Nor is it just the young people. In the June 1981 issue of
Esquire magazine, the liberal-minded editor Harry Stein
surveyed the plutocratic domestic policy and the militaristic
foreign policy of the Ronald Reagan administration and found
them wanting. What was the alternative? Stein called for the
American people to have a heart, to be sensitive and unselfish,
to brush up their moral sense, to cultivate a feeling of warmth
toward their fellows. At a commencement address the same
month, cartoonist Garry Trudeau admonished graduates
along the same line: we must not be so cynical. This, as we shall
see, was a very sixtyish way of approaching social problems,

and, more depressing than listening to an old Ted Lewis record on a rainy Saturday, some badly discredited gurus of the student movement of the sixties had the temerity in November 1981 to appear as main speakers at a conference to launch the student movement of the eighties in Davis, California.

Of course, it is everyone's right in the marketplace of ideas, as we know, to trade in these notions, as it is the right in that other marketplace for documentary film-makers and aging Movement veterans to trade in nostalgia. But I thought it might be well to announce the sale of a different merchandise, to say that the Movement was not humanistic, not selfless, not social, radical, or political. Indeed, to say that as historical forces go, it was not even very important.

This would seem an unlikely foreword to a book which the author hopes will be read beyond this early page. Let me clarify this point by saying that the Movement, the New Left and the Counterculture were not important for what their adherents said and did—not a radical social movement—but only for what their character and especially the widespread attention given to them tell us about the larger society. The Movement portended to be the cure for a social sickness. It seems rather to have been a virulent symptom of that illness and the attention lavished on it a confirmation of the diagnosis. Such is one theme of this book and, if I may continue briefly with the medical metaphor, I would add that the disease has not been cured simply because the troubles ended in the spring of 1970. It would seem that the affliction, like consumption or syphilis or any number of skin disorders, has merely gone into remission. If we examined the blood of the 1970s through a glass, we should observe squirming about in it the same microbes that used to cause such wrenching havoc.

But I am drifting into the future tense and, as a longtime admirer of John Dryden's lines, do not much like it there:

Sure there is none but fears a future state;
And when the most obdurate swear they do not
Their trembling hearts belie their boasting tongues.

The final chapters of this book touch on the 1970s—but not on the future. As promised above, this is no jeremiad but a book of history, albeit highly unacademic history, a series of reflections rather than a narrative, an attempt to put the Movement of the sixties into historical context. It has been researched according to unexceptional historians' methodology and pretends to no value other than that which the individual reader places on knowing one writer's view of the past. In fact, several years before I was motivated to revive this project, I set it aside because I felt too close in time and person to the subject to treat it as detachedly as, perhaps old-fashioned, I think history ought to be written.

Even after the "laid-back" 1970s, this has required some effort. The first anthologies of New Left literature I picked up were not my introduction to the Movement. Having been born in 1940, I came into my majority and first serious political interests at just about the time that the New Left was making its debut. As a college student and especially as a graduate student I dwelled in the homeland of the New Left. I sympathized with many of the Movement's avowed objects until about 1968 when I realized that, to most of my comrades, there were no *objects*. I marched in a number of civil rights and antiwar demonstrations and remain committed to the principles these movements seemed to represent. I delivered a speech now and then, participated in several teach-ins, and argued with friends and acquaintances late into many nights along the lines of "What Is to Be Done?" and "What's the Matter with Kansas?"

But I was never really a part of it. Even before I became a critic of the New Left, successively friendly and hostile (the Movement entertained no friendly critics), and eventually, detecting a certain shrillness in my voice, when I retired to a quiet corner of the room to be a silent observer, fancying myself Henry James, I was never able to "get into it." My social background was just different enough from that of most Movement militants to be obvious to both parties and to cause me to reflect before abandoning myself to songs about happy trails and vows of eternal brotherhood.

A trivial experience of the early sixties occurs to me. A comrade asked, a little timorously (it was such a delicate subject, like bad breath), why I customarily dressed in neckties and more-or-less pressed shirts instead of blue denim, collar to cuffs. I wish I had at that time heard historian Eugene Genovese's explanation some years later that this habit incontrovertibly established one's working-class origins, like simonizing the car on Sunday afternoon, that would have been true enough. Instead, I replied that by appearing indistinguishable from the enemy in the land I was able to sit unnoticed in their taverns and palestras and overhear what "they" were saying. (Which was also true in a way: at the peak of excitement I preferred to take my leisure at places where petitions were not circulated.) This proved to be a satisfactory response and, indeed, I was briefly regarded among the "radicals" of my acquaintance as a sort of ex officio intelligence officer, Our Man in Havana.

But mostly I maintained a little distance because I am not now nor have I ever been much of a joiner or (in both the theological and behavioral senses of the word) an enthusiast. When I was still accepted as a radical and not yet branded a reactionary, fascist, racist, sexist, etc., I always preferred to run the mimeographs and mop the floors or to do other routine tasks as my contributions to the cause ("shitwork" the New Left ladies came to call it) rather than announcing millennia in which I did not place full faith.

As Robert Frost tells us, a certain reserve in these matters whilst young helps one to avoid falling for the middle-age enthusiasms of the right wing such as, now and then, I take exquisite and unabashedly vindictive pleasure to see old Movement cronies embracing. But let that conclude the Confiteor. Unlike in almost every book about the 1960s I have read, the first person pronoun is absent in the text and I hope I have minimized unsignalled personal intrusions too. Forewarned of the nature of my involvement in the troubles, the reader can compensate for any lapses, just as he or she takes note of advice that the brakes on a borrowed car pull to the left. Or right. Or simply grab from time to time.

Some definitions of terms I have already used several times: by *the Movement* I mean the massive, shapeless protest and agitation of the 1960s, including the avowedly political Berkeley Free Speech Movement of 1964, Students for a Democratic Society, Black Power and antiwar movements, and so on (as I define *New Left*), and the so-called life-style rebellion of the flower children, hippies, and communalists (the *Counterculture*). These are common usages and should cause no problems.

Not so, however, with some other words that recur in this book because—one of the points I want to make—their meaning was changed during the sixties. Except when I refer to Movement militants as "radicals" or "leftists" sarcastically, I am observing the Old Style and beg readers' indulgence for the sake of communication.

So, by *left* I mean the political inclination in Western civilization which derives from the French revolutionary tradition as modified by nineteenth-century socialist thinkers, that is, the philosophy that envisions a freer and more equitable society through the elimination of social privilege and class power in property and its replacement with institutions guaranteeing economic justice. Property and class—not race, ethnic identification, sex, and sexual preference—remain in my age-bedimmed eyes the significant social categories, and by *radical,* therefore, when I use the word in a literal sense, I mean a person or a point of view moiling in the soil around these roots. By *political* I mean that having to do with power and the process by which changes are effected or warded off.

And finally to the period treated here, the sixties. Giving decades personalities can be a tiresome pedantry, but the history of the Movement, the troubles, coincides pretty closely with the years 1960–1970. If—as seems obvious—the distinguishing characteristics of the phenomenon were tumult, disturbance, and protest on a mass scale, the Movement was born in May 1960 when several thousand young people, mostly university students, demonstrated against the House Committee on Un-American Activities in San Francisco, and was ended, so very suddenly, in May 1970 when the Ohio National Guard opened fire on protesting students at Kent State University, killing four.

It is true that southern Negroes had been massively protesting racial segregation since the Montgomery Bus Boycott of 1955–1956, and I attend to them here. It is also true that the Mississippi Highway Patrol shot at a dormitory and killed two students at black Jackson State College on May 15, 1970, less than two weeks after the Kent State incident. However, black people were not a part of American society that "counted" in the 1950s as were the largely white, young, and middle-class protesters at the San Francisco City Hall. Rather more striking, despite momentous changes in the status of American Negroes during the 1960s (like turning into "blacks"), they still did not "count" quite the same in 1970. Kent State was a national tragedy, the center of national press and television coverage for months and the subject of several exhaustive investigations, official and private. The attack at Jackson State, although a less spontaneous and more cynical act than the Ohio incident, was practically ignored at the time and, immediately, almost completely forgotten.

Kent State was *the end of it,* the end of them, the troubles. People calling themselves Weathermen would bomb buildings after May 1970 (although that nihilistic group blew most of its frontliners to smithereens in an accidental explosion in Greenwich Village in March). It would take a few years before the last of the Movement mugwumps realized that no one was listening to them anymore. Some of the balmiest (and barmiest) books about the New Left bear post-1970 copyrights and subtitles like "Essays for the Future." Women's liberation, still in the morning papers as this page is written, albeit increasingly an occasion of popular boredom, is essentially a vestige of the New Left, deriving from it and never able to transcend its spirit. And, as I continue, it is impossible not to notice the antidraft grumblings among students, a phenomenon that takes one back, and the nostalgia I mention above, and to note that we had our first real race riot in a decade and a half in Miami in May of 1980, and that the desexed "Weather Underground" was back in the headlines in the fall of 1981. Perhaps the topic of this book will have, to haul out a catchphrase of the sixties, some "relevance."

But the troubles, a catchphrase I have borrowed from the Irish who apply it to their period of ugly and likewise not completely comprehensible civil conflict of the early 1920s, really ended during one night's sleep in the spring of 1970. When the nation woke up after the paroxysmic campus demonstrations that followed President Richard M. Nixon's invasion of Cambodia—Kent State was one of 450—the Movement was gone. Everything that followed was a postmortem spasm, kicking the bucket.

I believe I have come close to exhausting the *essential* sources for this study. But the mass of "material" in this verbose age is so awesome that significant oversights are highly likely. There were, for instance, several hundred "underground newspapers" with Movement connections published during the decade. I cannot pretend even to have scanned most of them, to know the names of many. I closed off my research and began writing when the material became so repetitious as to defy the endurance of even a habitually undiscriminating reader. The Movement was frequently clever but rarely profound. One can reread slogans only so often. I remain apprehensive that I have missed something important in thus breaking off research, but mere contemplation of the task of continuing made interruption seem worth the risk.

I think I have also been thorough in reading the analyses of the phenomenon (again, sometimes to my chagrin). Being but recently defunct when I started my work, the Movement was still inspiring gritty partisan polemics (the "Essays for the Future" and so on). I found my progress stalled repeatedly by the appearance of the hundreds of books and essays on the subject. Annoyance sometimes gave way to envy when I discovered ideas still raw fiber in my own mind finely spun and woven in the writings of others. It is, I expect, one of the nuisances with which a would-be historian of the recent past must learn to live and a daily frustration for the journalist.

So, older readers may find herein propositions that remind them of something they read long ago. Having been trained as an academic with a commitment to footnotes (here omitted with near hysterical pleasure), and a morbid fear of committing plagiarism in thought, word, or deed, I have credited all borrowings of which I am conscious. The others are not thefts, strictly speaking, but things I absentmindedly put into my pocket as at some long-ago party at an address I have forgotten. I hope their owners are indulgent. They can claim the goods—I hope I lifted only goods—with my apologies.

A true list of personal acknowledgments would have to include every person with whom I have discussed "affairs" over the past twenty years. There was scarcely an encounter from which I did not learn something. Such a list being untenable, I must nevertheless mention my friend, colleague, comrade, and sometimes critic of my cynicism, Thomas Wagstaff. The most consistently perceptive social critic of my acquaintance, bar none with ready access to print or television, he will be kind enough to accept my compliments and appreciation as compensation for what will exasperate or amuse him in the pages that follow. Mmes. Jean Harvey, Nancy Riley, and Cynthia Davis prepared the typescript. Elizabeth Hock, Senior Editor at Franklin Watts, Inc., was kind enough to encourage me to write this book and to cajole, pull, and push me through bad moments during the doing. Her editorial ministrations made it a better book.

J. R. C.

CHAPTER
ONE

FLASHBACKS

May 1980. Jerry Rubin, forty-one years old, is on tour: $1,000 plus expenses from New York for an hour lecture and another hour fielding questions from the audience. The old hell-raiser looks pretty good. The beard is neatly trimmed—a broker's, not a barbarian's. Indeed, within three months Jerry will take a job as a securities analyst investigating "companies of the future" for the Wall Street firm of John Muir and Company.

Jerry smiles pleasantly. He has kind eyes. A little trimmer around the middle and he could be the fellow in the television commercial who lifts a glass of beer on a beach and says languidly, "Here's to good friends."

Jerry Rubin has been on the university lecture circuit for a couple of years now. He has his entrance down pat: He glides onstage as smoothly as a lounge comic on fresh Friday wax, takes the microphone off the stand with a fumble, and nods toward the college student who has just introduced him. "Let's give *her* a big hand. *Mindy's* been learning that intro all day." Rubin tucks the microphone under his arm and claps.

His lecture is a breathless, pauseless reminiscence of his career in the 1960s as a Berkeley Free Speecher, antiwar activist, and leader of the Yippies. His topic is himself, and he does not shortsell his place in history. Rubin saw the tumultuous sixties coming, he says. He knew the seventies would be quiet, self-centered. And he tells his audience what they can expect of the eighties. The new decade will synthesize the best of what went before. The title of his talk is "Sixties Activism Plus Seventies Awareness." Every decade, in Jerry Rubin's dialectic, we are getting better and better.

But the slick entrance is deceptive. Rubin is a poor public speaker. His talk is confused, formless. He has changed a lot of his opinion since his heyday in the sixties, but he still believes in spontaneity. The lecture is a mishmash of chronology and sentiments. He describes "my first protest." (A star is born.)

But was it as an elementary schooler when the teacher told him to crouch under the desk for an A-bomb drill or when he was a cub reporter for the *Cincinnati Post and Times-Star*? Both episodes seem to have happened at about the same time. This auditorium is no place for someone who is "into" chronology.

Then he takes up his appearances in 1967 and 1969 before the House Committee on Un-American Activities. This is important. If Jerry inflates his role in the evolution of the American republic, he really was the man who, more than any other, slew that old dragon HUAC. For thirty years the committee obsessed, terrorized, and confounded the American Left, and liberals even more For a generation (Jerry Rubin's whole lifetime in 1967), radicals, liberals, and libertarians battled the committee, exposing its profanation of American principles and asking little more of the American people than a sense of decency. But HUAC lived on, thrived on the opposition like a movie dragon attacked by first-reel extras—until Jerry Rubin mocked its powers to intimidate by answering subpoenas in fancy dress. He came as a continental soldier, as Santa Claus, and in 1969 he came as Che Guevara with warpaint and a toy gun. The dragon that devoured appeals to decency like so many peasants could not take a joke. After Jerry Rubin, HUAC simply faded away.

It is worth hearing about that. HUAC, like Jerry Rubin's Movement, was a classic example of how Americans refuse to grapple with real political issues and, instead, divert themselves with symbols and shrieks. But if Jerry Rubin knew how to put the dagger to HUAC back in 1969, he did not know why it was worth doing. To Jerry Rubin in that half-filled college auditorium in 1980 the story is just another story, another grade-school bomb drill and his Sunday supplement–style account of a soldier who left his legs in Vietnam. The digressions are dizzying, the juxtapositions absurd. Suddenly Jerry is saying that all the United States needs to do to free the hostages in Iran ("the spies"—is that the way they talk on Wall Street at lunchtime?) is to list our national crimes on presidential stationery and say, "We apologize." It is all still "simple" for Jerry Rubin—he uses the word—all very much a matter of morality and witness.

He quotes a newspaper columnist who has written on "the impotence of the United States." Much approved by the audience, he explains that the key to understanding American imperialism is sexuality (on which he and his wife are writing a book). Americans think in terms of erections. There's the problem. "You don't need an erection to have fun in bed (general applause), but that's the title of another talk I give."

Rubin repeats himself, "I give another talk called 'You don't need an erection to have fun in bed.'" Is he fishing for another $1,000 date? Is this part of the activism or the awareness? Or is Jerry just not getting erections as often as he once did and spinning a cosmology out of this astonishing self-discovery? It would not be the first time Jerry Rubin and his generation found the center of the universe so close to their own navels. It would not be the first time Jerry Rubin and his generation failed to appreciate the objective reality of human catabolism until they experienced it personally, thence interpreting same as something like the discover of fire.

Back and forth he lurches, muddled recollections studded with quips. Rubin is "playing his audience," a technique he and his old pal, Abbie Hoffman like to talk about in their books. When he mentions that on the eve of his first Yippie prank "I was afraid people would think I was an asshole," and the audience roars at the word, he does five minutes on "assholes." We have been unjust to the rectum, he concludes because, "when you think of it, when you think of it, the asshole is beautiful, really beautiful." The audience thinks about it, solemnly and silently. It is not easy. They have been rolling in the aisles for five minutes as Rubin selects "asshole" as his every fifth word.

This would be the awareness part of the message.

This would be putting into practice the principles of oratory as enunciated by Abbott Hoffman of Worcester,

Massachusetts. "My speaking style was suited to the mood," Abbie wrote in *Steal This Book*. "Fire leaps from the tongue. Organizing tips. Some factual stuff on the war.... What's generally referred to in popular press as 'rhetoric.' I'd juice it up with cuss words, slogans, timely jokes...."

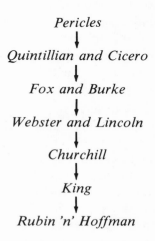

Pericles
↓
Quintillian and Cicero
↓
Fox and Burke
↓
Webster and Lincoln
↓
Churchill
↓
King
↓
Rubin 'n' Hoffman

Jerry Rubin has to make a living too. And the college lecture circuit is one of the few jobs there is for a man who spent the years he should have been learning a craft on the speaker's platform. He is trying to be a comedian: now Mort Sahl, now Lenny Bruce, even Jack E. Leonard ("I'm going to offend everyone here tonight"), now Abbie Hoffman.

But he is not very good at it! Small wonder he took a job on Wall Street. He has perfected his entrance and that is all. A boyish grin does not qualify as charm when the man is middle aged. The jokes are witless. His timing is atrocious. He takes himself too seriously to be funny and his preachments are as banal as a disc jockey's. No one is offended. A good many are bored, looking around, trying to remember why they came.

Is it—as much of the press will handle the Jerry Rubin of 1980—the familiar spectacle of the giant who has outlived his time? Is it Joe Louis up there, the shambles of a miracle reduced to wrestling in sequins in order to pay his income tax bill?

Or was Jerry Rubin always that way? Always muddled, ineffective, "not very good at it"? Even when in the late sixties he was one of the maximum leaders of the "Movement" which, everyone agreed, was profoundly changing America? When hundreds of thousands, maybe millions of young people looked to him for guidance? When the United States government found it advisable to single him out above most others for persecution and harassment? Could it be that this rather ineffectual . . . schlemiel . . . is precisely what the New Left and the Counterculture of the 1960s—the Movement—were always about?

It is necessary to go back twenty years to the beginning of it all when, if not quite young and gay, the United States was a little younger. The man up on the stage boasting to university students that he never reads more than thirty pages of any book was just twenty-one then and, as a graduate student in sociology, presumably more studious.

SPRING 1960

A very special spring. Change really was in the air. It was not just the new decade. It was also a presidential election year, an event Americans persist in celebrating as a jubilee. The incumbent, Dwight D. Eisenhower, a man recognized in his own time as a cultural symbol as well as head of state, had served two terms and would not succeed himself.

Liberals and intellectuals were particularly sensitive to the sense of passage from one era to another. Unlike the majority, they had never liked Ike and they loathed the smug, complacent 1950s over which the general presided like a Republican Queen Victoria. They were delighted to be starting anew as they were convinced they were doing. Writing in 1959 in anticipation of the event, the historian of presidents, Arthur M. Schlesinger, Jr., sensed the approach of "a moment." He wrote, "The beginning of a new political epoch is like the breaking of a dam. Problems which have collected in the years of indifference, values which have suffered neglect, energies which have been denied employment—all suddenly tumble as in a hopeless, swirling flood into an arid plain."

As a resident of the Commonwealth of Massachusetts, Schlesinger already had a pretty good idea as to who would personify the new decade as Ike had the old. By the end of May 1960, other liberals and intellectuals did too. He was the junior senator from the Bay State, John Fitzgerald Kennedy.

Sophisticated, self-assured, intellectual, said to be glamorous so often it came true, Kennedy associated himself with newness. He announced his candidacy for the presidency to coincide with the new year. (Actually, he declared on January 2, a Saturday; the scores from the bowl games would be digested so he got the Sunday newspapers to himself.) He turned anxieties over his youth (forty-three in May) to his advantage. When he won the Democratic nomination in July, he declared that "the old world is changing; the old era is dying; the old ways will not do" and announced that the United States stood "on the edge of a new frontier—the frontier of the 1960s—a frontier of unknown opportunities and perils—a frontier of unfulfilled hopes and threats." The following January, as President Kennedy, he repeated the theme: "Let the word go forth from this time and place, to friend and foe alike, that the torch has been passed to a new generation of Americans."

All these bold words were ahead of him in the spring of 1960, but the season went well enough. In March Kennedy won the first primary election, in New Hampshire. On April 5 he defeated his major liberal rival, the far more experienced (older) Hubert H. Humphrey in Humphrey's neighboring state, Wisconsin. On May 20 the rich Roman Catholic knocked the modestly fixed and Protestant Humphrey out of the contest, beating him soundly in poor and Protestant West Virginia. There was good reason to believe that the future lay in those freckled Irish hands.

It did not, of course. Kennedy would live through less than half the 1960s and, although as the victim of assassination he would be canonized, leaving those who revered him to contemplate into the 1980s "what might have been," he was not a very successful president. He botched his attempts at diplomacy and then claimed that taking the world to the brink of nuclear war in the Cuban missile crisis was a victory. In retrospect, he made several fatal decisions in America's rendezvous with disaster in Vietnam. Kennedy's domestic program, the "New Frontier," was bogged down in Congress at the time he was killed. Only the emotional reaction to his death and the accession of an old-time, backroom arm-twister, Lyndon B. Johnson, saw it through as "The Great Society."

Kennedy did not even launch the 1960s in that first spring, much as it looked as if he did. In the sense that decades have characters—Gay or Roaring or Red—that honor, if it is an honor to inaugurate a time of discontent, protest, riot, resistance, war, and trouble, belongs to another, much obscurer member of the American Congress, an unimaginative and singularly unglamorous old codger of sixty-six years, the Honorable Francis E. Walter of Easton, Pennsylvania. A member of the lower house since 1934, Walter was chairman of the House Committee on Un-American Activities or, as the acronym was rearranged for the sake of pronounciation and onomatopoeia, HUAC.

HUAC
The committee dated from 1938 when it was solemnly commissioned to investigate "the extent, character and objects of un-American propaganda in the United States." On the first day it met, HUAC observed that Nazis and fascists, then dragging the world into war, had some adherents in the United States. The next day, in the words of *Life* magazine, HUAC "switched to communism and stayed there."

Before long, in fact, the committee's investigations earned it the praise of the Ku Klux Klan, the Silver Shirts (a fascist group with a costume even catchier than the Klan's), the German-American Bund, and the extreme right-wing organizations of the 1940s and 1950s. Its first chairman, Martin Dies of Texas, cheerfully accepted commendations, plaques, sets of luggage, and what-all from quasi-fascist groups while defining organizations like the Milk Consumers Protective League as "Communist transmission belts."

HUAC's critics perceived from the outset that the committee served as a sniper's nest for anti–New Deal Democrats and conservative Republicans. Right-wingers had to move warily in attacking Roosevelt and his reforms before the working-class electorates that benefited from them. But they could, by smearing ancillary movements—supporters of civil liberties, racial justice, social welfare, pacifistic foreign policy, and later the outcry against nuclear weapons—as "red," obscure their own lack of alternatives and make the liberals more cautious.

In other words, while politically insubstantial—precious little legislation came out of the committee—HUAC could and did serve a political purpose.

To HUAC's critics, there was nothing accidental about this. They denounced the committee's members as totalitarian and racist and had little trouble assembling convincing dossiers on the likes of Martin Dies and the blatant anti-Semite, John Elliot Rankin of Mississippi. However, to define HUAC's purpose in terms of its effects would be an error as serious as to say that because the New Left killed radicalism in America, it was set up that way. On the contrary, from Congress's point of view, HUAC was a kind of storeroom, a place for the House of Representatives to keep, if not quite to hide, its embarrassments. From first to last, the one common characteristic of the HUAC Red-hunters was their mediocrity. Racist, anti-Semitic, pro-Nazi, or just pliant agents of conservative labor unions like Francis E. Walter, they were all men who, with a lot of luck and a lot of hard labor in local politics, drank and smoked good to poor cigars with the right people, demonstrated a heroic tolerance for lodge meetings and church dinners, and got themselves elected to Congress in disturbingly large numbers.

To judge by the membership lists of HUAC over twenty years, congressmen of integrity and talent avoided it as they would have avoided being photographed for *Sun Sports* magazine. HUAC was composed first to last of southern Democrats and northern Republicans who made a mark in few areas other than Red-baiting. Several of its members, includ- one chairman (the Republican J. Parnell Thomas), ended up in the penitentiary. The single alumnus who went on to bigger things only missed the Big House by an ace: Richard M. Nixon of Orange County, California, served on HUAC between 1947 and 1950.

Unhappily, the House of Representatives has always been crowded with this kind of fellow. It is in the nature of district politics in the United States that the man who serves the purposes of the local powers, rather than the individual useful to the nation, should be the ideal spokesman for the district. The survival of the Constitution for more than two centuries is evidence that these public servants are generally quite harm- less. Most of them are delighted with pay and perquisites that exceed anything their law practices back home might earn. Indeed, there is nothing like a seat in Congress to make that hometown career take off. Francis E. Walter, for example, although primarily a labor man, held directorships of several banks as well as maintaining memberships in the Elks, Odd Fellows, Eagles, and Junior Order of United American Mechanics. To him as well as to virtually every other congressman who sat on HUAC, it came as second nature, in the words of founder Dies, never to "participate in anything without consulting the American Legion or your local Cham- ber of Commerce."

Eloquent speeches were not expected of such men. Where the folks back home were concerned, a few mumbled pieties on the Fourth of July did nicely. All that was required, particularly in the one-party South, was that congressmen show up on the Fourth, lend august presence to a few other district functions, vote the way the local bosses expected, and get the district its fair share of end-of-session pork-barrel legislation.

The trouble comes because eminence goes to the weakest of heads. Boredom gets to the dullest. In a democracy, mediocrity is not only granted an equal chance, it can rise to be a tyrant, as de Tocqueville predicted and, in their different ways, Francis E. Walter and Jerry Rubin proved. In Congress long enough, some representatives began to think that as "statesmen," they should "shape" events. Or, through no fault other than seniority, they earned the right to a chair in the House's inviolable committee system. As Charles Frankel, among others, has observed, the committee system makes Congress more gerontocracy than democracy.

This does not really say so much. There are old men and old men, Charles de Gaulles and Winston Churchills, Ayatollah Khomeinis and Ronald Reagans. It is when the elderly incompetents or, in Somerset Maugham's phrase, the "ga-gas" begin to take themselves seriously that the elderly men who are capable get a bad reputation. A few Martin Dieses, Francis E. Walters, and J. Parnell Thomases (HUAC's chairman between 1947 and 1949) on every committee, distributed too thinly to form a bloc of ineptitude, and everything is all right. But when the seedy crew gets too numerous, committees which mean something, such as Ways and Means and Banking, cannot be allowed to fall into their hands.

Unfortunately, one irony of the Rooseveltian revolution in American politics—the construction of a generation-long Democratic majority—put a lot of Democratic hacks into office for a long time. Francis E. Walter, for instance, had twenty-six years of seniority in 1960.

HUAC was a solution for the presence of so many Walters. If the committee is pictured as a refuse dump, it is easier to understand why a basically New Dealish Congress gave Martin Dies his plaything in 1938 and why, despite fierce

denunciations of HUAC over the years by the labor movement, several Supreme Court justices, and an active liberal
lobby, liberal Democrats in Congress voted HUAC its appropriations every two years almost without dissent. (During the
1950s, only ten votes, total, were registered against funding
HUAC.) The committee was a way for Congress to keep its
incompetents out of mischief elsewhere.

Outside Congress, of course, HUAC did a great deal of
mischief and more than a little evil. No more seriously affected
by a conscience than by other higher processes, its members
subpoenaed schoolteachers, clergymen, workers in a dozen
occupations who had flirted with the Communist party in their
youth or, maybe, just the Milk Consumers Protective League.
If "hostile witnesses" stood on their rights of political advocacy, or privacy, HUAC harassed, bullied, and smeared them,
sending them out of the hearing room to social exorcism, the
loss of a job, anguish, or even a prison sentence for contempt of
Congress.

Timid witnesses recanted, purging themselves before the
inquisitors by divulging the names of old associates. At least
one, actor Larry Parks, did so between sobs. Technically
become "friendly witnesses" and congratulated by the likes of
J. Parnell Thomas and Francis E. Walter, such unhappy
people were the worst casualties of all. They were literally
looted of their souls, forced to gavotte for the amusement of
cads and boors. At least one person, a research scientist named
William K. Sherwood whose active subversive career seems to
have consisted largely of supporting the Loyalists in the
Spanish Civil War, committed suicide when, in June 1957, he
was ordered to appear before the committee. "I will in two days
be assassinated by publicity," the troubled Sherwood said.
Instead, he did the job himself, and Chairman Walter,
dependably tasteless, regretted that the witness would not
appear "because we have every reason to believe that he had
valuable information on the operations of the tax-exempt
foundations."

When he founded HUAC in 1938, Martin Dies said that he was not interested in the "old kind of investigation that would go after somebody only for cheap publicity." He was announcing the committee's mode of operation. Its glory days were between 1947 and 1953 when it went to Hollywood and basked in the glow of "the stars." Half of America's aristocracy lined up behind HUAC's campaign. Gary Cooper announced his opposition to communism because "it isn't on the level." Some resisted and survived. Humphrey Bogart snarled that "they'll nail anyone who ever scratched his ass during the National Anthem." The committee's greatest triumph in this shoot-'em-up was reducing movie tough guy John Garfield to a tearful repudiation of old leftist pals. So much for the sheeny Golden Boy.

After Hollywood, however, HUAC began to decline. It was eclipsed by Joseph McCarthy in the early fifties but also suffered when he was discredited.

At the end of the decade several Supreme Court decisions crippled the committee's power to nail uncooperative witnesses for contempt of Congress and, in 1959, hearings scheduled for San Francisco had to be canceled when the announcement triggered a broadly-based protest. (The suicide Sherwood had worked at Stanford University, just south of San Francisco.)

It may be that HUAC was dying a natural death by 1960, and, understandably reluctant to face such an unpleasant fact, Walter sought only to demonstrate its survival when, in the spring of 1960, he announced that the committee would make its debut for the decade in "everybody's favorite city." What he did, however, was to cause a riot and launch an era. What he did was to spawn a movement which, ostensibly opposed to what HUAC represented, came eventually to share many of its traits: imperviousness to real political issues, obliviousness to common decency as a handy tool in human intercourse, dependence on symbols and slogans for survival, belief in spectral evidence and intuition.

"OPERATION ABOLITION"

On May 12, the day before the HUAC hearings opened, about two thousand people, mostly students from San Francisco State College and the University of California at Berkeley, rallied in Union Square. They heard the well-rehearsed libertarian appeals of the anti-HUAC movement. The argument that HUAC's real target was loyal, progressive dissent was especially persuasive. Most of the forty-eight subpoenaed to appear the next day were old Depression-era Reds whose affiliations were known to all. But a few were new faces, leaders of the Bay Area's active civil rights movement that had offended right-wing Oakland publisher, William Knowland, and were very likely summoned at his behest.

When the hearings opened next day in the chambers of the county supervisors at San Francisco City Hall, a few hundred, mostly young people again, milled around the entrance, waiting to be admitted to the gallery on a first-come-first-served basis. Instead, they were held back while a parade of mostly older people with Republican blue dyed into their hair and white tickets gripped in their hands filed into the room.

There was nothing new in this. Wherever HUAC went it put on a show for its fans. Watching commies sweat, lick their lips, and take the Fifth was a popular pornography of the fifties. What was novel in San Francisco was the presence of a large number of hostiles who also wanted in. Before Friday the 13th, 1960, people who were not "for" the committee stayed away from it as they would from an alley full of glowering dogs. And so it was a more-or-less honest mistake when there were no seats for the protesters.

Angry and shocked, the students shouted, sang, and "sat in," imitating the tactic introduced a few months earlier by civil rights campaigners in Greensboro, North Carolina. They chanted the old gospel hymn which, following the labor organizing campaigns of the 1930s, the Negro movement had adopted:

We shall not,
We shall not be moved.
We shall not,
We shall not be moved.
Like a tree a-standing by the water,
We shall not be moved.

They were. The San Francisco police turned high pressure fire hoses on them, literally washing some down the long main staircase of City Hall. Then the cops waded in, swinging clubs and dragging about 150 stalwarts down the stone steps by feet and hair. Sixty-three were arrested.

The students were stunned. They had seen films of southern cops beating Negro protesters. But that was the movies. Alabama and Mississippi were a different part of the world, a *National Geographic* kind of place. This was San Francisco, a bastion of liberal-minded, easygoing tolerance. And the students thought they were what they actually were: decent, ordinary kids who were putting their civic lessons into practice.

In the end, official San Francisco agreed with them. Of the sixty-three who were arrested, all but one were exonerated immediately, and the last was acquitted of wrongdoing a year later. The cops and the committee were at fault, official San Francisco said, and even most of the police force seemed to agree. Two years later, the inspector who had ordered the hoses turned on retired early on the grounds of psychological stress. "I don't have any friends," he told the Police Retirement Board.

In the meantime, back at City Hall, a stunned and confused group of university students stood around soaked with water, blood, tears, and what Todd Gitlin would perceptively call "radical disappointment." They were not Reds or revolutionaries but trusting believers in the eternals of Constitution, Bill of Rights, and what the homilists of their childhood liked to call "the American Way of Life." And they had been beaten up because of that. The next day they were back, a little changed, joined by between five thousand and eight thousand others in a picket in front of City Hall. The New Left was born.

The midwife, HUAC, would stay on for a year as nurse. During the summer of 1960, the committee released *Operation Abolition,* a film about the "riot." It was put on national tour before church, lodge, and right-wing political groups (which were generally sympathetic) and the colleges (which were not). The message was as predictable as an episode of the red-scare television series of the fifties, *I Led Three Lives,* in which Richard Carlson (as Herbert Philbrick) saved a power plant, an elementary school library, or a swimming pool filtering system each week from Russian agents who numbered about an even third of the population. That is, the film presented the disturbance in San Francisco as a well-laid scheme fomented by communists whose "symps" and potential dupes—the students at City Hall and in the viewing audience—had better think twice about what they said and did.

From every campus were *Operation Abolition* was screened, small groups of students, larger after the new year, sent to Berkeley to learn what facts were distorted in the show and to get advice on how to counter the speech of Fulton Lewis III, a cynical smoothie who accompanied the film. *Operation Abolition* was a palpable fraud, filled with distortions by the admissions of HUAC's own investigator on the West Coast, William Wheeler. Lewis, an M.C. in the fashion of Art Linkletter—cool, a smiler, wholesome, and impeccably "square"—answered documented criticisms by ridiculing or smearing the questioner. If his audience was with him, it hooted critics down. If the hooting was hostile, it served Lewis and the local editor as evidence that the Reds were at their insidious work in Hometown, too.

However, what seemed to HUAC to be godsent grist for further machinations was nothing of the kind. By sending *Operation Abolition* "everywhere," the committee only spread

the radical disappointment that had cropped in front of the
San Francisco City Hall. But like the front line of May 13, the
student critics "everywhere" did not know what to do next.
They were simply bewildered by the contradictions between
what they had been taught by earnest schoolteachers, what
they saw in textbook cartoons, illustrating "Freedom of
Speech," and the reality they suddenly had experienced.

There is nothing in this reaction that needs explaining.
HUAC and its methods were venal civil hypocrisies. The
question is: why was there nowhere the students could turn?
Why did they have to start anew? Why didn't they turn to the
many groups that had been battling HUAC when they were
still sucking on tootsie-pops and chortling over Howdy
Doody?

They might have rallied to the Communist party,
HUAC's ostensible prey for twenty years. Finding that course
repellent for good reason or bad, they might have sought out
the Socialist party's campus arm, the Young People's Socialist
League, or "Yipsels." Or there was the Socialist Workers
party, a Trotskyist group which itself founded a youth group in
1960, the Young Socialist Alliance. Every large American
campus had at least one little claque of "lefties," the men in
blue workshirts and cloth caps, the women generally, in one of
H. L. Mencken's late *mots,* the kind that make you want to
burn every bed in the world. Indeed, when dozens of collegiate
anti-HUAC committees were organized in 1961, representatives of Old Left groups were dependably present, leaflets
and application blanks bundled under arm.

The Old Left was not large. There were perhaps two
thousand total in the Communist party, mostly New Yorkers
and pretty long in the tooth. (That is, as left-wing humor had it,
they would have been long in the tooth if so many of the
comrades had not been able dentists.) The Socialist party had
fewer than a thousand members. Adding up all the groups,
Milton Cantor estimates that there were no more than ten
thousand bona fide Old Leftists in the United States in 1960 or,

in HUAC terms, one Red to rustle around in the lint and foil wrappers under every eighteen thousand American beds.

This may be described as the institutional equivalent of what physicians call brain death, and it might have been the better part of decency if, sometime before 1960, some kindly sociologist in white could have pulled the Old Left's plug. Socialism, a movement which was, elsewhere in the world, one of the most important forces of the twentieth century, never secured more than a toehold in the United States.

WARUM GIBT ES KEINEN SOZIALISMUS?

The explanations alternately gloating and mournful, of why this was so, fill long library shelves. Some emphasize factors completely beyond the control of the radicals. Werner Sombart, a German sociologist, pointed to the vastness of American riches, the fact that there was so much to go around that American capitalism was able to provide basic comforts for its millions whilst continuing most fabulously to enrich its few. "On the reefs of roast beef and applie pie," Sombart wrote in *Warum Gibt es in den Vereinigten Staaten Keinen Sozialismus?* (Why Is There No Socialism in the United States?) in 1906, "socialistic utopias of every sort are sent to their doom." By the sixties, a substantial proportion of American whites, most notably the parents of the Movement generation, were faring much better than well-balanced diets. They were buying color TVs, second cars, vacation cottages, and cases of gin and vodka in record quantities. Because the essence of the Old Left's appeal was "more of the good things of life" and the attainments of the chief socialistic state, the Soviet Union, could be lovingly and accurately depicted in grays and queues by antiradical propagandists, the preponderance of the American working class, at least those capable of political action, was effectively immune.

Other scholars emphasized the social irrelevance of socialism in the United States. Following Louis B. Hartz, the

most interesting of the "consensus historians" (so called
because they posited an essential commonality of interests in
the United States), this school observed that, worldwide,
socialist movements succeeded not in well-developed capitalist
nations but in those countries where feudal or other precapital-
ist classes help power. In other words, whatever the pretensions of socialism as a postcapitalist form, socialism was in
fact, like capitalism, a mode of development, a way to
modernize. In the United States, where capitalism succeeded
so grandly at that task and where there were no feudal
survivals against which socialists might rally the masses, their
program was, simply, irrelevant, a rejected social alternative.

Leon Samson, a Depression-era American communist,
fastened on ideology as the key to the socialists' failure.
Americans found socialism unappealing, he said, because they
subscribed to a contending ideology, "Americanism":

> *Americanism is to the American not a tradition or a
> territory, not what France is to a Frenchman or
> England to an Englishman, but a doctrine—what
> socialism is to a socialist. Like socialism, Amer-
> icanism is looked upon not patriotically, as a
> personal attachment, but rather as a highly atten-
> uated, conceptualized, platonic, impersonal attrac-
> tion toward a system of ideas, a solemn assent to a
> handful of final notions—democracy, liberty, op-
> portunity, to all of which the American adheres
> rationalistically much as a socialist adheres to his
> socialism—because it does him good, because it
> gives him work, because, so he thinks, it guarantees
> him happiness. Americanism has thus served as a
> substitute for socialism. Every concept in socialism
> has its substitutive counter-concept in American-
> ism, and that is why the socialist argument falls so
> fruitlessly on the American ear.*

Save for that final, jarring audio-arboricultural metaphor, Samson is worth reading twice. Other peoples do not speak of "Britishism," "Canadaism," or "Congoism." They have their nationalisms, often highly silly ones, but they do not cast the net of treason so broadly as to catch tastes and crotchets as well as overt political acts. They search out and battle activities that are "anti-," but not those that are merely "un-."

The Movement activists of the sixties boasted of their lack of ideology. It was one of the particulars by which they distinguished themselves from the Old Left from the beginning. They scorned the old communist and Trotskyist cults for their allegiance to a comprehensive, all-explanatory system of thought. But they were ideologues. They were Americanists. In no significant respect did they transcend the vague "final notions" listed by Sombart. It is a matter to be explored. For the moment it is enough to note that even the protest against HUAC was frequently put in Americanist terms. The committee's investigations were described as the most un-American activity of all. Racial discrimination was wrong because it violated the American dream. A substantial part of the movement against the war in Vietnam was based on the conviction that in Indochina Americans were violating their national virtue. Americanism was everywhere in the sixties.

There are numerous other explanations of why socialism failed in the United States. Many old radical faithfuls liked to blame their failure on ruthless government intervention each time they showed signs of strength. Others fixed on the internal failures of the Socialist and Communist parties: the former's inability to offer a substantial alternative to Democratic party liberalism; the latter's tawdry self-pollution in the service of the Soviet Union and, to borrow from Daniel Bell, chiliastic commitment to dogma.

But the point is that, whatever the cause, the perplexed and restive young dissidents of 1960 and 1961 were unattracted to the old gospel and, in building their Movement on little but their radical personal disappointment, determined from the outset that it would be a failure. As the proverb implies, it is possible with a modicum of caution to see that the baby is set aside before dumping the bathwater. It was possible (desirable!) in 1960 to reject the organizations of the Old Left, to avoid the errors of both socialists and communists, while recognizing the valid, indispensable essence of radicalism to which the Old Left clung—that in a capitalist society the significant social fact is class, the relationship of people to property, the means by which wealth is produced. Without a class analysis of society there can be no radicalism, no politics of the root. If everything else is not quite bathwater, even if it is eminently worthwhile to fight Red-baiting, racial discrimination, mismanagement of education, war, sexual discrimination, and society's insistence that homosexuals keep their proclivities to themselves, none of these campaigns challenges the fundamental bases of society.

It was possible. But that was not the way the Movement developed. On the contrary, the Movement carefully set aside the bath water for loving ministrations and gave the baby a heave. Between 1960 and 1970 and after, America's "radicals" assailed just about every aspect of American life but the one that counted and counts, social class.

Such wrong-headedness, while colossal, is hardly unprecedented. Condemnation of "reformers" by "revolutionists" has been one of the staples of radical history. But before 1960 the argument took the form of the revolutionists calling the reformers "class collaborationists," sellouts, and the reformers responding by saying that the "r-r-r-r-red hot revolutionists" were dreamers, "impossibilities," ignorant of social realities. Both sides had a pretty reasonable idea of where they stood in relation to the established order and one another.

What was novel to the sixties was that people who abandoned radicalism insisted on clinging to the name, and American society obliged. The sources of this curious phenomenon are the subject of the next chapter.

CHAPTER TWO

MOM WAS A BEATNIK AND DAD WAS COLORED

Dissent was not a magazine which sold in drugstores. Indeed, if its list of subscribers had threatened to grow beyond a couple thousand, the editorial board of distinguished academics, writers, and intellectuals otherwise employed would have been thrown into agonies of introspection. What could they be doing wrong?

For *Dissent* was a leading and arguably the best periodical published during the fifties by and for a very small, very special group of Americans—people who thought of themselves as special. *Dissent* was the magazine of intellectuals who called themselves "radicals," people who might have flirted with the Communist and Socialist parties or even had a brief carnal fling with the "revolution" before concluding that the Old Left was morally bankrupt. Others of *Dissent*'s editors, contributors, and readers had maintained their chastity, even as youths. They were old liberals whose social consciousness had been forged by the New Deal and honed in the crusade against fascism. They were people who yearned for a concerned, ongoing struggle to make the world a better place, but who had no political medium through which to do so. They had minimal sympathy for the post-FDR Democratic party, although the reality of political choice and the wan personal appeal of Adlai Stevenson meant that many held their noses and voted that way.

Dissent people were arty people. Their primary interests lay in the life of the mind, especially that part of the mind which responds to literature and the arts, including the newly respectable medium of the film. A good many pages in most issues of *Dissent* were dedicated to such matters.

It is a legitimate subject. Arty people have as much right to their periodicals as fly fishermen, explorers, and the concupiscent. However, the people who edited and read *Dissent* were not content with a journal of the arts. They refused to give up the shadow of their old political commitment, the labels of "radical" and "liberal." They called *Dissent* a "Journal of Socialist Opinion," whereas in addition to their aesthetic interests, the *Dissent*ers had long since retreated into that eternal refuge of the disillusioned reformer, the radicalism of the personal statement, the rebellion of the life-style.

The Spring 1960 issue of *Dissent* included an article on beatniks (appreciative but worried about commercialization, false beatnikism); an article on juvenile delinquency (was it inarticulate social revolution?); a critique of the American university by a self-styled victim, a student; and a note on the non-programmatic leanings of the new radicalism which, perceptively, *Dissent* felt stirring.

In the letters department, Dwight Macdonald and Irving Howe engaged in some elegant hair-pulling over Howe's capitalization in a previous issue of the word "Him" in referring to Jesus Christ. Macdonald gloated that Howe had apparently converted. He (Macdonald) would never refer to Christ except in the lower case. With the ponderous jocularity one associates with London clubmen, Howe hastened to explain that he had capitalized the pronoun in the literary interests of his "fable."

It is a quality of precocious adolescents that they delight in mocking their childhood religious beliefs, at least between the time when the universities began to teach the higher criticism and the time when children ceased to have religious beliefs. Save perhaps for one's first sexual adventure, related nonchalantly to the boys on the corner as an everyday sort of thing—like shaving—nothing better advertizes the passing of a hormonal milestone than a bit of bold blasphemy, addressing the Lord contemptuously without a nervous upward glance. Or, by a sophisticated sophomore year at a good liberal arts college, a simple snort at the mere mention of His name. No silly, superstitious, orthographic conventions for the illuminated stripling.

But Macdonald and Howe were not striplings. They were two of the nation's dozen leading intellectuals who persisted in styling themselves radicals, leftists. And *Dissent* was no Seven

Sisters literary magazine bulging with self-discovery in un-rhymed stanzas. At least not in name. In fact, Macdonald and Howe's fatuous competition to decide who was less conventional than thou was all too common in its pages. In their isolation during the age of Eisenhower, the country's intellectual radicals and liberals had arrived at a pass where to mention something like religion without a hearty snicker was to risk the suspicion of one's nonconformist fellows that one was soft on "masscult," a term coined by Macdonald. It was tantamount to being seen exiting a Doris Day movie, humming a Perry Como tune, or watching Milton Berle when the gang dropped in to discuss the Buxtehude concert. One might as well have lived in Levittown or Daly City in a horrid little box made of ticky-tacky on a hillside. One might as well have belonged to the PTA, trained the boy for clean-up spot in the Little League, and trundled the girl off to baton-twirling lessons in a brand-new Oldsmobile Ninety-Eight hardtop convertible.

The rad-lib intellectuals of the 1950s did not do such things. The trouble was that observing a snarl of fashions and taboos was just about all that they did do. And yet, they called themselves *political* and waited for the opportunity, soon proffered them, to counsel their juniors.

Dwight Macdonald, one of the shrewdest political analysts of the 1940s, insisted on making a manifesto of the fact that he was disgusted with the futility of it all and would henceforth devote his time to movie criticism. Irving Howe retained his interest in the radical past, coauthoring what is still the best (and blithely devastating) history of the American Communist party. But his chief work was as a literary critic, at which last, like Macdonald at his, he was practically without a peer. Norman Mailer, also listed on *Dissent*'s masthead, had succeeded as a novelist and was enjoying, well deserved, the life of Tom Sawyer. None of them would admit, however, that going to the movies, extrapolating from Henry James, or recounting the experience of the battlefield with a new vitality were, perhaps, something other than radical political acts. To have done so would have been to admit defeat, to capitulate and come to terms with the complacency, conformism, and apathy of the age of Eisenhower which they despised, to lead a life that was *private,* something which, for that generation and the one to come, was immoral, an abdication of man's responsibility, self-stultifying.

So they simply puttered about a mildly bohemian intellectual existence and called it politics. Less celebrated old socialists and New Dealers did, too. They subscribed to *Dissent,* let the lawn go to dandelions under the neighbors' glares, drove "the-old-Plymouth-good-enough-to-get-me-around" while the neatniks frantically "traded up," refused to buy a TV (unless, of course, it was "for the news" or for Alistair Cooke's *Omnibus*), listened to folk music, sucked on a meerschaum instead of a Kent ("Don't touch it!"), dressed in tatty tweed jackets with suede elbow patches, or wrapped their undyed, unlacquered hair in a dowdy bun. They vacationed in the mountains instead of at the seashore or at the seashore instead of in the mountains depending on which opposite course was charted by their lemming neighbors.

As a matter of taste, it is difficult to fault those who disdained the popular culture of the fifties and strived at every turn to disassociate themselves from it. To recall or to study the vapid consumerism that absorbed so much of the white middle class during the Eisenhower years and the hypocrisy of masscult is to shudder, as if reliving an accident that took a leg.

However, when contemplating one's tastes, it is always well to remember that tastes are personal and aesthetic choices. When reveling in one's own excellent fashions, it is well to remember that fashion is one of the species' evolutionary weak points, usually harmless but, like the sheep's fatty tail, a thing that collects dung and burrs that are pretty much the same whether the animal is a plodding plain old Dorset or an exotic Himalayan Longwool.

It is impossible or at least pointless to fault the man who does not order scallops because he likes steak, the downhill skier because he will not fly to Kana-na-hula and try surfing, the tropical fish fancier whose eyes glaze over at the mention of stamp collecting, or the insurance man who would not be a college professor specializing in Coleridge for all the money in Macy's on the night before Christmas.

But, of course, steak eaters and scallop lovers and skiers and surfers and tropical fish people and stamp collectors and insurance men and college professors are apt to be very pleased with themselves precisely because of the little niches in which they shine, because they possess a virtuosity there that is entirely beyond everyone else. Members of the human species have more than once been likened to bullfrogs puffed proud of their lily pads.

Yet a certain obliviousness to or, at least, tolerance of the tastes of others would seem to be a desirable social trait, certainly for "the more enlightened members of society" who, at the drop of a copy of *Dissent,* talked of making the world a better, more humane place for all "the people."

Unhappily, it was just on the basis of their personal and aesthetic rebellion that the rad-lib intellectuals defined themselves. It was harmless enough as the pretense of a couple thousand people clustered in the less useful professions; however, the consequences of this habit of mind when transmitted to hundreds of thousands of children, such as happened in the sixties, were to be socially disastrous. This was one legacy which the fifties intellectuals bequeathed to the Movement their students founded: personal witness, an individual's statement in so trivial a thing as the cut of his hair was . . . radical.

It might also be called a cogenital deformity inasmuch as bohemianism, "culture radicalism" (Howe's phrase), has always been a major component of American leftism. But there was something new in the affectations of the fifties rad-libs.

Their styles cut them off not from the styles of the enemy, the exploitative ruling class, but from the popular culture accepted or at least aspired to by the vast majority of—what else to call them?—"the people"? When the Red intellectual of the 1910s or 1930s shed the necktie and waistcoat in which he had been raised and donned the blue workshirt and cloth cap of the proletarian, he was being silly enough for the most discriminating connoisseur of human behavior. But at least he was symbolically breaking with the fashions of "the plutocrats" and identifying with the working class, with whose plight he sympathized. When the literary critics of the "socialist realist" school scoffed at any work of art which did not advance the cause of revolution, they were making grand braying asses of themselves, but their line made some vague sense in Marxist revolutionary terms.

However, when the rad-libs of the fifties immersed themselves in Italian movies instead of Hollywood, in esoteric modes of picture painting and experimental novels as indubitably distinguished from the reading material of masscult, when they framed their tastes according to what was opposite the tastes of suburbia, they were denouncing and cutting themselves off from, indeed, *vide* masscult, the masses. The operative words are *opposite* and *instead*. Not only did the intellectuals define personal as political, but they said in effect that a privileged elite was radical, that the sigh of snobbery was the voice of social democracy.

Again, when the visible saints number in the thousands, they are as harmless as the Devonshire eccentric who lives in a teepee and beats on a tom-tom early on closing day. However, when preached to and adopted by hundreds of thousands, the effect would be grotesque.

The conformism of the nonconformists was (as it always has been), less tolerant and more demanding than that of the larger, conventional society. Aficionados of American social conformism since de Tocqueville have known of "no country in which there is so little true independence of mind and freedom of discussion as in America." Americans have never been a people who, like the gracious folk of Devonshire, take casual pleasure in their oddballs. But the herding millions have rarely been so absolute, so self-righteous, and so portentous about their fripperies and fashions as, to quote Ed Murray's article about neatniks, "the more enlightened members of society."

"The Neatnik" appeared in the Spring 1960 issue of *Dissent*. Its title subject was the majority American: "A creature who has sold his birthright for a mess of mortgages and traded in his masculinity for a tail fin. A creature whose intellect is as firmly buttoned down as the Ivy League collars he loves to wear, whose dreams may be as narrow as his tightly knotted ties."

The author touched on politics. *Dissent* always *touched on* "the political aspect." Thus, while the neatnik was most likely to be a Republican, he might also be a Democrat. "This doesn't matter very much. Democratic neatniks are transforming the party of FDR into an engine of enlightened conservatism."

What really counted was that the readership recognize the enemy and stick with its own kind. "The Neatnik" was a manual of etiquette with special emphasis on one's choice in a couturier and an acute hint that readers be sure that they were themselves truly, properly groomed, real radicals. It was a touchy business, fashion, as anyone in Cannes harbor might have told the rad-libs. Neatniks were themselves fascinated by the styles and behavior of their betters and "may even adopt some of the external features of the beat." Fortuitously, the phony could be distinguished from the genuine, for the neatnik was capable of emulation "only up to a point." Murray went on, "The young executive who sports a neatly trimmed beard is always dressed in a white shirt, dark suit and tie and polished shoes. His co-worker, who affects open collars and suede shoes, will be sure to appear clean shaven. The neatnik knows that when only a touch is used, taboo is a perfume. He won't go overboard." As would, of course, by definition the radical, the truly enlightened person who, *que audace!*, wore a beard *and* a colored shirt, with the collar open *too,* and *even* suede shoes scuffed like nobody's business! Thus the level of the radical dialectic in 1960.

OF BEATS, INTELLECTUALS, AND APATHY

Whither ever eccentricity, it is interesting that the beats should have appealed in any way to intellectuals who execrated masscult for its apathy and conformism. The beatniks (the burlesque of "beat" was coined by San Francisco gossip columnist, Herb Caen) were ostensibly a literary school but, in a way (because most of them wrote little or nothing), were simply the friends of poet Allen Ginsberg.

Later, due to the influence of Ginsberg's celebrated epic of 1955, *Howl!,* and Jack Kerouac's novel of wandering ne'er-do-wells, *On the Road,* beat became a life-style, the visible bohemianism of people who made no bones about their rejection of politics along with the other deadening requirements of the system, Moloch to Ginsberg.

The beatniks were rebellious all right, but they were also explicitly, ideologically *apathetic.* That word, as Daniel Boorstin points out in another context, is not synonymous with *lethargic* but means "a feeling apart from others" which was the crux of the beat style. The beatniks were lethargic too. Their style called for a languid lolling about dark coffee houses in Greenwich Village, North Beach, and Venice, California, for sipping red wine and black expresso while listening impassively to jazz and impenetrable poetic imitators of Ginsberg and Lawrence Ferlinghetti.

Work—regular labor, at least—was to be avoided like every other treadwheel in the middle class rat race. Just enough money to pay the rent on "a pad," named for the mattress on the floor—beds were "a drag,"—was quite enough.

It could be a pleasant life for young people. Self-immersion is the business of a certain stage in the process of maturing in societies where people do not have to harpoon wild pigs in order to put the next meal on the table. Indeed, beat was patterned in large part on the Greenwich Villagers of the 1910s, the *apaches* of nineteenth-century Paris, and assorted other *vies de bohème*, attractive interludes in Western cultural development by anyone's definition.

The point is that the beatniks said they were beat, both pummeled and defeated. Yet it was this attitude to which political intellectuals from Norman Mailer to Paul Goodman to Irving Howe, in various ways, looked as a bright spot in fifties America.

OF APATHY, COMMERCIALIZATION, HOODS, AND CONFORMITY

As for mainstream America in the fifties, it was annoyingly unaggravated by the beats, which should have taught the intellectuals something. Calamity-howlers in the Baptist churchs squeezed sermons and tracts out of the threat of uncleanliness, beards, sexual laxity, and obscene words in print, and a few police sergeants like Frank Rizzo of Philadelphia made their first splash harassing beatnik coffee houses. But the Baptists were no longer the opinion-makers they had been in the age of Mencken, and the avenging cops were ridiculed as much as lauded. As for the real "booboisie" of the time, the ostensibly timid and repressed middle classes, they were at worst amused by beatnik antics and, more likely, as Murray's false-beat neatnik, were apt to flit about gaily on the fringes of the phenomenon.

Howl!, despite the problems of distributing it—because of them, of course!—was a huge success. "No poem written by a thirty-year-old," writes Godfrey Hodgson, "has ever so totally rejected so many of the beliefs of the society it was written in. No poem, certainly, has lived to see so many of its heresies so widely accepted before its author turned forty."

This process began right away. For Moloch could, can, and does merchandise everything from noxious diseases to slavering demands that he be strangled with his own entrails by

Saturday next. Beyond Ginsberg's and Kerouac's literary successes, beatnik coffee houses did an attractive business in tourists and neatniks, charging seventy-five cents for a cup of coffee and an hour of Negro jazz groups or poets with a positively electronic command of the human monotone. Along with the other buyers came the rad-lib intellectuals who somehow exempted themselves from the denunciations, which they articulated, that beat was being corrupted by dabblers.

It boggles the best-anchored mind to pause on a vision which damned the typical American for apathy and social sloth, celebrated the genuine apathy and idealized sloth of beat as an admirable alternative, and then condemned neatnik for partially absorbing beat styles, and finally declared that these harbingers of the future were corrupted because somebody listened!

Is there true sound in the forest only when there is no one to hear the falling tree? This is the pass of cultural analysis to which America's intellectuals had come.

Their "reasoning" was even more perplexing in that, however persuasive their criticism of fifties masscult, the people they poked at most, the suburbanites, were neither apathetic nor lethargic. It is true that suburbia was uninterested in preserving the spirit of FDR and the élan that had brought down fascism. It is also true that suburbia reveled in the dubious baubles that had been won for them by New Deal reforms (for the suburbanites were the children of the working class). Middle-class America did accept the tacit proclamation of Eisenhower Republicanism that, although a good thing, the reform movement had done its work and was at an end. But even in caricature, the suburban world of flower bed competitions, cocktails-and-steak barbecues, ballet lessons, Little League, canasta clubs, and PTA was a dizzying whirl. Vapid, perhaps, trivial and empty—but eminently dynamic.

Moreover, if the folkways of suburbs are examined with the same open-minded tolerance with which anthropologists examine Italian mountain villages, English pubs, and New

Guinean potlatches, it is difficult to sneer and snort at Mr. and Mrs. Neatnik as particularly wretched representatives of the race.

The suburbanites were co-operators (a word a rad-lib sociologist would use), inter-relators (a psychologist's favorite), and tireless devotees of ritual (which mystics admire awfully). Most of all, the neatniks were ingenious creators of communities (which radicals have said they sought) in a new world, seeding and nursing new ways of coming together with all the attention they lavished on the saplings they planted amidst the bent nails and plaster droppings of "the tract."

Again, it is not necessarily petulant to be apprehensive of the eternal value of such communities. Daniel Boorstin's identification of "consumption communities" as the equivalents of family, village, church, and covered wagon train—the Volkswagen owners' community: "Wave!"; the community of Pepsi drinkers: "Join!"; the community of those who smoke the same brand of cigarette: "Show us your Lark pack!"—is as depressing as it is ingenious. But he is right. Communities they were, and powerful ones at that.

So was the generational community of the adolescent. This group, which was first haltingly identified as a community during the Great Depression (the word *teenager* seems to date from the thirties), first became "a problem" with the juvenile delinquency scare of the 1950s. Ravaging gangs of slum kids did not disturb conventional America any more than beatniks did. They could be avoided and served as a distant reaffirmation that the life in suburbia was indeed the good life. As for the radical intellectuals, they were not sure. They could attribute the world of zipguns and "hoods" to poverty and lament it, or they could make Romeo and Juliet out of ethnic gangs and tout *West Side Story* as so much more meaningful than Rodgers and Hammerstein.

But when the children of the suburbs and even the offspring of the more enlightened members of society took to aping Puerto Rican styles and occasionally to breaking loose with senseless vandalism and "rumbles" of their own, America scrutinized its children as never before. Whatever they were—a threat to decent people or evidence of discontent in Eden or even harbingers of a new age—adolescents had become a distinct group, to be taken very seriously.

This marked a major shift in the way society conceives of those who are no longer infants but not yet adults. Traditionally, the adolescent was a bumbling, lovable fool, the occasion of sometimes malicious but usually good-humored fun. The teenager had been tricked by the process of growing up into stumbling over his own feet, having his voice crack into falsetto at the most awkward moments, newly and compulsively worrying about his appearance at just the time his face broke out in pimples, and drowning in puppy love and other harmless enthusiasms.

During the fifties, however, from *Look* magazine to *Dissent,* in church and on TV, and at deadly serious meetings at Town Hall, America began to wonder if the adolescent as lovable fool had not been replaced by the adolescent as the barbarian at the gates, if Henry Aldrich had not become Attila the Hun.

What the fifties could not know was, whereas Henry had always grown up a little at the end of each show, as he was expected to do, Attila would not. Attila would explicitly revel in his childhood (his barbarity), and the rad-libs, while hardly positive in the fifties that the Hun was a desirable fellow to have around, would come to terms with him by paying munificent tribute. Just as they twisted the meaning of terms like apathy and radicalism, they simply changed Attila's identity. They came to call him John the Baptist. The adolescent as barbarian became, in the sixties, without changing very much, the adolescent as prophet.

As for conformity, another favorite devil of fifties and sixties intellectuals, the indifference of the apathetic to it and the hostility of the eccentric both go without saying. However, to those who spoke of reforming society, of longing for a more meaningful cooperative, communitarian, humanistic world, a certain (rather considerable) degree of conformism would seem to have been part of the package. Nothing in the intellectuals' legacy to the sixties was more mischievous in consequence than the contradiction that nonconformism and community went together, that antisocial aesthetics, beatniks and, just maybe, destructive children, had a lesson for those who dreamed of a more abundant, more justly ordered society of 180 million souls, all of whom had appetites and partiality to leak-proof roofs over their heads.

Finally in this discussion of the leisured middle classes of the fifties—for neatnik, beat, intellectual, and rebellious suburban hood were all members of that class—it needs to be pointed out that there was an "Other America." When Michael Harrington rediscovered America's poor in a book of that title in 1962, not only the readers of *Look* and the viewers of television were astonished. The radical journals fluttered too, as if they were the crew of a demasted windjammer which had been blown aground on the beaches of Atlantis to find a world unlike anything of which they had ever dreamed. If masscult was unaware that over a quarter of the American people merely aspired to their comforts and peccadillos and actually lived below a conservatively defined poverty line in want and with untreated disease, the socially-aware intelligentsia were too. So far had the left strayed from the class it supposedly spoke for. Not only had they been wrong-headed across the board in their response to fifties America, but the only America the intellectuals knew or at least concretely cared about proved to be the world of the middle classes.

The most conspicuous bloc of Harrington's Other Americans was the Negroes, nineteen million of them in 1960, a majority of whom still lived with Jim Crow laws in the southern states. The dissenters had by no means ignored the problems of segregation and racism during the 1950s athough, once again, they were aroused on the subject at the same time as the larger society, with the Supreme Court's momentous decision of 1954 outlawing segregation in the schools.

However, in rallying to the cause of the civil rights movement, they treated it much as they treated the comparative use of image in Emily Dickinson and Antonioni or as Leonard Bernstein treated juvenile gangs in *West Side Story,* as an occasion for personal expression, as a point of personal aesthetic reference.

It is the nation's, rather than the intellectuals', tragedy that the chasm between white America and the nation's blacks was so broad that no one, at least among the whites, could see Negroes as other than vaguely animate objects, meaningful only to the extent that they served the cause of personal catharsis. In any event, the fifties looked rather different to black Americans than to whites. Far from an age of consumerism, poetry, apathy, conformity, and delicious self-righteousness, the fifties were a time of rebirth, a time of elemental political action of some considerable meaning indeed.

THE DECLINE OF JIM CROW

In 1954 seventeen states and the District of Columbia observed laws that segregated the black race from the white in schools, transportation, and in the use of other public facilities. In parts of the South even drinking fountains in the public parks were marked "White" and "Colored" and there were countless invisible lines which canny Negroes knew not to cross.

The seventeen included all the old slave states, Union as well as Confederate, plus Oklahoma. Four western states— Arizona, New Mexico, Kansas, and Wyoming—allowed local option on segregation questions, although no county in Wyoming exercised the option. (There were only two thousand blacks in the state, about one person in 165. Wyoming's law was if nothing else a triumph of principle.) Sixteen states explicitly prohibited racial segregation. Eleven had no legislation pertaining to relationships between the races.

Jim Crow had an uneven, mostly quiet history after the decline of northern interest in the civil rights of Negroes in the late nineteenth century. In 1896, the Supreme Court tacitly gave the go-ahead to those who wished to institute Jim Crow when, in the case of *Plessy* v. *Ferguson,* it found that segregated public schools violated no citizen's rights under the Fourteenth Amendment so long as the separate schools (by extension, all public facilities) were equal in quality. Along with the right to vote, the schools were the clearest cut public issue on which civil rights advocates could fight, so that decision wrote the end of Civil War idealism in the matter.

By the time of *Plessy,* white Americans either approved Jim Crow or were indifferent to him. Black America put up with the laws because of the atmosphere of terror on which they rested. Lynchings rose to an average of more than one a week nationally through much of the 1890s and again after World War I.

Nevertheless, there were sporadic outbursts of black protest throughout the first half of the twentieth century, and organizations such as the National Association for the Advancement of Colored People (NAACP) fought a constant, low-key legal battle to erase the demoralizing and psychologically destructive "mark of oppression" Jim Crow laws placed on every Negro.

The courts occasionally threw out the most blatant racial laws. In 1917 the Supreme Court refused to swallow a Louisville ordinance which forbade Negroes and whites to move into houses on streets occupied by a majority of the opposite race.

In 1927 the Court declared state laws forbidding Negroes to vote in primary elections to be unconstitutional, and in 1938 the Court said that for Missouri to pay the tuition of a black law student at an integrated out-of-state law school did not meet *Plessy*'s separate-but-equal test. (Missouri had no law school for Negroes.)

Much more important than this case, because it closely

scrutinized the separate-but-equal doctrine itself, was the Court's finding in 1950 that a separate Negro law school in Texas did not meet the *Plessy* test because, in the opinion of Chief Justice Fred M. Vinson, "reputation of faculty, experience of the administration, position and influence of the alumni, standing in the community, traditions and prestige" were all part of the equal rights the Fourteenth Amendment guaranteed all citizens.

"It is difficult to believe," Vinson continued, "that one who had a free choice" between the prestigious University of Texas School of Law and the state's Jim Crow school "would consider the question close." Although segregationists would later revile the "Warren Court"—Earl Warren succeeded Vinson as Chief Justice in 1953—for introducing a sociological rather than legalistic perspective into racial cases, it was this decision that actually marked the shift.

It is not irrelevant to the story of a social upheaval to linger so long in the halls of justice. When the Supreme Court unanimously struck down the principle of school segregation in *Brown* v. *Topeka Board of Education et al.,* it very literally launched the great civil rights revolution of the mid-twentieth century just as—despite delusions that it was a spontaneous, popular phenomenon—the Movement of the sixties took many of its cues from decisions made on high. By holding out the promise of civil equality to blacks and then, a few months later, by prescribing that school districts should integrate with "all deliberate speed," the Court managed both to arouse black hopes and to provide segregationist whites a way to defy the decision.

Jim Crow was dying. The provincial taboo, the "Whites Only" signs, were made untenable by the experience of black soldiers in the armed forces and the whiff of a world in which there was no relentless, official racial insult that the millions who went north to work during the war caught. "Sociological" as they might have been, the *Brown* findings merely ratified what was already under way socially.

Nothing better demonstrated this than the fact that, in the two or three years immediately following *Brown,* a large number of school districts in the border states, especially those in the more cosmopolitan cities, desegregated without incident. The whites seemed as relieved to be rid of a burden as the blacks were.

However, the opportunity to procrastinate presented by the "all deliberate speed" directive was too tempting for southern politicians accustomed to building their careers on smokescreen issues like HUAC and racism. For over half a century the South had evaded the Fourteenth and even the Fifteenth amendments by "Grandfather Clauses" combined with literacy tests, white primaries, and poll taxes. These enabled the southern states to deny the right to vote to anyone whose grandfathers had not voted before 1866 (when slavery was abolished), to ask educated Negroes to demonstrate literacy by interpreting a subtle point of law (one was turned down because of an "error in spilling") while asking whites to interpret, as in Mississippi, the constitutional provision that "there shall be no imprisonment for debt." (One cracker passed by writing "I thank that a Neorger should have 2 years in collage before voting because he don't under stand.")

So they stalled until finally, in 1957, a reluctant Dwight D. Eisenhower was forced to send in ten thousand members of the National Guard and a thousand paratroopers to protect nine Negro children who tried to go to a high school in Little Rock, Arkansas.

From this point, the segregationists fought like bayou panthers, obstructing and deflecting court orders to desegregate. The example of Arkansas governor Orval Faubus, a colorless and previously rather moderate politician who became a pop hero for resisting the federal government, encouraged other southern politicians, notably Ross Barnett of Mississippi and George Wallace of Alabama, to capitalize on and further stir up grass-roots racism. Wallace had begun as a trimmer on the race issue in the Huey Long–Big Jim

Folsom school of southern demagoguery. But, after losing an election for a minor statewide office to a race-baiter, he vowed that he would never be "out-niggered again." He was not and, in September 1963, made a phony stand at the entrance of the University of Alabama to prevent its defilement by the registration of a Negro student, Autherine Lucy.

With this kind of leadership coming to the fore, Little Rock's vicious, screaming crowds proved to be just the beginning of the ugliness. For almost a decade, a reliable staple of the evening news was the story of nasty crowds, brutal southern police, church bombings, murders, and southern statesmen egging it all on. By way of contrast, the Negro protesters and their few white supporters were peaceful, passive, and patient.

Most of the violence came when the civil rights movement confronted the two sturdy legs of Jim Crow, school segregation and black disenfranchisement. However, the ideology of the movement which eventually won victory on both questions was formed in a dispute over discriminatory public accommodations in Montgomery, Alabama.

THE MONTGOMERY
BUS BOYCOTT

Sociologists and historians frequently point out that revolutionary upheavals do not occur when the upheavers are in the deepest troughs of oppression. Those are a fatalistic people, rarely capable of resistance, let alone protest. It is in a time of rapid change, whether technological, social, or legal, when improvement is promised or hinted at but flies more quickly than the fact of the matter, that people rise.

This is true of the great revolutions of modern history, the French, the Russian, and the Chinese. All occurred at a time of ferment rather than despond such as all three societies had known and borne with. It has been true of the national liberation movements of the final third of the twentieth century. It is also true, on a more trivial level, of contemporary

American "upheaval" in which the banners of women's, gay, and ethnic lobbies were unfurled when the protesters were better off as groups than ever before.

It was hardly the case with American Negroes in the mid-1950s that they were well off as a group. But they were, even those who lived in the first capital of the Confederacy, Montgomery, and shared the crumbs and an odd bite-size bit of the cake that white America was wolfing down so greedily.

Large numbers of blacks were employed, as never before, in secure, high-paying jobs protected by strong and generally antiracist industrial unions. A growing black middle-class of professionals and small businessmen, prospering because of the large concentrations of Negroes in the northern city ghettos and because of the extremity of Jim Crow in the South, was better educated than ever before and ambitious for opportunities in the larger society.

Even in the worst parts of the South, the situation had changed. A lynching, previously little more notable than a speeding violation by Big Daddy's little boy, was now news. Even in the remotest pinewoods of eastern Mississippi, one could no longer get away unstained with "stringing up a buck." Lynchings made the front page, and if their perpetrators were still acquitted as often as not, they were at least brought to trial. Such piquant local methods of social control could no more withstand the cultural homogenization of fifties America than the Mom-and-Pop grocery stores of Tuscaloosa, Chicago, and Boise could resist the grand openings of new supermarkets.

On December 1, 1955, the patience of one black woman ran out. Mrs. Rosa Parks was on her way home from her job as a secretary. An attractive woman, just a few years shy of "matronly," neat as a pin, a churchwoman, and an NAACP volunteer, she could not have been better designed if a conspiracy had selected her to strike the first blow (as the Montgomery establishment was sure had been done, saying in effect that it was dirty to use a nice person for the job).

What Mrs. Parks did was to refuse to give up her seat at the front of the bus when, according to tradition and city ordinance, a white wanted it. She refused, sat tight, staring out the window. Mrs. Parks was arrested and later convicted and fined.

Such things had happened before. Indeed, unnumbered and unnoticed times tired black women like Mrs. Parks had raised little defiances of Jim Crow and been laughed off. "Good ol' Mammy." But in 1955, the southern whites were as nervous about changing racial relations as the blacks were impatient with delays. Establishment stupidity led to the bus boycott which, in fact, had been planned in outline by Jo Ann Robinson, head of the NAACP's Women's Political Council, and was just waiting for a Mrs. Parks to refuse to stand up.

On December 2, 1955, fifty leaders of Montgomery's Negro community, many of them ministers, met at the Dexter Avenue Baptist Church. They called for a boycott of the city's bus system and, by December 5, an estimated 90 percent of the city's Negroes were observing it. Their demands were hardly "excessive." In fact, they did not at first call for the complete removal of racial separation on buses but for an elimination of the gross indignities such as that to which Mrs. Parks was subjected. Insofar as the boycott had a program, it was merely that, with blacks first taking seats in the back of the bus and whites in the front, nobody had to move when the seats were all occupied. Hardly a "Declaration of the Rights of Man."

But official Montgomery held on despite a 65 percent cut in bus revenues which led to a raising of fares and a reduction of schedules. They arrested the young minister who had become the most conspicuous leader of the movement, the Rev. Martin Luther King, Jr. That led to a dramatic statement by the city's Negro community.

On February 22, 1956, Washington's Birthday, with dozens of newspaper reporters from all over the country puzzling about Alabama's odd racial and liquor laws, Montgomery's blacks not only stayed off the buses, they also refused to drive to work. They walked. Since they constituted more than half of the population of 125,000, their action emptied the streets and filled the sidewalks. The scene—and it was a scene with television journalists present—won widespread sympathy for the protesters and, more important, showed black people all over the country a way to voice their discontents: direct, nonviolent, mass civil disobedience.

The Montgomery Bus Boycott also created the single most important figure in the history of the civil rights movement, the pastor of the Dexter Avenue Church, thirty-six-year-old Dr. Martin Luther King, Jr.

DR. KING

Perhaps in the early thirteenth century, Assisi was as unlikely a place to produce a great saint as Montgomery was in 1956. But Martin Luther King, Jr., was that, a man from out of nowhere who, in the great moment, rose from being a pretty conventional black Baptist preacher, albeit a well-educated one, to become the eloquent teacher of a coherent, popular, and effective political philosophy. Neither the initial foot-dragging of the Eisenhower and early Kennedy administrations, nor the hatred for King by J. Edgar Hoover and other powerful men who efficiently and indefatigably gathered information about King's eye for the ladies, nor even King's later attempts to accommodate fools within his own movement can obscure the greatness of his message and the heroic response of the people to whom he preached. There are occasional bright moments in the unhappy history of humankind.

Martin Luther King was born in Atlanta in 1929, the son and grandson of ministers at the Ebenezer Baptist Church. He went to Morehouse College, a better than average Jim Crow school, and then to Crozer Theological Seminary in Pennsylvania and to the Boston University Divinity School. There he took a doctorate and continued a study of the formulators of nonviolent resistance and massive civil disobedience, Thoreau, Tolstoy, and Gandhi. He got his chance to articulate his ideas when his home in Montgomery was bombed. Speaking from the rubble on the front porch, he told his supporters, "We want to love our enemies. We must love our white brothers no matter what they do to us."

King's ethereal vision was given its most eloquent statement eight years later, on August 28, 1963, when, to a quarter of a million people in front of the Lincoln Memorial in Washington, he delivered his "I Have a Dream" speech.

> *I have a dream today.*
>
> *I have a dream that one day ... little black boys and black girls will be able to join hands with little white boys and white girls and walk together as sisters and brothers.*
>
> *I have a dream today.*
>
> *I have a dream that one day every valley shall be exalted, every hill and mountain shall be made low, the rough places will be made plain, and the crooked places will be made straight, and the glory of the Lord shall be revealed, and all flesh shall see it together.*
>
> *This is our hope. This is the faith with which I return to the South. With this faith we will be able to hew out of the mountain of despair a stone of hope. With this faith we will be able to transform the jangling discords of our nation into a beautiful symphony of brotherhood....*

For blacks and his white supporters, King constructed a *praxis* of direct-action, nonviolent civil disobedience. Black people would tumble unjust laws by disobeying them. They would submit without resistance to arrest, appealing to King's vision of brotherhood by contrasting their witness—their Christian faith and example—with the ugliness and brutality needed to enforce evil laws.

It was no pie-in-the-sky theory. As Gandhi and, in the United States, the old Wobblies had shown, massive disobedience of a law accompanied by a willingness of the violators to go to jail deftly shifts the burden of enforcement from the shoulders of the violators to those of the enforcers. The dependably high-handed brutality of southern police forces meant that the Christians would suffer. But Christianity was synonymous with suffering to people like King, and the public could not fail to get the message. Moreover, it cost money to keep hundreds of protesters in the worst of jails. What was right was also effective.

King did not reach the black masses of the South with expositions on Thoreau and Gandhi. As the rich gospel imagery of the "I Have a Dream" speech shows, he reached them because his message—just the opposite of the message of the rad-lib intellectuals in their world—was rooted like an ancient hickory in the culture of the southern Negroes.

Irving Howe and Dwight Macdonald never made fun of southern Negro religion although, given its hysterical side, they might have had quite a good time with it. They, like their successors in the sixties, were always quick to make exceptions for Negroes, to patronize them. In fact, the spiritual life of the southern blacks was real and vital. They responded to King's gospel because he appealed to the ancient buttresses of the Christian faith, buttresses which stood firmly on the experience of a people not unlike that of the raggedy mystery cultists of Antioch, Corinth, and Rome.

But like St. Paul and St. Francis, Martin Luther King was never simply a mystic. He may have seen great lights and chatted with starlings and sparrows now and then, but he also understood political and social realities, the importance of exposing to national publicity the folkways of the white South, and the importance of winning or forcing the support of powerful politicians who dealt in something less than moral ultimates. King was always ready to deal, from the compromise settlement he offered in Montgomery to his endorsement of politicians who voted for the civil rights acts of 1964 and 1965.

THE SIT-INS

The preachments of King were transmitted to the movement generation by the sit-in movement which began in Greensboro, North Carolina, in February 1960 and by the Freedom Rides of 1961, both of which were carried out under the auspices of King's Southern Christian Leadership Conference (SCLC). The first sit-in began with another spontaneous, individual act of "intrepid affirmation" (to quote King on Mrs. Parks), "an individual expression of a timeless longing for human dignity." This act was by Joseph McNeill, a freshman at North Carolina Agricultural and Technical College, a Jim Crow school.

On January 31, 1960, McNeill tried to get something to eat at the Greensboro Greyhound Bus Terminal. Like Rosa Parks, McNeill had little more in mind than satisfying a homely biological need. He knew well enough that most such eateries in the South were legally and customarily closed to Negroes, but he also knew that the slender profits in a tuna fish sandwich were sometimes enough to win a variance.

Not in McNeill's case. He was turned down, and that night, in a dormitory discussion with his roommate, Ezell Blair, Jr., he decided that he too had had enough. Next day, February 1, 1960, he and Blair and two others walked into the Greensboro Woolworth's (they were not gourmets), asked for a cup of coffee, were turned down, and stayed for several hours, uneasy, self-conscious, even frightened but, again like Mrs. Parks, "anchored by the accumulated indignities of days gone by and the boundless aspirations of generations yet unborn." At closing time they left.

There was no excitement that first day. A few jokes by the whites at the counter, more nervous than witty. White people in Greensboro read the national news too and knew what could come of such things. But there were no arrests as there was apparently no inclination to call in the cops. One of the race's less harmful impulses is to long for troubles to fade away as painlessly as possible.

But the next day, McNeill and Blair and their friends were back, and this time both the national press and the local yeomanry picked up on what was happening. By February 4 the counter at Woolworth's was lined with black students from A & T plus a few white supporters who tried unsuccessfully to get coffee for their friends. Tuna and egg salad sales took a nose dive as the sitters-in relieved one another on the stools, monopolizing the counter. Behind them white teenagers and more than a few of their elders milled about jeering, jostling, spattering the protesters with mustard and catsup. By the middle of the month, similar groups had organized all over the South. There were sit-ins of various duration in over a hundred southern cities, especially in the border states. King was arrested for ordering something or other at Atlanta's Rich's Department Store.

The lunch counter was not a difficult part of the color line to flank, especially at national chain stores such as Woolworth's. In addition to the discomfiting scenes at southern stores, northern whites and blacks set up pickets outside quite unsegregated Woolworth's in their towns, probably not hurting the trade much but, once again, disrupting the day, day after day. Moreover, in the cosmopolitan border state cities, few people defended the Jim Crowing of Woolworth's lunch counters. Few police forces actually arrested sitters-in, and even the nasty crowds of white teenagers that gathered at the news of an incident soon returned to the streets to listen to the squeal of rubber and the deep boiling of glass mufflers. Greensboro held out six months.

By the end of 1960, most large border cities quietly integrated their lunch counters and similar facilities, many without a sit-in.

THE FREEDOM RIDES

The deep South was another matter as CORE—the Congress of Racial Equality—discovered when, in the Spring of 1961, it launched its direct action campaign against back-of-the-bus seating on long distance coaches of the Greyhound and Trailways lines. In Alabama, an integrated busload of Freedom Riders was beaten with chains, kicked to the ground, and stomped. Their bus was stoned and then burned.

In May 1961 CORE launched its challenge to both Jim Crow and the new Kennedy administration. On May 4 a Freedom Bus left Washington, D.C., bound for New Orleans and traversing eight southern states. At first the bus was only mildly harassed, but in Alabama segregationists spoke openly of violent action. Before they could deliver, Attorney General Robert F. Kennedy dispatched five hundred federal marshals to Montgomery where the Freedom Riders planned to rally. There was the usual foofaraw about states rights and the competence of the law enforcement officials of the sovereign state of Alabama to maintain law and order for all its citizens and visitors to the land of camellias, but Kennedy did not relent. Prodded by King's march on Washington, he and his more reluctant brother, the President, pushed through the Civil Rights Law of June 19, 1963, which, among other things, outlawed discrimination by race in interstate travel.

Moral upheavals have political shortcomings by definition. Preoccupied by the Christian admonition to witness, the Montgomery, sit-in, and Freedom Rides movements struck Jim Crow at dramatic but nonvital points.

The protesters could leave school desegregation to the federal government which, after Little Rock and especially after the Kennedys came to power, moved deliberately with its suits.

However, until 1964, the King-SNCC-CORE movement also virtually ignored the issue of Negro voting rights, an obvious key to black equality. Even when, at the tail end of the Eisenhower administration, Attorney General William P.

Rogers tried to interest the civil rights groups in the voting problem, he was ignored. They seem to have thought his motive was to distract them from the public accommodations fight. When the Kennedy administration repeated the suggestion, it was "met with suspicion."

A few years later, a new young generation of civil rights activists did attack this problem. In doing so they showed a greater appreciation than the King movement of the political realities of the republic, due in part to their northern upbringing, secular mainsteam educations, and insensitivity to the southern Negro Protestant culture.

In fact, these new activists prided themselves on their awareness of the need for "black power" and they were inclined to sneer at King as Uncle Tom, D.D. However, their "political realism" was not so far beyond Dr. King as they believed (not to mention being three years behind William P. Rogers). Rather than transcending or even building on King's and SNCC's and CORE's beginning, they perverted it and, in the end, turned out to be less political than their predecessors.

THE LEGACY OF THE
CIVIL RIGHTS MOVEMENT

Martin Luther King was never a New Leftist. He never thought of himself as a radical and when, late in the sixties, he tried to accommodate "revolutionaries" like Stokely Carmichael and the Black Panthers, the effort was awkward and half-hearted. He could persuade neither them nor himself that separatism and antagonistic confrontation had a place in his essentially Christian philosophy.

Although SNCC, an offshoot of SCLC, evolved into one of the groups that rejected King's message, few of the sit-in leaders were members when it happened. If they had not drifted away in order to pursue private careers, they broke with SNCC when, in the turn to Black Power, SNCC rejected the southern rural Protestantism that had given it birth. CORE was a little different. A largely urban, northern organization, it

came late to the struggle against segregation in public accommodations in the South, a never quite comprehending tail of
the dog. CORE found it easy to convert to Black Power. Its
leaders, especially the gloriously inarticulate Floyd McKis-
sick, found it easy to make the shift from integration,
brotherhood, nonviolence, and witness to racial separatism,
antagonism, force, and pseudo-revolutionism.

But the legacy of nonviolent, mass civil disobedience was
a large one. Personal witness, rooted in and given meaning by
the religious background of the early protesters, remained an
integral part of the Black Power movement. However, di-
vorced from its Christian context, gussied up by courses in
liberal arts, witness was transformed into the existential act,
less important for its objective purpose—setting an example to
edify others—than as self-affirmation and self-gratification.
What was to King a holy, spiritual act became a pose.
Necessarily, the moral self-limitations on the principle of
witness ceased to apply when the purpose was personal
gratification.

Civil disobedience, always defined by King and SNCC as
including the willingness to accept without wincing the
prescribed civil penalties—the object being "a higher law"—
became, in the minds of northern blacks raised in the tradition
of you-do-what-you-can-get-away-with, and northern middle-
class whites accustomed to getting away with everything, an
occasion for juvenile mischief or worse. They called breaking
the law "revolution," and then felt misused when authorities
tolerated neither the crime nor the ostensible insurrectionary
act. Despite the Movement's penchant for quoting revolutionary writers, it was from the nonrevolutionary civil rights
movement that they learned their tactics. The difference was
the New Leftists' inability to comprehend the foundations of
their predecessors' actions.

King's movement also had unfortunate consequences for
the radical-liberal intellectuals who not only supported him

but also rushed to defend and explain the perversions of his successors. Never fully able to understand the vitality of the anachronistic southern black religious tradition (as much as they liked the songs), not to mention what King knew—that he was no radical—they were attracted to the southern blacks as victims of Moloch.

The coherence of the King movement was no more important to them than the incoherence and social emptiness of beat. Both were rebellions. The fact that American society dictated black inferiority while the beatniks had to manufacture their alienation, to strain at it, was of no importance. Both blacks and beatniks were underdogs. As a result, when the Negro movement shifted to an aimless thrashing about under Stokely Carmichael, Hubert Geroid "H. Rap" Brown, and Huey P. Newton, it made no difference. Were not the Black Powerites rebellious? Were they not victims? *Like* Martin Luther King and his people? Undeniably. Therefore, what they said—whatever they said—was O.K. and more than that. The intellectuals who had been smitten by the Wild Ones, Jets, Sharks, and Purple Gougers of the 1950s found juvenile delinquents who talked revolution too good to be true.

The Establishment also learned a few lessons from the King movement which were to help it contribute to the troubles of the sixties. Looking back, the politicians and bureaucrats of the mid- and late 1960s saw that, time and time again, moderate black groups presented just and reasonable demands. Time and again they saw the southern power structure greet these demands with procrastination or with German shepherds, cattle prods, fire hoses, and billy clubs. Time and again the result was a larger, angrier, and more demanding black protest plus instability—dreaded instability—and worse, a loss of money, from a near bankrupt bus system to, periodically all over the South, boycotted business sections.

After the breakthrough of the civil rights acts of 1964 and

1965, the result was an inclination to respond *immediately* to *all* demands made by *any* blacks or, in time, any group that defined itself as oppressed. Tom Wolfe described these tortured bureaucrats as "Flak-Catchers." He called the technique of sparking them to dance, which was not difficult to learn, "Mau-Mauing."

From a cynic's seat in a corner of the room, the antics of the Mau-Mauers could be highly diverting. Blacks and students and women and homosexuals and what-have-you convinced themselves that unless they received government grants or a share of jobs in a bureaucracy, all was not well with the world. They screamed, as close to the face of the appropriate perspiring bureaucrat as could be done without kissing. The bureaucrat and his boss buckled. They would not be George Wallaces, Bull Connorses, racists, fascists. They heard a peep and they jumped. They heard a shout and they flew. It was immaterial that there might be a difference between Martin Luther King's pleas for simple human dignity and the "needs" of the grant-gouger and the seventeen-year-old student who thought it would raise his self-esteem if old P.U. instituted a course in Masai shield painting.

All this was to come. But the immediate consequence of SNCC's appeals for northern white support was to provide uneasy, questing university students with a focus for their discontents and energies. HUAC did not actually raise the white flag until Jerry Rubin's assault at the end of the decade. But the committee was badly wounded by the campaign of 1961 and spent its appropriations quietly through most of the decade. By 1962 the young people whom *Operation Abolition* had aroused were looking for a new cause, and racial inequality provided it. Students for a Democratic Society (SDS), the central organization of the Movement, adopted civil rights as its first arena of operations. But before looking at the origins of SDS, it is necessary to look more closely at the character and assumptions of the generation that was at the center of its decade.

CHAPTER THREE

WE
THE
PEOPLE
OF
THIS
GENERATION

A biology professor at a western university was easing new students into their introductory course. It was 1975. That year, more college freshmen and sophomores sat in Biology I than ever before. In 1975, the people born in 1957, the peak year of the great American baby boom, were eighteen years old.

The professor was only vaguely aware of such sociological niceties. He was old enough to have noticed the steadily rising enrollments. He was close to retirement. But academic scientists had not been so profoundly affected as social scientists and humanists by the population explosion on campus during the sixties. Furthermore, the biologist's lifelong research project—on the reproductive system of some sort of winged insect or another—had climaxed during the decade of the Movement; while the demonstrations raged outside, he had been sealed in a soundproof laboratory with microscopes and long lists of data, only vaguely aware that "something's happening, baby."

Indeed, he was quite one of those "dull, doddering, irrelevant specialists" the Movement scorned for their insensitivity to the plight of humanity, and he had been lucky enough to be left alone with his preoccupations.

He devoted scarcely more time to his Biology I lecture notes than to current events. Pretty cut-and-dried stuff it was. There was little one could do with fundamentals but explain them, crisply and clearly. Because the students were still nervously settling in during the first days of the course and the order of the day was mere definition of basic biological processes like reproduction, anabolism, catabolism, and so on, the professor was not accustomed to interruptions as he toiled his way through his notes.

He illustrated each definition with a homey human example. For catabolism—"the degradative chemical reactions in a living cell"—he noted the visible signs of aging in human beings. As the components of subcutaneous fats broke down into their chemical constituents, "deteriorated," he droned on absently, leaving the skin too large for its contents, people's faces "wrinkled." It was a throwaway line, filler, a little color, and he turned a page to the next definition.

Up shot a hand. Could the professor repeat his last point? He did, and also reassured what he took to be an uneasy student that it was the definition of catabolism that was important, not his example. He joked weakly that there would be no questions about wrinkled faces and jowls on the examination.

Another hand. Another student wanted this wrinkling thing cleared up. A little exasperated—there are a great many definitions to be mastered in the first days of a basic Biology course—the old professor repeated once again that it was simply an obvious, visible sign of aging in humans. "Look around at old people," he said. "Look at me. I'm wrinkled. (Nervous laugh.) It's part of life. Catabolism." He also emphasized that the class was wandering from the point. They would be studying amoebas and paramecia and other rather simple creatures in Biology I, not humans.

He never saw such an inquisitive group of students. The hands waved like flowers by a freeway. Scratch one day's progress through the syllabus. He could not escape dry skin and wrinkles and, truth to tell, as an insect man, he did not know a great deal about the specifics of the process in humans.

He did know that he would not use the illustration again. It was only later, at home, while ruminating over the odd experience, that he realized what it was all about. It was not that his students had mistaken a throwaway line for a "main point." Students had trouble distinguishing essentials from trivia at the best of times. His colleagues in the history department told him that their students would rather chatter about George Washington's wooden teeth than about the Founding Father's world view any day of the week.

But no, the trouble here was that these students did not believe in aging. They did not know what it was. They were trying and failing to grasp a concept that might as well have been a tenet of Shintoism because they could not "relate" to it personally. They were writhing in anxiety in that lecture hall as they might have writhed at age six when they lay under the stars and tried to grasp the fact that, unlike Anaheim, the space above them went on forever. "Wrinkling" was as boggling a concept as infinity, as mysterius as the Trinity, as frustrating as the first moment on a bicycle. In drawing attention to his own wizened face, the professor had helped them no more than wheeling a lifelong paraplegic into a basketball game would help him understand what it means to get up on his own two feet and go after that ball.

The professor's shortage of subcutaneous fat was not "relevant." That was a word the full life cycle of which the professor had missed. Like newborn infants, his students' universes ended with the tips of their fingers and toes. In a way, they had not progressed to that stage of development the psychologist Jean Piaget described in which the human creature understands that the feces he evacuates is no longer him.

The good professor had not vivified a biological concept by means of an everyday sight. He had obscured it.

Were the students merely stupid? In part, perhaps. In *Great Expectations,* his insightful book on the baby boom generation, Landon Y. Jones discussed the steady decline of scores on the Scholastic Aptitude Tests between 1963 and 1979. (SAT is an examination virtually all people applying for a spot in a university must write.) Despite some evidence that the test grew easier during the period, the average score declined from a 1963 high of 478 on verbal skills and 502 on mathematical (within a range of 200–600) to 427 and 467 in 1979. "After believing all along that they were the best and the brightest," Jones comments, "the baby boomers were suddenly facing distressing evidence that they were the dumbest."

By the seventies, any university professor who was not a fool—they could be found, with diligence—had a repertory of anecdotes suitable for cocktail parties that dramatized the SAT data. The students of the late sixties and the seventies seemed generally dimmer, less able to cope with difficult study, and more lacking in basic principles by which to organize what they were capable of learning than any previous generation of students and, as seems to be the case, the one presently attending high school.

It is not beyond the realm of possibility that the general intelligence of the race is in genetic decline. Just as primitive society put a premium on the physically prime, and industrial society favored those best equipped mentally to contend with new complexities, postindustrial society, with its even minimal social welfare programs, burdens the physically and mentally unblessed with no great handicaps. With the decreasing value of literacy in contemporary times, it is not farfetched to imagine a human population in a few centuries that is dramatically more stupid than any since Neanderthal days. In *Brave New World*, Aldous Huxley thought this could be accomplished only through the wonders of chemistry. Maybe it is a simple matter of biological adaptation?

However that may be, the laws of natural selection do not reveal their workings in a decade. The "disappearing scores" on the SATs can only reflect a cultural origin.

In *Great Expectations,* Landon Jones makes a persuasive case for the fact that the sheer size of the baby boom generation—those born between 1946 and 1964—accounts for the declining scores and for much else that has characterized and troubled American culture since World War II. There is more to it than numbers, but because Jones is so persuasive, and because the first wave of the baby boom *was* the Movement generation (a person eighteen in 1970 was born in 1952), the significance of the boomers' millions must be understood.

BOOM!

In 1946 one of the smallest generations in the history of the American population began to beget the hordes of children known as the baby boom. After virtual stability in the birth rate during the twenties and thirties and unsteady spurts during World War II, the number of new squalling infants rose to a record 3.4 million in the first postwar year.

Demographers expected that. For four years, marriages had been deferred by the mobilization into the armed forces of one age cohort of young males after another. (*Cohort* in this context refers to people born in the same year, of the same age.) However, almost to the last man, whether employed by census bureau or university, the demographers said that 1946 was an aberration. A high birth rate would endure for a year or two, at the most. Subsequently, as the nation readjusted to "normalcy," the century-long trend of a birth rate in decline would reassert itself.

They were wrong. Indeed, one of the most fascinating revelations of Landon Y. Jones's study is how dependably demographers are wrong. Jones is too much the gentleman to put it so bluntly, but it is obvious that those who predict population trends are less often on the money than those who apply science or the tarot to the selection of bingo cards. Apparently, the unseen hand that determines who rises to the top in the profession of demography is the same one that taps the shoulders of the leaders and the eminent in other areas of American life.

For, in 1947, as the demographers continued to draw their salaries, the total of births in the United States rose to 3.8 million. After a negligible dip, the upswing started again in 1951 and climbed and climbed until 1957 when American births peaked at 4.3 million.

The last year of the baby boom was 1964 (4 million). From then until 1976, despite a bulge in the cohorts of women of child-bearing age—the baby boomers themselves since nearly all the female boomers were in that category by 1980—the number of births dropped steadily and sharply.*

---

*In 1977 a slight increase began that may or may not augur a trend. The best gauge as to the significance of the climb is the opposite of the demographers' most recent projections.

If the post-1964 decline is a long-term phenomenon, the consequences of the bulge in the American age profile will continue to influence—even determine—the development of society well into the twenty-first century, and the consequences of the "baby bust" of 1965–?, somewhat longer. The consequences have already been immense. There is no way they could not be. However inept the demographers were in predicting them, they displayed a happy faculty for metaphor when they described the phenomenon of the baby boom as "the pig in the python," quite as traumatic to the society as the snake's big lunch is to its digestive process.

"The pig in the python" can be understood by imagining a line depicting the annual number of births in the United States between 1910 and 1980. That great bulge on the right center is not stationary. Just as the python's clever musculature forces the meal through it, eventually to oblivion, the baby boomers grow older, forming a domineering bloc of age cohorts when they are infants, when they are adolescents, and when they are adults in the prime of life. Eventually they will dominate the society with their numbers when they are ancient.

Perhaps the best-known social consequence of the aging of the baby boom is what it meant for the American educational system. Beginning about 1952, the boomers entered elementary school. In that first year there were fully 350,000 more first graders than there had been the previous year. When the age cohort of 1945, the final preboom group (2.8 million), were in their final year of high school in 1962 and 1963, more than four million children were in first grade. Almost 1.5 million more schoolchildren were hunched over their coloring books that year than were fretting over locating a date for the senior prom. Such "mere numbers" inevitably disrupted a school system that had annually processed approximately the same number of children for half a century.

Landon Y. Jones explored many more implications of the phenomenon than the well-known overcrowding of schools and the near panic in which the country hastened to build classrooms and train teachers through the sixties. Inevitably there was a lag. In the meantime, the overcrowded facilities and half-day schedules of the era provide a *prima facie* explanation of why, while much-schooled, the baby boom generation was not as well educated, not as bright, as the one that preceded it. The nation's cadre of experienced teachers could not grow as quickly as the number of children in schools. Experience is a matter of years on the stick. In the meantime, the new and sometimes hastily-trained teachers could not do the same job as the cranky old maiden lady who, through the forties, still exemplified the American schoolteacher.

It is also pertinent to the subject at hand that, because they were so numerous, baby boomers found it easy, even incumbent upon them, to fraternize largely, even exclusively, with people their own age. There were so many of them that they did not need to look farther, to those older or those younger, in order to find companions. This was particularly true in that cultural sink of the fifties radicals and that breeding ground of the Movement, suburbia, to where the parents of the baby boomers flocked.

It is conceivably quite natural that, free of external pressures, children gravitate to those of their own age. (Americans are particularly notorious for age segregation.) But, like many things "natural"—typhoons, belladonna weed, wolverines, and that sort of thing—it is not necessarily "good for you." Because they had comparatively less to do with their juniors than previous generations, each age cohort of baby boomers failed to develop the habits of responsibility that protecting the less mature seems to cultivate in a person, whether as big brother or baby-sitter (a characteristic that helps explain the narcissism of the seventies when the first boomers were in their twenties and thirties, the trend-setting prime of life, as well as the sharp decline in childbearing after 1965).

Because they had less to do with their elders, including their parents, even as measured by simple shared time, the baby boomers were less acculturated in the values of the past than has been customary in American or other cultures. Instead, in fraternizing principally and constantly with those of their own age cohort, they evolved an unguided, uprooted, infantile vision of the world that was at most only mildly challenged at home and in school. There are no "authorities" in an age cohort, as there cannot be, only people who are "popular," particularly apt at attracting attention to themselves.

In his chilling novel of 1954, *Lord of the Flies,* William Golding dealt with the consequences of children left without moral authority and, therefore, cultural links with the past. A group of English public school boys, about as civilized and regimented a lot of lads as can be imagined, were stranded on a tropical island where they reverted to savagery, including the attempted extirpation of one another. *Lord of the Flies* was a smashing success, the inspiration of a cult. But somehow, preposterously, until the general record of fifties intellectuals is recalled, especially that of the radical aesthetes, Golding's millions of readers seem to have missed the point. During the sixties when youth ruled supreme and played out a version of Golding's story, the book fell into obscurity.

What few challenges to their peer culture the baby boomers were confronted with, as in *Lord of the Flies,* were easily shaken off. A Labrador retriever has less trouble drying down after a dip. An age cohort is quite as conditioned to be suspicious of outsiders as a tribe of headhunters that discovers another tribe's hunting party or maybe just some university's anthropology department cutting its way through the local brush.

Unless, that is, the strangers come laden with attractive goodies. America's consumer orgiasts came laden with plenty for the kids of the baby boom and it was, perhaps, through the baubles of the fifties that the culture got through to "the kids." Shrewd entrepreneurs presented the huge baby boom market of the fifties (baby boomers 0–14 years of age) with a galaxy of fad items: hula hoops, Davy Crockett caps, Barbi dolls, a popular music dedicated to juvenile themes at prices to suit juvenile allowances (89 cents per 45 rpm disc). Ephemeral by definition, fads reinforced the peculiarly fragmentary quality of television entertainment in depriving the boomers of a sense of continuity, historical or otherwise, instilling in them instead a reliance on novelty for their "fulfillment."

Biologically, childhood passes. But, as the old biology professor's discomfiting experience indicates, a childish conception of the world does not necessarily respond to altered rates of hormone production. Writing as early as 1960, when only a few age cohorts of baby boomers had entered adolescence, Grace and Fred M. Hechinger already feared the significance of their numbers. The United States was in danger of becoming "a teenage society, with permanently teenage standards of thought, culture, and goals."

It was during the 1960s that the Hechingers' dream came true. The first reason for the triumph of "youth culture" was the boom generation's numerical dominance during the troubled decade. Between 0 and 24 year of age during the sixties, the boomers became what the Italian magazine *L'Europeo* called the most "pitiless, ineducable, indestructible dictatorship in the world."

But were their numbers really the whole of it? Writing later in the decade Philip Selznik suggested that the New Left was a temporary distemper because it was so clearly an adolescent phenomenon and adolescence passes. Landon Y. Jones expresses the same point of view in a somewhat different way when he argues that there was never really a kiddie culture in the 1950s or a youth culture during the 1960s but only the domination of a particular generation which, like the pig in the python, moves on to dominate in another fashion.

With time, the baby boomers will indeed be hobbling about the Santa Monica boardwalks and Broadway median strips of the twenty-first century, and, assuming their numbers still disproportionate compared to those who come after them, they will make the United States a nation of old women and old men. Will the United States then be a "geriatric culture" or simply still under the sway of its dominant and tragic generation for one last time? Will the elderly baby boomers be the first generation that comes to old age presenilized?

One thing is sure. When the baby boomers are on their canes, whether gutta-percha, stainless steel, or, God forbid, plastic, America's intellectuals will swoon about the profound beauties of senescence that, somehow, all previous generations failed to see. Already (in the early 1980s) the trendy social scientists have launched the campaign to deny the very existence of biological senility or a decline in sexual powers.

The shallowness of America's thinkers, an apparently irreversible disease, is the second element in explaining why the kids of the Movement generation were able to make the impact they did.

Children will be children, and perhaps the peculiar and severe emotional handicaps of the children of the baby boom—due to their numbers alone—could not be avoided. Nevertheless, it is also pertinent to the troubles of the 1960s that the people society entrusts with thinking did not think straight. The Movement was not just numbers. Instead of casting the doleful eye, watching the pig in the python with a healthy skepticism and warning society of the problems of a culture dictated by the immature, a large part of the American intellectual community crawled into the snake's maw to join the pig. In part, the baby boomers never "grew up" and likely never will because their home experience as infants and the thrust of their schooling as children was such as to urge them to remain kids. To the extent that childhood can be defined as a time of irresponsibility and dependence, when one's soul cannot be damned, then the sins of the decade must be laid not on the hysterical "long-haired kids" of SDS and Woodstock but on their elders. The elders offered the juniors no incentive to embrace their culture.

"If manhood, if the good life in the good community," sociologist Bennett Berger wrote in 1962, "is the goal of adolescence, then the goal is clear, and with it the direction and the path. But what if existing manhood is viewed as empty, static, obsolescent," not only by adolescents but by the men and women of that society? "Then becoming a man is death, and manhood marks the death of adolescence, not its fulfillment."

It was, of course, an Everest of stupidity to look to children as saviors. But this book is about a whole Himalayas of stupidity; the Sherpas of the range were not "the kids"— they never got out of the hash shops in the valley—but the adults, who had no demographic excuses for their behavior.

Perhaps the ultimate demonstration of the "older generation's" responsibility for the troubles of the sixties can be most clearly seen by scanning a brief but entirely representative list of Movement leaders and their birthdates. *None of them were baby boomers!*

Leaders of SDS

Al Haber, 1936
Tom Hayden, 1940
Todd Gitlin, 1943
Paul Potter, 1940
Carl Oglesby, 1935
Jim Mellen, 1935

SNCC Leaders

Robert Moses, 1935
John Lewis, 1940
Stokely Carmichael, 1941
Hubert Geroid "H. Rap" Brown, 1943

Black Panther Leaders

Huey P. Newton, 1942
Bobby Seale, 1936
Eldridge Cleaver, 1936

Free Speech Movement Leaders

Mario Savio, 1942
Jack Weinberg, 1940

Antiwar Movement Leaders

Benjamin Spock, 1903
David Dellinger, 1916
Staughton Lynd, 1929

Yippies

Abbie Hoffman, 1936
Jerry Rubin, 1939

Balance of the Chicago Seven of 1968

Lee Weiner, 1939
John Froines, 1939
Rennie Davis, 1940

Gurus and Jesters

Herbert Marcuse, 1898
Angela Davis, 1944
Timothy Leary, 1921
Charles Reich, 1928
Bob Dylan, 1941
Beatles, 1940, 1940, 1942, 1943

Ten years was more than sufficient time for the Movement to have raised successors to these pioneers. By 1970 the first baby boomers were twenty-four years old, senior to many of those listed above when they launched their careers. But it did not happen. The nearest thing to a baby boom leader of the New Left was the ludicrous Mark Rudd (born 1949) of Columbia University and the Weathermen, and he was quickly eclipsed in the terrorist group by Bernadine Dohrn (born 1943), closer in years to middle-age spread and wrinkles, as the Movement calendar had it, than to her jacks and Raggedy Ann doll.

The baby boom did provide victims. Those who were beaten up in demonstrations and the few killed in New Left battles with authorities were boomers. Black Panther martyr Bobby Hutton was born in 1952. The four students shot at Kent State were born in 1950 and 1951. The overdosers of the drug culture were virtually all kids. The bodies found and yet to be found in shallow graves in commune country like the Santa Cruz mountains of California had not begun to catabolize naturally when their processes were interrupted by the tantrum of some other flower child. Perhaps the incidence of suicide among baby boomers in the seventies, not paralleled in any other age group, ought to be included as a species of victimization. And then there was the raft of Weather Underground and Black Liberation Army militants arrested and alleged to have killed several police in an incompetent robbery of a Brink's truck: Most of those "revolutionaries" were born about 1950.

The boomers were top quality cannon fodder. As Landon Y. Jones points out, one of the generation's most chilling characteristics was its propensity to move as a mass. Whether the impetus was Davy Crockett hats, "revolution," disco, women's lib, Eastern religious cults, jogging, or the motherhood craze of the early eighties, thanks both to their total numbers and their mass personality, the baby boomers formed a great responsive flock. Open the right gate. Set the right dog on them. You had them.

"Sheep" and "dogs" may be the wrong images. Somewhere in the Aldous Huxley–D. H. Lawrence correspondence the human race gets divided into three more appropriate zoological specimens: apes, asses, and dogs. The apes of the sixties were the Movement generation, the first wave of the baby boomers, dull-witted, lazy, sociable, negligible creatures but for the strength of their numbers. But the leaders of the

Movement and the intellectuals who made straight the way for the Movement were not so much dogs—manipulators, vicious often enough, the kind that snarl and nip their way to what they want, the Nixons and Agnews of the decade—they were asses, fools with little to say, but they were always braying nevertheless, braying, braying, braying. By the fifties, when the vast numbers of baby boomers were in junior high school, they had been braying so long they were in charge.

PRAGMATISM AND PROGRESSIVE EDUCATION

The modern American intellectual's world view has its origins in the thought of a group of late nineteenth century philosophers known as the pragmatists. These men were themselves schooled in what is known as the "common sense" philosophy of the Scottish realists. Believing that man was rational and that God was real and coherent, the system taught that common sense guided by divinely revealed absolutes was sufficient to know what could be known and thereby serve as a basis with which to order human affairs. Among other things, Herbert W. Schneider writes in his *History of American Philosophy,* "the safe and sane system . . . was an ideal pattern for preventing youth from indulging in speculative excesses."

Why just "youth?" For the philosophical system that replaced Scottish realism among American intellectuals cut them loose to some pretty wild philosophical philandering, too.

This new system was "pragmatism." Surrounded by collapsing verities in the late nineteenth century, stunned as others were by the brilliance of Charles Darwin's evolutionary explanation of the biological world but disturbed by his and the social Darwinist Herbert Spencer's determinism, men like Charles S. Peirce and William James renounced the very concept of philosophical absolutes—immutable or at least stubborn principles. They argued that truth evolved to accommodate the times. Indeed, there was no truth, only *truths,* always changing, always evolving. Process, not a standard, was the key. Ideas could be evaluated only in terms of their consequences.

In a famous essay, "How to Make Our Ideas Clear," Peirce said that an idea is nothing more than the sum of its consequences. Ideas and theories mattered (were "relevant," to call on sixties jargon) only in terms of specifics.

In *Principles of Psychology,* published in 1890, William James added another dimension to Peirce's theories. If ideas mattered only in terms of their consequences, the effectiveness of an idea—James liked the term "cash value"—could be enhanced by the extent of a person's "will to believe." The truth of a point of view could be increased by the intensity with which one believed it. ("Are you really committed, really sincere?") Conversely, doubt—skepticism—increased the like-lihood that the idea would fail, that it was wrong, false.

Readers who are fond of old movies will recognize the philosophical underpinnings of those hospital scenes in which a poor soul flattened by a steamroller is given a chance to survive and live happily ever after by the attending physician to the degree that he or she possesses "the will to live." More to the point at hand, the triumph of the pragmatic view of the world among the American intellectual community during the twentieth century helps explain why the simple size of the baby boom generation is not enough to account for the sixties. As children they might have been imbued with any of a dozen philosophies. As it was, through the pragmatists' application of their point of view to education and child rearing, they were made into the ultimate pragmatists, which is to say, with apologies to the thoughtful Peirce and the eloquent William James, wishful thinkers.

It needs to be said that pragmatism was in many ways a mere codification of the way Americans already thought. Since the decay of Puritanism in the colonial period, and excepting anomalous groups ranging from the nineteenth century Mormons through the urban, ethnic Catholic Church of the twentieth century, and some Old Left radicals, Americans have not been idealogues with a central, unifying vision but engineers, isolators, and solvers of specific problems.

Sir Isaiah Berlin illustrated the distinction between ideologues and engineers by calling on the Greek fabulist, Archilochus, who divided the human race—more animals!—into foxes who know many things and hedgehogs who know one big thing.

Americans were foxes. They never had a taste for the one big thing. They have always, long before Peirce and James, preferred the pragmatic accommodation to the specific problem. The role of the pragmatists was merely to elevate this habit of mind into a coherent philosophy, an . . . absolute.

Perhaps the ultimate weakness of pragmatism is the fact that, much more than religious zeal, it works dependably for only one generation. Thinkers well educated in principles and the stuff of wisdom—facts—could have a reasonable go at testing ideas by their consequences because they were capable of understanding the nature of those consequences. They could rebel against the verities taught to them as children with some authority. Jesuit education could produce a Stephen Daedalus worth listening to. But people educated by pragmatists had neither a fortress against which to hurl themselves nor a body of knowledge to serve as ammunition. They had neither anything worth rebelling against nor anything to offer. Ultimately in such circumstances—very soon—pragmatism degenerates into intuition.

This was particularly true when the pragmatists' philosophy was applied to elementary and secondary education, as was done through the theories of "progressive education." It is one thing when learned men and women try to test ideas according to specifics; it is quite another when children innocent of specifics are allowed—instructed—to do so.

During the 1960s, the unsavory likes of Spiro Agnew and Richard M. Nixon appealed to their troops of apes with nasty words about progressive education as the source of the troubles, making it easy to pooh-pooh the idea. To do so, however, is to test an idea by consequences, its unsavory associations. The most striking characteristics of the Movement are too clearly related to the prevailing attitudes of the education schools of the period to reject the point. The ignorance of the people of the New Left and Counterculture, their rejection of the very idea of program, their reflexive belief that wishing will make it so, their refusal to be held accountable to objective standards, all—however diluted and however obnoxious doughty William James would have found it—were at least partly the fruit of the pragmatists' success.

Nor was intellectual slovenliness the only disservice rendered by pragmatist educators. To emphasize process rather than goal, to encourage children unequipped for testing ideas to do just that, to believe in the insipid "will to believe" and the corollary that potential believers be encouraged to work on their own rather than to look to others for answers involve, in the end, a lot of outright lying. The subjective individual, not the objective standard (which did not exist), was important. As Grace and Fred M. Hechinger, two waspish critics of progressive education, put it in 1960:

> *The child who just smeared paints across the pad was seen as expressing himself as usefully as the child who showed the beginnings of a sense of color and pattern. Were not both letting the individual soul speak? And who was to pass judgement on the expressions of these sacred individuals? In fact, there were some who began to define the "correct" expression as society-dictated and therefore destructive of individual expression.*

Another villain of the Nixon-Agnew, right-wing gang of the 1960s, and a far less culpable one, was Dr. Benjamin Spock. The vilifiers of the New Left and Counterculture accused him of extending indulgence down from the schools into the at-home years. Although surely within the pragmatist tradition,

Spock preached anything but "spoiling" children. As historian William Graebner points out, Spock tried to devise a system of childhood discipline suitable to a democratic society. Far from "anything goes," the tenets of his *Common Sense Book of Baby and Child Care,* first published in 1946, aimed at bringing order into the lives of children who lived in a world shattered by disorder: economic depression, the crimes of fascism, world war. Spock was trying to find a rational middle ground between the regimentation by which Hitler trained his robots and the anarchy that Spock may have seen emerging in American homes and schools.

But if Spock was a handy fellow at diaper folding and commonsensical when it came to treating measles and mumps, he was and remained a sloppy philosopher. He never could make up his mind about human nature. On one evening a Little Mary Sunshine, on the next he was capable of calling man "distinctly more aggressive, cruel, and relentless than any of the other apes" and the child "a potential tyrant, and incipient demagogue." Most often he equivocated: "If the infant is not born a barbarian, the potential for a twentieth-century version of savagery is never far below the surface."

It is curious that the apostle of *consistency* in disciplining and otherwise dealing with children should have been so inconsistent on the question that would seem to be funda-mental to any philosophy of child rearing. But Spock's confusion was not untypical of pragmatists when they are held accountable to the norms they denied existed.

Spock was also faulted by his critics for calling for the coddling of children. Once again he was not so guilty as he was said to be. He did emphasize demonstrating love for children more than any of his predecessors had done. The gist of Spock's forerunners in the baby book market (none nearly so successful; *Baby and Child Care* sold four million copies by 1952 and thirty million by 1980) was sternness and distance. However, the most recent scholarly commentators on Spock are surely correct when they emphasize that discipline was at the center of his theory.

CHILD WORSHIP

Spock took the rap for the fruition of an old American tradition. If the Duke of Windsor could set a roomful of his friends to snuffling gaily when he remarked that Americans obeyed their children wonderfully well, and if Marxist Eugene G. Genovese could condemn the mass media in 1970 because they "hail everything young as intrinsically good and misunderstood," they were merely echoing what foreign and jaundiced domestic observers of American folkways had said for two centuries.

In 1855 an Englishman wrote that "baby citizens are allowed to run as wild as Snake Indians and do whatever they please." Half a century earlier a Londoner commented that "to see sensible people smile with secret admiration at the spirited exhibition of rebellious will on the part of their offspring excites in an English mind a sense of lurking danger."

It is an old story and quite rooted in the American character. Americans' deference to their children was owed in part to a nebulous but compelling belief in the future and in the inevitable progress toward happiness that the younger were destined to taste better foods than the older, a fact that merited for them a certain indulgence and even awe. In part it has to do with the chronic inability of Americans, *vide* Dr. Spock, to believe, despite the evidence, in original sin, a flawed human nature. Children, to such a people, far from being "vipers and infinitely more hateful than vipers," were, by virtue of their proximity to pure human innocence, superior to adults. The English romantics did well enough by this notion, but only in the United States did it deeply permeate the society. William Wordsworth might have been named poet laureate. Ralph Waldo Emerson could not find the time to appear before the hundreds of large audiences that slavered to sip his cup of bubbly good cheer.

If the indulgence of children has deep roots in American culture, however, it is important to recall that the observers of it dealt exclusively with the privileged and comfortably-fixed classes. The troubled British observers of the early nineteenth century were not speaking of the brats of Molly O'Rourke and the snot-faced bairns of Kentucky's hill folk. Edward and Wallis, one may be sure, never laid eyes on the children of the American working class save, red-eyed from good brandy, through the smoked glass of a limousine. Eugene Genovese was talking about the privileged middle-class children that comprised the New Left.

Consequently, although ancient, American deference to children did not become a *social* problem (any more than impotence among million-dollar Arabian stallions is a social problem) until such time as significant numbers of people were well enough off to indulge in it. Before the post–World War II period, only leisured elites with no productive tasks to assign to their infants and adolescents could, therefore, not only indulge them as children, but prolong their childhood.

It is back to numbers again. The postwar period not only brought bumper crops of babies to America, it brought unprecedented mass prosperity to their parents who were few enough to enjoy it. Like most classes on the rise, the parents of the baby boomers emulated the life of those who were a niche above them. Among the wallowing in creature comforts, Florida holidays, and golf was the indulgence of their bright-faced lads and lasses.

SDS, SON OF LID

The history of SDS, the central institution of the New Left, illustrates from first to last the significance of the baby boom's numbers and the unfortunate philosophical legacy of half a century of American thought. SDS was sired out of youth culture by LID, the League for Industrial Democracy, one of the intellectually most vital sections of the radical avant-garde.

LID had a distinguished pedigree. Founded in 1905 as the Intercollegiate Socialist Society by Jack London, Upton Sinclair, and other radical writers and intellectuals, LID was designed to be a kind of parlor for the Socialist party's intellectuals.

In 1905, the Socialist party could still conceive of a future in which the working class ran the house. Therefore, recognizing intellectuals as a distinct group with interests peculiar to them and valuable to the rest of the movement, it was reasonable to set aside a room they could call their own. Perhaps more interesting from the perspective of the late twentieth century, the Socialists of 1905 viewed university students as adults, grouping them with older intellectuals on the basis of their common interest in the life of the mind rather than drawing lines on the basis of age or student status. LID was not itself a working-class organization, but it reflected working-class attitudes.

LID's history paralleled that of the larger party. With the waxing of American Communism during the 1920s and 1930s, the Socialist party, and LID with it, drifted into an anti-revolutionary reformist politics, filling a niche between the mainstream liberals and the revolutionist, pro-Soviet Communists. Like Norman Thomas, its leader for almost forty years, the party functioned somewhat as the conscience of the liberals. Socialist policies did not really differ from what the New Dealers preached. Simply, the Socialists believed in ideals the New Dealers found merely useful.

The Socialists also served the liberals as the shock troops of anticommunism. The Socialists were "other-directed," to play around a bit with David Reisman's famous phrase. They came to define themselves in terms of what they were not: not quite liberals and definitely not communists. As a result they were far more militant than New Deal liberals in execrating the Reds. So strong was their anticommunism that they attacked many liberals who tried to maintain an open mind. Thus, Thomas dedicated his presidential campaign of 1948 not to appealing for social democracy but to following Progressive party candidate Henry Wallace around the country, ragging him because he was supported by American communists. The former vice-president was no bolshevik. He was more of a mystic. Had he lived he might have contributed marvelous pieces on feelings to *Dissent* and, in the late sixties and seventies, made a fortune dressed in a caftan. But he called for accommodation with the Soviet Union and the CPUSA backed him. That was enough for the Socialist party and LID. As during the two previous decades, they devoted their energies to attacking him.

By 1930 LID's charter members had grown old. Like the people who belong to Junior Chambers of Commerce, the old socialist grads woke up one day to realize that they were no longer so junior as they had once been. It is not clear how Junior Chambers of Commerce respond to such awakenings. (Young Junior Chambers of Commerce?) LID's response in 1930 was to found SLID, the Student League for Industrial Democracy.

The implication in the new auxiliary's total orientation toward the campus is worth a nod. Defining students as a group distinct from intellectuals has more than casual meaning. It was not that college attendance was so large in 1930 as to merit organization separate from intellectuals. Nor, with the exception of a few places like City College of New York, was the social composition of the university much different from what it had always been—well-to-do and privileged. The fact is that LID and the SPA were abandoning any pretense of appealing to the working class. Instead, they decided to appeal to a group of people who, if not vital to society, augured to be so in the future.

By the fifties, the radicals' disillusionment with the working class was complete. It was put into its most systematic form, however, by a decidedly non-LID sociologist, C. Wright Mills. Mills coined the term "New Left." He also argued in a series of strident essays and books that students would form the spearhead of a revived radicalism. Mills died in 1962, but those early New Leftists who believed in reading, like Tom Hayden, read him closely.

From a peak of several thousand during the thirties, SLID sloughed off during the fifties to perhaps a hundred faithful nationwide and only three locals with mailing addresses—at Yale, Columbia, and the University of Michigan.

There was little "socialistic" about the group by then. But like *Dissent,* LID kept "socialism" on the letterhead. Also like *Dissent*'s subscribers, LID members were aesthetes more than *politiques.* Al Haber was known as "the campus radical" at the University of Michigan because of his beatnik appearance, not because of what he had to say. Indeed, the most dynamic figure at LID's central office, Michael Harrington, was one of *Dissent*'s editors and among its most perceptive contributors.

In 1959, perceiving the stirring on the nation's campuses, LID's directors, prodded by Harrington, decided to revive the youth group. In keeping with the theme of newness as promoted by politicians like John F. Kennedy and corporations like Proctor and Gamble, they rechristened SLID Students for a Democratic Society (SDS).

Thus did the whorl of the Movement emerge, not from the sternly ideological communist tradition but from the loins of eclectic, some would say "fuzzy," socialists. SDS's commission was characteristically pragmatic and nonprescriptive: "raise issues," discuss social problems, and so on. So totally did the socialists define themselves in reference to the communists by 1960—so much were they within the pragmatist tradition—that they abhorred the very notion of laying down a *credo* for their youngsters. Even the new, improved name represented a retreat from the traditional radical assumptions that, whatever the role of other groups, it was the working people, those who produced the wealth of the world, who were at the heart of the struggle. The imputation of "Industrial" was unmistakable and utterly irrelevant, even offensive, to the aesthetic inclinations of the fifties rad-libs. LID kept it for old times' sake. But you could not appeal to "the kids" with that kind of stuff. From the beginning, in other words, the New Left lacked direction, ideology, program, and even concrete purpose.

LID's leaders were by no means bohemians themselves, especially not the no-nonsense Harrington who, as a graduate of the Catholic Worker movement that worked among skid-row derelicts, knew better than to romanticize sleeping on floors and letting the teeth go. Whatever the discreetly ordered quality of their personal lives, LID people did define their remote, sentimental patronization of "the oppressed," a category including beatniks as well as blacks, as the barometer of their radical commitment. SDS's two prime movers during its formative years, Al Haber and Tom Hayden, were both the sort of fifties youth who drifted casually from interest in liberal politics to the murky cafes of beat without sensing any tension between a narcissistic personal life and a vow to toil on behalf of the millions.

EARLY SDS
In May 1960, the month of the HUAC incident in San Francisco, SDS held a conference in Ann Arbor. The subject was the civil rights movement and what it meant for America. Shortly after the meeting, the United Auto Workers granted the organization $10,000 to rent an office in New York City, purchase a mimeograph machine (a "means of production" American middle-class revolutionaries have always understood), and hire a full-time president. He was Robert Alan "Al" Haber, the former head of the SLID chapter at the University of Michigan.

On first glance, the contrast between this first leader of the Movement and the chiefs of its Wounded Knee period— zanies like Rubin and Hoffman, and the "Weatherpeople" Mark Rudd and Bernadine Dohrn—appears as sharp as the genetic evolution of the screeching baboon of Abyssinia from a seaborne cell of protoplasm. In fact, Haber felt out of place with the Movement before very long.

Nevertheless, this short, unprepossessing, even colorless young intellectual, introspective but given to incessant talk, the son of a Michigan academic and LID member, was very much the father of SDS. He fixed on the organization and the Movement it spearheaded certain patterns of behavior that evolved directly into the patent nonsense of Yippie and the pathos of the Weatherman underground. Chief among these was Haber's assumption that action, any action, was constructive, desirable, progressive, *radical* in and of itself. From the very beginning of his stewardship, instead of organizing SDS chapters, "laying the groundwork" as, it would seem, a first president of anything from a Ladies' Aid Society to an aircraft manufacturing plant must do, Haber encouraged SDSers around the country to attach themselves to the innumerable single-issue protests that were erupting on campuses, including campus political parties.

LID was as happy as Haber to see all this activity. The signs of discontent were what had motivated the parent organization to set SDS up. However, whereas the LID directors regarded Haber's job as the delivery of an organization out of this furor, Haber was content just to hop on for the ride. He never suggested that he and SDS were responsible for the demonstrations against everything from the bomb to dress codes, dormitory closing hours, and the ineptitude of cafeteria managers. Indeed, it was the spontaneity of the uprisings that appealed to him, that demonstrated their meaningfulness. They justified his policy, a point LID could not quite grasp. They wanted to see members, an organization, and a program.

SCREW PROGRAMS!
Perhaps the significance of Haber's aversion to programmatic radicalism and his love of any kind of action can best be understood by quoting New Leftists prominent later in the decade. Gene Marine, a writer with a knack for stating things at their most simple-minded, wrote toward the end of the sixties, "Let man be free first, and let him define his freedom afterward." Mitchell Goodman, a pacifist of some learning

who might have known better but did not, clung to this sort of nonsense even in 1970, after it had demonstrably led to the mindless terrorism that he must have abhorred.

> *Where's your program? They taunt, the critics—*
> *those who do nothing, who play it safe. Where's*
> *your theory? They don't see what's happening; it's*
> *beyond their horizon. We don't have a road map*
> *because there are no road maps. There are no roads*
> *until we make them. We're in the wilderness,*
> *exploring the unknown. We're in the early stages of*
> *creating a new society! We have migrated; we are*
> *what Camus called "strangers," aliens (in our own*
> *country), a new culture that contains a new politics.*

Within this tidy paragraph are allusions to the four sources of the "action" generation: pragmatism; a repudiation of the ways of the Old Left, the self-centered narcissism of beat and its hangers-on, and the moralism of the civil rights movement.

That is, people like Haber and his successors recoiled from the long period of radical inactivity during the Eisenhower years and associated it with the sterile, incestuous haggling among Old Leftists over (in *Village Voice* editor Jack Newfield's phrase) "the alien cobwebbed doctrines of Marx, Lenin, and Trotsky." To Haber, it was of small moment that the various demonstrations he supported seemed to lead nowhere. They were a refreshing new departure from nothing at all. It was the same within SNCC, more or less SDS's black counterpart. During the first summer of 1960, Julian Bond recalled, "we really weren't doing much.... The executive committee would gather and the exchanges would go something like this:... 'I was arrested four times in the last thirty days, how about you?'... 'Well, I haven't been arrested but I've been beaten up twice.'"

To call on Jack Newfield again, this time criticizing the Movement, "Another demonstration seemed to be the stock recipe for all intellectual problems, another chorus of a freedom song a substitute for analysis."

Relief at having escaped the snare of the Old Left was reinforced by the narcissistic lethargy of beat. Anything smacking remotely of serious discussion soon became a drag. Of a radical conference at Denton, Michigan, in June 1967, Abbie Hoffman wrote, "The seminars drag on... a total bore... Jim and I are avoided, except by a small group. They do socialism, we blow pot on the grass, they do imperialism, we go swimming, they do racism, we do flowers for everybody and clean up the rooms."

On the face of it, this was not Al Haber. He loved the discussions. But in his policies, once again, he encouraged the Hoffman types to believe they were, in their personal rebellion, "radical."

Finally, the moralistic cast of the Movement, absorbed from the civil rights agitators as well as from the existential writers then in vogue, was expressed not only in Haber's explanations to the LID board of why it was irrelevant that he organized no chapters—the wholesome spontaneity of the demonstration—but in SNCC workers like Norm Fruchter. Reporting on SNCC's project in Mississippi in 1965, Fruchter wrote that the success or failure of the voter registration drive there would not be determined by "standards of efficiency of progress towards a solution," that is, by old objective political measures, but by the "quality" of relationships within the Movement. Process was the key, and commitment to one another.

This kind of argument failed to impress LID during the winter of 1961. Ironically, while the directors were delighted to see Haber abjuring the communist way of doing things, gabbing among others, it was their old hostility to the CP that made them wary. Old scars, long experience with CP cant, and deviousness has made LID extremely sensitive to associating with party members in any way whatsoever.

There was an element of defilement theory in LID's aversion to the Reds. Anything *they* touched was fouled. Moreover, the LID directors feared that any association with communists would bring HUAC and its ilk down on their heads. LID's exclusion clause was more thoroughgoing than most government loyalty oaths:

> *Advocates of dictatorship and totalitarianism and of any political system that fails to provide for freedom of speech, of press, of religion, of assembly, and of political, economic, and cultural organization; or of any system that would deny civil rights to any person because of race, color, creed, or national origin are not eligible for membership.*

Just as Haber pooh-poohed the extension of this principle— that SDS should have nothing to do with communists even informally—it would be on the issue of the "exclusion clause" that SDS and LID would eventually rift.

In 1961, however, it was the ectasy of *acting* that underlay Haber's policy. He agreed that communists should not be allowed to join SDS. However, to foreswear any contact with them whatsoever meant to do nothing for, during those same months, the Trotskyist Socialist Workers Party launched its very active youth arm, the Young Socialist Alliance, and the communists were gearing up toward forming their DuBois Clubs.

Neither group hesitated to join in the same local movements with which Haber wanted to ally. The party policy of both of them was still imbued with the spirit of the "popular front," alliances with less revolutionary single-interest groups. Indeed, Michael Harrington's chief line of argument to Haber and the SDSers was that the socialists, LID, had settled the popular front question "ten or twenty years" previously.

Appealing to something "settled" had little meaning to a product of pragmatic progressive education. To people like Haber, nothing was settled. Enamored of action, he was not about to cut SDS off from what action there was. He was enough of a hereditary LIDer to oppose admitting communists to membership, but he would not refuse to cooperate with them on battles against HUAC, censorship of student newspapers, and dress codes.

It would be a mistake to attribute Haber's conflict with his employers entirely to different points of view. The fact is that Haber was simply not the administrative type, just as some people cannot whistle for the life of them. Indefatigably he could compose letters, newsletters, and pamphlets. Usually, he remembered to crank them off the mimeograph machine he sometimes slept beneath. Less usually, however, did Haber remember to mail his manifestos. He began composing new ones amidst stacks of the old, unread, and unmailed. To have expected someone of his type to construct a membership organization was folly. Facing up to this in March 1961, LID fired Haber.

Then, in a literal precedent of what would happen many times figuratively during the decade, Haber's dad bailed him out. In a letter to Frank Trager, a Columbia professor and chairman of LID's Executive Committee, Haber *père* wrote that he was sure Al "has a deep sense of responsibility and he has a deep sense of mission. In all fairness, you and I had it at his age and we cannot be too hard on young people who exhibit it at his age."

This expression of parental solicitude, on one level touching and so entirely unextraordinary, is also a document that explains much about why the Movement developed in the way it did, that is, as a childish thrashing about that was tacitly, when not explicitly, encouraged by the militants' elders. About 1600, George Chapman wrote that "Young men think old men are fools; but old men know young men are fools." In the 1960s, while the young acted true to their mission, the old men of the left did not. They became the rooters-on of a generation whose problems and deficiencies were not, of course, of their own making. Therefore, assuming the old have a greater responsibility to know better, they were ultimately responsible for the human waste and tragedies of the decade.

Rehired in May, Haber introduced to the Movement a man who would remain at the center of events until the end of the decade. In February 1961 he persuaded LID to hire SDS's second full-time employee, a University of Michigan crony named Tom Hayden.

In addition to being older than most Movement militants, Hayden was unlike them in his social background. His childhood Catholicism was probably not too important in accounting for this, unlike in the case of Berkeley's Mario Savio. Hayden abandoned churchgoing quite early. However, rather than coming of age in a cozy *Leave It To Beaver* suburban family, he was raised in an indifferent, later broken, household.

Pocked, homely, with eyes that seemed eternally rheumy, and conscious of his appearance, as he later told it, Hayden was a searching intellectual of a kind that was found on every fifties campus. One day he was attracted by the "beat" poets and *la vie de bohème*, the next he threw himself into organizing VOICE, a student party designed to move student politics beyond "Let's-have-more-school-spirit." Hayden spent a summer in Berkeley alternately studying the first of such parties, SLATE, and sampling the beatnik scene in San Francisco's North Beach.

The Movement would never quite untangle politics and "culture radicalism," the difference between fundamental social relationships on the one hand and life-style—fads and fashions—on the other. Indeed, it will be seen that the Movement lost sight of the former and degenerated into a craze little more substantial than Davy Crockett hats and hula hoops. Not Hayden, however. If he was not immune to fashion, he was and remained principally a *politique*. As the editor of the *Michigan Daily* during his final year at the university, he transformed it from a review of fraternity-sorority fluff and football hoopla into a well-informed liberal newspaper. As SDS's field secretary he went to Atlanta and reported intelligently on the emergence of SNCC, the Student Non-Violent Co-ordinating Committee, which was the vanguard of the civil rights movement (and soon the other pivotal organization of the New Left).

Under Haber and Hayden, SDS grew from perhaps 250 members in the fall of 1960 to more than 600 in twenty chapters in the spring of 1962. It was at this point that Haber called for a national conference which, reflecting his obliviousness to the nuts and bolts of administration, had no venue until two weeks before it was scheduled to begin. In a pinch, SDS fell back on the original benefactor, the United Auto Workers. No one in SDS much liked the idea. The antilabor bias of the Movement was already taking shape. But Haber had as usual put off too long the unspiritual task of reserving a hall. The UAW offered its members' summer camp at Port Huron, Michigan, forty miles north of Detroit.

THE PORT HURON
STATEMENT
On June 11, 1963, forty-three members of SDS and sixteen other young people, including one "observer" from the "Communist Progressive Youth Organizing Committee," assembled at the pleasant lakefront site. For five days the more earnest delegates discussed the sorry plight of both the nation and the left and poured over a long manifesto which Hayden had pieced together while traveling about the country, in consultation with many of those now present at Port Huron. The conclave made a few changes in his draft, but the manifesto that emerged was essentially Hayden's definition of what was wrong with America and his and Haber's call for a movement of university students to take the lead in changing it.

The preamble to the *Port Huron Statement* succinctly if abstractly expressed the disillusionment of the students who feared nuclear war, were disgusted by racism, and were

disappointed to discover that the United States did not live up
to its avowed devotion to peace and justice. A goodly part of
the long second section, elaborating on what was wrong with
America, fastened on the university and the SDSers' disappointment with their collegiate experience, the topic of one
article in that watershed issue of *Dissent*. It is, as Milton Viorst
has noted, the most flaccid part of the document. Hayden was
not, and never convincingly would be, committed to the idea
that the world could be remade in the nation's Trinity Halls,
classrooms, and resident cafeterias.

What there was of a program in the statement pretty
much resembled what LID and the liberal wing of the
Democratic party espoused: a realignment of the major parties
along "liberal" and "conservative" lines, a program which
amounted to expelling the right-wing and racist southern
Democrats from the Democratic party; the abolition of
repressive institutions such as HUAC; the regulation of
corporations for social ends; and a reallocation of national
resources so as to "abolish squalor, terminate neglect, and
establish an environment for people to live in with dignity and
creativeness."

It was hardly "revolutionary." It reflected a point of view
of people who, as Hayden described himself from the vantage
of 1972, were very much "tied to the Kennedy image . . . . The
appeal of the New Frontier and the Peace Corps was pretty
great." It was also high-flown and abstract enough that, with a
few changes, President Kennedy might easily have signed it
himself and brought Vice-President Johnson along to whip up
some Pedernales barbecue. The only thing remotely "radical"
about the *Port Huron Statement* was the hopelessly vague call
for "participatory democracy" and Hayden's very nonliberal
argument, derived from C. Wright Mills, that the various ills of
America were interrelated.

When criticized for vagueness, Hayden responded by
pointing out that the statement was not a comprehensive
program but a stimulus to further analysis. To be specific on

every point, to build a "platform," would be to replicate the sectarian failing of the Old Left, to alienate at the outset discontented people who might disagree with one "plank" or another. Hayden, like the other people at Port Huron, believed he was "starting a journey," the goal of which would be set as they traveled.

During the sixties, both activists and observers considered the *Port Huron Statement* the basic document of the New Left. They were right. But they understated it. The statement proved to be the *only* comprehensive statement of principles the Movement ever produced. The New Left (and Hayden himself) failed to take up the challenge to pause on the road, reflect upon the route they had traced, and sketch out the rest of the trek. They just kept moving.

As a result, they never got anywhere. A New Leftist of 1970 quizzed on his or her principles (as opposed to the whim of the day) would have responded with a rehash of the principles of Port Huron, only less articulate than those admittedly half-formed ideas. The New Left expanded, but it never grew. Like a balloon, the Movement got bigger and bigger. But also like a balloon, it was at the end, when it burst, substantially the same thing it had been in the beginning.

In part this was due to the belief of the Port Huron students that, as Haber put it, "any really radical force . . . is going to come from the colleges and the young." The final section of the *Port Huron Statement* was devoted to demonstrating that the university was at the center of the American experience and that students, therefore, were a vital social force, veritably a social class, capable of changing the society.

Unfortunately, this was not only a delusion in the best of circumstances, but it was propounded and it swept the campuses at the precise moment when the American university was on the verge of intellectual and structural decay, an inclination the New Left accelerated. The *Port Huron Statement* was widely distributed. By September 1962 perhaps a thousand mimeographed copies had been mailed to SDS chapters and sympathizers throughout the country. By the fall of 1966, the national office had mimeographed or printed sixty thousand copies. These, in turn, were retyped and duplicated on dozens of campuses. The *Port Huron Statement* was surely, in Kirkpatrick Sale's words, "the most widely distributed document of the American left in the sixties."

And yet . . . and yet, it may also have been the least read manifesto in the history of rebellions. In mimeographed form, the statement ran to sixty-four single-spaced, typewritten pages, over thirty thousand words. Any academic on a payroll during the 1960s might have informed a reporter who was poring over the *Port Huron Statement* for "background" that students simply did not tackle such large blocks of type. Some professors would have told him that they warned against it, as a dermatologist cautions against lying on the beach too long. Godfrey Hodgson slyly points out that the only passage of the statement which was ever much quoted was the preamble, because it came first. As with so much, the message of Port Huron was understood only to the extent that it could be conveyed in "rap sessions." Thus the fact that, at the end of the decade, the statement's principles were not only not amplified, but they had decayed like the old professor's facial fat into slogans. Whatever the inadequacies of the manifesto, Hayden cannot be held responsible for the fact that, whilst much printed, he was not much read.

LID read the *Port Huron Statement,* however, and as Michael Harrington, LID's representative at Port Huron predicted, they went "through the roof." The problem was not with Hayden's analysis or ideals. They were pretty much identical to those of the social democrats. The problem was the reflexive anticommunism which stood at the center of the old socialists' psychology.

Although it repeatedly criticized the Soviet Union, the statement focused on American contributions to the cold war. Objectively, this was fair enough. Americans could not directly influence Soviet policy, only their own. However, LID's social democrats had long since abandoned the hope of influencing anyone's policy. Their role in the Great Chain of Being, like that of the communists, was to repeat old incantations. Even worse than SDS's failure to bait the Soviets quite enough, the youth organization modified LID's communist exclusion clause. Not in substance! The SDS membership clause provided that "advocates or apologists" for "any totalitarian principle as a basis for government or social organization" were not "eligible for membership."

But the words, *the words!*, were not the same. Not having experienced Stalinism as a part of their lives but recognizing the similarity between LID's exclusion clause and the tactics of HUAC, the Port Huron group decided to tone the words down.

It is difficult to sympathize with the paranoia this amendment and the admission of a communist observer to the proceedings unleashed at LID headquarters after the conference, especially because Michael Harrington gave in to SDS symbolism for three years and tried to make them see the substance of LID's anticommunism. Haber and Hayden were hauled before an inquisitional meeting of the board of directors and forced in the end to accept an administrative reorganization of SDS.

In the end, however, LID relented. Despite suffering regular resignations over the next several years as SDS opened up to more intimate collaboration with young communist groups, LID continued to sponsor and subvene SDS until February, 1965. Ironically, the New Left had a healthy influence on the old socialists. In an effort to maintain a relationship with the tumult among the young, they shed the rabid anticommunism that had preoccupied them since the 1930s. Unfortunately, in opening up and mustering the capacity to lead a new radicalism, they were also passed by.

As for the SDSers, it is interesting to observe that while they mocked the parent group, they were very good at depositing LID checks. Only when SDS grew larger and richer did the group find the "conflict of principles" insufferable and decide to go its own way. It was not so very different from the arrangements the young revolutionaries of the sixties had with their real Moms and Dads, cultural Moms and Dads as well as the biological ones.

CHAPTER FOUR

FREE SPEECH, FREE CAMPUS, FREE KIDS

In the past, beyond memory it sometimes seems, social rebellion was a thing oppressed people did: gladiators, peasants with scythes, weavers working sixteen-hour shifts, and so on. In this scheme of things—quaint now, like a maple Hoosier with a built-in flour sifter—the privileged classes resisted as best they could with the exception of a few individuals who, out of idealism, eccentricity, or an eye for the main political chance, threw in their lot with the rebels. The civil rights movement of the fifties and early sixties fit this description.

It was therefore the last old-fashioned social upheaval in American history. For, midway through the sixties, social revolution took on a different shape. "The people," including most blacks, sat out while university students, a privileged group, handled the rage and rampage. The Movement's militants were not members of the ruling class by any means. But as the *Port Huron Statement* had it, they were "bred in at least modest comfort, housed now in universities," not exactly what might be called the wretched of the earth. Moreover, as 3 percent of the population at their most numerous, students were something less than the masses.

More to the point, unlike revolutionaries as traditionally defined, the student militants never challenged the ruling class or its prevailing ideology. They believed that they did. But they actually confronted people much like themselves, who also lived in at least modest comfort at universities and whose world view, it turned out, the students shared. Not surprisingly, after first balking at the impudence of the student protesters, the university administrators caved in. Quite easily, of course, once they discovered that the challenge the students flung at them was no challenge at all but an opportunity for their own aggrandizement.

The student revolution was a colossal sham. Professors and pundits and politicians expended millions of words, thousands of unoffending pulpwood trees, and years of solemn meetings and hearings agonizing over what might as well have been grumblings about watered Jell-O in the university cafeteria. They called the campus movement a crisis in the structure of higher education. When they were done, the students' reforms accepted across the board, the American university was substantially the same as it was before the troubles began, only—as the phrase goes—worse.

The New Left chose the campus as its principal battleground because its "radicalism" failed elsewhere, and the Movement "transferred," like a flunking chemistry major switching to psychology. Or, more precisely, the Movement did what those students of the fifties did who found campus life so congenial and the baccalaureate degree's implied commission to venture forth so disconcerting. They hung around and hung around, the aging beatniks in the corner of every large university cafeteria, the balding regulars at every free concert and poem reading.

Students for a Democratic Society tried the outside world. Beginning in 1963 (and funded by another United Automobile Workers' grant), SDS organized the Economic Research and Action Project. The brainchild of Tom Hayden, who would never be quite comfortable with the delusion that the campus was "where it's at," ERAP opened offices in blighted neighborhoods of Newark, New Jersey, Chester, Pennsylvania and other wretched, politically corrupt, largely black cities. The idea was to organize a movement of poor people to work for their own short-term benefit and to take a step toward building a radical coalition through action. The poor were fashionable at the time, thanks to Michael Harrington's *Other America*. To that extent ERAP was doomed to an early flagging interest like any other adolescent fad.

ERAP survived in name until 1965 because Hayden was capable of sticking to a job. In fact, the project flopped almost immediately. Saul Alinsky, a no-nonsense professional in the business of advising poor people's pressure groups, spotted ERAP's dilettantish character right away. The students who manned ERAP's storefront offices thought that they could carry the day on the basis of their earnestness, sincerity, and dedication. That these were words favored by Miss America finalists does not seem to have occurred to them. Indeed, like the ingenue in some of the Tarzan movies, the students who joined the collegiate safaris into darkest Newark and Chester had a patronizingly romantic view of the poor, and especially of blacks.

Alinsky, whose favorite word was "bullshit," recognized that the ERAP workers were more interested in tickling their own psychological tender spots than in working for concrete gains. They were incapable of taking satisfaction in the drab, piecemeal concessions that it was possible to wring from hardheaded and powerful municipal machines and their businessmen patrons. As a result, they did not win even those. Alinsky's first admonition to groups he counseled was to forget the personal vanities and lower the sights. The ERAP kids believed that their bohemian life-style and easy informality would somehow appeal to the hard-bitten black denizens of the inner city. Alinsky's second admonition to his clients was that they were going to have to do what he told them to do; he was the expert and they were amateurs. The romantic ERAP kids—the revolutionaries!—asked the poor of the cities to illuminate them! ERAP was a crushing experience.

The several hundred white university students who, in June 1964, trekked to Mississippi to help out in SNCC's "Freedom Summer" were also quickly disillusioned. The Mississippi Project was designed to sign up Negro voters, much as Attorney General Rogers had suggested. In the long run this campaign was not a failure—if successful black politicians who act like successful white politicians are accounted a victory. But, like adventists on a hilltop, the Movement was looking for great things by Labor Day.

The Movement claimed that their campaign was ruined by the Democratic party establishment when it refused to seat the Mississippi Freedom Democratic party at the 1964 convention. In fact, the registration-drive workers were languishing in frustration within a month of their arrival. White resistance, even murder, was to be expected. But the caution, fear, and sheer desuetude of the rural southern blacks, and their suspicion of the shiny white kids from . . . "Where you say you from, Honey? Rho 'Islan'? Where dat?" . . . was beyond comprehension. Even Miss America, frequently a representative of the Magnolia State in those years, could have told the SNCC kids a thing or two. It was a revelation—or should have been!—that flesh and blood Negroes did not measure up to the images created for them by Allen Ginsberg, Norman Mailer, and any number of bohemian-radical writers.

One of the most revealing documents of the student experience in Mississippi was a letter written from Tchula in August. "There is some ambivalence which goes with this work," an idealistic young lady wrote friends back home. "I sometimes fear that I am only helping to integrate some beautiful people into modern white society with all its depersonalization. . . . It is somewhat annoying to see a grubby little Negro cafe with a four foot by six foot tall full color picture of a young handsome Negro in a white dinner jacket next to his beautiful young Negro wife in a $200 cocktail dress in the backyard of their $40,000 brick home standing in front of a massive barbecue with prime rib of beef and tender young duckling in beautiful glistening copperware serving Pabst Blue Ribbon Beer. A typical American Negro couple on a typical Sunday afternoon."

Not if the SNCC militants could help it. It was the grubbiness of the cafes and the poverty of the blacks that was to them the Moor's primal strength. They could not comprehend that the minds of black people worked much like the minds of their own parents. They were appalled that, given a choice between authentic grubby cafes and plastic Howard Johnson's, between rattling old Dodge pickups and red Buicks with four portholes in the fender, the blacks would opt for the latter, soul-killing dullness and all. In offering as an alternative nothing but swooning admiration of the blacks' natural vitality, the students offered no alternative at all.

One had to get back to one's university housing in September, and there was no Freedom Summer II. What was the use in being part of a social drama if, unlike the dramas in foreign films and coffee-house poetry, it could not be brought to a cathartic conclusion in one episode?

So, with ERAP floundering aimlessly and the Mississippi Project a disillusionment, the Movement was spent by September 1964. Saving those parts of the world which could have used a little salvation proved to be something of "a drag." Then, in this trough, the Movement discovered that it had not come to the end of the road after all. The young people bred in at least modest comfort discovered that by stretching definitions a bit, an old rad-lib specialty, they could be just as oppressed as the black fellow. It proved to be a propitious discovery because black students, as unsettled as themselves, were about to expel them from their revolution.

It was not difficult to put the student revolution on a par with the powerlessness of the Newark poor and the heroic movement among southern blacks. Asking why the student uprising occurred first in Berkeley, California, the first leader of the campus movement said, "is like asking why Negroes, and not Americans generally, are involved in securing access for all to the good which America could provide for her people." The University of California, Clark's Kerr's multiversity, was the model for higher education throughout the nation which, the students decided to discover, was the source of all the problems.

There is another way of looking at Berkeley which helps explain why the student movement should begin there. The student movement was an easy, fun rebellion, and, in 1964, Berkeley, California, was just about the easiest, most fun place in the United States. Berkeley was an idyll.

BERKELEY, 1964

As with the rest of the idylls, that is no longer so. Today, much of Berkeley is a slum. Not in the gutted tenement style of New York City slums or the chilling twenty-story "public housing" slums that places like Chicago have so proudly erected. Whatever her problems, Berkeley is still a California girl. Her slums are "single family dwelling" slums, made up of California cottages long paintless, falling down, guarded by derelict automobiles in tall grass. To the extent that Berkeley is a student slum, and not the slum of poor people, it is a slum of deliberate neglect.

On the western edge of the city, rimming the bay, Interstate 80 has spun off one of those strips of franchised drive-ins that northern Californians used to call "Los Angelization" but which, nearly facing up to geographical reality, they now describe as "like San Jose."

Much of Berkeley is clogged with traffic much of the time. Prostitution is semi-public ("College Girls—Coed Massage"). Telegraph Avenue is a skid row distinguished from others only by the youth of its "bums." The pathetic, bedraggled young people with bad teeth may remember but no longer bother with sixties euphemisms like "street people." A quarter here, a quarter there will do quite nicely.

Hardly an idyll. To have known Berkeley before 1964 means not to know her today or at least to pretend—unless, closer to home, one has watched a bouncy young girl dabble in exciting ideas and end up a burned-out old bag in a misbuttoned blouse.

Back in the forties and fifties, and into the sixties, Berkeley was an idyllic place. There was the kind cool climate the city shares with San Francisco but improves on: "never too hot, never too cold," with sun instead of San Francisco's fog. Berkeley was close enough to "America's Favorite City" to hop over on a whim, but Berkeley itself was peaceful, quiet, not quite urban. People who lived there knew that, like the mountain, San Francisco was better to look at than to look from.

Of course, Berkeley was not for everyone. That was a big part of its appeal. Berkeley was, most of all, the University of California. It was for college professors and students, other professionals, liberal lawyers, excruciatingly sympathetic Protestant clergymen who lived in elm-shaded houses they liked to call "vicarages," people who worked in broadcasting or for publishers, people who were interested in the worlds of art and ideas and who subscribed to journals like *Dissent.*

If other kinds of people lived in Berkeley, they did not set the tone of the place. There must have been working people, of course. But they were quiet, invisible—the way, in the best possible of all worlds, the people who cut the lawns and stoke the furnaces at universities and colleges are supposed to be. There were not many blacks in Berkeley—they lived in bordering, unmistakably urban Oakland—but by 1964 few in Berkeley objected to Negro neighbors.

The University of California was both unique and a prototype. It reeked of dignity like the heliotrope that grew here and there on a campus that was also a horticultural exhibit. Its fine gray buildings were so quintessentially collegiate that Hollywood regularly used it for academic locations. More than any other place, Berkeley looked the way that Americans thought a great university should look. Jimmy Stewart was a professor there at least once. Ray Milland must have had tenure. Other movieland instructors, alternately eccentric and just brilliant, included . . . it was a handsome and ingratiating staff.

In real life the professors tended to paunches and spectacles, but they were far more distinguished than Hollywood could convey in a ninety-minute comedy or murder mystery. Famous physicists, chemists, historians, logicians, sociologists, and literary critics liked California too. The faculty numbered more Nobel laureates than any other single institution in the world. In the United States, the University of California's Berkeley library was excelled only by Harvard's and the Library of Congress. The noble gray buildings housed the best laboratories in their fields. In the Berkeley Hills behind the university, a professor could buy a comfortable and palpably *not* ticky-tacky house with views of the flats, the Bay, and the City of St. Francis at a trying but manageable price.

Berkeley was also an interesting place. It was big—huge, the largest single university campus in the United States. Until 1964, this size was celebrated as a virtue and a strength. Presiding over Berkeley and the whole of the state system, President Clark Kerr boasted that the multiversity offered something for everyone. "What the railroads did for the second half of the last century and the automobile for the first half of this century," Kerr suggested, "may be done for the second half of this century by the knowledge industry: that is, to serve as the focal point for national growth."

Until 1964 few found this vision amiss or unattractive. Berkeley attracted California's best and brightest students and an even more select group from other parts of the world. In 1964 academics were inclined to look at the parochial, small eastern liberal arts college as stultifying; Edward Albee's New Carthage College only dated from 1962, and his scathing portrayal of life there was still packing them in two years later.

Berkeleyans also liked to contrast their university with nearby Stanford. Stanford was big enough and physically even more striking than Berkeley, but Stanford was private, appropriately the alma mater of Herbert Hoover, peopled with rich, dull nitwits who talked about "The Big Game" and really meant it.

Berkeley's tone was cerebral, tolerant, sophisticated, and progressive. Politically the university and city were seedbeds of the new discontent. There had been a socialist mayor early in the century and, during the 1930s and 1940s, Berkeley was rivaled as a center of leftism only by City College of New York and the universities of Chicago and Wisconsin. Through the 1950s, all the old dispensations survived in the odd corners of the town.

These were reinvigorated after the anti-HUAC demonstrations of 1960 and 1961 and they overlapped with an assortment of ad hoc, mostly single-issue organizations: antinuclear weapons and pacifist societies (SANE, Fellowship of Reconciliation, etc.), pro-Castro groups (Fair Play for Cuba), and civil rights organizations (CORE was active in Berkeley and the campus produced one of the first chapters of the informal support organization, Friends of SNCC). Fully 10 percent of the student body was actively involved in the civil rights movement.

Mostly, this activity consisted of support for the southern campaign, raising money and recruiting workers for SCLC, SNCC, and CORE. However, Berkeley's students also cooperated with CORE in attacking racism locally. There was little to arouse them in Berkeley itself, but there were plentiful manifestations of racist hiring practices and the like in San Francisco and especially in the heavily black but reactionary city of Oakland to the south.

Oakland was the political fief of William P. Knowland, former U.S. Senator and still publisher of the *Oakland Tribune*. Knowland, a glowering, feisty man who was once a supporter of Joe McCarthy, had grown nastier after his self-inflicted decline in state politics. Knowland's redeeming quality was that, like most American right-wingers, he was a blunderer. Even when the wind is blowing their way, right-wing politicians manage to turn around when they have to spit. Thus, in 1958 Knowland decided to abandon his secure seat in the Senate and establish a machine based on the governorship. He bullied the incumbent Republican governor, Goodwin Knight, a well-meaning gent of "Big Game" cut, to swap nominations with him. Knight ran for the Senate. Senator Knowland ran for governor. The cynicism was too much for

California and both were defeated. It ruined Knowland's never equanimous disposition and swept liberal Democrats into power two years before Kennedy's election.

In the *Tribune* Knowland took to railing against subversives in every quarter. He was a dependable screamer in the HUAC fracas and took one of the frankest prosegregationist stands to be found outside the South. He smeared King and other civil rights leaders as, at best, dupes of the Kremlin. Not unreasonably, young idealistics at the university believed that Knowland's encouragement, if not his directives, were behind the city of Oakland's refusal even to entertain the appeals of the Negro organizations. Periodically, they picketed the *Tribune*'s offices, each time spoiling yet another of Knowland's bilious lunch hours.

THE TROUBLE
WITH LIBERALS

The administration of the University of California was by no means a part of Knowland's shrinking realm. They were estabishment liberals such as Knowland loathed, "pointy-heads." Clark Kerr had been a pacifist and a member of SLID, the predecessor of SDS. His minions were committed to the extension of the public sector both because of their New Deal background and because tax dollars paid them salaries which, since Sputnik in 1956, had become almost handsome. After 1960, with Kennedy in power, they could realistically think in terms of moving higher and higher in the government apparatus.

However, like most old liberals who had made it through the fifties, Kerr and his assistants suffered from Roderick Usher Disease, "a morbid acuteness of the senses" when it came to the sight, sound, and scent of right-wingers like Knowland. When he grumbled, it sounded to liberals like the rebel yell at Shiloh Church. To make matters worse, they suffered from Madeline Usher's malady too. When it came to the complaints of their own students, they were positively catatonic.

The issue which laid the Kerr liberals in the tomb was the university's "Rule 17." This regulation forbade political advocacy on the campus. Not even presidential candidates were permitted to speak on university property.

However, because of the configuration of the main entrance at Berkeley, there was some question as to where political groups might hand out their literature and hook new recruits and where they might not do so. To be precise, there was no question about it but an incorrect answer until the summer of 1964. To understand the problem requires taking a short walk.

A stranger approaching the university from Telegraph Avenue crossed Bancroft Way, entered what was called Sproul Plaza, and was then, to all appearances, "on campus." University buildings, most notably the administration building to the right—Sproul Hall—were all around. The crowds that milled about were diverse—beatnik types, perky coeds, and professors with briefcases and bent pipes—but unmistakably collegiate.

It was universally assumed, even by the U.C. administration, that Sproul Plaza was city property. It was universally assumed that until the pedestrian, presumably dazzled by the electric atmosphere that reigned in the plaza, entered Sproul Hall or another building or continued straight ahead, passing through Sather Gate, a handsome stone and iron monument to some dead dignitary, he or she was legally under the jurisdiction of the city of Berkeley.

In fact this was not so. Sproul Plaza was university property. It had been transferred to the university by the city in 1959 when the new Student Union was built (to the left as one entered the campus). But for reasons lost as irretrievably as Leviticus's pork taboo, the university administration never interfered with political activity there and directed interested groups to apply for permits at city hall, which continued to issue them.

The political activity took the form of two lines of card tables flanking the last part of the stroll from Bancroft Way to Sather Gate. At these tables, representatives of student organizations, including the political groups, proselytized, harangued, recruited, and just enjoyed the warm sun and cool air. If the letter of the law was not observed, tradition was— fastidiously. The politicking ended abruptly at Peder Sather's portals.

In the summer of 1964, a reporter for William Knowland's *Oakland Tribune* discovered that Sproul Plaza was under university jurisdiction and, therefore, legally off limits to "political advocacy." The newspaper, actually less rabid than usual, called for a halt to it. The Kerr administration was presented with a problem, or at least it decided that it was.

Administrative decisions may be made on the basis of principles, that is, according to what serves the purposes of the administration's underlying philosophy or ideology. These principles, of course, can vary quite wondrously or not exist at all.

In the latter case, when like American liberals the administrator lacks a guiding philosophy of any kind, there are at least two ways in which he or she can act on problems. One, which doubtless dates back to the day of the first easygoing neolithic headman, is to do nothing. This was earliest defined as an actual technique by the first prime minister of Great Britain, Robert Walpole, a lazy, contented fellow who liked his comfortable Queen Anne divan, his jeroboam of best port, and his graft. Walpole had the good luck to bring these tastes to the fore during good times when he could approach administration as a matter of "salutary neglect." That is, his administration left "well-enough" alone and also "not-quite-well-enough-but-not-too-bad." When he was confronted by a screamer, an eighteenth-century William Knowland, Walpole made some symbolic or rhetorical gesture to throw the troublemaker off stride and then . . . he left well-enough alone.

It worked wonderfully—as it did for the foremost American practitioner of the craft, Calvin Coolidge. He did not share Walpole's interest in port, witty conversation, and graft. Coolidge just liked to sleep. But he also thought that "one of the most important accomplishments of my administration" was "minding my own business."

Kerr and his assistants could have minded their own business. For them, the sixties were quite as good times as the twenties were for Calvin Coolidge. They could have made some symbolic gesture toward Knowland's half-hearted protest and turned the *Tribune*'s alleged "conservatism" on its head by pointing out the obvious, that political advocacy on Sproul Plaza was traditional and therefore sacred.

However, there is another approach to running things when the administrator lacks principles. It is what American liberals dignify as "pragmatism" and it is something like the stimulus-response mechanism with which researchers do such marvelous things with white rats and lobotomized dogs. That is, deriving from the theories of John Dewey and the Action-Any-Action-But-Always-Action approach to government of the New Deal, American liberals developed the reflex of responding, quite as thoughtlessly as Pavlov's dogs, to every problem placed before them, even when, as with the political advocacy on Sproul Plaza, there was no real problem and when any change in the situation (if one bothered to think about it) was bound to cause trouble.

And so, on September 14, 1964, Dean of Students Katherine Towles issued a memorandum that, henceforth, Sproul Plaza was closed to political groups.

Nineteen affected organizations, mostly leftist and liberal groups but including, at first, a right-wing student club, petitioned Towles to rescind her directive. While they waited for a reply, they met and agreed to adopt the tactics of the civil rights movement—demonstrations and civil disobedience—if Towles held out.

Towles did not quite hold out. Pavlov's dogs did not merely salivate upon stimulation, they ceased to salivate upon receiving another kind of message. White rats can be conditioned to scamper gleefully in circles at the sound of a buzzer and then, at the ringing of a bell or the dousing of a light, to jump up and down and squeal. Likewise the American liberal. Having foresworn the existence of principles, he (or she) does *something* no matter what the action of the previous day or the gist or intensity of "the problem." Every request is a stimulus. Liberal bureaucrats respond to pressure from all directions. It is what makes them so much fun to watch when one is in a good mood and has a few minutes to spare from the personal rat race. It is also what makes American liberals so easy to trap.

On September 21 Dean Towles announced that the plaza might be the scene of "informational activities" but not of "advocacy."

The solution was absurd, as the protesters immediately pointed out. What was a group's informational officer to do when someone picked up a pamphlet and wanted to discuss it? Was the table-tender to clear his throat, point to his sealed lips, and walk his mark to the Bancroft Way sidewalk a hundred yards away, glancing about furtively like a man with stolen Seiko watches for sale? About seventy-five activists staged a brief sit-in upon receiving news of Dean Towles's memo and called for a picket line the next day. Large numbers of students joined them, "took a few turns in front of Sproul," in the words of the *Daily Californian,* "and then turned their signs over to others."

It may have been too late already. In September 1964 the frustrated Movement was aching for action and an enemy. The crisis may have been irreversible with the release of the original, thoughtless memorandum.

However, it is also possible that the Berkeley administration might have salvaged the situation (and at least its own moral position) as late as September 22 by retreating in good order. Knowland and his gang would have screamed, but then they were always screaming. On the other hand, it should have been obvious from the broad-based participation in the picket line that the Towles directives displeased not simply a few true believers but a large number of otherwise placid students.

Four years later, at the tumultuous Democratic National Convention of 1968, an obscure figure by now, sitting in the galleries watching chairman Carl Albert fence with a rebellious Wisconsin delegation, Clark Kerr turned to the driver he had been assigned, a graduate student named Spencer LeGate, and said, "He had better give in now or he's going to lose it all." Kerr paused a few seconds and added, *"I know."*

In 1964, Clark Kerr did not know. He was still in the fifties habit of worrying about right-wingers, HUACs and Knowlands. Students, on the other hand, could be ignored. In his Godkin Lectures of 1963 on "The Uses of the University," Kerr remarked that "one of the most distressful tasks of a university president is to pretend that the protest and outrage of each new generation of undergraduates is really fresh and meaningful."

He was right and he was wrong. He was right that there was nothing essentially new under the campus sun. He was right in his intuition that students could offer no realistic alternative to serve their interests better than his bloated but intricately complex multiversity. He was dead wrong in estimating the scope of disruption with which he was dealing. He thought he had a handful of troublemakers whom he could isolate from the docile majority. Kerr was also on record as saying, "The employers are going to love this generation. They are going to be easy to handle." A legatee of American liberalism, he could hardly be expected to see that some of its fabulous crop was rotten.

Chancellor Edward Strong reiterated the Towles compromise and, on September 25, Kerr strongly condemned the daily demonstrations outside Sproul Hall. With Knowland growing shriller, the administration escalated on September 29. Five students who set up card tables on the plaza—civil disobedience—were told to report to the deans. Somewhere between four hundred and six hundred students signed statements of complicity in the act. (There was the usual complement of Jesus Christs and Elvis Presleys on the petition—which seemed to confirm Kerr's reading of the situation.) They insisted, in SCLC-SNCC fashion, that they receive identical punishments.

The chancellor ignored the petitions and suspended eight students. Then, on October 1, more card tables appeared and a rally was scheduled for noon. With magnificently poor timing, a police car arrived to make arrests shortly before the rally was to begin, not to mention the daily crush in the plaza from people who were interested in nothing more than a sandwich. The police arrested a CORE worker, Jack Weinberg, and put him into the car.

Several hundred students surrounded the car. At noon there were three hundred; by 12:30, at least two thousand. It was an historic moment for the New Left. The issues were not entirely clear. No doubt many of the crowd would have gathered as quickly around a good juggler or a demonstration of some new contrivance for chopping vegetables. There was no plan. There never was a plan in the free speech fight. Hal Draper, an old-time socialist who worked at the university library and a sympathizer with the Free Speech Movement, later observed that the students' actions consisted of a series of responses. The administration came "to their rescue" time after time. "The students were spared the burden of working out a strategy."

If American liberals act pretty much like Pavlov's dogs, the American student movement learned at Berkeley to act like pups in experiments run by Pavlov's dogs.

But what exhilaration! What euphoria there was in that throng around the police car, the sense of community that any crowd generates, the illusion of power—the reality of power on that acre of concrete! These ceased to be sensations known only to southern blacks on October 1 and for the thirty-two hours the crowd remained to hear dozens of speakers—administrators, students, professors—who first removed their shoes and clambered atop the automobile with poor Weinberg still inside like an old-fashioned vaudeville prompter. Jerry Rubin was in the crowd. "As we surrounded the car," he remembered, "we became conscious that we were a new community with the power and love to confront the old institution."

MARIO SAVIO

It was not yet Jerry Rubin's day to mount automobiles before large crowds (without removing his shoes). The leader of the Free Speech Movement was a young man who had as little in common with Rubin and the Movement that elevated Rubin into greatness as Girolamo Savonarola had in common with reformation sectarians who preached that God wanted people to shed their clothes and howl like wolves.

The student movement's Savonarola was Mario Savio, born in 1942 into a working-class family in New York. His father was a sheet-metal worker, and the family was both piously Catholic and "ethnic," active members of an Italian fraternal society.

Mario was an excellent student. He attended Manhattan College, a small school in New York operated by the Christian Brothers, a largely Irish order in the United States, better known as disciplinarians than as scholars. After a year with them, Savio transferred to Queens College, a part of the City University of New York. The switch did not mean that Savio was now thinking of the Lord in lower-case letters. He wanted a more rigorous education than the Brothers offered, but he clung to Catholicism. At Queens he became president of the

Confraternity of Christian Doctrine, an organization for Catholic students who, while electing a secular education, wanted to keep their Thomistic training honed keen.

Mario Savio's social class and his roots in ethnic Catholic culture help explain why he leapt so quickly to leadership at Berkeley and also why, within a few months, a Movement made up of people with rather different backgrounds repudiated him and he them.

Savio came to the fore and awed his fellow students and the liberals who ran the University of California because of a clean, sharp intelligence that was trained to cut to essentials, an ability to articulate clearly and stick to principles, and more than a dollop of the sophistry that Catholic educators fingered as delicately as the Eucharist. These faculties, which would lose their value to the Movement within months, can be traced to his peculiar background.

Savio was the product of an era in the history of American Catholicism that was drawing to a close in 1964. Symbolized by Kennedy's election to the presidency and even more by his funeral, when a requiem high mass was the focal point of a whole nation's grief, American Catholicism ceased in the early 1960s to be not quite acceptable. During the 1960s American Catholics paddled into the mainstream of American culture.

Previously, largely working class and palpably ethnic, they had cleaved to the Church—Holy Mother indeed!—as a buffer against a society they perceived as hostile. Victims of the mild disdain of real Americans, the masses of Catholics consoled themselves that they, at least, unlike their bosses and fellow citizens, observed the one true faith. Although less extreme, their clustering and exclusiveness are comparable to the social history of Jewry in Western culture. Although, again, their exclusion from full participation in American society was not comparable to that of southern blacks, their religion played a role similar to that of southern Negro Protestantism in the lives of its people.

Simple piety, adherence to ritual, and a sense of community served well enough for the majority of Catholics. The Church guaranteed the loyalty of its elite by training them rigorously in Scholastic philosophy and in apologetics, the highly rationalistic, systematic, sophistic defense of Catholic doctrine. Organic and medieval in character, Thomistic philosophy provided educated Catholics a world view that was not only persuasive, it was fundamentally at odds with the prevailing pragmatic liberalism. No matter how successful and apparently comfortable in corporation board room, government, country club, or intelligentsia, the educated Catholic was as apart philosophically as the Polish miner whose guttural English kept him in his place. It is no coincidence that the staff of William F. Buckley's *National Review,* tatty and temporizing as that magazine's conservatism was, could have formed a sodality without offending any coworkers.

Thomistic philosophy trafficked in absolutes, steely logic, and a rational, if accommodating, ethics. Catholic education of bright students emphasized skill in disputation. A clever lad like Mario Savio could not help noticing that he ran circles around liberal Protestant friends whose Sunday schooling had been devoted to rubbing Crayola crayons on Bible story coloring books and around liberal Jews for whom the temple was a place where one was introduced to potential spouses.

The system was falling apart by the early sixties. Not only had Kennedy's presidency destroyed ancient apprehensions of the Catholics among all but fundamentalist diehards, but fifties prosperity and mobility destroyed the old class and ethnic foundations on which the Fortress Church was built. In Rome, the Vatican Council absolved Catholics of the symbols of their apartness: mysterious Latin rituals, meatless Fridays, and other token "mortifications of the flesh"—rejections of the world. Guitar-playing priests as "groovy" as the loosest limbed Unitarian minister were only a few years away.

But Mario Savio was a product of the old tradition. His working-class family subscribed to the archaic notion that childhood was a preparation for maturity and not something to be prolonged. Children were indeed (so much for the disapproval of progressive educators and the likes of Margaret Mead) to be "jerked toward adulthood as rapidly as possible." A good working-class boy, Savio believed that one donned a jacket and tie when one was going to meet with deans or deliver a speech. Even at the start of the Free Speech Movement, when he was indisputably its leader, some Free Speechers worried darkly that Savio still attended mass each week.

However, Savio was still a rational Thomistic moralist, an ethician. He was an old hand at thinking syllogistically, of "proving that natural rights exist" and solving problems like "give and explain a definition of sacrifice." By 1964 Savio was also a political activist. During the summer of 1963 he did social work in Taxco, Mexico. During the summer of 1964 he taught at a SNCC Freedom School in Mississippi. It was the relationship with SNCC that involved him in the card table controversy.

Savio was tall, skinny, with an ordinary face, a rather over-solemn and brooding young man as a Savonarola ought to be. He was not, however, a flamboyant orator. The reminiscence of the fifteenth-century agitator breaks down there. Savio tended to "a certain shyness," and he stuttered a little. It may be that his lack of a feel for show biz played a role in his early downfall, too.

By October 2, 1964, Savio was the informal leader of the protesters. At a meeting held that day to resolve the impasse over the police car, he took over. While the details of the discussions between the Free Speech Movement and the university administration remained secret, Savio's mark was on the directness, workability, and rationality of the six points to which the administration and the Free Speechers agreed. It is impossible to imagine them originating with Kerr and Strong, whose specialties were obfuscation and evasion, or with, as a short time would tell, Savio's softer-headed Free Speech Movement allies.

The "Pact of October 2" provided that the demonstration be ended immediately; that Weinberg be arrested but the administration not press charges against him; that President Kerr create a special committee to study the whole question of politics on campus; that the Academic Senate—a faculty and therefore a neutral party—consider the cases of the suspended students; that political activities conform to existing regulations while the university initiated the steps necessary to deed Sproul Plaza to the city of Berkeley and therefore open it legally to political action.

The pact saved everyone's face (another often overlooked specialty of Thomistic ethics), ended the disruption of campus life, and provided the means to legitimize the obviously inevitable student political activity without disturbing the principal functions of the university.

Although ingenious, however, the plan was not foolproof, as Kerr and Strong soon demonstrated. They immediately set about to pack the special committee with stooges. The president gratuitously smeared Savio and other FSM leaders in terms better suited to Francis Walter. When the Academic Senate counseled merely nominal discipline of the suspended students, the administration ignored the recommendation.

The Free Speechers waited patiently for two months. On December 1 they demanded that the promises of October 2 be implemented right away. When they were ignored (Kerr was looking forward to Christmas vacation more avidly than any Tahoe skier), there was an illegal rally in Sproul Plaza followed by a sit-in by about eight hundred students in the administration building.

Hal Draper, a supporter of the FSM, later reflected that even then the administration might have squelched the movement with "a waiting game." The sitters-in, like those young men at the Greensboro lunch counter three years before, were frightened and confused. Instead, with less sense than the mayor of Greensboro (which is surely saying some-

thing), at 3:45 A.M., December 3, Governor Edmund G. Brown
dispatched 635 police to Sproul Hall to arrest the students. The
result was a strike. The 800 hostiles of December 2 became
5,000 by December 4. Most observers had the impression that
the overwhelming majority of the Berkeley student body sympathized with the militants.

At an extraordinary convocation of the university on
December 7, Kerr made his customary effort to obscure the
issues. Only eighteen more days until Christmas! Then, Mario
Savio rose to speak and was seized by the police. He was
released immediately and did address the crowd. But the
shades of deep Dixie and HUAC falling so soon after Kerr's
glowing liberal pieties destroyed what was left of the president's authority.

In effect, the faculty took control of the university and
established policies which permitted political advocacy and
organization on campus. On January 4, 1965, a legal rally was
held in Sproul Plaza. Two days before, Chancellor Strong had
resigned. Kerr stayed on for a while, but he had been
completely discredited. The governor and the faculty were
allowing him the courtesy of departing during a slow month.

The free speech fight was over. The students had won
their point, one so clear-cut that even anti-FSM professors
agreed that they were right.

But the troubles were not over. The student movement
had only just begun. Like the civil rights fighters, the students
at Berkeley and elsewhere (the battle was watched closely from
many campuses) discovered not only that they had specific,
definable, and negotiable grievances, and therefore ones which
could be redressed—like Rule 17—but that they were also
suffering from a vague emotional malaise for which the
university was responsible.

THE CRITIQUE OF
THE UNIVERSITY

Before the Free Speech Movement, New Leftists looked upon
the university as a kind of sanctuary. The FSM itself began

because the University of California's administration refused to serve this traditional function as fully as the student militants believed it should.

The pre-FSM New Leftists were friendly to the university because they were intellectuals. They believed in knowledge and learning and, to that extent, cleaved to the place where those ideals were the object. The founders of *Studies on the Left* at the University of Wisconsin in 1959, according to James Weinstein and David Eakins, were mostly graduate "students who planned to make academic work their life's activity." The same was true of other campus radicals. Graduate students in the humanities and social sciences comprised the leadership of the early FSM.

To such people, whatever was wrong with the university was due to the fact that it reflected to some extent the structure and ideology of the larger society. To some extent the university housed flunkies of corporate capitalism and to that extent it prostituted itself. But, as Marxists (in the general sense of the word), the early New Leftists, like the *Studies* circle, believed that the university could be reformed where it needed reforming only by striking at the fundamental questions of property and social class. If anything, the university was remarkably "clean." More than any other major American institution, the university preserved traditions independent of the system. Indeed it was "an ivory tower," and a good thing too. Radicals at Wisconsin were vividly aware that their state university had stoutly defended leftists on the faculty and freedom of inquiry during the highest-flying years of Senator Joe McCarthy, when practically every other institution buckled under before him. Was this a malignant institution?

Conscious of the university's role as a sanctuary, pre-FSM New Leftists inclined to be academic traditionalists at the same time they were social rebels. University radicals would participate in the Movement as intellectuals. Leftist professors would "participate in the development of a body of theory to stimulate the creation of a new revolutionary movement in the United States." SDSers Tom Hayden and

Carl Wittman wrote of the university as a place where students could organize research projects "which any self-educating and program-centered movement needs." They assumed that the battle would take place in the outside, real world. Hayden and Wittman also saw the student's principal if temporary role as that of student. They, too, respected learning as a good in itself. Radical groups on campus would act as "recruiting agents," but students would foray into society as "a crucial volunteer force" only "in their spare time."

But foraying out of the university was less inviting after the ERAP and Mississippi Project debacles. Like so many people before them, the Movement students discovered that the real world was not so cozy and accommodating a place as the well-mowed campus lawn. Indeed, if a person could live in Berkeley or Madison or Morningside Heights or even in leafy, bucolic Chico, California, site of one of the hundreds of less notorious but no less tumultuous student rebellions of the late sixties, who would want to live in Tchula or Newark and worry about rednecks with shotguns and black muggers who had not yet shed false consciousness?

So the Movement withdrew to the campus. All that remained was to scratch that infernal itch, more fashionable each year, and to play revolutionary.

In fact, there was another vision of the university abroad in 1964, one which allowed the students to be revolutionaries without risks and frustration. Minutes before his arrest, Jack Weinberg gave voice to it when he told a heckler, "This is a knowledge factory. If you read Clark Kerr's book, those are his words. This is mass production. No deviations from the norm are tolerated."

What did he mean? He meant that the university was too big, too impersonal, was run like a factory in which students were products with serial numbers punched in tiny rectangular holes on IBM cards. Weinberg himself may only have meant that the university was a symbol of what was wrong with American society. But students are like other people and like cats who lick themselves in the warm sun. They tend to think of themselves as the center of things. Soon enough, the university was not merely a symbol of the whole of American society, it was the malignant heart of Leviathan.

Writing in *Liberation*, Sol Stern summed up the critique of the university that the students made their own:

> *The new undergraduate learns quickly that of all the functions of the Great University, his own education is perhaps the least important. He has almost no contact with the famous professors he has heard about.... Graduate teaching assistants do most of what face-to-face teaching the undergraduate encounters.... A student organization, SLATE, publishes a* Supplement to the General Catalogue *every semester, which advises the undergraduate on ways to beat the "system" and get a reasonable education in spite of it. Whether the undergraduate is morally revolted by the system, or whether he shrugs it off as merely another facet of the lifemanship he must master, it is as a "system" that his education is commonly perceived and becomes a central part of the undergraduate folklore.*

Stern was wrong about some things. The *training* and *conditioning* of technicians and bureaucrats were surely the most important functions of the university. But he was right when he implied that large university education was inferior to what a college degree meant ten years before and what four years at a good, small liberal arts college still did mean. He was partly right when he attributed the emptiness of a Berkeley-type education to the size of the place and the depersonalization of bigness. When FSM protesters hoisted placards that read I AM A STUDENT. DO NOT FOLD, SPINDLE, OR MUTILATE ME, a parody of the legend on the first generations of IBM cards, they were pungently describing how it felt to be a Berkeley undergraduate. The multiversity was indeed a machine.

Mario Savio and his fellows were the first to resent the superficiality of multiversity education because they were the brightest. When the inevitable statistician got loose among the arrest records of December 3, it was revealed that 47 percent of the sitters-in had "B" averages compared to 20 percent in the student body at large. There were twenty Phi Beta Kappas in the bunch, eight Woodrow Wilson Fellows, fifty-three National Merit Scholars or Finalists, and twenty students who had published in scholarly journals, still something of an accomplishment at that time.

When such students complained of "the factory-like mass miseducation of which Clark Kerr is the leading ideologist," and of courses of study which had "little or no logical relationship to one another," they meant it. They wanted an education that would test them. They were the kind of students who thrived under a demanding intellectual regimen.

However, what they wanted without quite recognizing it was an elite education. Their emotional commitment to the ideals of democracy and equalitarianism would not allow them to admit that. Nor, given their adversary habits of mind for which HUAC, the southern racists, blundering Clark Kerr, and their parents' encouragement of "spunk" were responsible, were they capable of seeing that what was at the source of inadequate education, bigness, was not the consequence of corporate interests so much as of American democracy. Called upon to make degrees available to all who wanted them—to process seven million young citizens a year during the mid-sixties—it was not possible for the great public university to cater to the talented few. As for bureaucratic depersonalization, it was hardly the corporation's doing. With ten thousand to thirty thousand students on a campus exercising their equalitarian rights to a college degree, poor old, good old Mrs. Davis in the purple dress, upper lip quivering under her downy mustaches, simply could no longer handle the paperwork as she used to do.

In anger and thoughtlessness, the FSM and the student movement impaled itself on a dilemma which it was incapable of recognizing. Mario Savio, suckled on such things as dilemmas, did face up to it and, during 1965, made his break with the Movement. By the spring of that year, the Free Speech Movement degenerated into the Filthy Speech Movement. A small group of students claimed their sacred rights and intellectual needs to shout "Fuck," *et al.,* into the Sproul Plaza public address system. When they were arrested and the crowds of protesters gathered quite as indignantly as they had the previous fall, Savio the intellectual and moralist divined that something had gone wrong. He disappeared, retired into a cloistered personal life, un-New Leftishly rebuffed all interviewers, and worked as a bartender. When after a year or so of reflection, he returned to the university, it was as an apolitical student of pure science.

Savio realized that the Movement was no longer concerned with definable rights or, indeed, with the "real education" he had been talking about and about which the Movement still did talk. His solution was an old one, always open to a clever person in any large institution. Sol Stern alluded to it distastefully when he mentioned SLATE's *Supplement.* The solution was to beat the system. The multiversity curriculum was filled with loopholes of all kinds. One could get through with a minimum of work. Or one could get himself quite a fine education . . . if one was willing to go it lone wolf, to abjure politics, solidarity, the Movement, and the interests of all one's brothers and sisters. It was for this that a disillusioned Mario Savio opted.

There was another alternative—in theory. A serious student could go to one of the small eastern liberal arts colleges which specialized in just the unbureaucratic, personal education for which the protesters called. However, the students of the sixties, including the militants, did not flock to Amherst, Franklin and Marshall, and New Carthage. Such places closed their doors by the dozens each year of the decade while the multiversities grew larger, and middling-sized old teachers' colleges—the West Chester and Chico States—turned into large universities. The "community colleges," two-year public-supported institutions that offered vocational courses but also a freshman-sophomore curriculum, boomed. Places like Foot-hill Junior College in southern California were larger than the Big Ten universities had been in 1960.

In part the growth of the large institutions was due to the fact that the students of the sixties did not really want the demanding curriculum the small colleges generally offered, something Savio seems to have recognized by 1965. They wanted the diversions and excitement of the multiversity, the diversity and color of life in places like Berkeley. In truth, members of a big generation, they wanted the bigness which, among other things, meant as few personal and intellectual demands as being a one-inch firecracker in the baby boom had meant.

Or, they simply could not afford the small private schools. Amherst and New Carthage cost lots of money. The personal intellectual education the student movement *talked about* was reserved for the wealthy.

From that observation, the students might have deduced, as traditional radicals had, that the problem with higher education in the United States lay not in the university itself, but in the structure of society: good education was a privilege of wealth, not talent. The battle, therefore, lay not on the quad where that situation could not be altered, but in the great white world beyond the gates.

Such a conclusion would have brought the Movement back once again to the frustrations of ERAP and the Mississippi Project. Instead, they called for the impossible, the ludicrous. The student movement that was born in Berkeley called for a personally responsive education for all.

As long as university administrators took the students at their word, they resisted, as indeed they had no choice. Some took a hard line, like Samuel Hayakawa of San Francisco State who parlayed his battle with students into a U.S. senatorship. The majority of university administrators, good liberals, fell back on the time-honored devices of evasion and equivocation.

Both hard and soft lines fed the Movement. The administration's "failure" to make students feel at ease provided "evidence" that universities were in fact the enemy. While antistudent speakers and journalists hastened to point out that the majority of American university students, even at the height of the commotion, were not activists, activism was surely the prevailing mood on American campuses through the rest of the sixties. If most students did not sit in at the doors to the dean's office demanding that he or she respond to them and institute more "relevant" courses, neither did the mass of students much object.

Increasingly during the final years of the decade, university administrators recognized the fact that they could accommodate the protesters. If the students were demanding the impossible, American society delivers the impossible quite regularly. American society delivers the impossible by making it out of plastic.

There was no substance to the student movement's demands. They called for administrators who would respond to them. The university hired more administrators to walk around campus and respond.

The students demanded accessible professors? The university hired more professors.

The students demanded "relevant" courses? The university dropped English I and Freshman Math and replaced them with a panoply of choices ranging from literature through the film to massage to self-examination for women.

Mario Savio had complained about "unrealistically long reading lists"? The university abandoned reading. By 1980 it was possible—not uncommon—for an illiterate to be crowned with the laurel.

The students complained that the university was cold—it did not accommodate their emotional needs? The university piled counseling program on counseling program. A distraught sophomore could not "relate" to the Freudians at the counseling office? The university hired a Jungian.

Blacks felt out of place? Or white students said they did? The university authorized a Black Studies program. Chicanos? Ditto. Women? *Ad inf.* "Line up" was the word of suddenly generous administrators.

The American university was able to accommodate student demands down the line because, far from challenging Clark Kerr's vision of the multiversity as an expanding empire serving society, the students provided university bureaucrats with whole new theaters for the expansion of their bureaucracy. In so doing, of course, they contributed further to the dilution of the university's traditional functions of transmitting and increasing knowledge. But few, least of all the students and their trendy faculty supporters, had any commitment to such archaica.

Kerr and Daniel Bell and other liberal theorists of the multiversity had defined it as serving the needs of the corporate economy, training technicians and pursuing research for business, agriculture and government. The "radicals" got the university into the emotional mollification, Third World, and minority groups businesses, too. The end result was a larger, less efficient, more stultifying, and less competent bureaucracy and faculty than any Berkeleyan, Class of '64, could have imagined possible.

When something is easy, it is well to pause and wonder if it is worthwhile. The university revolution was mighty easy once administrators realized that the protesters demanded nothing but more of the same. It is of no great moment to a bureaucrat if the functionaries under him, whose existence justifies his job, are directing programs researching new fertilizers or studying the impact of living on a street corner upon feminists. If the money to support them is forthcoming—

and politicians are willing to fund the most remarkable programs—that is the point.

As for the Movement, its leaders and rooters-on concluded that the greater multiversity was both an ideal and an accomplishment. In 1970 two professors of English at the City University of New York crowed that, thanks to the New Left, the university was no longer "an ivory tower or medieval fortress where graying professors meditated and students endured a sometimes jolly period of adolescent incubation." They continued that "the American university through its recent upheavals has thrust itself into the forefront of the nation's political life. Now the world is in the university and the university is in the world." They defined as radical and progressive what, in 1964, had been condemned as reactionary. They claimed what Clark Kerr had called for as a fruit of the student revolution. As indeed it was. The student revolution of the sixties was a mirror image of Kerr's flaccid liberalism.

REVOLUTION MADE EASY
Not every professor of the sixties was so inane. Inasmuch as the student revolution was a tacit conspiracy of student hell-raisers and administrative bureaucrats, some academics resisted the further dilution of the university's function as a place where knowledge and truth were the prey. Some, able to do so, wrote off the large universities and escaped them for the small colleges where, if only the wealthy and a few token blacks enjoyed the pleasures of genuine study, at least study was encouraged. Others fought a wan rear-guard action in the public institutions.

Curiously, they were themselves a queer alliance. The academics who resisted the students and administrators were in part fusty old conservatives and in part old radicals. They were not a powerful group. The administrators shrugged them off as cranks. The student revolutionaries denounced them as fascists. This latter group included such people as William

Appleman Williams, the author of the century's major critique of American foreign policy (he fled to an engineering school in Oregon); Eugene Genovese, one the nation's leading Marxist historians; Harvey Goldberg, a historian at Wisconsin notorious for his solicitude toward students; and, outside the academy, even Paul Goodman, one of the founding fathers of the New Left. Their crime was to question the wisdom of ruining the university, of turning it into a playhouse where knowledge and study counted for less than the students' definition of what made them happy.

They pointed out that rather than the key social institution in modern America, as Kerr and the Movement agreed it was, the university was in fact a fragile institution, highly vulnerable. Robert Brustein of Yale University, another early supporter upon whom the Movement turned, thought that picking on the university was a little like the old game of "get the guy with the glasses."

Precisely because the traditional university had remained aloof from society to some extent and therefore had not fully absorbed the practical, purpose-serving "relevance" of other American institutions, it was necessary to protect it, to maintain its separateness. When the student movement culminated in 1967 in the students' seizure of several buildings at Columbia University, Daniel Bell and Irving Kristol pointed out the ultimate defenselessness of the university against physical attacks because the university commanded "its loyalty through the moral authority growing out of the idea that the university is a special institution, drawing its grace from the most 'sacred' source of rights in a free society—the commitment to open inquiry and truth."

It is difficult to be overly sympathetic with Bell's anguish. Second only to Clark Kerr, he had helped construct the idea of the multiversity as a servant of corporate capitalism, a denial of the "ivory tower" ideal. The student movement did not challenge the social university. It merely shifted its direction and served to move the university more deeply into the larger society.

The university was fragile. It was an easy target, exactly the kind of target a movement needed which failed to recognize what real change was, let alone effect it. Eugene Genovese, not yet denounced by the New Left as a fascist, tried to point this out in *Studies on the Left* in 1967. "It is, of course," he wrote, "easier to provoke a bitter quarrel with an administrator than to organize a movement for peace and socialism." The organ of Students for a Democratic Society, *New Left Notes,* confessed as much during the same year when a contributor wrote, "Since we cannot yet take over the whole society, let us begin by taking Columbia."

CHAPTER FIVE

BLACK MISCHIEF, WHITE SKIN PRIVILEGE

The campus movement was launched by civil rights activists who believed that the university was essential to the campaign against racism, "the most important issue in the United States today." When the students turned inward and defined the university as at least as insidious an enemy as racism, they lost interest in the continuing struggle of groups like King's SCLC. They did not withdraw their moral support of the blacks, but they thought of them as Free Norwegians must have thought of the Kuomintang during World War II: as remote allies fighting the allies of their enemies in a place so remote as not to have really existed.

The student movement itself was pretty much a lily-white affair. It could hardly have been otherwise. In 1965 and 1966, with the exception of athlete mercenaries, there were few black students in the universities which the white students attended.

The tackles, guards, and pivot men had other things to think about than anomie and the right to shout dirty words into a microphone. They were mostly poor kids who did not know much of anything about universities except that they were way stations for a cat with a salable body or skill. The few genuine black university students who were interested in political or social causes inclined to see the fight against racial discrimination in the larger society as a fight more pertinent to them. Negro students who were aware that their mere presence in the university was a fluke, like the white working-class students who never did join the Movement in any numbers, could not get too excited about being computer cards.

By the end of the sixties, when the black student population had grown considerably (as a result of Leviathan's own policies), a black student movement also emerged, but it was just as segregated from the white student movement as the toilets at the Yazoo County Jefferson Davis Day Picnic. By the end of the decade, whites and blacks mixed nowhere on the American campus except on the football fields and basketball courts, and even in those one-time sanctuaries of brotherly idiocy, the "jocks" clustered by race once the game was over. It is difficult to imagine why in the world athletes should make race second only to sport as the most important fact in their lives. But it is not difficult to show that, in the sixties, they did.

Black Separatism—Black Power! Black is Beautiful!— these slogans represent one of the most remarkable social phenomena of the sixties. The decision of new black leaders to withdraw from all dealings with whites (and the response of many blacks to the impulse) was unsettling to people of both races who had worked—some since the fifties, some their whole lives—for racial understanding and cooperation, for Martin Luther King's "dream." In a way, however, the sudden emergence of the Black Power movement in the summer of 1966 should have been a consolation both to those who insisted there was nothing radical about the demands of American blacks and to those who sincerely believed in the equality of humanity's races.

Black Power was a retreat to the liberal mainstream from the radical humanistic challenge to American society which integration presented. Integrationism called for a good society, Black Power only for goodies for some of the colored folks too.

As for racial equality, it was not preposterous before 1966 to look at the heroism of the southern blacks and the simultaneous nobility and shrewdness of the leadership of the civil rights movement and wonder if these people were not in fact annointed. They acted with such infinite decency and forbearance compared to the whites they confronted, and they were winning nonetheless. Was George Wallace "the equal" of Martin Luther King?

After the black activists repudiated King and made the likes of Stokely Carmichael, Eldridge Cleaver, and the Black Panthers their leaders and ideals, it was clear once again that the color of a man's skin had nothing to do with his quality. Given a fair chance, blacks were as asinine as whites.

In order to understand the emergence of Black Power, it is necessary to understand that in the mid-sixties, the black movement had, like the white New Left, reached a trying impasse. With the adoption of the Civil Rights Acts of 1964 and 1965, the black movement won a victory which was, by its own terms, a complete triumph. The 1964 law struck down nearly every legal barrier to integration. The 1965 law put the federal government's muscle behind the blacks' right to vote in the southern states. From a historical point of view, the civil rights movement was easy. It took only ten years from the Montgomery bus boycott to the 1965 law.

In another sense, of course, the victory was hollow. Race relations remained much as they had before. The universal recognition of human dignity for which King called was nowhere in sight. The economic plight of American Negroes did not improve. On the contrary, the employment levels and earning power of blacks actually declined relative to that of whites during the prosperous middle sixties. Between 1964 and 1968 an epidemic of riots in the black ghettos of the major northern cities unpleasantly dramatized the problems that Lyndon Johnson's milestone bills did not touch.

It was not that the Johnson legislation was a failure. The two acts did just what they were intended to do and what they were capable of doing: put the Fourteenth and Fifteenth amendments into practice. The problem rested in the fact that the civil rights movement was based on a broad humanistic utopianism while it proposed a narrow legislative program. King and his movement (and the New Leftists who supported him) had a dream of brotherhood. But the black groups, at least, were also realistic. Their program—the abolition of one legal code and its replacement with another—was attainable. (The New Left continued to dream.)

This program tacitly assumed either that the fabric of American society was sound and that the problem was the "dilemma" that Gunnar Myrdal had defined, or that a moral end could be accomplished by a strictly legal program. No civil rights or New Left leader ever said in so many words that a humane society could be legislated by a majority of the United States Congress, but that was the implication of the thought, policies, and expectations of the campaign.

Few "organizations" voluntarily dissolve themselves, especially ones that, like the civil rights movement, thanks to its comparatively quick and easy victory, were bursting with energy. So, in the face of the mockery that the results of the Civil Rights Acts made of their dream, a mutation was inevitable. The catalytic incident was rather an eccentric action than in the old style civil rights tradition. The incident painfully and vividly illustrated the delusions that New Leftists had wagered on "rights."

James Meredith was an army veteran who "integrated" the University of Mississippi. He had gone on to put his Ol' Miss degree at work as a part-time mystic, part-time landlord in New York City. In 1966, he announced that he would stage a "March Against Fear" through the truculently white suprema- cist delta country of Mississippi. Meredith would walk alone by day and night through a region where random bullying of blacks was a folkway and terrorism as common as midsummer thunderstorms.

Meredith was one of the first Movement creatures of the mass media who never grasped the fact that his role in history was symbolic and passive, the body that was presented to Mississippi by changing times, and nothing more. After his university career, he chafed under the obscurity that followed the dimming of the TV lights. He had liked the attention and he had a message with which to frame his comeback: the age of fear and deference was over; blacks in even the bleakest corner of Dixie ought now to take in hand the equality that the rights laws guaranteed. It was a stunning statement of the civil rights movements's non sequitur, that race relations could be legis- lated. Meredith had barely started on his hike when he was shotgunned from roadside brush by a local yeoman.

The reaction of the drifting Negro leaders was galvanic. Thousands of blacks and whites—all of the civil rights movement leaders—rushed to Mississippi to complete Mere-dith's march. Stokely Carmichael, recently elected the head of SNCC, worked his way to the middle of the throng. Soon he had the marchers responding to the question "What do you want?" not with the traditional "Freedom Now!" but rather, "Black Power!"

POWER!

"Black Power" meant as much and as little as "participatory democracy" or "women's liberation." Carmichael himself could and did assume all the different definitions in articles for the *New York Review of Books,* in a book coauthored by sociologist Charles Hamilton, and in sermons from torchlit platforms. Black Power could mean a "closing of ranks," the creation of political blocs along the lines that Mormons and Irishmen had devised a century before, Jews a millennium. It could mean a Freemasonic sort of tribalism, patronizing only businesses owned or managed by soul brothers. Or a demand that a certain area of the country be ceded to blacks for their own nation. Or ghetto political autonomy. Or paramilitary defense. Or even attack against the white racist society. Or back to Africa. (Carmichael, well-married to folksinger Mir-iam Makeba, eventually did just that.) Or it could mean nothing more than new duds and hairdo, an affectation of "African" ways, a "natural" where, before seeing the light, one wore a "conk." Or incantation: "Black is Beautiful." There can be no defining Black Power because, like all New Left leaders, its proponents would not be pinned down to specifics that might be subjected to rational analysis. It was an impulse, not a program, a fad rather than an ideology. The black New Leftists had caught up to the whites at the part of the trip where everyone bogged down in the ooze.

Historically, "Black Power" was an extrusion of the black nationalist tradition in American Negro political thought that has always survived alongside the integrationist tradition and sometimes submerged it. One historian of the phenomenon wrote:

The Black Power Movement is a conscious attempt to harness the emotional power of Black Nationalism to a practical program for the elimination of oppression in America. The strength shared by all American Black Nationalist movements has been their ability to engage the pride and imagination of the Black community, in ways that integrationist leaders cannot. For a Negro to seek integration into American society means to identify with the values of a society that has oppressed and degraded him, to repress his natural hostility against a people who have mistreated him and to seek their approval and acceptance by continually proving his worth. The Black Nationalist, venting his hatred and freely accepting his own identity, has obvious psychological advantages.

But, as Thomas Wagstaff continued, "Black Nationalist movements have... historically been unable to direct the emotional commitments of their followers in functional directions.... The most powerful critique of the Black Nationalist tradition has always been that it provided no realistic hope for the material advancement of the race." In the late sixties, with the legal force of racism prohibited by the acts of 1964 and 1965, the material legacy of discrimination was precisely the crux of the Negro's problem.

There were various options open to black leaders. Bayard Rustin called for an expansion of the corporate liberal solution: more legislation, won by a coalition of black pressure groups and white liberal centers of power, to accomplish in ameliorative New Deal fashion the economic improvement of the nation's Negroes. This was the course to be followed by Martin Luther King's SCLC, civil disobedience and demonstration, this time for jobs and training. The traditional radical's alternative, assuming the economic problems of blacks no more soluble under capitalism than the reform of the university, was for blacks to work in union with whites for revolutionary social change. The alternative *actually* selected was, as Rustin described it, to give priority to "the issue of race precisely at a time when the fundamental questions facing the Negro and American society alike are economic and social."

Few ostensibly political movements of any time or culture have been so consistently off the mark as the Movement of the 1960s. Black Power was the issue of mating a narrowly legislative liberal program to problems which were versed in terms of the most ethereal of ideals, and calling in fools to be midwives. Black Power was not only as fuzzy-minded as the student movement, it also rejected the sound and defensible core of the movement from which it emerged. Like reformed drunkards smashing table lamps made from wine bottles, black university students, ghetto adolescents, even the tiny privileged Negro elite in lucrative and high status positions seized upon social as well as political isolation from whites as the proper course of action. "Radical" being the vogue word in the mid-sixties, that was how separatism was defined.

The Black Power era produced more celebrities than rock-and-roll. Stokely Carmichael was the first. The head of SNCC who turned it from a biracial organization striving for brotherhood into a pile of paper was a flashy West Indian who had excellent teeth. LeRoi Jones, a playwright, took the stage name Imamu Baraka. Malcolm X (Malcolm Little), a one-time pimp and convict who converted in prison to Black Islam, turned what had been just another ghetto racket into a significant if ephemeral social force. By the time he was assassinated in February 1965, Malcolm had abandoned black separatism and appeared to be embracing a traditional anticapitalist radicalism.

Even Martin Luther King, Jr., found it expedient to genuflect to the black-is-beautiful idol. *Even* Bayard Rustin, a lifelong social democrat, agreed to be photographed playing ring-around-the-rosie with the silly Carmichael. They were a diverse lot. No one could impugn the integrity of King or

the abilities of Malcolm X. But the Gresham's law that ruled
Movement development as ruthlessly as Vlad the Impaler soon
drove out or drove into obscurity the spokesmen of substance
and raised to the top people like Hubert Geroid "H. Rap"
Brown, Carmichael's successor as head of a then moribund
SNCC whose contribution to radical theory was the aphorism
"Burn, baby, burn." The maximum hero of Black Power was
as fluffy a character as ever Oscar Hammerstein had sing a
waltz.

HUEY P. NEWTON

Huey Pierce Newton was born February 17, 1942, in Oak
Grove, Louisiana, and was named for the Kingfish of Depression politics, Huey P. Long. Newton's father was a laborer and
preacher who went west to take advantage of wartime
employment opportunities in Oakland, California. By 1948, he
was working with the Streets Department in the East Bay city.

Later, black movement rivals said Huey Newton was
bourgeois—"bourgie." In the Oakland ghetto that meant little
more than that his father was employed, the family was stable,
and there were regular mealtimes. In a relative sense, Newton's
status was "privileged," and that might have contributed to the
fact that Newton as a "political leader" had more in common
with the white New Left than with black liberals. Within his
family, Newton's childhood was even more untypical of ghetto
blacks and again reminiscent of the archtypical New Leftist
that Kenneth Keniston described. Huey was the darling.
"Huey never had a hustle during high school," a brother said.
"He never had to; he was always taken care of by our parents,
and he had several brothers and sisters who were already
married . . . . And Huey was everybody's pet, so he didn't have
to worry."

Bright but pampered and lazy, Newton did poorly in his
classes. At the prestigious school he attended in Berkeley, he
was too quickly written off by counselors no doubt predisposed to dismissing Negroes. Big, muscular, strong, and

cocky, Newton spent most of his time on the streets, earning a reputation as "a bad-ass motherfucker" and, in the fashion of the ghetto, a worshipful but shifting following. Newton's handsome face radiated friendliness rather than intelligence. With a thick head of hair and a wide brow, he took flashbulbs poorly for a black leader, and looked rather Caucasian. His most famous photograph (Huey posed as Poseidon on a raffia throne, holding a rifle for a trident and glowering theatrically) accomplishes its purpose of sub-Saharan ominousness thanks only to underexposure.

Newton really was charismatic in something like the old-fashioned sense of the word. He compelled personal loyalty. As Bobby Seale put it, "if you knew Huey and liked Huey, you would be pro-Huey when it came to an argument." It was a magnetism unlikely to attract adults, based as it was on Newton's "tough guy" street-fighter bravado. But Newton's Black Panther Party comprised ghetto youth, and the "real-ness" of black toughness was just the sort of thing to enamor suburban whites with a gnawing sense of the artificiality of their own "plastic" lives. "Huey always hit a corner, his car speeding down the road," his Boswell wrote. "Once he turned the corner, and a block up there was a railroad crossing with a little red light swinging, signalling that a train was coming. There was also a big building right on the corner that you couldn't see around. Huey started speeding up. He didn't know exactly where that train was, but he knew it was around that building somewhere. The next thing you knew, Huey had driven straight over that railroad crossing, and all the dudes in the car were cussing him out."

Of such stuff were made the maximum leaders of the New Left. "They would say he was crazy when he did things like that, but they thought his mind was out of sight."

Newton matriculated at Oakland's Merritt College, a two-year county-financed institution which was to some extent a ghetto continuation school. Already the ferment among urban blacks had spawned what Eldridge Cleaver called "the archipelago of one-man showcase groups that plagued the black community." At Merritt, a student organization called the Afro-American Association had sprung up in the early stages of the black-is-beautiful boom and Newton naturally gravitated toward it.

But it did not suit him. For one thing, Huey was accustomed to driving the car and the Afro-American Association was registered to someone else, a faculty member at the college. For another, Newton had begun to think of black association in terms of "politics"—"power." He apparently had acquaintances among campus radicals around Oakland and Berkeley (Newton retained a shrewd understanding of their psychology), and he read at least desultorily in political literature and pseudopolitics, like the works of Frantz Fanon, several months on the *Times* best-seller list at that time. He gained a reputation for confounding teachers at Merritt with quotation and a facile tongue. Finally, Newton disliked the "cultural nationalists," those whom he saw as so blinded by racial hatred that they isolated themselves from possible alliances with whites and ended up supporting reactionaries simply because they were blacks. Papa Doc Duvalier of Haiti was "an excellent example" of the result of "reactionary nationalism," according to Newton in 1968. "He oppresses the people but he does promote the African culture. He's against anything other than black, which on the surface seems very good, but for him it is only to mislead the people. He merely kicked out the racists and replaced them with himself as the oppressor. Many of the nationalists in this country seem to desire the same ends."

The mass media portrayed Huey as a racist. His white apologists responded that Newton unequivocally rejected the racism of the "cultural nationalists." Huey's defenders were, of course, correct. Any misconstruction among the Panthers lay not in their affinity for the white New Left but in their concessions to "black is beautiful" and the African affectations which had become publicly *de rigeur* for activist blacks.

There is no evidence whatsoever that Newton felt the pull of Africanism or Negritude. There were no dashikis and few other import shop accessories in the Black Panther wardrobe. Organized in a parody of a para-military corps, the Panthers spoke the language of Warner Brothers' Junior G-Men and affected the habiliments of the 1950s ghetto street gang: powder blue T-shirts, motorcycle boots, leather jackets, and, for just that touch of revolutionary contemporaneity, black berets.

Newton was articulate in conversation and on the platform but lacked the ability or patience of the white militants to sit down and write. He was also given to the pose and the theatrical gesture as the instruments with which to sustain the Black Panthers as something more than a street gang. Fortunately, his weaknesses were compensated for by the complementary cofounder of his movement, Bobby Seale.

FOOLIN' AROUND

Seale was another type altogether. Born in Dallas in 1936, he was raised by a poor but stable family which was also swept to Oakland in the great black migration of the 1940s. Without any of Newton's electricity, Bobby Seale was rather one of the sort in the crowds that formed Huey's sustenance.

Seale joined the air force where he learned sheet metal work but, after a series of incidents, was discharged. He was a drummer and worked, while in the service and after, both in bands and as a stand-up comic. Seale's early life is a document of the waste wrought on American Negroes. Intelligent, sensitive, personable, social, skilled, of some substance, he found no outlet for his energies but bounced around from poor job to worse. But for the emergence of the Black Panther movement, Seale's future was as typically uncertain as that of most of his peers in the ghettos: like a cat poised on a board fence, he was just as likely to leap into a life of petty or serious crime as into a reasonably stable round of routine work, diversion, and some contentment; the direction of the leap more likely determined by a stroke of luck—the bark of a dog—than by any individual merit or volition.

Bobby Seale was never political. Hanging around on street corners until he was thirty, he was like most ghetto blacks entirely innocent of interest in the civil rights movement. When he was mustered out of the air force and asked what he thought of Martin Luther King's movement, he mumbled in all sincerity that he thought it was run by communists. That was what he had heard. After completing high school, Seale entered Merritt College with the idea of becoming an engineer. There, however, he was taken up in the excitement of the new studies in black history, began reading extensively, and moved on into what was popularly regarded as revolutionary thought. It was Seale who introduced Newton to Fanon's *Wretched of the Earth.*

Seale was a member of the Afro-American Association and more comfortable in it than Newton. Definitely not a flashy personality and with no illusions on the matter, he found companionship there and a place to discuss his intellectual discoveries. Older than most of his fellow students, Seale was still a juvenile of the Studs Lonigan cut, given to adolescent escapades and associations rather unlikely for a thirty-year-old husband and father in the mainstream of society. The beginning of his friendship with Newton has the pathetic ring of a change of gangs in a high school student's short story. Seale was sitting in his car at night, drinking beer. Newton came by and beamed a flashlight on him. "He said, 'What's happening, man?' I said to myself, now *this* is who I ought to be running with."

The ponderings over the Panthers during the late sixties—apprehensions of danger to the republic from the party's enemies, salutes to the vanguard from its white supporters—obscured the fact that the organization was little more than an incredibly well-publicized teenage club. When Newton and Seale completed the first and final draft of the Panthers' program, the whole enterprise was set rolling by

Newton's question: "We've got to have some kind of structure.
What do you want to be . . . Chairman or Minister of Defense?"

"Doesn't make any difference to me," Seale said. "What
do you want to be, Chairman or Minister of Defense?"

"I'll be the Minister of Defense," Huey decided, "and
you'll be the Chairman."

"And that's just how that shit came about," Seale wrote
later, "how Huey became the Minister of Defense and I
became the Chairman of the Black Panther Party. Just like
that."

Seale's account of the establishment of the Panthers'
headquarters is likewise revealing: Mickey Rooney and Judy
Garland putting on a show. "Let's get those brothers together
and let's get us an office," Newton said. "That was very
important to Huey, because the establishment of an office
meant that something was functional."

By 1972, when he stood unsuccessfully for mayor of
Oakland, Seale was at last on his own, but his relationship to
Newton never really changed throughout the 1960s. He was
the attentive, worshipful, reliably self-effacing second-in-
command, and happy for the honor of proximity to what he
and the sixties called "the genius of Huey P. Newton." When
the Panthers split into so many cults in 1971, with Newton
holed up in a $600-a-month apartment, Eldridge Cleaver
running the "true" BPP from exile in Algeria, and Seale
fighting jail in several states, Bobby remained Huey's dependable aide, hoping for a détente with Cleaver but maintaining
the personal faith that was the substance of his commitment:
"if you knew Huey and liked Huey; you would be pro-Huey
when it came to an argument."

Newton was lucky to have Bobby Seale. He was the black
Huck to Huey's Tom Sawyer, enamored of his romantic pal
but commonsensical, moderating Newton's more frivolous
fantasies, acting as a restraint on Newton in several incidents in
which Huey would otherwise have been quite capable of the
rashest stupidity. Had it not been for the faithful Seale, the

BPP might have died in a bull session. Huey dictated the platform but Seale immortalized it—by the simple expedient of writing it down. It may have been the seven times seventh time Newton had spun out a master plan of one sort or another.

Seale was working on a project of the Office of Economic Opportunity at the time, in October, 1966. Not only did that job provide the raw paper, pencils, and Ditto stencils for the inauguration of a "political party," but the job had honed Seale's natural steadiness and tact. He was the sort who actually could remember that rent needed to be paid on the clubhouse, that the day's receipts needed to be counted and handled with some care. Huey could dream, strut, pose, harangue, transfix the yokels, and photograph well. But it was Bobby Seale, scowling silently at his side, cropped out of half the pix in the papers, who gave it all some reality. Huey would free Nigger Jim by sawing through the table leg to which he was chained. Bobby would suggest, quietly and deferentially, that they just lift the table.

THE PANTHERS

Founded by a Tom Sawyer and Huck Finn, the Black Panther Party for Self Defense actually was, as if by the inevitable stroke of luck in a game of chance, a weirdly successful synthesis of several strains in the black ferment of the sixties. The name came from SNCC's Black Panther Party of Lowndes County, Alabama. Stokely Carmichael gave it to them when, on the verge of winning the election there, Carmichael called off the project and dissolved it. The *Self Defense* in the title came from the Deacons for Defense, a short-lived organization of the mid-sixties which attracted some attention when, breaking with the absolute nonviolence of SNCC and Martin Luther King's SCLC, its founders—a group of southern Negro farmers who armed themselves— announced that they would retaliate in kind to violent harassment.

The Panthers appealed to black nationalists with a blacks-only policy and token gestures to the black-is-beautiful mystique. From the white New Left the Panthers took a concept of themselves as revolutionary and in time the romantic white vision of the blacks as the vanguard. To the restive young people of the ghetto, the Panthers offered the catharsis of defiant assertion, replete with the guns and military paraphernalia which seemed to them to symbolize power. From the fading legacy of Fidel Castro and Che Guevara, the BPP arrogated a military discipline which frequently degenerated into street-gang martinetism but was appealing just the same. To the intellectual radical-liberals who would defend them, the Panthers offered flagellation, gracious acceptance of contributions, and a bonus: a veneer of "ideological" roots in the fashionable writings of Fanon, Malcolm X, and Eldridge Cleaver.

Seale and Newton formally promulgated the party on October 15, 1966. They published a program of ten points, each divided into statements of "What We Want" and of "What We Believe." The dichotomy is an insight into the ambiguity of New Left revolutionism as late as 1966. The "Wants" consisted of edifying generalities and concrete demands either quite within the competence of the liberal establishment to approve and even to accomplish, or so farfetched as to be easily ignored. (These latter, of course, were the part that appealed to the white New Left.)

Thus, Newton dictated and Seale transcribed: "We want freedom. We want power to determine the destiny of our Black Community.... We want full employment for our people.... We want an end to the robbery by the white man of our Black Community.... We want decent housing, fit for shelter of human beings.... We want an immediate end to POLICE BRUTALITY and MURDER of black people.... We want land, bread, housing, education, clothing, justice, and peace." To none of which, denotatively, President Johnson would have taken exception.

Demands that blacks be exempt from military service, that education for Negroes expose "the true nature of their decadent American society," that all blacks held in jails be released, that only blacks sit on juries that tried blacks, and that the U.N. be petitioned to hold a plebiscite in the ghettos to determine their "national destiny"—these were extravagances neither unprecedented in political programs nor the sort of thing ever taken seriously by sensible men. The platform ended with a long extract from the Declaration of Independence, not popular with the white Movement but seemingly relevant to Newton.

The only point of the ten to which the Panthers paid much attention in practice was the seventh, concerning police brutality. Here was an issue of constant interest in the ghetto and in vogue among white liberals after a decade of well-publicized beatings and mistreatment of civil rights demonstrators and other militants. Oakland's police force was worse than most. The city actually advertised in the South for recruits, and lower-class southern whites were conspicuously over represented in the department.

The Panthers' innovation was dramatic. "We believe we can end police brutality in our black community by organizing black self-defense groups that are dedicated to defending our black community from racist police oppression and brutality. The Second Amendment to the Constitution of the United States gives a right to bear arms. We therefore believe that all black people should arm themselves for self-defense."

The Panthers secured a few firearms from a local Japanese radical who collected the things. Later, in one of the brilliant insights into the white New Left mentality that was to stand Newton in good stead for three years, he organized a sale of "Little Red Books," the compilations of Mao Zedong's aphorisms that had just made their appearance in the news. The campaign made considerable money for the party, and the Panthers purchased additional weapons. "You know what," Newton told Seale, "I know how we can make some money to buy some guns.... We can sell those Red Books. I know that many brothers on the block would not even buy a Red Book, but I do know that many of those leftist radicals at Berkeley will buy the Red Book." Newton knew that the publicity given Mao's book in the papers would create a bonanza market among the university's rad-libs. Even at that the Panthers were "shocked" at the ease with which they disposed of them and amused by the perplexed clerk in San Francisco's China Book Store who wondered what the blacks were doing with all "them motherfuckers."

Now armed, the Panthers began parading by day and following Oakland police cars after dark. The explanation was that police would be afraid to bully or brutalize ghetto residents when they knew or thought that armed Panthers were also on the prowl. A few early encounters with police seemed to bear the Panthers out. Stunned by the specter of young blacks with guns spouting a litany of statutes that justified their right to have them (Newton and Seale were amateur experts on the firearms codes), the police retreated indecorously from their first confrontations with the new group. The element of sheer adolescent fantasia that went into the idea in the first place was fired by the heady elation of these early encounters. The Panthers set themselves up for a denouement that, in the excitement, they seemed to have forgotten (if they ever knew) was inevitable.

In 1967 a group of Panthers went to the State Capitol in Sacramento to protest a bill aimed at bearing arms which was then under debate. Inadvertently, they entered the State Assembly Chambers with their guns. In the aftermath, the anti-Panther "Mulford Act" passed, and, worse, the episode was depicted by the media as proving the Panthers to be ruthless revolutionaries. In fact the legalistic Newton had enforced gun handling practices on his Panthers that were just as stringent as the laws he quoted to the police. (The Panthers were strict beyond the comprehension of white middle-class New Leftists in obeying laws and even proprieties: no shoplifting, no marijuana or alcohol on party business, etc.) But, after the Sacramento incident (with which, again fantastically, the Panthers were actually elated), the Oakland police force was able to rally public support as it regrouped for revenge.

The attacks on the Panthers extended far beyond Oakland. Black Panther Party headquarters was shot up. Individual local leaders were harassed and arrested. Newton was arrested, tried, and convicted of murdering a policeman; Eldridge Cleaver was wounded in a gun battle that left a companion dead (Bobby Hutton, Newton and Seale's first recruit and literally no more than a child). The organization was a shambles.

Black Panther lawyer Charles Garry claimed that twenty-one Black Panthers were murdered by the police in a national conspiracy to extirpate the organization. The claim was discredited, but there is no doubt that police despised the Panthers' arrogance and feared the guns. When their opportunity came, they acted neither delicately nor circumspectly in confrontations with the party. Newton's murder case was highly suspicious. Precisely what happened is impossible to say, but the Panther claim of self-defense seems more credible than the prosecution's case of unprovoked murder. In the least defensible police aggression, a Panther leader in Chicago was murdered in bed at the party's headquarters. After a well-planned police blitz of the building, which was practically torn apart by the gunfire, experts determined that no more than a few bullets could confidently be said to have been fired out of the house at the police. Yet, public opinion accepted the official account that the police had been attacked and generally, if tacitly, approved whatever the Panthers got.

What was done to the Panthers was a hideous injustice for which they were certainly not "responsible." At the same time, it cannot be said that the actions of the police were unrelated to Panther activities. If the party was frequently discreet, it was also incredibly foolish and naive, practically inviting its destruction.

PANTHERMANIA

The fascination of the New Left and many white liberals for the Panthers was distilled into a single exclamation put into the mouth of a Park Avenue matron in Tom Wolfe's *Radical Chic*. "These are no civil-rights *Negroes* wearing gray suits three sizes too big," she said when a group of Black Panthers entered Leonard Bernstein's apartment, "these are real men." Gene Marine, one of the earliest New Left promoters of the Panthers, gushed that for the sense of euphoria he felt about them, one needed only "see a line of uniformed Panthers guarding a building in solemn dignity."

This titillating sense of being in the presence of something elemental was nothing new in the history of middle-class radicalism. During the 1910s, schoolteachers were delighted to consort with Wobblies. Dentist and college-professor communists in the 1930s fastened on blue-collar workers, deferred to them, and affected their manners. Stephen Spender saw the connection between the white black-worshipers of 1968 and the middle-class proletarian-worshipers of the 1930s. "One reason why the bourgeois turned anti-bourgeois found it difficult to criticize the Communists," Spender wrote, "was that they were to him 'the workers.' He brought in consideration of their case a sense of guilt that washed away any sins of the proletariat, just because it was the proletariat." To the guilt-stricken, affluent New Yorkers of "radical chic," and to their children in the Movement, the Panthers were the black oppressed, and any apparent foibles were illusory, not to be mentioned—or even pondered—simply because the Panthers were the black oppressed.

Ironically, the assumption on which this impulse was based was itself not true. In the beginning, the Panthers (and most Black Power cadres) were no more "typical" of the Negro population than was the leadership of the now vilified civil rights movement. The active support of the Black Power groups was far less representative of American blacks than King's disciples were. For all the yammer about hog's jowls and chitterlings, the Afro-Culture and Panther types knew little of the typical American Negro experience. They came from a relatively privileged, thin stratum at the "top" of the ghetto pyramid. Or, if individually they rose from the mass of blacks, they were those few tokens cut out of the herd by liberal establishment programs for special privileges. The sudden shift from integration to black separatism in SNCC was marked by a shift in leadership from generally rural blacks of traditional religious orientation to secular urban Negroes who came from a more sophisticated background. The John Lewises, Bob Parrisses, and Ivanhoe Donaldsons of early SNCC had passed through segregated southern agricultural and mechanical colleges. The Stokely Carmichaels had attended the Bronx High School of Science and elite Howard University.

Nor, as the Panthers grew, did they represent the black population—rural South or urban North—any more closely. The movement drew its recruits from a social group regarded as typical of American Negroes by only New Leftists and right-wing racists: the teenage gang members and petty thugs who were the most immediate bane of ghetto life.

With a leadership that paralleled the relative social station of New Leftists in white America, it is not surprising that the Black Panthers had much in common with their white allies in terms of political weakness. The differences are significant but the similarities are striking. With the white Movement, the Panthers and their fellow travelers shared a pathetically romantic self-image, a sub rosa belief in violence as a viable revolutionary tool in the United States. Both groups shared the same naive confidence in school-taught American institutions. Both rejected programmatic radicalism and ideology in favor of "action."

The Saturday matinee romanticism of Black Panthers was never better expressed than by Eldridge Cleaver. He was one of those characters white liberals loved. Cleaver was a rapist who sent chills of excitement rather than horror down rad-lib spines when he pointed out that when he raped someone, it was "an insurrectionary act." He wrote *Soul on Ice* in prison. It was rewritten at *Ramparts* magazine, a San Francisco publication that combined well-researched exposés with "Oh Wow!" bohemianism, and was touted in the salons as a masterpiece. (It is a remarkably slight book.)

In December 1966 Cleaver was paroled and went to work for *Ramparts*. He fell in with a Black Power group in the city and was at one of its meetings when he met the Panthers.

> *Suddenly the room fell silent. The crackling undercurrent, that for weeks had made it impossible to get one's point across when one had the floor, was gone; there was only the sound of the lock clicking as the front door opened, and then the soft shuffle of feet moving quietly toward the circle. Shadows danced on the walls. From the tension showing on the faces of the people sitting before me, I thought the cops were invading the meeting, but there was a deep female gleam leaping out of one of the women's eyes that no cop who ever lived could elicit. I recognized that gleam out of the recesses of my soul, even though I had never seen it before in my life: the total admiration of a black woman for a black man. I spun around in my seat and saw the most beautiful sight I had ever seen: four black men wearing black berets, powder blue shirts, black leather jackets, black trousers, shiny black shoes—and each with a gun! In front was Huey P. Newton with a riot pump shotgun in his right hand, barrel pointed down to the floor. Beside him was Bobby Seale, the handle of a 45 calibre automatic showing from its holster on his right hip, just below the hem of his jacket. A few steps behind was Bobby Hutton, the barrel of his shotgun at his feet. Next to him was Sherwin Forte, an MI carbine with a banana clip cradled in his arms.*

This melodramatic squib rivals anything fantasized by a highly wrought teenage girl on a snowbound cattle ranch. The uniforms and posing are comprehensible. The symbolic significance of the paramilitary paraphernalia is obvious. The question that renews itself is, what was an ostensibly sophisticated intellectual community thinking of when it adjudged this to be a momentous political phenomenon? Certainly not the social realities of the black ghetto or, indeed, of American society as a whole. The paramilitary posturing represented at best a politically foolish policy and, eventually, self-destructive delusion. Sensitivity to the rage of the Panthers may have demanded considerable tact in pointing this out to them. But what the Panthers actually got from the white Left was awe and admiration.

The Panther regalia aped the uniforms of the juvenile hoodlum gangs of the 1950s. This was not likely to appeal to the mass of ghetto blacks who were the principal victims of ghetto crime, petty and grand. The Panther playacting was no different in effect from the personal bohemian rebellions of white suburbanites who attempted to outrage their world with long hair and beads on the fellows. The white rebellion was conscious, the Panthers' merely obtuse. In both cases, the posturing was not the action of a *political* movement.

The Panther jackets and jackboots were patterned after the costume of the Oakland ghetto's juvenile underworld in which Newton had moved and with which he was smitten. Gaining his recruits there in addition to a small circle of college students, Newton was to see from prison the Panthers lose in jigtime the superficial political gloss he had put on a ghetto gang. In the absence of his discipline, the party reverted to petty protection rackets, bullyism within the ghetto, and other gang activities. The Panthers had recruited hoods not to reform them, as did the Muslims and Malcolm X, but to be absorbed by them. The irony atop the irony was that while the white militants and liberals stood agog before Huey P. Newton as the salt of the earth, a real man, Newton himself slavered

after and envied the ghetto hoodlumism of which the "bourgie" had never quite been a part.

THE GRAND ILLUSION

A more tragic effect of the guns and paraphernalia was that
they instilled in the Panthers an illusion of power (again shared
by the white New Left) which, in its turn, produced an
arrogance and recklessness that, while psychically rewarding,
contributed in confrontation with the real world to the party's
debacle. In his "Letters from Jail," Cleaver recounted a visit to
San Francisco of the widow of Malcolm X, Betty Shabazz. It
was a kind of Ruritanian State Visit. She had been met at the
airport by an armed Panther escort, led by Newton, which
accompanied her to Cleaver's office at *Ramparts* magazine. By
the time the party was ready to leave the downtown building,
the street outside was filled with police and a crowd of
curiosity-seekers. A television cameraman who had been
denied entrance to the building at the request of Mrs. Shabazz
attempted to shoot his film on the sidewalk. Newton held an
envelope or small card over the camera lens. The cameraman
knocked his hand away and Newton asked a policeman to
arrest him for assault. "If I arrest anybody, it'll be you," the
policeman replied. There was another scuffle with the cameraman and Newton pushed him, throwing him off balance.

> *Bobby Seale tugged at Huey's shirt sleeve. "C'mon
> Huey, let's get out of here."*
> *Huey and Bobby started up the sidewalk toward
> their car. The cops stood there on the point, poised
> as though ready to start shooting at a given signal.
> "Don't turn your back on these back-shooting
> dogs!" Huey called out to Bobby and the three other
> Panthers. By this time the other Panthers and sister
> Betty and Jamal had gotten into cars and melted
> into the traffic jam. Only these five were still at the
> scene.*

At that moment a big beefy cop stepped foward. He undid the little strap holding his pistol in his holster and started shouting at Huey, "Don't point that gun at me; stop pointing that gun at me." He kept making gestures as though he was going for his gun.

This was the most tense of moments. Huey stopped in his tracks and stared at the cop.

"Let's split, let's split," Bobby Seale was saying.

Ignoring him, Huey walked to within a few feet of the cop and said, "What's the matter, you got an itchy finger?"

The cop made no reply.

"You want to draw your gun?" Huey asked him.

The other cops were calling out for this cop to cool it, to take it easy, but he didn't seem able to hear them. He was staring into Huey's eyes, measuring him.

"OK," Huey said, "You big fat racist pig. Draw your gun."

The cop made no move.

"Draw it, you cowardly dog." Huey pumped a round into the chamber of the shotgun. "I'm waiting," he said, and stood there waiting for the cop to draw.

All the other cops moved back out of the line of fire. I moved back too, onto the top step of Ramparts. *I was thinking, staring at Huey surrounded by all those cops and daring one of them to draw: Goddam, that nigger is crazy.*

Then the cop facing Huey gave up. He heaved a heavy sigh and lowered his head. Huey literally laughed in his face and then went off up the street at a jaunty pace, disappearing in a blaze of dazzling sunlight.

"Work out, soul brother," I was shouting to myself.
"You're the baddest motherfucker I've ever seen."
I went back into Ramparts *and we all stood around chattering excitedly, discussing what we had witnessed with disbelief.*
"Who was that?" asked Vampira, Warren Hinckle's little sister.
"That was Huey P. Newton," I said, "Minister of Defense for the Black Panther Party for Self Defense."
"Boy, is he gutsy," she said dreamily.
"Yeah," I agreed, "He's out of sight."

It is not particularly important that the incident might not have conformed in all its details to Cleaver's Dodge City melodrama, replete with tense moments, cowardly dogs, "draw-your-gun's," and jaunty exits into a sunburst. The point being the lesson that its readers were expected to draw and did. That lesson was that the combined police power of the Bay Area cities melted away before the steely gaze of Huey Pierce Newton. Cleaver and Newton and the Panthers and the white New Leftists who read this seriously believed that the incident said something about the power of the Black Panther Party.

In fact, assuming something like this narrative actually occurred, a more sober interpretation might be: the unnotified police were caught completely off guard by the Panther visitation; they did not like "the terrain" (daylight, at the office of a nationally-circulated magazine on a crowded San Francisco street with a small horde of newspaper and television reporters on the scene). And, of course, they had their revenge: Cleaver wounded in a gun battle and kicked into exile with, by early 1973, no influence of note on anyone but his wife; Huey Newton occupied for several years in averting a lifetime prison sentence; Bobby Seale with a brace of indictments hanging over his head; Bobby Hutton dead, killed after a police ambush at night on a battlefield of the police's choosing; and the Panthers in disarray, bound for oblivion. All of which is rudimentary common sense. But it was beyond the comprehension of a Movement drowning in its own fantasies.

Game playing became the core of the movement. Panther rallies as early as mid-1967 consisted of little more than empty bravado. According to Sol Stern, "At these rallies small groups of young bloods gather to hear Bobby Seale and Newton tell them how, when the time comes, they can 'take care of business' in groups of threes and fours. The 'business' they are talking about is 'executing white racist cops' or dropping Molotov cocktails into strategic industrial installations. It is all suddenly very real and serious when [Newton] tells you confidently that when the time comes, it won't be just the killing of a couple of cops but part of a whole nationally coordinated effort aimed at the entire white occupying army."

GREASY KID STUFF

Officially and formally, the Black Panther Party never advocated the use of offensive violence. Violence was justified only in self-defense and then in accordance with Newton's strict rules of discipline. This principle was especially emphasized when the party was fighting off a dozen legal attacks and seeking the protection of civil liberties. But there are plenty of indications in early, obscure Panther documents, intended principally and perhaps wholly for Panther consumption, that this is really what the party meant. Or, meant to mean.

Thus, "Item #7" of the October 1966 "Black Panther Party Platform and Program" reads clearly and simply that the organization believes "that all black people should arm themselves for *self defense*." The third "Main Rule of Discipline" provided that the party shall "turn in everything captured from the attacking army." "Attacking" is gratuitous; a conscious extra effort by Newton to emphasize to members, catechumens, and observers the defensive nature of Panther arms. And, early in 1968, by then in disastrous retreat, the party organ urged: "Let us make one thing crystal clear. We do not claim the right to indiscriminate violence. We seek no bloodbath." A white hanger-on pleaded that whites were attracted by the party's antipolice line but "do not yet see the hard core of love in the ten points." And Huey Newton, all the time he drew interest from the white radical euphoria over his police confrontation, wondered whether white radicals were "going to be disappointed when they find out I didn't shoot those cops."

The hell-walloping infant organization that mellows as it ages is a familiar phenomenon in the history of dissidence. The Black Panthers, and the New Left generally, developed in quite another manner. Relatively circumspect in inception but lacking any sense of direction, both movements moved on the basis of frustration and unfounded deductions to progressively less responsible behavior. For, whatever the official line and the sincerity of it, the Panthers were capable in other moods and on different occasions of voicing an altogether different sentiment: that violent revolution was imminent and violence on the offense, therefore, the order of the day. In the excitement of the rally, in opportunistic appeals to ghetto lumpen in "Tomming" sessions for white audiences, in private—the Panthers, like the white militants, were wont to forget official strictures and their own better judgment. The Panthers did frequently call for serving the people and liberating the colony "by the only means necessary—the GUN."

Every Panther leader was culpable of such extravagances. At a rally on San Francisco's Potrero Hill in June 1967, Newton redefined "self defense" in a manner he considered clever: "Every time you go execute a white racist Gestapo cop, you are defending yourself." A New Left man of one season at San Francisco State College: "Change. Freedom everywhere. Dynamite! Black Power. Use the gun. Kill the pigs everywhere." David Hilliard played Peck's Bad Boy on his day at

Yale University, April 21, 1970: "Everyone knows that pigs are depraved traducers that violate the lives of human beings and that there ain't nothing wrong with taking the life of a motherfucking pig." Boola, boola. And there was the sort of thing favored by Black Power leader, H. Rap Brown, who presided over the merger of paper SNCC into the Panther Party in February 1968. "You call yourself revolutionaries?" Brown would leer. "How many white folks you killed today?"

This was adolescent bad-mouthing. It was seized upon by the police and makers of opinion friendly to them to prepare the public for an eventual suppression. The jolly rhetoric was in abysmally bad taste and eventually became a bore to even the most sensation-starved liberals. Few, including the Panthers, took the boastfulness seriously, and the old truism that real terrorists go about their business—they do not broadcast their deeds—is relevant here.

If a bad mouth does not warrant being riddled with bullets or locked into a penitentiary, however, neither is it the mark of a political movement to be taken seriously. It is impossible to say that the police would have acted differently or that the Panthers would have survived had the party been more sensible. During World War I, a conscious governmental effort to depict the Industrial Workers of the World as a violent and subversive organization deserving peremptory repression succeeded despite the union's frantic attempt to assert its nonviolence and even to waffle on its opposition to the war. But for a movement claiming to be political to be so irresponsible was, simply, stupid. And the Wobblies knew, one does not invite a suppressor that is perfectly able to let itself in.

THE NAIVETÉ OF
THE MOVEMENT

That is, if such a movement believes repression possible in the first place. For this temptation of Nemesis illustrates not only the juvenile romanticism of the Panthers and what I.F. Stone correctly labeled as "not practical politics" but "psychological therapy." It also evidenced a naive faith in American institutions. Like the early New Leftists, the Black Panthers indicated in their actions a fundamental belief in the essential fairness and justice of "the system" that was immeasurably more naive than the cynicism of the workingman who shrugs that "You can't fight city hall."

Implicit in the way the Panthers acted was the assumption that city hall would do right in the long run. For example, Brown's statement: "How many white folks you killed today?" To make such a statement and then to cry "repression" and "racism" when called to account for it signifies a profound faith in the society's definition of the First Amendment. Or, it signifies an adolescent dilettantism that counts on the indulgence of kids' "fooling around." In either case, it is a characteristic generally associated with the middle-class white movement.

The Panthers not only expected better of the police than the bestiality with which they verbally attributed them, they expected better than would occur to any sensible suburbanite stopped for speeding on a freeway. The Panthers were quite as shocked by the blitzkrieg that killed Bobby Hutton and wounded Cleaver in Oakland and the action against the Chicago headquarters as the "revolutionaries" at Columbia University in 1968, who could not believe that the police were actually beating them up just for starting an insurrection.

The split depiction of the Panther martyr Bobby Hutton is another case in point. On the one hand he was the Guevarista revolutionary: grim-faced, cold-blooded *macho,* weapon ever ready. On the other, killed by the police, he was "Little Bobby," sweet infant, Hugh of Lincoln, taken from his Momma, slaughtered by pigs. The Panthers believed they could have it both ways. In one sense, the black movement had come a long way since 1961. In another, this was the same implicit faith that the SNCC sit-in campaign had evinced: the world was essentially well; one needed only to point to the evils in society to see them remedied. However, where the SNCC workers shunned violence in word as well as deed and stood ready to take responsibility for their actions, the Panthers wanted to attack and be indulged. It was not politics and it was certainly not revolutionary.

Nor were the Panthers' policies, such as they were and forgotten as they were when the game was well under way. Like the essential reformism of the white Movement, the Panthers, when pressed to be concrete, came up with principles like "employment" and "guaranteed income," "decent housing," a well-balanced breakfast ("the most important meal of your day"), and stoplights at dangerous intersections. All salutary and desirable, none precisely the cooperative commonwealth to which white liberals and militants trusted the Panthers to lead them. Like the New Left, the Black Panthers believed that their actions, even their posturing, was itself "revolution." Even before the party was founded, Irving Howe pointed out exactly where it would lead. Writing in 1965 of the nascent Black Power militants, he noted that they were acting out social motives like those of the Russian *narodniki* "who also tried to substitute the intransigent will for the sluggishness of history." Howe added that "the consequences may be similar: the best cadres exhausted in isolation and defeat."

WHITE SKIN PRIVILEGE

It is a commonplace that the central tragedy of the black experience in America is the fact that the fate of black people has always been almost wholly in the hands of whites. The Black Powerites constantly reiterated this in reference to "the first 350 years." But the sad fact is just as pertinent to the history of the Black Power movement itself. The human waste and woe entailed in the debacle of the Panthers owed a great deal to the white militants' and liberals' response to "Black Powerism." It is impossible to say to what extent the whites were "responsible" for the bloody endpiece. Early Panther setbacks such as Huey P. Newton's arrest grew out of incidents quite within the indigenous Black Panther concept of "self-defense."

But in the end the black movement was taking its cues from its white supporters as mechanically as seasoned actors in a long-running play, jumping Jim Crow as ever it was jumped. The white activists devised ornate theories to justify complete deference to the blacks and rooted on the blacks in their accelerating irresponsibility. There was no cynicism or calculation in this patronization. It was impelled by guilt and fostered by a world view as foolish as that of the blacks. But there was such a thing, as the catchword had it, as "white skin privilege." The Panthers and their ilk suffered a loss of blood for their foolery; the white New Leftists sustained nothing more gory than disappointment, and, when Rolfing, the Guru Maharaj Ji, and jogging came along, they got over their disappointment quickly enough.

The relationship of the Movement of the late 1960s to the blacks had its roots in the motives of the earliest white SNCC workers. These college students envisioned their treks south not simply or even primarily as assistance in the political struggles of others. They sought quite as much to shrive themselves, to identify with and be subsumed in the black experience. With their expulsion from SNCC in 1966 and the head-over-heels development in 1966 and 1967 of social exclusionism among blacks, white radicals found themselves completely awash. Stokely Carmichael offered something of a program to the white ex-SNCC workers along with his antiwhite diatribes. White radicals should return to their own communities and labor there against racism, at its source. But this was out of the question. As the young lady who winced at the Pabst poster in Tchula made clear, the whole idea for the whites had been to get out of that society. "Radicals" imbued with the bohemianism of beat were not going to return to suburbia and mix with neatniks. As a result, when they were thrown out of the civil rights movement as reformed by S. Carmichael, they went back to the university.

They were hurt. But the New Leftists never for a moment thought to criticize the blacks. On the contrary, as Greg Calvert of SDS wrote, "We owe SNCC a deep debt of gratitude for having slapped us brutally in the face with the slogan of black power." With nothing to offer themselves but screaming at perspiring deans, the white New Leftists devised a new identity for themselves. This was obligingly phrased for them by a person named Bertram Garskov at the New Politics convention of 1967 when he assumed for whites the role of "the white tail on the real movement."

MAN, CAN
THOSE COONS DANCE!

Howard Zinn, a historian, published *SNCC: The New Abolitionists* in 1964. He had the bad luck to predict a new era of white-black radical collaboration on the eve of the racial split. But Zinn was resilient. It was vital for New Leftists that they not be dismayed by being dead wrong. Zinn rebounded immediately with a fantastic adaptation of Marx that included the black vanguard idea among other curiosities. "Recent experience suggests," Zinn wrote, "that Negroes, especially those in the ghetto, may be the most powerful single force for social change in the United States." Zinn, an aging academic, differed from the younger New Leftists only in his attempt to dredge out an "ideological" rationale for this act of faith.

A writer later in the decade was even less circumspect in his use of the saints, calling the Black Panthers (of all things) "a Marxist-Leninist party heavily influenced by Maoist teachings." (The notion is all the more engaging in view of the fact that Newton's crowd appears to have sold a thousand "little red books" to white radicals before they read it themselves.) "Unquestionably," he continued, "the Black Panthers have been able to demonstrate the relevance of Marxist theory to conditions in the ghetto. This is owing in large part to their intelligent adaptation of Marxist maxims to the concrete experience of the black community and especially to the anti-colonial nature of the black struggle."

Weatherman, the final incarnation of SDS, took the idea to its extreme. The group devised an analysis of American society and the possibilities of revolution based on a healthy dose of white liberal masochism and a bizarre view of world politics. The entire world was a macrocosm of the Marxist class model in which the underdeveloped countries represented the revolutionary proletariat, and the *entirety* of American society, including white workers, were the exploiting capitalists. The exception was the American black community which was actually a colony within the mother country. (This sort of doodling with Marx had been applied a year or so earlier to the university, the students being the proletariat.)

Only the proletarian colonies should conceivably be revolutionary. Hopelessly corrupted by their "white skin privilege," white radicals could contribute only by sniping behind the lines, thus softening up behemoth for the final coup. The Weatherman apocrypha actually saw the post-revolutionary world much as the John Birch Society saw it: a sea of grinning, many-colored peoples washing down Main Street, Disneyland, wreaking cruel vengeance on American whites (hopefully but not necessarily sparing the Weatherman) and living something like sultans on American wealth— which the suburbanite Weatherman thought of in terms of Master Charge with no reckoning—in just compensation for two thousand years of white-inflicted misery.

American blacks were naturally accorded an awesome power by this frame of mind. The first Weatherman manifesto somehow deduced that blacks were an essential part of the work force (some said *the* critical segment) and posited that a move to self-determination on their part would itself mean the end of the American Empire. And blacks *could* do this: "If necessary, black people could win self-determination, abolishing the imperialist system and seizing state power to do it, without the white movement" because blacks are critical to the system, "economically and geo-militarily, and because of the level of unity, commitment, and initiative which will be developed in waging a people's war for survival and national liberation." This at a time when serious analysts of black America were troubled by the economic superfluity of blacks and the potential (often apocalyptic) implications they divined from this observation.

Weatherman actually attempted to act according to its analysis, sponsoring a series of terrorist bombings on the assumption that the international uprising was imminent.

Most other post-1966 white militants, however, were content with solemn deference. It became impossible to look on the blacks in any other mood but dead seriousness. Abbie Hoffman, Jerry Rubin, and Paul Krassner built careers on a jesting nihilism, but they mustered with the solemnity of Irish altar boys when the black question came up. Hoffman, who had been closest of the three to the civil rights movement as a SNCC field worker, was most obvious. His *Revolution for the Hell of It* is one long guffaw: cynical, nihilistic, indiscriminate jibing. Everything was fair game; there were, in *The Realist's* phrase, "no sacred cows." Except on the matter of blacks; that was nothing to clown about; that was a serious matter. Hoffman quotes a letter from "Stokely" in the book. It stands out an inch from the page, a totally gratuitous sentimentalism in some hundred pages of zaniness. Hoffman was establishing his honorary negritude according to highest authority. With the benediction completed, back to the fun!

By 1970, even the addle-headed Timothy Leary (rescued from prison by Weatherman) was calling the Black Panthers the vanguard in his newly perceived revolutionary cosmos: "It hardly seems necessary to repeat what is obvious to any clear-seeing person that the vanguard leadership of the freedom movement in the United States is provided by the Black Panthers who for three years now have stood up to protect their homes and offices against genocidal attack." Leary had no time for the argument from Marxism-Zinnism, of course: "You can talk and protest as loud as you want to but when it comes right down to it, it has been the Panthers who have showed us in Zen, existential fashion that if you don't stand up and defend yourself you will lose your freedom, if not your life."

The accumulation of this sort of thing had a remarkable effect. European radicals who avidly followed developments on the American New Left through movement prisms adopted and sometimes distorted further the deference to the blacks. At a "Congress on the Dialectics of Liberation" in London in the summer of 1967, a large number of European radicals heard papers of some erudition from Paul Sweezy, Herbert Marcuse, Paul Goodman, R.D. Laing, Lucien Goldman, and others. Their analyses covered a broad range of topics and stimulated extensive discussion. But, in collecting these papers for publication, British radical David Cooper concentrated almost exclusively in his afternote on the talk by Stokely Carmichael. This had been a frothy dab of nonsense, much sillier than Carmichael's usual pitch, filled with wild factual errors and analytical absurdities. It was the sort of thing by which Carmichael flourished for a season before audiences of American white liberals. The British audience took it less well than the Americans, and Carmichael got some criticisms (to which he was utterly unaccustomed) from the auditorium. But Cooper pleads for forbearance in his note on the grounds that this man has *done* something, unlike ourselves.

As perceptive a critic as the Belgian Ernest Mandel was capable of writing that while students had launched the American movement, they had eventually drawn in "masses of adult black workers and now [are] beginning to affect white workers also."

BLACK POWER—
THE NEW UNCLE TOMS

This fantasy of what was going on in America by a leading European Marxist was rivaled by the delusions on the scene, in the United States. Not only did white radicals talk themselves into the most incredible nonsense, the activist blacks began to believe it. Thinking that "Black is Beautiful" actually meant

something, and startled by the masochism with which whites
accepted the best laid-on stripes, groups like the Panthers
actually envisaged themselves not only as protectors of the
ghettos and as a lobby seeking jobs and decent housing and as
the black wing of a revolutionary movement. They came to
subscribe to the white definition of themselves as *the* vanguard
of it not the revolution *in toto.* "Once again," wrote Julius
Lester, a Negro New Leftist who was an early exploiter of
bourgeois white guilt as well as a victim of its delusions, "it was
left to SNCC to act as the vanguard, the prod, pushing and
forcing whites deeper into a confrontation with political
realities." Lester was writing about the Chicago New Politics
Conference, one of the New Left's greatest fiascos. And he was
writing at a time, late 1967, when SNCC, his vanguard, had
ceased to exist.

The oratorical excesses of SNCC leader H. Rap Brown
and Panthers like Bobby Seale and David Hilliard were played
out within the context of their role as defined by white
militants: the leaders of the social upheaval. They bought the
Weatherman-type dictum that a black "uprising is imminent
and will wipe out American fascism/imperialism." It is not
impossible to imagine this notion developing within an
isolated Black Panther politics. Huey P. Newton and Bobby
Seale were as capable of nonsense as their white counterparts.
Nevertheless, the idea was developed by the white New Left
and was kicked back to the blacks. "Violence is not good or
evil. It is necessary," Julius Lester wrote. "Today we have our
Nat Turners on the street corners of every ghetto, but where
are our John Browns?" Lester eventually got his John Browns
in the form of Weatherman, and he eventually sobered up to
recant both them and the Panthers, recognizing that the Nats
of the sixties were really Toms. In the meantime the Movement
managed to huzzah many "revolutionaries" to the scaffold.

"SOUL"

A more intelligent white New Left assessment of the black
movement was impossible because, as part of the whites'

deference, they accepted and expanded the black concept of "soul." Steeped in irrationalism from interaction with the Counterculture, white militants made into a self-evident truth what had been to early black nationalists a tool to effect racial pride. "Perhaps no white man—and I am white," wrote Gene Marine, an early booster of the Panthers, "can adequately convey the background of being black which is necessary in order really to understand the Panthers." How, then, could Marine excuse his own lengthy book on the subject? He came up with a magnificent further insight: "On the other hand, and always excepting a couple of outstanding novelists, if a black man expressed it adequately, he would have to be talking in black terms, and if you're white, you probably wouldn't understand him anyway." *Quod erat demonstrandum.*

This was in one sense simply a new example of the awe of black "realness" that permeated the white SNCC workers from the beginning of the 1960s. Yet it also represented a more explicit recognition of the political consequences of "soul," the sort of thing Weatherman was apparently referring to in its talk of black "geo-militancy." It became at times the white racist notion of black sexual superiority turned at least on its side. Mary Moylan, writing from underground where she had fled to escape the prosecution of her Roman Catholic group of draft-file burners, told of her discomfiture at being unable to act. "How do you operate?" she wondered. "I don't think we have the mechanisms set up for that. I think the black community does but not the whites."

The belief in a vast, highly synchronized black movement was as much a staple (and an object of envy) to New Left activists as it was to right-wing hysterics. The belief that here was a people with a certain veritably racial knack for revolution was reminiscent of American socialists in the wake of the Bolshevik revolution who stood and applauded when a Russian immigrant recruit happened to enter the hall. At the least, the belief in a peculiarly black insight into social problems (a matter of personal experience, not rational deduction) provided reason not to criticize the actions of black movements in any way. When Saul Alinsky was told of the muted chagrin of some white militants that a number of blacks had "rewritten" the American Constitution without them, he noted, "as long as blacks wrote it they wouldn't dare open their mouths." What white could possibly know better than any black?

"Because *all blacks* experience oppression in a form that no whites do, *no whites* are in a position to fully understand and test from their own practice the real situation black people face and the necessary response to it . . . ." wrote Gene Marine. "It is not legitimate for whites to organizationally intervene in differences among revolutionary black nationalists. It would be arrogant for us to attack any black organization that defends black people and opposes imperialism in practice."

The policy had its pathetic-comic relief, chronicled most famously in Tom Wolfe's description of a fund-raising party for the Panthers at composer-conductor Leonard Bernstein's plush apartment. The concept of "radical chic" is a valuable one. The implication of it that Wolfe did not develop was that this entire black-worshipping phase of the white New Left was itself nothing more. The young militants were the children of the Park Avenue matrons, on the surface less ridiculous only because they gathered in musty garrets rather than Leonard Bernstein's *salon*. The eyes through which they looked at the Panthers were quite as bourgeois and romantic.

There was a good example of this in a women's liberation picture portfolio. On one page, the bust of Nefertiti is depicted as an example of idealized feminine beauty, and therefore, presumably, of the dehumanization of female by male. "In the name of Beauty," the caption read, "her hair was shaved from her head and her eyebrows plucked one by one." Having winced compassionately, the reader turns to the page opposite, a photograph entitled "Profile of a Black Woman" by Owen Brown. It was captioned: "The elegant beauty and regal bearing of Queen Nefertiti finds a modern equivalent in this profile." In one roll of the eye, what is sneered at is admired.

The difference is that the subject is black. As blacks are exempted from political criticism, even a movement committed to the "pro-woman line" will exempt black women from the doctrine of dehumanization by cosmetic companies. In fact, the women's liberation movement generally absolved blacks of the otherwise absolute sexual dichotomy. There was a slogan, possibly but not necessarily coined to mock women's liberation: "Our black brothers are our sisters."

About the only guru of the period who actually put the word "soul" to paper was Charles Reich. The codifier of American suburban fantasies, he writes of rock music that it "tells of the discovery by whites of the quality known as soul— a depth of feeling long denied to most Americans."

PATRONIZATION
The British poet Stephen Spender spent some time among American New Leftists and their liberal hangers-on during 1968. He noted among other observations that their personal sense of guilt for the oppression of blacks had generated a masochistic relationship with them. "I imagined a musical called *The Last Liberal*," he wrote. "During a strike on a great American Campus, the blacks seize a building.... A liberal professor—white—joins them, and is received with enthusiasm. All contact with the world outside is cut off, and there is nothing to eat. After several days all supplies run out. The liberal professor has to offer himself to be eaten. There is a party."

Spender was neither alone nor first in recognizing the pathological willingness of white liberals and New Leftists— their anxiety to be rhetorically flogged by black militants. In fact, long before intellectual analysts described the phenomenon, various prominent Black Power leaders, if momentarily stunned by the fact, were quick to take advantage.

Malcolm X had a different sort of speech for the largely white audiences at the colleges he began touring as a Black Muslim in the early sixties than what he presented to all-negro

groups. To the latter, Malcolm wasted little time cataloging
the white man's depredations against his race. He assumed
they were well enough known. What he spoke about to other
blacks was the need for unity and, like the good revivalist he
was, he prepared the ground for conversion with a recitation of
black peccadillos. To generally white audiences, on the other
hand, Malcolm gave what he knew they wanted: a good
whupping. If, as the pioneer on the trail, he was at first startled
by the thunderous applause that followed his performance, his
imitators were not.

"The least you can say about white skin," quipped a New
York City journalist, "is that it seems to be pretty thick."
Stokely Carmichael, H. Rap Brown, and a whole galaxy of
even lesser Panthers and local black Chautaquans made a
lucrative career out of addressing liberal and New Left college
students, denouncing and vilifying them in the foul language
the FSM won the right to use in academe. They could not elicit
a reaction less favorable than lusty cheers. On the rare
occasion that a game heckler opened his mouth, the result was
a perfunctory drubbing by the toughs that Black Power
spokesmen took some pleasure in carrying along with them, all
to the approval of the rest of the audience.

There was a large element of psychological exploitation
in the craft. The black rage orators also discovered that the
technique was the best means of raising funds: the worse the
abuse, the bigger the collection. The baldest profiteer of "Mau-
Mauing," as Tom Wolfe called it, was LeRoi Jones. Little
recognized until he discovered white masochism, Jones lived a
dual life of interracial aesthetics in private life and avenging
scourge of the white devils on platform and stage. A typical
Jones performance occurred at a fund-raising benefit for
Eldridge Cleaver at the Fillmore East Auditorium in New
York City. To a mostly white audience who paid to get in
because they were sympathetic to Cleaver, Jones shouted,
"The same people who killed Bobby Hutton... the same
people who jailed Rap Brown, are the same white people who

are sitting in this room." "The same white people" cheered and whistled.

Jones profited handsomely for the season or two that this sort of therapy was in fashion. Not only was he in demand at university "lectures," his plays and films, most of them flaccid little sob stories of no apparent literary merit, were well attended. As the master of "Mau-Mauing," Jones received several poverty program grants apparently on the grounds that he was so very angry.

Bobby Seale was another example of the black militant who consciously employed vilification of supporters as a rhetorical tool. At the same benefit for Cleaver, Seale said, "We hate you white people! We hate you white people! And the next time one of you paddies comes up here and accuses me of hating you because of the color of your skin, I will kick you in your ass. We started out hating you because of the color of your skin...." Seale knew how to play on the New Left preoccupation with complicity. He told of an incident from his high school days when he cornered "a little white liberal" and made him give up his lunch money. Later, as Seale told it, he forced his mark to bring him two dollars. "And the next day he'd bring me two dollars. Because that two dollars was mine. Mine because of 400 years of racism and oppression. When I take two dollars from you, pig, don't you keep nothing."

What was this fad all about? It may have had something to do with the angers and resentments of would-be black political leaders at the meager response that met them in the ghettos. Some black teenagers fell in behind them. Virtually all blacks resented mistreatment at the hands of the police. But, in the end, their base was minuscule. At a march against the war in Vietnam in New York City in 1967, Stokely Carmichael announced that "the black contingent" against the war would not befoul itself by assembling in the Sheep Meadow of Central Park with the whites. The blacks would march down Fifth Avenue from Harlem behind Field Marshal Carmichael. The black march, a ragged hundred or so, would have been called off in embarrassment by a leader more substantial than Carmichael. It would have been laughed down or at least been accepted as demonstration that Stokely Carmichael was not quite the King of Harlem by any movement not predisposed to regard one black marcher as, in "soul," the equivalent of ten thousand whites. But neither Carmichael nor the hundred thousand whites got the point. When the whites saw the man with the Pepsodent scowl and his tiny group of supporters, they cheered.

The incident was typical. The Black Power movement consistently failed to elicit a mass following from beginning to end, from Mississippi to Oakland, California. The white New Leftists decorously refused to notice, as they had been trained not to notice when someone broke wind in church. They spun fantasies of an imminent black rising. The Black Power leaders acted as if the whites were right and took out their frustrations on their only and unfortunately colorless supporters.

There was also the matter, related to this, that the Panthers and their like had simply nothing to say but bad words. Like the white movement, they were not primarily political but merely an expression of the impotent fury of a few. With no black following, no power with which to make demands outside white imaginations, no program—what was there to do but shout epithets and vulgarities? Soon enough, like everything that represented no threat to the social order but satisfied uncertain masochistic yearnings among the *grand bourgeoisie,* the black art was incorporated into popular culture and whatever sincerity the black spokesmen brought with their aimlessness was formalized into an opera bouffe. If the genteel liberals of Tom Wolfe's "Radical Chic" were stung into at least partial retreat by his satire, it never penetrated their nonreading sons and daughters of the New Left. As late as 1971, three California state colleges in one day paid $1,500 each for a talk by the shopworn Stokely Carmichael. Even he seemed surprised that there was still that much money in the racket.

The Black Powerites were Toms. They delivered what "the man" wanted to hear! It was easier, and no doubt more gratifying to the psyche, than organizational work in the ghettos, than the painful effort and small results of real political organization. Lacking the privileged adolescent cynicism of the Yippies, the black leaders who made a career of wielding the lash in a sense opted for the same course as Jerry Rubin and Abbie Hoffman. Without admitting that there was to be no revolution, they decided to have fun. The difference was the same as that between greenbelt and inner-city ghetto: there are more opportunities for fun for the kids in the suburbs.

THE RACISM OF
THE NEW LEFT

As for the whites, their Simple Simon encouragement of the detractors indicated a sort of racial discrimination not found in most other groups in the society. These New Leftists were from neighborhoods and classes in which they never really had contact with Negroes until, as college students, they joined the civil rights movement. Their fantasies about Negroes were never, in the most basic sense, broken down by the integrationist period, and they were reinforced when, after 1966, all blacks within earshot withdrew into homogeneous, exclusivist groups, alternately cackling and glowering from the corners of university cafeterias. One of the pathetic ironies of the young generation of the 1960s is that for all the thunder about "real human relationships," in connection with the blacks at least, the young white radicals were never able to see them as other than depersonalized objects, first as "the oppressed" with whom to identify and whom to elevate, then as the remote, steely, romanticized "vanguard" whose racial depth of the soul was, alas, never to be attained by bloodless whites. Blacks never ceased to be "invisible" as human beings in Ralph Ellison's sense of that word. The meeting of Weatherman at Flint, Michigan, in late December 1969 is an instance. It was held at a black-owned ballroom in the Flint ghetto. No sooner did the group assemble, slavering in anticipation of the black rising against white America, than it was swept by a paranoiac fear that the conventioneers would be pummeled by local Negroes. In the abstract, the blacks were the worshipped leaders. Suddenly, in the streets surrounded by the dusky Moor, the young suburbanites quivered like dogs in recollection of puppyhood horror stories.

Even when this inability to see individual black people as other than members of "the race" did not obtrude in terms of fear, the New Leftist attitude toward the blacks was, ultimately, rank patronization: the *noblesse oblige* of their liberal parents rather than the hostility of the white working class. The preferential treatment accorded to the blacks in the 1968 occupation of Columbia University illustrated this. The blacks, naturally, had occupied one building themselves. While demanding that the white rebels capitulate, the university administration offered a deal, including amnesty, to the blacks. The blacks took it, in effect selling their white allies out. Vice-President David Truman accounted for the kid-gloves treatment of the blacks in Hamilton Hall (as opposed to a brutal police attack on the whites) on the grounds that the blacks were "a totally different cut as far as performance is concerned.... I must say I admire the way they conducted themselves." The facts were that the only firearms reported in the disturbance from beginning to end were in black-held Hamilton Hall, and the blacks were, additionally, the only group to hold hostages, and therefore technically guilty of kidnapping. Truman and Columbia's president, Grayson Kirk, apparently felt that Harlem would rise if the blacks were mistreated, a delusion both black and white militants shared. But the point is that no white militant raised a peep about the episode, about neither the liberal administrators' indulgence nor the blacks'... what was it?... cowardice? treachery?

George Kennan realized that both liberals and New Leftists were patronizing the Negroes. He noted that the New

Left attitude toward the blacks blames their plight "exclusively" on the "cruelty and indifference of the white community now alive," thus ignoring the historical roots of the problem. This makes the Negro "a helpless ward of public authority." The New Left's refusal to criticize black politics meant in effect that "the American Negro is to be held to no standards." Kennan continued: "The image is left only of a cold heartless, cruel white society, encumbered with total guilt and total power, facing a Negro population marked only by helplessness, innocence, and nobility of spirit."

Kennan was right. And this end product derived from New Left opinions, policies, and practices. In fact, what he described is the traditional white American dehumanization of the black man which, depending on class of origin, geographical region, or other factors, has variously manifested itself in history as conservative noblesse oblige, liberal leadership in the civil rights movement, and the guilt-stricken patronization of the New Left and the 1960s liberals. LeRoi Jones's dramas were not to be judged by the same critical standards as a white playwright's. An individual Negro's technical competence was not to be critical in consideration of him for a position. For blacks, mere literacy was to be no entrance requirement to a university. There was a racial debt to be paid, a penance to be made.

The frantic rush of liberal academics to meet black demands for "black studies" programs illustrated this patronization at its most ludicrous. Black campus groups began challenging the fact that courses in history, social sciences, and the fine arts had traditionally and habitually skated over or ignored Negro contributions to especially American development. Operating on the then current principle that "black" was unique, various campus groups began to insist on special programs devoted to these studies. (A few at first insisted—unsuccessfully—that only blacks be permitted in these courses. As it turned out, the failure of this demand was fortunate for the people who got jobs as professors of black studies. After a semester or two, their courses were supported mainly by whites.)

The white campus penitents were quick to take up the cries and, by 1970, it was a rare college of any size which did not have such a program. On many campuses, including some of the best, professors who would have bought small arms at the suggestion that their own disciplines be subject to the whims of those whom they were teaching cheerily put programs under the control of the black students. This was the absence of standards of which Kennan wrote. As a physics professor at CCNY who shrugged approval of the program said, "It is their funeral. They will suffer or they will prosper; it will have very little effect on the rest of us." Newspaper columnist Murray Kempton observed, "Even Harvard... agrees to give its Negro students control over their own black-studies program. After all, it is their funeral. Yet none of these institutions would grant its students any such power in any other department; men do not that easily give away anything they think worth having."

Of his arrest on a drug charge and subsequent fear that he would be beaten by police, Jerry Rubin wrote: "At the end of the corridor I saw a black cop and felt less uptight." The New Leftists, so accustomed to patronizing black people and exempting them from standards, did not—inevitably to their chagrin—hold Negro policemen to what the Movement conceived of as a standard of brutality-potential. Movement people took wry pleasure in the way in which courts and police forces methodically loaded riot-control contingents with black officers and officials when a black power incident was involved. They apparently were never capable of thinking of such individuals as individuals and thus as policemen whose ideas were closer to those of Patrolman Murphy than of Bobby Seale.

The radicals indulged black militants and Negroes generally as slave owners had indulged them—as if they were children. When the Black Panthers in Oakland established a free breakfast program for ghetto school children, this admirable social action was vaunted in the Movement as something very marvelous indeed, akin to a moon voyage. Saul Alinsky jibed only a little too acerbically: "Oh well, look, the breakfast stuff is real chickenshit, let's face it. If you had a white group going around setting up little Sunday breakfasts, who'd give a damn about it? But the white liberals get so *captivated* with the *romance* of the whole black business."

Perhaps white Movement patronization came to its critical head (as did so many New Left absurdities) at the Conference on a New Politics at Chicago in September 1967. When a small black contingent (mostly Negro teenagers from the neighborhood) demanded for their separate caucus one-half of the convention votes and, in effect, a pre-endorsement of everything they did, the assembly—summoned to bring order and good sense to the chaotic movement—capitulated almost immediately. On the Israel issue, this policy turned its neatest tricks. First, after prodding by the blacks, the whole convention (including its chief organizer, Arthur A. Waskow, an Orthodox Jew) condemned the "imperialistic Zionist war" in the Middle East. Then, probably because of charges of black anti-Semitism then in the air, the black caucus reversed its stand *in camera* and dropped the condemnation. Renata Adler wrote, "the convention found itself in the position of having both endorsed a proposal and pre-endorsed, *carte blanche,* so to speak, its reversal." Toward the end of the convention, the white rump did little more than wait silently, hands in laps, for their cues from the blacks. At one point, when the white half was attempting to conjecture the black caucus position on one matter, a black man in the hall stood up and "reported" it. The whites then voted to ratify, only to learn later that the black caucus had decided just the opposite. The Negro "liaison" turned out to be a good-humored fellow who walked in off the street, was amused when he sized up the situation, and had some fun with it. But his credentials were convincing: you could see them in his face.

The conference sank into ultimate absurdity when it solemnly accepted a black proposal to send "white civilizing committees" into the white society "as exemplified by George Lincoln Rockwells and Lyndon Baines Johnsons." It ended its proceedings with an automatic endorsement of the resolutions of a Black Power Conference then meeting in Newark. Renata Adler wrote an appropriate *coda:* "Many did not know what the resolutions of the Newark Black Power Conference were, since no official list was ever issued, and it is not certain that any was ever drawn up." About the only salutary result of the convention was to the benefit of the group of Negro kids who, figuring that there was more to be wrung from white guilt than a few resolutions, ate an expensive supper in the Palmer House Restaurant and charged it to the convention. Of course the bill was paid.

Unfortunately, this glad story was not the whole consequence of the white patronization. That deference encouraged militant blacks, whose energies might otherwise have been directed toward genuine social goals or even toward their own personal careers, into the same kind of aimless foundering that characterized the white Movement.

CHAPTER SIX

WAR IS HELL ON THE HOMEFRONT, TOO

During the winter of 1963, the Marxist Study Group of Madison, Wisconsin, devoted one of its regular meetings at the Women's Peace Center to a discussion of the guerrilla war in Vietnam. Appropriately, it was not a big meeting, for the war was not very big at that time. Nor was it a "protest." The Marxist Study Group was not a protest organization. It was an informal, almost cliquish seminar of radical graduate students at the University of Wisconsin and half a dozen leftist townies, remnant Bob La Follette progressives and Victor Berger social democrats whose survival made Madison as politically peculiar in its way as Berkeley was in its.

Madison's way was different from Berkeley's. The Madison radicals were by no means oblivious to the civil rights struggles of the day and, in 1964, they sympathetically followed the course of the Free Speech Movement out west. But just as a Wisconsin FSM would have been superfluous—political advocacy at the university was not only untethered, the Left actually "set the tone for campus political discussion"—Wisconsin's radical tradition was more intellectual than activist, armchair rather than picket line.

Madisonians held rallies against the bomb on the steps of the State Historical Society. Protest marches were common enough, but they were decorous, highly-structured affairs, almost British in their propriety, snaking around the state Capitol, with coffee and doughnuts available in the basement of the Episcopal church across the street. Even the sound of Madison demonstrations was distinctive, the murmur of a hundred small disputations rather than a chant.

A few Wisconsinites participated in projects such as SNCC's Freedom Summer. But a leftie earned status in Madison in arguments around a table rather than in speeches from a platform. And when Madison's radicals of the early sixties took up the subjects of civil rights and civil liberties and what have you, they wrung every droplet of dialectical pigment out of the ink of the news. Indeed, they could read more between the lines than could conceivably have been recorded there before the age of silicon chips.

Madison's Left was decidedly on the Old Left side of the time warp that, in 1963, was trembling in the moment of birth. They more likely sucked bent pipes than "reefers." They listened to classical rather than popular music. Indeed, they favored baroque in those days, formal, rational, and as finely structured as a Washington (or Moscow) bureau. They were puritans more than hedonists. They were far less likely than Berkeleyans or even the run-of-the-mill fifties rad-libs to agonize over their personal alienation. Every Sunday in season they assembled at a Madison park with a few cases of the cheap local beer and played all-comers softball until dusk. Everyone owned mitts in that cell. A few could still locate their old team caps. Madison was not Berkeley.

Perhaps it was the durable influence of the hereditary communists? A large number of CP stalwarts sent their heirs to the University of Wisconsin where they took a leading part in the loquacious, heady discussions that were the regimen leftist community. These heirs were not merely second generation in the cause, thereby wearing their politics with a grace beyond Berkeley *nouveaux,* but had been conceived, delivered, nursed, and weaned during the party's Popular Front period. Except for their unusual political affiliation, that itself seemed rather like the Republican affiliation of little old Vermont ladies, they felt quite at home in America. In an expansive mood they made gentle sport of the bohemians with whom they shared several bars. Feeling peevish, they called the campus beatniks "bourgeois decadents."

Then again, it may have been the climate. The New England Puritans occasionally explained their moral and intellectual superiority to Virginians in terms of weather. In Wisconsin, where the thermometer typically dropped below zero in January, sometimes not to rise above it for the better part of a month, what better to do on an icy Wednesday evening than to amble on over to the Women's Peace Center, gather around a hissing radiator, and enjoy a nice shout at one's running-dog revisionist friends?

Rather more likely, it was the continuous and established tradition of intellectual freedom at the University of Wisconsin as opposed to Berkeley's rather erratic adventurism in alternately tolerating and harassing its left-wing faculty and students. The question of intellectual freedom had been settled early and decisively at Wisconsin, shortly after the turn of the century. Periodically, right-wing state legislators had a go at the "campus communists," but there was no Bill Knowland in the state. Wisconsin's intellectuals took a peculiar sort of pride in the fact that, at the height of his popularity when he was assaulting even the U.S. Army, Senator Joe McCarthy never even looked crooked in the direction of the University of Wisconsin.

Madisonians believed that thinking and reflection were worthwhile activities for radicals. Consequently, comparatively few of them ever made the transition to New Leftism. With the possible exception of Clark Kissinger of SDS, whose methodical ways offended his New Left comrades, no one from the Madison radical community of the early sixties made a mark in the Movement.

The most influential radical faculty member at Madison was the historian, William Appleman Williams. An Annapolis graduate and former naval officer, Williams wrote an incisive history of American foreign policy, *The Tragedy of American Diplomacy,* that showed that national policy toward the world had been framed not in terms of American political ideals but in the interests of American business. Williams's presence in Madison drew dozens of young graduate students interested in research that would expand on his insights. In 1960, several of them founded *Studies on the Left,* a scholarly journal widely respected for its demanding standards.

Late in 1962, however, prompted by James Weinstein, an earnest democratic socialist who kept the journal going through most of the sixties, *Studies* moved to New York where it evolved into a "relevant" New Left organ and nearly immediate oblivion. With the *Studies* office abandoned, Madison's lefties adopted the Women's Peace Center as their informal headquarters.

The Women's Peace Center was located in a former food market on University Avenue. It was run by pleasant Quaker-type ladies with gray-streaked hair done up in buns. They sold second-hand clothing and battered Little Golden Books reinforced at the spine with Mystic Tape. They gave away crackling new tracts and the tabloid periodicals of a dozen pacifist and radical organizations to anyone game enough to push through the door. The pacifists ran the place and saw to it that the telephone cartel was paid and the landlord stalled to the brink each month. But, being even fewer than they were eclectic, they did not set the tone of the place. The center was known, not unfairly, as the left-wing hangout.

The juxtaposition of the squeaky wholesome and the creaky didactic at the Peace Center could have delicious results for the regular with a sense of humor. (A sense of humor being a function of reason, Madison's radical community was much longer on those than Berkeley's.)

At one meeting of the study group, a doughty Marxist rose and proposed as the question of the evening: "*Resolved,* that a sunset, not being man-made, is not beautiful." They were crackpots who were willing to grapple with that kind of problem, but they were not oh-man-right-on-far-out pot-heads.

Unhappily, to the irretrievable loss of the Western intellectual tradition, the debate was terminated during the second sentence of the affirmative statement by the request of a Sane Nuclear Policy lady that a few of the "fine young men" of the group help take out the garbage. Madisonians were no longer on that kind of exercise than Berkeleyans. They took the stuff out. But it always cast a pall over a promising evening.

On another occasion, the group fell to squabbling in pairs and trios when the daughter of a communist orthopedist from

Brooklyn denounced the Beatles as social-fascist and announced that a truly proletarian rock group, the Rolling Stones, was about to emerge from the revolutionary cauldrons of Liverpool.

Just a month or so before the Vietnam discussion, a somewhat older Trotskyist woman broke down in tears when a graduate student named Steven Anderson suggested that the group schedule a session to examine the Marxist definition of property in terms of the intriguing phenomenon that, through their retirement fund, the employees of Sears Roebuck appeared to own controlling interest in the great chain store. That session was terminated when, from over the pipe racks came the voices of a dozen pacifist children rehearsing their Christmas play: "I am the king with the big feet! I am the king with the big feet! I shall tromp and stomp upon the message of this man from Nazareth!"

The seminar on the war in Vietnam was not interrupted; nor was it as boisterous as the study group's typical meeting. Few people knew much about Vietnam in early 1963, and for all their vagaries, the Madison radicals were always willing to listen when knowledge new to them was on the agenda. The consensus that came out of this first formal discussion of Vietnam in one of the sixties' centers of the antiwar movement was that here was another Portugal, another Dominican Republic or Cuba, one more wretched little country where the United States supported a venal dictatorship and pretty much had its way. No one thought anything out of the ordinary would come of it. Business and antibusiness as usual.

RADICALS AND THE PEACE MOVEMENT

Thus was spun, independently in dozens of similar groups all over the country, the radical skein that wove into that complicated and profound phenomenon, the movement against the war in Vietnam. It was the greatest mass protest movement in American history since the Populists, larger even than the civil rights agitation. To the radicals, the United States' actions in Southeast Asia followed inevitably on the nature of capitalism. The Vietnamese were fighting for socialism, for independence from imperial exploitation, and for human justice, as "the people" were supposed to do.

The United States, the bulwark of the old order, was fighting to maintain its hegemony. It was true that Lenin was little help in explaining Vietnam. Before the massive intervention, American capital had little stake in Indochina. But, especially at Wisconsin, William Appleman Williams provided another subtler and more persuasive explanation of such interventions. In order to maintain its potential to expand, American capitalists, the dictators of American foreign policy, insisted on maintaining a door open to economic penetration throughout the world. It was an ideological rather than a dollars-and-cents position. Communism—even socialist states independent of Soviet or Chinese domination—closed the door just as the old colonial empires had done. They must not be allowed to do so, no matter that the price was the nation of Thomas Jefferson supporting brutal "tinhorn" dictators elsewhere. Indeed, the survival of American democracy depended upon stifling democracy in Vietnam and where have you. As Williams told a teach-in audience at the University of Wisconsin in April 1965,

> *Our leaders are clinging to the old analysis and the old policy because these worked surprisingly well over a period of two generations, because they seriously believe that any change in these attitudes and policies would severely damage or destroy the essence of American democracy and the basis of American prosperity, and because they have enough power at their disposal to postpone the final and complete breakdown of the old outlook and policy.*

Radicals like the Madisonians assumed that the final breakdown was inevitable. On precisely how it would come about and as to what kind of America would be built atop the rubble, they differed—in glorious variety and ambiguity. That was what kept them going, just as chess players never cease to be engrossed in the infinite insolubility of their game. But the radicals mostly agreed that, as intellectuals, their own job was brain work, to keep "working on" these problems while waiting for the mass movement to develop. At the very most, their task was to explain to the people the radical implications of social and political problems like Vietnam.

The difficulty of putting such an analysis across to Americans is obvious. It called for putting across the same view of American society that socialists, communists, and anarchists had been unable to convey when they pegged it to everything from low wages through the lynching of sassy blacks to the cowing of dissent by HUAC and Joe McCarthy. Working people did not like their low wages. Most people found lynching reprehensible and, in time, they repudiated the excesses of the Red-baiters. Few were ever persuaded that these abominations proved anything about capitalism itself.

To most Americans they were aberrations, horrible mistakes of a basically beneficent social system, problems to be solved rather than symptoms to be traced to their source. The American people's tenacious loyalty to democratic capitalism remained the frustration of the American radical. The country's way of thinking, quite opposite to that of people like the Madisonians, is explanation enough of the weirdness of that isolated little world of the Peace Center.

During the sixties, however, it appeared to some radicals that, at last, thanks to the enormity of the war, they had finally overcome the barriers between them and the American people. Those Old Leftists who became New Leftists believed that in their growing opposition to the war in Vietnam, a goodly part of the American people were "radicalized."

On the face of it they were right. Not only did the number of critics grow from a few huddled little Marxist study groups in 1963 to, by the end of the decade, demonstrations by 750,000

people, active resistance to the government, and even plural-
ities in the public opinion polls on some war issues, but the
rhetoric of the antiwar movement was also "radicalized."

That is, when the antiwar movement first came to
national attention in the spring of 1965, the radical line was
only one of several critiques of the war, and by no means the
dominant one. The radicals were only a small part of an odd
alliance of pacifists, idealists, and cold war realpolitikers. By
1969, however, the cold war realists were no longer heard at
antiwar protests. The idealists had ceased to appeal to
American decency because they ceased to believe in it. And the
pacifists were making distinctions between just warriors and
unjust ones. By the end of the 1960s, the dominant color in the
fabric of the antiwar movement was apparently red: the United
States was wrong and the revolutionary people of Vietnam
right.

It was a very odd hue of red because it was an optical
illusion. The color of the antiwar movement was not dyed in
the wool but cast upon it as light through a prism. When the
lamp—the faddish, self-serving appeal of being thought "radical"—was extinguished, the radicalism disappeared. For
radicalization means building a rational conviction that the
social structure must be altered at its roots, that phenomena
such as the Vietnamese war were symptoms. Vietnam radicalized no one. On the contrary, the experience of participating in
the antiwar movement—of being part of a massive, seething,
electric phenomenon—had the effect of *de-radicalizing* many
of those who at the beginning, like the bright young men and
women of the Madison Marxist Study Group, believed they
had a fairly coherent idea of what was going on in the world.

When the ashes finally cooled in the early seventies, the
American Left was weaker than it had been since Karl Marx
shipped the First International to New Jersey, weaker even
than during the fifties. It was reduced to a few tiny sects, tinier
than before, and a few subscription lists shorter than *Dissent*'s
had been. In 1980 the CPUSA still existed. So did the

Trotskyist Socialist Workers party and the Socialist Labor party. Here and there, as always, a few academics preached Marxism to their undergraduate students. Many of the Madisonians of the early sixties—then "students who planned to make academic work their life's activity," in the words of Weinstein and another *Studies* regular, David W. Eakins— fell into that category.

But most of the stalwarts of the American Left in 1980 had been radicals before the troubles. For all the comical aspects, there was a substance to the old Marxist study groups, a commitment based on reason and study. To the New Left there was none. During the seventies when old radicals like James Weinstein were still slugging away at corporate capitalism, the New Left "militants," those supposedly "radicalized" by the antiwar movement, were jogging, kowtowing before overweight, underage gurus, waving the flag, and experimenting with vegetarianism or just simple vegetation.

But the absence of radicalism in the Movement is a subject for a later chapter. Here the purpose is to show how the antiwar movement served to destroy much of what there was of the old radicalism in the United States.

THE MAKE-UP
OF THE ANTIWAR MOVEMENT

It would take a Linnaeus to sort out all the subtle variations on the arguments that, during the Vietnam war, were mounted against American policy in Indochina. From pulpit, from congressional committee hearing room, from hastily erected platform, from roofs of cars, in the columns of periodicals as diverse as the *New York Review of Books, New York Times, New Republic, Nation, Old Mole,* and *Fuck You: A Magazine of the Arts,* in mimeographed leaflets handed out at supermarkets—a bewildering and often contradictory array of critiques went into the Movement.

However, a case can be made for grouping the antiwar activists into four broad categories: the radicals, already

noticed; the pacifists; the patriotic idealistics; and the realpolitikers. In appreciating how people who came to the antiwar
movement with these points of view were befuddled, so carried
away in the excitement of it all that they lost sight of their once
coherent thoughts, it will be easier to understand both the
enormity of the war in Vietnam and the pathetic collapse of
American radicalism.

THE PACIFIST PLEA:
NOT SO EXTERNAL AFTER ALL

Jesus may have been speaking as much of pacifists as of the
poor when he said they would always be with us. Surely that
has been true of the United States, thanks particularly to the
fact that three of the earliest colonies—Pennsylvania, New
Jersey, and Delaware—were founded by a pacifist sect, the
Society of Friends. In eastern Pennsylvania the Quakers
maintained a continuous and noticeable presence into the
national period.

In the early nineteenth century, recoiling from the
unprecedented bloodletting of the Napoleonic Wars, absolute
Christian pacifism spread throughout the conventional American denominations. The reasoning of pacifism was unexceptionable. The commandment said "Thou shalt not kill." Jesus
seemed unequivocally to confirm and define the prohibition:
war meant killing. No more war.

In the nineteenth century, as at other times, reason was all
very pleasant as a master but more congenial as a servant.
When, with the coming of the Civil War, American pacifists
were confronted with the choice of sticking to their antiguns
or killing and dying to make men free—to destroy slavery—
they chose the latter.

Something similar happened during the late 1930s.
Although it was less explicitly rooted in Christianity, absolute
pacifism spread during the Depression decade through the
student community. Thousands solemnly swore the Oxford
pledge not to fight for king and country under any conditions.

This avowal evaporated when the generation was faced with a choice between their pacifism and joining in a war against the monstrosities of fascism and Nazism. With the exception of Quakers, Jehovah's Witnesses, and other sectarians, there were comparatively few conscientious objectors during World War II.

Pacifism revived during the 1950s, especially as a consequence of the threat of nuclear war. Indeed, on the A-bomb and H-bomb issues, the pacifists displayed their pragmatic side, seemingly political wisdom but also fraught with difficulties for their philosophy. That is, in devoting themselves to the antinuclear cause, and not necessarily or at least explicitly to the position of no-more-war-of-any-kind, they made more converts. But they also exposed themselves to the danger of abandoning the essence of their position.

It is difficult to beat up on pacifists. It is impossible to criticize them because, in their horror of nuclear holocaust, they were willing to join hands with anyone who shared an aversion to the new weaponry. Their belief in the necessity of witness justified cooperation with nonpacifist opponents of nuclear war in the hopes that, eventually, their coworkers in that cause would join them in the farther reaching pacifistic crusade.

During the sixties, it appeared as if pacifism made just such gains in the United States. Antiwar speakers of many stripes picked up on pacifistic rhetoric. Substantial minorities on most large university campuses vowed they would not bear arms for any reason whatsoever. The number of conscientious objectors increased almost as quickly as the monthly draft quotas despite the Selective Service System's systematic attempt to avoid a crisis by deferring students.

However, as with the other catchwords adopted by university students, the pacifistic ideal meant little to most of those who voiced it. Lacking a principled conviction in what is, after all, a demanding if unsubtle creed, not to mention one that is probably unnatural, the hundreds of thousands of young people who said war was wrong were simply funning. The apparent popularity of their gospel confused the pacifists. No more than revivalist preachers were they inclined to be skeptical about anyone's conversion to the faith. Holding to tenets rooted more in a moral sense than in reason, they accepted the new pacifists at face value. In intermingling with them, in their gratification that their cause was growing so quickly, the pacifists lost their grip on the core of their beliefs. If some well-known folksingers, eminent writers, and movie stars stated that they were absolute pacifists and then proceeded to say that the National Liberation Front had a right to fight in Vietnam, as the United States did not, even the old pacifists inclined to accept their illogic rather than question the credentials of their prestigious converts. When tens of thousands of students said they were pacifists and then cheered Viet Cong victories, those few pacifists who sensed something was funny kept their mouths shut.

The enormous injustice of the American war effort must not be overlooked. So indefensible was it that American pacifists forgot that barbaric actions were not new to the race nor unique in the American intervention in Vietnam. There was good reason to focus single-mindedly on the war in Vietnam. No other war in the world during the sixties rivaled it in size, duration, and the tenacity of the American government in the face of widespread repudiation.

Once again, however, in their revulsion, American pacifists transformed *the relatively more justifiable cause* of the Vietnamese into *the* just cause of the Vietnamese and then into *a* just cause, a just war. In doing so they ceased to be pacifists.

The case of Mitchell Goodman is instructive as well as depressing. He came to Movement activism via the absolute pacifist tradition. Until the late sixties he probably considered his politics liberal rather than radical. So appalled was he by the war, however, constantly escalated in the face of damning indictments of it, that he lost all sense of discernment in regard to those who opposed American policy.

In 1970 (just in time for the Movement's demise),
Goodman supervised the production of a telephone-directory-
size book called *The Movement Toward a New America: The
Beginning of a Long Revolution.* A collection of newspaper
and magazine clippings about every aspect of the sixties
tumult, from SDS and FSM through Black Panthers and
flower children and the antiwar movement, the book was
necessarily eclectic. But the gist of it was "revolutionary"—
something is happening and I am for it. Necessarily, this
required Goodman to smile upon some pretty violent people.
Their cause was just, ergo, their actions are justified. There is
nothing unique in this kind of thinking, but it is a long way
from the coherent and absolute pacifism for which, just a few
years before, Goodman was an eloquent spokesman.

Liberation, a journal of some distinction published by
pacifists such as Staughton Lynd and David Dellinger, took a
similar route. Dellinger, in his fifties, and Lynd, in his forties,
had spoken unwaveringly for the necessity of peace before
social reconstruction. During the years before the sixties, they
had no difficulty parrying the antipacifistic arguments of both
American patriots and the Old Left. During the sixties,
however, they were persuaded—by what? the excitement of a
mass movement? the enormity of Vietnam?—to justify, tacitly
and often enough explicitly, the violent resistance of revolutionaries.

By the end of the decade, pacifists justifying some wars
were as easy to locate as oilmen justifying the depletion
allowance. By the time the war ended, the integrity of
American pacifism was lost as irretrievably as the virginity of a
Tennessee town punch. The pacifists of the seventies could
continue to act as if they were chaste. They could talk as if they
were still virgins. But those who knew better could be excused
for knowing better.

This is the legacy of the sixties. The decade transformed
the principles of the most principled into an ooze, the tough
inflexible absolutes of centuries-old traditions into sponge. If

Christian pacifism, the legacy of two millennia, was destroyed by Vietnam, it is not surprising that American radicals, drawing on a short and flimsy heritage, made fools of themselves too.

AMERICANS DON'T
DO SUCH THINGS

Media portrayals of the early antiwar demonstrations focused on the youth of the protesters, their bohemian scruffiness, or their association with pacifist organizations like SANE or the Fellowship of Reconciliation that could still be written off in the wake of the fifties as far-out radical.

The newspapers and television news producers were promptly taken to task by the substantial number of people who opposed the war but also wore pressed shirts, neckties, and lintless dark dresses, who bathed regularly and belonged to no organization of which the American Legion would not approve. There were, it seemed, a great many neatniks opposed to the war.

The newsmen, either because they were chastened by the criticism, or because many of them were both mainstream in their tastes and increasingly disturbed by the war, quickly obliged these critics. They adopted as standard operating procedure in reporting on antiwar demonstrations a few words or a few feet of film showing that normal people opposed the war too.

What motivated these people? To a large extent, the mainstream antiwar opposition was made up of people who were suddenly ashamed of their country. Their opposition to the war was rooted deeply in their patriotism. They expected the United States to act according to higher standards than other nations did. They were the legatees of a tradition that held America to be unique and exemplary, the "citty on a hill" of the Puritans, gleaming in the sun for the edification of all people, a "beaconlight of freedom," as some of the Founding Fathers secularized the conviction that their nation had a mission to inspire all peoples to emulation or, at least, admiration.

Students of American history know that the belief that the United States is not "just another country" but a very special place has generally been a harmless conceit and even a wellspring of social vitality. However, it has occasionally taken on very odd shapes.

During the 1840s, the conviction that American institutions were demonstrably superior to Mexican institutions was read to mean that the United States had the right to attack Mexico and detach a third of its territory for the purpose of institutional plantings. The American people were mobilized into supporting the allied cause in World War I for the purpose of "making the world safe for democracy." It was not enough to keep the beaconlight burning. The light was to be mounted on a machine gun far from the walls of the "citty."

Indeed, Lyndon Johnson and other defenders of the intervention in Vietnam drew generously on this tradition, arguing that the United States was solemnly commissioned to defend democracy in Indochina. Unhappily for the President, he could not rally everyone who shared his belief in the peculiar virtues of the American way of life. Others weaned on the conviction that their country was special insisted that the government act special. Least of all should the United States support "tinhorn dictators," in the words of Senator George McGovern of South Dakota. Nor should a nation of such exemplary virtue use its superior technology to crush a whole people, or employ weaponry such as napalm that was peculiarly vicious, or literally destroy the earth as with the defoliants that some clever Pentagon official decided were the key to rooting out an enemy that was everywhere. Was that any way for a "citty on a hill" to behave?

The patriotic idealists were not pacifists and they were certainly not radicals. They were quick to point out that they would take up what arms were necessary to defend Old Glory. Painfully, they explained that, no, they did not believe the

communism of the Viet Cong was the best way to order
Vietnamese society. But they insisted that American actions
accord with American ideals. They differed from the liberals
who designed and fought the war only in their lack of
hypocrisy.

When the cant of the prowar liberals continued to pour
out of Washington, the patriotic idealists found themselves
associating increasingly with pacifists and radicals, they easily
absorbed the rhetoric and impulses of both groups. In doing
so, they abandoned their principles as surely as President
Johnson and his lieutenants abandoned theirs. For it is not a
logical hop and step from finding the napalming of children
indefensible to opposing all war. Nor does it stand to reason
that because a government is hypocritical, the principles
underlying the system of that government are spurious.

Some years later, Eugene D. Genovese observed that
"those who find America an especially violent and oppressive
country ('Amerika') have apparently never read the history of
England or France, Germany or Russia, Indonesia or Bur-
undi, Turkey or Uganda." Whatever the reading habits of the
liberal opponents of the war in Vietnam, they indeed jumped
from considering their country superior to such benighted
lands to concluding that "Amerika" was uniquely brutal and
evil.

Psychologists are not surprised to run across such
behavior on the leather covered couch. But the fact that it is
irrational and yet characterized the Movement indicates once
again the insubstance of the decade.

LET'S BE REALISTIC
In the earliest days of the antiwar movement, when it was still
largely a matter of discussion, cold warriors and realpolitiker
diplomatists actually dominated the protest. While the radicals of the Marxist study groups were still sequestered in their
cells, at the most issuing a few wan mimeographed "position
papers," troubled politicians such as Senator William J.

Fulbright, Chairman of the Senate Foreign Relations Committee, were inquiring as to the strategic wisdom of warring in Indochina.

The most eloquent of the realpolitikers was not a public official but a German refugee become American university professor, Hans J. Morgenthau. A minor architect of cold war policy, Morgenthau will likely be lumped in the post-holocaust histories with such more successful immigrant geopoliticians as Henry Kissinger and Zbigniew Brzezinski. His view of the world had no room for the sentiment that social revolutions were de facto "good things" like the Norman Conquest and the Magna Carta. Nor did Morgenthau, who cultivated a solemnly portentous manner, have much time for arguments about the superior humanity of this weapon over that, punji sticks over B-52s and so on. To Morgenthau, the purpose of diplomacy and war was to serve a nation's interests, quite including its standard of living. In his seminars at Chicago, his eyelids drooped if anyone were so foolish as to use words like ethics, morality, ideals, bullying, and the human race. Except for the fact that he did not grin and clown like Edward Teller and Henry Kissinger, he could as well has been the model for actor Peter Sellers's Dr. Strangelove. During World War II he had argued that Germany be transformed into an agricultural and pastoral country.

It was because of his coldblooded view of the use of war that Morgenthau vociferously opposed the intervention in Vietnam. The United States had no interests in Indochina. It did not and could not matter a whit to the prosperity and security of the United States if Ho Chi Minh, Mao Zedong, or Ming the Merciless told Vietnamese peasants what and how much to plant in their paddies and where to buy their tunics. Vietnam would never pose a threat to the United States. As for Chinese domination of the area, it would make no difference in the realities of geopolitics even if it came to pass. Geographically, the Chinese had very real interests in Southeast Asia. Indeed, the realpolitiker critics pointed out, a united

Vietnam would be nothing but trouble to China (a real "good thing" geopolitically) because of the ancient animosities between the two peoples.

Ironically, the realpolitikers who supported the war responded to the Morgenthau critique with moralism, gracelessly spouting of the Americans' sacred obligation to defend liberty and democracy among the Vietnamese. (It was not only the opposition during the sixties that was mixed up.) But here the issue is the fact that despite the utter incompatibility of the Morgenthau opposition with pacifism and radicalism and patriotic idealism, the people who clung to all three of these gospels lionized Morgenthau and made the distinguished and very conservative Senator Fulbright their hero in Washington. Pacifists quoted Morgenthau, a man ready to turn a Central American banana republic into a sandlot, in the same sentence as Henry David Thoreau. Radicals invited a man with the social attitudes of a Prussian Junker to speak to their assemblies. Morgenthau's chief medium of expression was the trendy-radical *New York Review of Books,* a journal that, in alternating issues, simpered over the lightweight likes of Stokely Carmichael and printed diagrams of bombs that, well-placed, could knock out a think-tank in a twinkling. Moralists claimed as their own the professor who took pompous pride in his amoralism.

Again, it is important to know that this misalliance was not based on expediency. The radicals did not push Morgenthau, the antiwar generals, and the warmer-blooded arguments of Fulbright in the belief that, because the goal was a Viet Cong victory and the American people would more likely support the realpolitiker argument than their own revolutionism, the nonradical antiwar people should be allowed to take the fore. (Conservatives often attribute such Machiavellian cleverness to radicals because they are also fools.) Nor did the pacifists and moralists "use" Morgenthau as, arguably, they were incapable of "using" anyone. Simply put, they did not notice that Hans J. Morgenthau was not one of them.

Morgenthau, on the other hand, did. As the four skeins of the antiwar movement wove to form a crazy tartan, a feeling rather than an argument, he withdrew from the debate and returned to the pleasant offices and seminars of the University of Chicago, home of the Great Books program and bastion of "eternal values."

TEACH-IN
The four skeins of the antiwar movement were woven on that curious loom of the mid-sixties, the teach-in. If one wished to devise a mechanism that ensured what was already a mess remained one, one could not have done better than to hand the movement against the war to the kids and their followers, the professors.

By March 1965, when the first teach-in was held at the University of Michigan, the American university was falling apart, and the principal cause of the breakdown was the delusion that students as students were a vital social group. On the one hand, this made professors seem like very important people indeed. On the other, it was to make them awestruck trundlers in the van of a leaderless army.

On March 11, 1965, a group of Michigan professors got together to draft a newspaper advertisement announcing why they opposed the war in Vietnam. A sociology professor, William Gamson, suggested that something more was needed. His idea was a one-day strike of scheduled classes and, in place of them, a faculty-supervised discussion of the "concealed story of Vietnam." If his method was gamy, his assumptions were unexceptionable: if the truth behind the American intervention were revealed, the people would not permit the war to continue. And who else to see that the people were informed—that they *learned*—than professors?

Because of administrative pressure and the reluctance of many faculty to suspend classes—what they still regarded as their duty and what militants dismissed as exposing their cowardice—the group decided against cancellation. Instead, with reluctant university approbation, the teach-in would be extracurricular, held at night. Mark Pilisuk, one of the organizers, noted that "many students felt betrayed" by this decision. In other words, before the first teach-in assembled, there were those who felt that the object was not *educational* or even the war in Vietnam but the fulfillment of a psychological need to rebel within and against, to defy, the little institution in which students dwelled, the university.

Before the Michigan teach-in actually assembled on March 24, at least thirty-five other campuses were planning their own affairs. As at Ann Arbor, local organizers seem originally to have conceived of their teach-ins as educational exercises, designed to disseminate information. With few exceptions they also turned into occasions of personal existential statement, witness, not to mention a diversion little different from a night in the bar or at the basketball game. There were very few actual *teach*-ins. The sixties were just a little slow in finding the right name for what those 3,500 people at Michigan started: the "*be*-in."

From the start, the teach-in audience cheered indiscriminately the coldblooded arguments of the realpolitikers, the appeals of Quaker ladies, the speeches of people who called on Americans to behave decently toward other races, the difficult reflections of political philosophers such as William Appleman Williams, and the frank radical statements of men like Eugene Genovese of Rutgers University who caused a statewide fracas in New Jersey in April by saying, "I do not fear or regret the impending Vietcong victory in Vietnam, I welcome it. I do not believe that American foreign policy is stupid or irrational. I believe it to be intelligent, if crude, rational and predatory."

It bears repeating that the teach-in movement did not begin as an educational phenomenon and degenerate into an exercise in mass personal therapy. In part because there were precious few Southeast Asia experts at large in 1965, in part because, with a few exceptions, apologists for the war refused to participate, but largely because the American intelligentsia of the period was not primarily interested in knowledge and learning, the teach-ins started out that way.

Writing up the Michigan experience shortly after it ended, Professor Pilisuk said that its most important consequence "was the germ of an idea which permitted the *concerned* professional *to envision himself* as the conqueror not of governments but, rather, of *his own sense of impotence.* This dimly formed *vision of self,* perhaps more than anything else, links the professor *garbed as guerrilla warrior* with the professor debating in a marathon teach-in."

Pilisuk spoke of the transformational quality of the long night in Hill Auditorium: "For it seems obvious that we are not now wholly the same people we were before the teach-in." He brushed aside—indeed he did not even brush by—the informational contributions of the night. "For all of us, the most interesting aspect of our metamorphosis was the realization that our purely academic work was virtually irrelevant to American policy in Vietnam—unless we chose to make it count."

The historian, James Gilbert, then a graduate student at the University of Wisconsin, conveyed in the same message in his account of an even larger teach-in held a week later in Madison. (Five thousand attended.) Only four of twenty-six speakers at Wisconsin dealt with subjects "directly concerned with Vietnam as such." Some others, like William Appleman Williams, dealt with related questions of substance such as the assumptions underlying American foreign policy. But at Wisconsin as at Ann Arbor and at dozens of other universities, the audiences fairly fidgeted through these *lectures.* The speakers who got the biggest hand were those who prefaced their talks with statements that they knew nothing about Vietnam and little about how the State Department made its decisions but that they did know what was right and what was wrong (by gum!) and they—speaking as persons!—did not like the smell of Vietnam.

Universally, commentators on the teach-ins celebrated the "human-ness" of the atmosphere as opposed to the impersonality of the lecture hall. Even William A. Williams felt constrained to introduce his lecture at Wisconsin by saying, "we have the makings of a community here."

The trouble is, the teach-in crowds were bigger than the largest course ever ventured at multiversity. It is true that the crowd was informal and relaxed, very much like (contrary to Williams) the "crowd at a football game or... other entertainment." But genuine personal intellectual interaction such as the Berkeley Free Speechers seemed to call for in 1964? No.

What excited the students at the teach-ins was the fact that their professors presented themselves as "ordinary fellows" and not just "some guy who knows a lot about math or something." Far from "educational," the teach-ins were most successful in their stridently uneducational aspects. The statements that were most popular were those in which professors asserted their lack of expertise but, instead, savored the common feeling of revulsion and opposition they shared with their students.

At Wisconsin, James Gilbert correctly sensed, "the most important" lecture had nothing to do with Vietnam. It was the testament of a professor of French, Germaine Brée, who had been an associate of Camus and a fighter in the French Resistance. Brée's message was the stock existential call for self-assertion. It was popular because, by touting commitment over conviction, moral decision over rational deduction, the will to believe over the grounds for belief, Brée provided students with a high-flown version of what they had heard through elementary and secondary school, with what was easy to grasp and easier to act on, with exactly what they wanted to hear.

If *commitment* was the whole of it, it did not matter that one antiwar activist believed the war stupid, another criminal, another the rational, amoral act of a political adversary. As long as they were all committed in their heart-of-hearts, they were all brothers and sisters.

Of course, they were not. There was no more substance to the antiwar movement than there is to the delicious sense of solidarity in rooting the home team on to victory in the Rose Bowl in communion with tens of thousands of others. And had the American government been capable of bringing about diversions as regularly as major university athletic programs do, the antiwar movement might have lasted just that long.

THE GREAT
DEMONSTRATIONS

The personal sense of being a part of a meaningful community was all the more exciting when the teach-in gave way to the mass demonstration as the antiwar movement's chief medium of expression. In the sense that radicals and pacifists began picketing, leafletting, and marching locally as early as 1963 and 1964, demonstration preceded the university meetings. But the first truly massive demonstrations began in the spring of 1965 when SDS expected two thousand people to show up at a demonstration in Washington and twenty-five thousand actually came. I.F. Stone, Senator Ernest Gruening, and Staughton Lynd gave speeches. Folksingers Phil Ochs, Joan Baez, and Judy Collins provided entertainment.

In October, a hundred thousand people demonstrated simultaneously in ninety cities and, on November 27, forty thousand gathered in Washington alone. In April 1967, three hundred thousand people demonstrated in New York and San Francisco. In Washington in the fall of 1969, perhaps 750,000 gathered to testify against the war.

Such exponential growth was heartening in a nation of quantifiers, especially when prowar groups like the American Legion took up the challenge, called counter-marches, and could not mobilize even half the number of patriots. But as exhilarating as it was to feel kinship in righteousness with people who were willing to "put their bodies on the line," the demonstrations actually indicated how big a failure the Movement was.

There was no doubt it expanded. But where was the Movement in 1967 that it had not been in 1962? Did the demonstrators have a better understanding of their enemy or what they had to do than the founders of SNCC and SDS had? Did they have a better understanding of the meaning of the war in Vietnam than those who attended the comparatively cerebral teach-ins?

They did not. For all the failure of the teach-in movement to serve as intellectual exercises, the idea was, initially at least, to disseminate information and appeal to reason. In theory, they were attempts to communicate ideas, but the demonstrations were by definition personal statements of dissent. When demonstrations concluded with public statements, the best of them showed that the Movement had gone nowhere since it was born.

Perhaps the two best speeches delivered at the antiwar demonstrations were those of two SDS presidents, Paul Potter and Carl Oglesby. Potter's speech at Washington on April 17, 1965, was strident and eloquent, but all he said was what Tom Hayden had said in the *Port Huron Statement*. "We must name it," Potter told the crowds, "describe it, analyze it, understand it, and change it." It was still time to define the trouble with the United States. And few paused to reflect on the fact that in more than three years no one had done so.

Oglesby, a successful engineer who dropped out of the corporate world believing that SDS was the medium through which a coherent radical challenge to corporate liberalism could be mounted, ended up, despite serious efforts, turning a social, economic, and political issue into a moral one. Pointing out that a series of "liberal" politicians and statesmen had begun and sustained the war, he concluded: "They are not moral monsters. They are all honorable men. They are all liberals." Oglesby wanted "a closer look at this American liberalism." But just as the Movement named Potter's *it* by simply calling names, "Pig" and "Fascist," they responded to Oglesby by concluding that liberalism was immoral and that was enough to know.

In effect, the speeches at the demonstrations were sermons and, as at the First Presbyterian, they were interspersed with hymns. Popular performers like Pete Seeger, a veteran of labor struggles of the thirties and forties (blacklisted in the fifties), and Joan Baez, who built a remarkable career on a maudlin whining voice and an Aimee Semple McPherson aura of spirituality, were joined by other show business personalities in making the early demonstrations explicitly at least half entertainment. With such dazzling casts, no one was going to "name it" or try to understand the nature of American liberalism.

The greatest of the demonstrations were nearly pure symbol and show biz. At the Pentagon in October 1967 protesters satisfied themselves by putting flowers into the muzzles of soldiers' rifles and attempting to levitate the building by chanting Hindu mantras along with Ed Sanders, Tuli Kupferberg, and the Fugs, a clever musical group from New York. The chronicler of the great climax was Norman Mailer, as much persona as writer by this time. In *Armies of the Night*, he referred to himself, the central figure of the book, in the third person, as "Aquarius." As he often did, Mailer hit on the crux of the demonstration movement. *Everyone* was the center of the demonstration. The Movement was no social or political movement at all but a most astonishing collection of individuals doing their own thing.

The great demonstrations also revealed the bankruptcy of the Black Power movement. Few blacks marched as individuals in the great marches although, as John Helmer showed in his *Bringing the War Home,* blacks opposed the war in Vietnam proportionately more than whites did. (As, indeed, they had good reason to do. While white middle-class youth were being deferred wholesale from the draft, blacks were the Defense Department's cannon fodder.)

Was the lily-white complexion of the typical demonstration a result of lower-class black aversion to what was in effect middle-class therapy? Was it simply another manifestation of Negroes' enforced alienation from the mainstream of American life for over three hundred years? Or was the failure of blacks to participate in the protest a consequence of the inane separatism preached by Stokely Carmichael and privileged blacks in the universities and professions? Carmichael and his ilk, of course, liked to think they were responsible but Stokely revealed how inconsequential he was (except in the media) when, in 1967, he announced that he would lead the Harlem contingent in the huge New York demonstration from 125th Street down Fifth Avenue. Waiting to cheer their black half-brothers and -sisters, the several hundred thousand protesters in Central Park beheld about two hundred kids following Carmichael. They cheered anyway.

The fun, fulfillment, and undemanding ease of marching on a sunny day to hear singers and chanters was a troubling portent to some of the genuinely political New Left activists. Even the issue of the war, not in itself radical, was arousing not so much a political movement as a crowd interested in having a good time. In a few years, of course, the excitement of demonstration was bound to wear thin and the hundreds of thousands would turn elsewhere. Indeed, by 1967, many of them already were—to the "hippie" counterculture. Before considering this, however, it is worthwhile to notice another kind of mischief worked by the size of the demonstrations in the minds of many Movement people: the delusion that because of their numbers, they were possessed of a great power.

DELUSIONS OF POWER

When Staughton Lynd led the antiwar marchers through the streets of Washington in April 1965, he believed that the crowd would follow him anywhere. Up the steps of the Pentagon, over the fences of the White House, into the corridors of the

Capitol. The thousands of people who ringed the Oakland Induction Center in 1968 really believed they could close it down. An antiwar movement organizer told Kenneth Keniston that he "enjoyed being cast as a world historical figure."

But the delusion that they possessed real power was by no means restricted to the people who found themselves in the midst of hundreds of thousands of antiwar marchers. In addition to the exhilaration of that kind of experience, black, student, and SDS leaders and troops were convinced by media attention, the dependable hysteria of the far right, and the prattlings of the intellectuals and politicians who rooted them on that they were part of a great movement very near to success. Gene Marine, the San Francisco chronicler of the Black Panthers, wrote that "white Americans watched—and shuddered" when Stokely Carmichael spoke. "The more he talked, the more baffled—and afraid—white America became." He believed this stuff. So did Stokely Carmichael, his handful of black followers, and the rather more numerous white students and kids who believed in Black Power.

Congresswoman Shirley Chisholm of New York believed. She was quoted in 1969 as saying that college students and black people would eventually "save American society." An undereducated, heavily unemployed, unskilled, and partially "unacceptable" 10 percent of the population plus the liberal arts and sociology majors of the United States would save American society! When Timothy Leary fled prison to Algeria, his attorney called a press conference to announce that the professor would return in about two years. A reporter observed that there was no statute of limitations on jailbreak. "Oh, that's got nothing to do with that; it's going to take two years, possibly twenty-five months for the revolution to overthrow the government and then it will be safe for him to come back."

Saul Alinsky remarked that "I looked at this silly son of a bitch! How whacked out can you be?"

Quite a bit. As chagrined as Alinsky, another old veteran of the social battles fought by working people, Murray Kempton, noted that "we have in general led lives so protected from historical disasters that we have trouble distinguishing the merely disturbing from the apocalyptic." Kempton noted that even heads of academic departments believed that because a handful of black students yelled at them that they were in the Winter Palace in Petrograd. And "dissident junior instructors" worried about getting tenure talked "as though they are in the Sierra Maestra."

Even Tom Hayden, who generally avoided overreaching and maintained for the most part a rational comprehension of the real power of the agitation, was carried away when, in 1968, students seized several buildings at Columbia University. In an article entitled "Two, Three, Many Columbias," not a joke on Mao Zedong but a belief that an outbreak of varsity high jinks was the same thing as a popular revolution, Hayden was "certain" that the Movement was "moving toward power—the power to stop the machine if it cannot be made to serve humane ends."

Evidence that the Movement was going nowhere in terms of power as in terms of analysis did not stifle these optimists. As SDS turned into a memorandum factory, Black Power decayed into black university students cordoning off a Jim Crow section of the cafeteria, and the antiwar movement, for all its arguments and numbers, failed to halt escalation, the shouts of apocalypse grew louder and louder.

No longer, in fact, did they depend on numbers of protesters or ostensibly political action. The belief that revolution was right around the corner reached its peak when the Movement divided into two streams that unequivocally bespoke its and not Moloch's last days: the counterculture and the terrorism of Weatherman.

At the famous Woodstock rock concert of August 1969— a rock concert!—Abbie Hoffman wrote, "On Saturday night up on the stage"—the stage!—"you felt the monster was going

to crush the American Dinosaur. You could see the distant
bonfires on far-off hills and sense thousands of soldiers
resurrected from the Macedonian army hammering out their
weapons."

Harold Jacobs thought that Weatherman, a ragtag
couple dozen rich kids, was important enough to collect their
documents into a book of 1970, a kind of twentieth-century
Federalist Papers. He called Weatherman "second only to the
Black Panthers in its ability to conjure up the specter of
Revolution within America" which, in its cleverly ambiguous
phrasing, may have been quite true. However, he and
numerous other intellectuals did not disassociate themselves
from American middle-class hysteria, a phenomenon that has
had its moments. "Owing to Weatherman's efforts," he wrote,
"and those it has inspired, there is hardly a symbol of racist and
imperialist oppression secure from violent attack."

Symbols! There was the sixties in a word. The Movement
never got around to the substance symbols are supposed to
represent. By the Summer of Love and the occupation of
symbolic Columbia University—Roar, Lion, Roar—the radicals of the sixties did not know the difference.

By the end of 1967, they were at a dead end. Shunning the
need to sit down and hammer out a program had not yielded a
program. SDS's ERAP, going to the poor, had been a flop.
The civil rights movement had reached its limits in 1965 and
gave way to the Black Power silliness. The antiwar movement,
although peaking in numbers after 1967, already displayed the
impossible contradictions that would render it meaningless.
The war would survive it.

But excited, mobilized people do not calm down and
demobilize in the United States simply because they have
gotten nowhere, especially when there were money and fame to
be made from them. Instead, the Movement was redirected in
1967 and 1968 and, once again, definitions were changed to fit
the new direction.

Directions. For the Movement took two in its final

phase, both confessions of failure. Those activists would have insisted in the face of reality that they were still "political," turned to forceful confrontation and that dependable receiver of bankrupts, terrorism. More durable in its influence on American society was the Counterculture, the turn of thousands from public affairs to private, personal fulfillment.

CHAPTER SEVEN

O FAR-OUT NEW WORLD

The Haight-Ashbury district of San Francisco was, until the mid-1960s, an undistinguished residential section little noted beyond its boundaries. It took its name from the two shop-lined streets that intersected at its center and was colloquially called after the principal of the two, "the Haight." The Haight sidled up to Golden Gate Park at the point where the old earthquake-days city meets the twentieth-century subdivisions. Its houses were typically half a century old. They were modest, two- and three-story wooden structures with only the coyest hint of San Francisco's vaunted Victorian charm. In 1965 they were rundown, as *House and Garden* standards went, but they were liveable. Socially, the district was for white people a last step before seaside suburbia just over the hill; and for blacks, a first step out of the ghetto, even closer.

The Haight was integrated. It had been a white area into the fifties but, abutting as it does on the black Fillmore district—something of a slum—the neighborhood was inevitably attractive to Negro working people who were more or less securely employed and searching for some relief from ghetto crime and social chaos. They moved in, but the whites, perhaps only because they could not afford to do so, perhaps because they were attached to their homes (a sociologist, of course, would know for sure), did not all disappear into the ocean fogs.

The Haight had its problems. As late as 1962, muggings and teenage gang brawls were common enough and police ministrations so lackadaisical that residents formed vigilante patrols. Nevertheless, it struck many observers that this was a neighborhood genuinely striving to solve its problems and maintain a community, a formidable chore in urban America.

The Haight failed. Today it is a dump, much worse than the Fillmore district in some ways. However, it was not racial conflict or the carry-over curses of ghetto life that proved its undoing but the attentions of refugees from the privileged classes. In the United States, no matter what the Irish of South Boston and other warlike tribes believe, neighborhoods are "ruined" as often from above as from below, by the slumming of the privileged as often as by the aspirations of those on the bottom.

What happened is that, in the middle sixties, the Haight came to the attention of a completely new element. The district's low rents, the romantic allure of the black presence, and the Haight's proximity to San Francisco's largest park attracted bohemian types who, thanks to tourism and Telegraph Hill swells with fat wallets, could no longer afford or bear to live in their capital of the fifties, North Beach.

In New York similar developments drove graying beatniks from Greenwich Village to the borderlands of the Lower East Side which, nostalgically, they renamed the "East Village." But because cultural sensations are so easily swallowed up in New York, it was the Haight that came to epitomize the bohemia of the sixties in the American mind.

The "flower children" or "love generation" or "hippies," as the phenomenon was variously known, also made a much greater impact on American consciousness than the beatniks had done. This was due in part to the fact that the new bohemians were, at first implicitly, and then without making bones, "political." They wanted to change things, an impulse contributed to their jumble of sentiments by dropouts from the New Left who joined the emigration to the Haight. The impact of the love generation was also due in part to the simple demographic fact that it, like everything in which the baby boom generation took an interest, was big, much bigger than beat had been. For, along with the politically minded New Leftists, teenagers flocked to the hippie centers as soon as they heard about them in the recorded music and on the television shows that were tailored to their immature minds.

OLD LIGHTS AND NEW
Like the beatniks, the Haight people scorned regular work and all habits measured by the clock. They were fond of "blowing

grass," or smoking marijuana, a custom absorbed by the
beatniks from Negro jazz musicians and widely regarded in
middle America as a practice dangerous both to its devotees
and to themselves. The new residents of the Haight shared
beat's disdain for "square" America all around. Like all
bohemians they were first of all rebels, rejecting the ways in
which they were raised.

But they were not simply beat revived. In sexual matters,
for instance, although beatniks had scorned marriage vows,
they had been generally a monogamous lot at any given
moment, or at least as secretive ("discreet") about irregular
couplings as any shoe salesman or legal secretary. The hippies,
on the other hand, repudiated the very idea of monogamy. To
them, sex on a whim with whomever was convenient and
(more or less) willing, without "hang-ups," a sense of guilt, or
impropriety was an article of faith. If one wanted to do "it," the
sixties' favorite slang for genital diddling, why, then, one ought
to do "it."

This startling and significant reformulation of sexual
morality was, of course, not so very repugnant to "straight"
America. A few years' passage would demonstrate that sex on
whim was in the works for the whole society. The oral
contraceptive pill and other effective means of birth control
made it possible for women and girls to indulge their urges as
liberally as men and boys had always wished they would. The
hoary ideal of female chastity and the clear-cut distinction
between good girls and sluts could not survive such a
technological breakthrough.

Nevertheless, there was in hippie sex a quality that set it
apart from traditional morality (including the beatnik
variation) and the addle-brained singles-bars promiscuity of
the "straights" of the seventies. Hippie sex was grim and
determined for all the la-di-da language that surrounded it. It
was not really a matter of "if one wanted to it, one ought to do
it"; it was a matter of one ought to do it, whatever one wanted
at the moment, because if one did not want to do it there was
something wrong with one—lingering straightness. Only the

hippies themselves ever said they were a liberal-minded folk, and they, as shall be seen, were handicapped when it came to judgments more subtle than those involved in the motor functions.

Perhaps a certain intellective inadequacy along these lines explains that it was not paradoxical that while the flower children severed sex from sentimentalized romantic love, they turned around and attached it to love in its greater *caritas* sense. That is, promiscuously "doing it" was defined as an expression of the principle by which, according to the Movement, war, racial injustice, economic exploitation, and poverty would be abolished, *i.e.*, people feeling nice about one another.

Far from Rabelaisian, far from sex as an entertaining sneeze in the pants, flower children made sex a very serious thing indeed. They turned the Victorian attitude on its head. Doing it—"balling," another bit of the sixties argot—was not so much a matter of fun as a moral duty. Jerry Rubin chose *"Do It!"* as the title of his first "political" tract.

Hippiedom approached dope differently from the beatniks too. Beat looked on the use of the forbidden plant as an assertion of their alienation from masscult. However, they regarded the weed mostly as jazz musicians did, as a way to wind down, a harmless tranquilizer, a pleasant recreation. The flower children, on the other hand, invested "pot" and "grass" and a new drug all their own, LSD, with sacramental meaning. Ingesting drugs was not merely a kick; it was a holy act. Lew Yablonsky, a sociologist who wrote a worshipful account of hippie culture, had no compunctions about putting it directly. "Drugs are not for the single purpose of getting high and having fun," he wrote. "They are . . . a sacramental part of daily existence." Once again: drugs were something very serious indeed. In time, they would be defined as revolutionary.

The new bohemia was not, like the beatnik world, a jazz culture. Instead of clustering in obscure Negro jazz joints such as survived on the obscure fringes of masscult and creating a school of caterwauling folksingers who played autoharps and other archaic instruments—things the larger culture did not much fancy—the hippies took their music directly from the commerical recorded music industry of New York and Los Angeles. Where beat created its own art, whatever the eternal merit of the product, the flower children merely accepted what was given to them at a fair market price.

"Acid rock" was a technologically sophisticated music. To make it required a lot of money; to disseminate it, a highly efficient, highly rationalized business structure. The anomaly that they supported plastic show biz in what remains its most prosperous era never occurred to the hippies as an index of their superficiality.

Quite unlike beat, the love generation was aggressively anti-intellectual. The beatniks may have shunned the academic life as arid, but no self-respecting Greenwich Villager of the fifties would have stepped out for groceries without first tucking a dog-eared Bantam Dostoevski under arm. Coffeehouse conversation was often turgid, but beat's topics were heady enough, and status in the crowd demanded that a raconteur have strong opinion of a large and shifting cast of authors and philosophers. The *Village Voice,* originally the organ of the New York beatniks, set high standards of serious, literate journalism.

But if hippies read at all, it was in tabloid picture sheets like San Francisco's *Oracle,* a mess of multicolored, poorly-printed photographs of nudes, lots of white space, comic strips, and free-form verse prominently featuring the forbidden four-letter words. The distinctive graphic art form of the Counterculture was the poster advertising a Bill Graham rock concert. "Psychedelic" posters defied all the principles of the art. One did not read them and take in the pertinent information at a glance, but one had to pick carefully through a swirling mess of color and hidden images. Who, What, When, Where, and particularly How Much were hidden like the cow in the tree in a *Weekly Reader* "Can You See the

Animals" puzzle. It helped if the object of psychedelic advertising was in a stupor such as required time to answer a simple question, and that fact did not hurt business.

One source of Counterculture illiteracy was the ill-education foisted on the baby boom generation by the progressive educators triumphant. Another was the exaltation of feelings—sensations—over the intellect, a judgment, if that is the word, in which (of course!) the intellectuals soon justified the young primitives. Finally, having been educated to believe literacy was unnecessary and having confirmed it when the university proved "a drag," the Counterculture made itself incapable of literacy through drugs (of which more below).

Hippie conversation was restricted to a vocabulary that paleolithic man would find inadequate. Mostly, observers noted, hippie talk consisted of a series of slogans and exclamations aspirated languidly at one another: "Do your own thing"..."Get it together"..."Oh wow"..."Far out," sometimes expanded in a moment of articulate enthusiasm to "Out of sight"..."Groovy," and so on. Surely there was never a cultural phenomenon accounted portentous by society less able to verbalize what it meant.

The most obvious difference between beat and the love generation was the world of fashion. The new dropouts dressed exotically rather than casually. Jack Kerouac and Allen Ginsberg could outrage by leaving their neckties home. The *ne plus ultra* of beatnik style was a beard. The hippies, in startling contrast, sported hair to their shoulders and knee-high, lace-up boots. They dressed in ankle-length madras skirts and ballooning peasant blouses, in babushkas and gypsy cummerbunds, in caftans and dashikis, in whatever was the weekly loss-leader at the Salvation Army or St. Vincent de Paul Society: Eisenhower jackets, coonskin caps left over from the Crockett craze, Mouseketeer beanies, cowboy hats, old broad-brimmed, plumed bonnets from the thirties, helmets from the twenties.

The new wave liked jewelry, too, with the gents only half a sparkle behind the ladies. The men put on earrings. The women kept ahead by piercing the flanges of their noses and inserting a button of birthstone. Both subcontinent India and astrology were big in the Haight. And beads. Beads were bigger—"far out" and "groovy"—almost but not quite the trademark of the new bohemia. Beads of wood, glass, nuts, brass, teeth—anything but plastic—seemed to dangle from every neck.

In fact, the flower children were most remarkably encumbered with *things,* from cheap beads and secondhand togs to expensive electronic gear. Somewhere during the boom years of the fifties and sixties, bohemian America lost sight of the fact that to shake off the dead hand of American materialism meant to abandon material things. It was this curious turn of mind that made hippies more congenial to businessmen than beat had been, and also less substantial as a cultural as well as a social rebellion.

Also unlike beat, which clung to the stark, pallid Charles Addams look, the new generation had a penchant for cosmetics. Neophytes daubed brightly colored paints on their bodies. Fluorescents, tellingly known by a brand name, Day-Glo, were most popular. Hippies a little farther out got tattoos, "Love" and "Peace" instead of "Mother" and "Irene til I Die." Here and there, the intrepid explorer into the Haight might locate some intentional as opposed to slip-of-the-needle scarification among some group "into" pygmies or Amazon Valley wisdom. No doubt about it. The beat look might catch your eye. The *nouvelle vogue* made it difficult to look away.

And that, it turned out, was the whole idea. For where beat was morose, taciturn, retiring as a point of first principle, with no message for outsiders but "Leave me alone," the new bohemians were blissful, "mellow," gently bubbling with the joy of living in this great big wonderful world. They were exhibitionists and they were preachers. Quite unlike beat, jealously guarded by its adherents as a sect, the deity's gift to a chosen few that was by definition fouled when too many noticed it, like the early Islam of the Arabs, the hippies practiced a proselytizing faith, a Turkish Mohammedanism, conquering not by the sword, but by the easy pleasures it offered: sex and the euphoria of drugs.

When kids from uptown showed up in Greenwich Village coffee houses during the fifties, the regulars groaned and groused and eventually withdrew. Their intellectual champions spoke of defilement by false beatniks. But when kids from Marin and Contra Costa county and Queens and Rockville Centre dabbled in and selectively adopted the fashions and values of the sixties dropouts, the full-timers beamed glassily, celebrated with a more ebullient "Far out" than usual, offered their services as tutors ("Let's ball!"), and urged the potential recruits to plunge a bit more deeply into the way, the truth, and the life. Quite unlike *Dissent* back in 1960, the hippies' interpreters applauded weekend hippies. It meant that the Counterculture, the redeeming gospel of this new nation, was spreading. Prairie fire! Far out, man!

The proselytizing impulse of the hippies was another contribution of the large number of New Leftists among the first immigrants to the Haight, the East Village, and new bohemias in other cities. For by 1965, with the hard work of ERAP-type projects having evaporated in frustration, with the civil rights movement at a less than utopian conclusion and their expulsion from SNCC leaving them adrift, with Lyndon B. Johnson escalating the war in cowboy disregard of their moral anguish, with the easy conquest of the university by the student rebels turning sour, a large number of militants moved on—moved back—to the pursuit of self-fulfillment such as had been the theme of their lives as schoolchildren.

Abbie Hoffman, who had worked in SNCC Freedom Schools before being tossed out by the Black Powerites, conveyed the sense of disappointment and failure that sent him and many others into bohemia. "Once upon a time," he wrote, "about a generation ago, right after the thirteen-thousand-seven-hundred-and-sixty-fourth demonstration against the war in Vietnam, young people started to congregate in an area of San Francisco known as the Haight-Ashbury." A correspondent for the *Berkeley Barb,* a profitable organ of the Movement, an "underground newspaper" that sold from sheet-metal vendors at important intersections in the Bay Area, reported that "almost everybody here"—in the Haight—"was at one time or another engaged in some form of political activity."

Youngsters from Berkeley with Movement pasts were right behind the North Beachers in relocating in the Haight. Dropouts from eastern universities were among the trailblazers in the East Village. Sociologically, they looked much like a sample of any active Movement group. Lewis Yablonsky, an academic who briefly moved among the new bohemians, estimated that 70 percent of those he met had middle- and upper-class backgrounds, half of them from families with annual incomes of $15,000 or more.

At the beginning, some hippies closer to the beatnik spirit bemoaned the political element in their midst. A few leaders of the Haight–East Village community thought of their discovery of unrestricted sex, love of all in brotherhood and sisterhood, and the use of drugs as an exculpatory sacrament as something to be kept to themselves. When New York's bohemian community sponsored a "be-in" in Central Park in the spring of 1967, a paean to existence, they objected to the participation of antiwar demonstrators. To them, according to a reporter from the *Village Voice,* the be-in was "a sacred event, harking back to medieval pageants, gypsy gatherings, or the great pow-wows of the American Indians." They had no objection to onlookers from among the unregenerate, any more than, it may be noticed, Navajo rain dancers refuse to jig for paying tourists. They delighted in envy, not to mention an opportunity to pass the hat. But they believed that their example should be passive.

Nevertheless, as Don McNeil continued, as a medium of witness, the be-in was "political" in spite of itself. It was "a new and futuristic experience which, once refined, offered great promise." There was no way that the ostensibly antipolitical flower children could have remained outside what was, during the sixties, defined as politics. Everything, even the predilection of a teenager for lots of sex partners, was imbued with apocalyptic political significance during that parlous decade.

AMERICA AND HER YOUTH

But more directly on bliss and saving America. These possibilities were just hatching in the Haight in the summer of 1966. In that season the new immigrants seemed merely to be improving the ambience of a neighborhood that could have used some. They recovered decayed shops and homes, brightened the place with their clothing and jewelry but did not appreciably drive up the cost of living for the old timers.

The burglary rate was up, to be sure, but such is cold reality in urban America that this is always an encouraging datum, almost the sort of thing a neighborhood improvement association might crow about in a brochure. It meant there was something worth stealing around.

Another problem was the dope. The Haight's natives, black and white, just a few strides from middle-American respectability, were not particularly keen on the newcomers' insistence on smoking marijuana on the curbstone and roaming around on one or another sort of capsule.

But violent crime was way down and, as one of the earliest publicists of the love generation put it, there were few old residents "who wouldn't rather step over a giggling freak on the sidewalk than worry about hoodlums with switch-blades," hoodlums that seemed briefly, in 1966, if you squinted into the sun, to have taken their custom elsewhere. Indeed, there was reason to believe the new immigrants were a boon to the Haight. "The fact that the hippies and squares have worked out such a peaceful coexistence seemed to baffle the powers at City Hall."

America was not long in finding out what hippies were and only a little slower in taking them to its heart. The success story in the Haight and the colorful habits of the newcomers—exotic fashions, and free sex, the sitting about passively zonked on "grass"—drew droves of feature writers from the newspapers and television "spot crews" much more quickly than the beat had done. Beat needed the literary success of Jack Kerouac and Allen Ginsberg to give it a start. The hippies' poet laureate, Rod McKuen, emerged—was created and embraced in a smothering sea-to-shining-sea bear hug—only after the brave new world of the Haight was known to everyone.

Bennett Berger noted early on in the media discovery of the phenomenon that "far more interesting than the hippies themselves is America's inability to leave them alone." Other intellectuals later said that the saturation media attention given them destroyed what augured to be a portentous and salutary cultural revolution. Could Jesus Christ, someone asked, have promulgated the message that transformed the world had he been subjected at the conclusion of every parable and little throwaway miracle to the relentless glare of television lights and "inquiring reporters" who clamped on like snapping turtles? It is not a question without speculative interest. Nevertheless, it was not in the nature of social analysis in the sixties to ask further if any gospel so vulnerable to sensationalism and commercial packaging was worth promulgating. Everyone, from Bible-thumping moralists warning of a new Sodom to some of the nation's leading intellectuals, thought hippies very important indeed.

The hippie–Counterculture–flower children–love generation phenomenon was short lived. Of episodes that merit a paragraph in every American history textbook, only the Pony Express rivals it for temporal insignificance. Consider this chronology. The first big splash came in 1966. The golden age coincided with the summer of 1967 and was called "the summer of love" (as in National Secretary Week, etc.). Beginning with June graduations that year, over a hundred thousand youthful pilgrims were drawn to San Francisco by a popular song exhorting them to wear a flower in their hair, and sung in the mid-pubescent tremolo Americans have favored in their bards since the 1950s. And by the summer of 1968, in the Haight-Ashbury and the East Village and in hippie neighbor-hoods in other cities, the brave new world of beads, flowers, and love had degenerated into a pestilence of disease, addic-tion, big-time vice, and brutal crime such as few racial ghettos suffer.

By the summer of 1968 the far-out new world was discredited. As early as August 1967, equinox of the summer of love, when a 16-year-old girl was shot full of Methedrine by a Haight Don Juan and gang-raped by an uncountable number of young gentle people there, a group of locals calling themselves the Communication Company issued a broadside that asked, "Are you aware that Haight Street is just as bad as the squares say it is? . . . Haight Street is an ugly shitdeath" and all its leaders suggested was "more elegant attire."

Nevertheless, the Communication Company blamed not the imbecility of the love generation for the problem but only media exposure. So did a group of Haight Street hippies who announced a funeral in Golden Gate Park for "A. Hippie, Beloved Son of Mass Media." Implicitly they said that when the cameras departed—there were plenty at the requiem—when straight America left them alone, the new culture would resume its salubrious evolution.

It was not media exposure that destroyed the new world aborning. Like the political New Left from which in part it sprung and back into which it merged, the world of the hippies was without substance. It was the play-acting, with increas-ingly dangerous toys, of the children of the American middle class, an orgy of self-indulgence dependent entirely on the sufferance of an indulgent society in need of amusement.

The world of the Haight and the East Village was a reflection of middle America, not a challenge to it. If the farmers outside Keokuk loved to watch and cluck over CBS documentaries on the hippies, and tourists in San Francisco lined up at the Gray Line Tours bus company to take "the only foreign tour within the continental limits of the United States," the daughter of the Keokuk farmers, renamed Sunshine Love somewhere along Interstate 80, thrived on the attention. In New York, hippies responded to the bus tours down MacDougal Street by lining up on the curb and pointing cameras back at the gawkers. *Touché* indeed! But they scored the hit on themselves as well as on all those moms and dads in polyester and white shoes.

Writer Don McNeill, who wrote on the East Village scene for the *Village Voice,* noted that the hippies "arrived long before the label. At least there were kids with long hair and a passive manner who smoked grass and got stoned on acid and felt free in their sanctuary of a slum. But when the label came, they were ready to respond."

WHAT'S IN A LABEL?
As has been noted, the phenomenon went by different names. The Haight people themselves preferred "love generation" and "flower children." The media liked these well enough but preferred the tag tied on them by the waspish chronicler of San Franciscana, columnist Herb Caen. It was he who came up with "hippie." "Hip" was a jazz crowd adjective, doubtless of black origin, for those who were "with it." Norman Mailer had immortalized the white "hipster" for breaking with fifties culture. In making a diminutive of "hipster," Caen was pointing to the fact that the new with-it generation was very young indeed, as many in their teens as over twenty, more than a few of the girls still carrying a doughnut of babyfat around their waists, more than a few of the boys with pimple problems. And "hippie" was the name that struck fastest in the cafes and barrooms, lardooned with the usual working-class contempt for the fripperies of their betters.

Some Movement activists were at first dismayed at losing so many young, *ergo* progressive, troops to baubles, bangles, and stupor. Carl Davidson of SDS saluted hippies for their disillusionment with American life, but he condemned the phenomenon for making "many of our people withdraw into a personalistic cult of consumption. These aspects [of the love generation] need to be criticized and curtailed. We should be clear about one thing: the individual liberation of man, the most social of animals, is a dead-end—an impossibility." Liza Williams, writing in the *Los Angeles Free Press,* tried to shame hippie ex-activists back into the political movement:

> *OK. So you are wearing beads and your hair is long and from the back you might be anyone, and from the front your face isn't too different either. Your expression, is it an expression, is non-attendance, and your style is all I ever know of you. Style, it's all style and not much content, but what is the definition of a decadence? Is it the substitution of style for content?*

But the most striking aspect of the New Left's response to the hippies was how very quickly they adopted it as their own, defining it as yet another leap forward. Being new, and obviously popular among the young, offending much of "straight" society, the hippies must be all right. Indeed, they must be revolutionary. All it required to confirm this analysis was, as usual, a new label. If the facts do not fit, rename them. The New Left, and its elder boosters, adopted the name given the phenomenon by a California historian, Theodore Roszak. What was fermenting within the entrails of American society in places like the Haight, they said, was (sip of coffee, suck on pipe) nothing less than a "Counterculture," a social antithesis within the deadening American way of life. Abbie Hoffman was even more grandiose. After a hippie rock and roll concert near Woodstock, New York, in 1969, he called hippies a nation, the "Woodstock Nation." A Yale professor went further. To Charles Reich, the hippies created a new "consciousness" such as the world had never seen.

The different nomenclatures have some significance. Flowers, for instance, as in flower children, symbolized peace and love and warmth among people, and niceness generally. The cheery ancient symbol was given a new freshness during the sixties by a regiment of mysticism mongers such as periodically part the American middle classes from some of their filthy small change.

Hindu showmen have been around this country for a long time. Frances Trollope, an acerbic English lady who lived in Cincinnati, subsequently birthplace of Jerry Rubin, observed that "I sincerely believe that if a fire-worshipper, or an Indian Brahmin, were to come to the United States, prepared to preach and pray in English, he would not be long without a 'very respectable congregation.'" She was probably playing with hyperbole. At the time Mrs. Trollope wrote, only a few American proto–flower children like Ralph Waldo Emerson had displayed any knowledge of, let alone interest in, Oriental mysticism. However, beginning in 1893, when one Swami Vivekananda was booked into the Chicago World's Fair and found Americans willing to pay premium prices to hear his antimaterialistic, antitechnological messages (in the midst of a celebration of money and machines!), Hindu fakirs have regularly trekked to Moloch's shores.

Allen Ginsberg, the only beatnik who was also a prominent citizen of the hippie era, was the principal source of flower child interest in Oriental mysticism. He had traveled to India after the furor over *Howl!* abated and returned to preach the attainment of higher levels of consciousness through either (it is difficult for a non-mystic to say) loss of selfness in the Godhead through chanting "Ommmm" or loss of the world in selfness through chanting "Ommmm." The hippies were not high on the study a book like the *Bhagavad Gita* requires, but they could get into "Ommmm." It was easy enough to understand the message that the anxieties of life in an avaricious, capitalist, technological society could be allayed by a charm. Moreover, the lesson that happiness was attainable,

attainable *only* through self-fulfillment, was palatable to the baby boom generation no matter what the form.

If Ginsberg represented a continuity with beat, the Maharishi Mahesh Yogi spanned the apparent gap between the hippies and middle America. The mentor of the Beatles and actress Mia Farrow (although not Frank Sinatra), he was a congenial, monkeylike little man who giggled when, during his appearances on talk shows, people asked him difficult questions. His "Transcendental Meditation" (the name was copyrighted) involved taking a course in Yoga exercises through the Maharishi's extensive network of teachers and seminars. Classes met in Unitarian church basements and at Holiday Inns, and local gurus worked on commission. Among the guidance novices received for a couple hundred dollars was a mantra, or syllable, all one's own with which to induce the desirable trance. To critics who suggested that the confidentially whispered mantra was *all* the bang one got for one's buck, TM replied with the eternal and broad-sweeping explanation of the mystic: unless one did it, one could not understand it.

Like the raft of imitators that followed him, the Maharishi liked to be photographed clutching a blossom. This appealed to the dropouts. So did subcontinent fashions, saris and nose jewelry and the like (so long as they could be mixed with Native American accessories) and the whole far-out idea of trances (which went nicely with sweat baths).

Moreover, the Maharishi's techniques dealt with releasing energies that were already within everyone. There was no difficult objective world with which one needed to cope, no stubborn facts. All that was required for happiness, fulfillment, and accomplishment was already within each self, and needed only to be liberated. For a generation programmed to fasten on themselves, TM was ready-made. To flower children who had been New Leftists and found the world beyond the fingertips so unyielding, it was an irresistible consolation. All the successful exploiters of the sixties (and seventies) would preach one variety or another of self-fulfillment that was completely within the individual's competence, what Norman Vincent Peale called "Positive Thinking" in the fifties.

However, the Maharishi's direct influence on the flower children was limited and short-lived—for the same reason they never hung beads on Peale. Transcendental Meditation cost money, rather a lot of it for people who, whatever their expectations when mother and father moved on to the great ashram in the sky, were generally poor in the present, living day to day. Moreover, the Maharishi was a businessman who knew what a mass market looked like. The really big one in the sixties was not made up of the drop-out kids but of their parents.

After 1970, in fact, the Maharishi began to deal directly with corporations, administering the TM program to employees not as a means to karmic bliss but to spur greater sales and more efficient production. Any such explicit concession to the straights was enough to disgrace a gospel in the eyes of the flower children.

Finally, the Maharishi forbade the use of drugs as destructive (not to mention illegal), and the flower children would have none of that heresy. Hindu trances were okay, but for quick relief, you could not beat a little pill. The fact is that, in the end, the hippie phenomenon was about drugs. Nicholas Von Hoffman, one of the few liberal intellectuals of the late 1960s who did not, at least briefly, go ga-ga over the hippies, caught this when he wrote in *We Are the People Our Parents Warned Us Against,* "there are hippies who hate the establishment and hippies who are indifferent to it; there are hippies who love money and there are hippies who love love, love free food, free rent, free everything. But if the word means anything, it means a hippy is a dope dealer."

Consequently, the flower children found a guru who dealt dope. He, too, was big on sniffing posies while he spoke, was cheaper than the Maharishi (only $3.50 per *son et lumière* show plus sermon), and was in many ways an awful lot like a situation comedy Dad.

THE DRUG CULTURE

This was Dr. Timothy Leary, a Harvard psychologist. Born in 1921, Leary was raised in comfortable circumstances, was well educated, and took a Ph.D. in psychology. Except for a few writers, like Aldous Huxley, and bohemian roustabouts (beatnik Ken Kesey), he was one of the pioneers in experimenting with the synthetic chemical lysergic acid diethylamide or LSD.

Huxley thought of LSD as a means of augmenting rational knowledge. He compared the discovery of LSD with Leeuwenhoek's contriving of the microscope. LSD opened a whole new world of perception not previously known to have existed. Kesey, a writer who scored a big success with *One Flew Over the Cuckoo's Nest,* a trite adolescent novel about an insane asylum that could be touted as a masterpiece only in the sixties, thought of acid as a lot of fun, a better booze. He became a direct precursor of the hippie phenomenon by leading a tour of "Merry Pranksters" about California in a Day-Glo painted bus. Leary, however, was pure bench chemist, a plodding academic who published the results of his LSD experiments in the kind of scholarly journals kept handy in the bedroom by some insomniacs.

Another of the early LSD researchers was Jolyon West, later of the University of Oklahoma, who headed a program to investigate the federal government's suspicion that, during the Korean conflict, the enemy had used LSD as part of its mysterious "brainwashing" program. West said his findings were inconclusive but, along the way, he administered the drug to an elephant (which expired) and to Siamese fighting fish (which swam up and down instead of forward and backward).

West was wary of taking the drug himself because, as he told Nicholas Von Hoffman, the IQ of one chronic user he observed dropped from 140 to 122 within two and a half years. "He reminds me," West said, "of teenagers I've examined who've had frontal lobotomies.... This boy likes himself better. You have to realize that lobotomies make people happy. They attenuate those inner struggles and conflicts that are characteristics of the human condition."

Whatever Timothy Leary's intelligence quotient at the beginning of the 1960s, no such observations deterred him. Along with an associate who later renamed himself Baba Ram Dass, he did administer LSD to himself, found himself increasingly happy, and went public, not as a scientist but as a priest with a prescription for a better world.

This disturbed the overseers of Harvard University, a notoriously morose lot, and they sacked Leary in 1963. He tried to get his job back, the first of many incongruities in a life pathetically spent. However, when all his efforts failed and he found himself faced with criminal charges, too—LSD had been added to the dangerous-drug list—Leary founded, in September 1966, the League for Spiritual Discovery, a church.

By tying LSD to religion, specifically the peyote cult among southwestern Indians, but also to other primitive cultures that employed drug-induced trances, Leary hoped to win First Amendment protection (and tax-exempt status) for both his gospel and his indicted person. In order to raise money, he went on tour, presiding over services in movie houses. Appropriate to his costumed audience, Leary donned flowing white robes of the sort seen frequently on wise men in science fiction movies, his handsome mane of gray hair clipped to the tonsorial perfection that ten dollars bought in the late sixties.

The service itself was a simulated LSD "trip." Lights flashed; colors danced on the walls of movie theaters; "acid rock" blared from loudspeakers.

Amidst it all, Leary fondled a bloom, and from the stage delivered a quiet sermon, always on the same theme, the credo of the League for Spiritual Discovery: "Tune In, Turn On,

Drop Out." Tuning in was listening to the word. Turning on was, of course, dropping LSD, the customary technique being to soak the liquid into a sugar cube. Dropping out was simple enough, what the Counterculture, even before Leary, was based upon: repudiating not only the competitive, plastic, uptight, and repressive larger society but also the misguided attempts of the New Left to change things through political and social action. To Leary, the solution was individual—pharmaceutical—and not social. The answer to the troubles of the times was not action but personal redemption, and the key to that was a drug.

The lights and music were the best part of Leary's show. Journalists noted that those of the congregation who were not semicomatose, having already received the Eucharist, were disappointed by the pontiff. One critic observed sourly that Leary was "virtually incapable of intelligible thinking even about the implementation of his own doctrine." By this time the psychologist become priest was in his sixth or seventh year of regular trips and might have been at the back of Jolyon West's mind when he warned against LSD.

Leary had his enemies in the Movement. In August 1967 the Communication Company railed against him as another exploiter, like sensation-mongering reporters. "Why hasn't the man who really did it to us," created the "shitdeath" of Haight Street, "done something about the problem he has created? . . . He's now at work on yet another Psychedelic Circus at $3.50 a head, presumably to raise enough cash to keep himself out of jail and there isn't even a rumor that he's contributed any of the fortune he made with the last circus toward alleviating the misery of the psychedelia he created."

It would be a mistake to paint Leary as Elmer Gantry or Maharishi, a cynical hard-headed businessman who knew he had a good thing and let his customers take care of themselves. A better analogy would be those tobacco company officers who regularly appear on television to pooh-pooh the American Cancer Society and the surgeon general, puffing frantically and happily on their own products. Leary believed in his inchoate message, and if circumstantial evidence indicated that he was a mental wreck by the late sixties, the better point would seem to be that most Movement leaders did not notice. They honored him as a people's leader, and intellectual hangers-on, who would not themselves dream of dropping Leary's wonderful elixir, strained and groped to accord meaning to his gospel.

Theodore Roszak did not believe in drugs. His book on the Counterculture was based on the assertion that hippies offered something else but marijuana and LSD to the world. He suggested that, perhaps, only responsible, learned adults should use LSD—and then cautiously. Referring to Huxley's microscope analogy, he pointed out that "a microscope in the hands of a child or the laboratory janitor becomes a toy that produces nothing but a kind of barbarous and superficial fascination. Perhaps the drug experience bears significant fruit when rooted in the soil of a mature and cultivated mind. But the experience has all of a sudden been laid hold of by a generation of youngsters who are pathetically acultural and who often bring nothing to the experience but a vacuous yearning."

Nevertheless, the possibility that drugs in the right hands might produce insights underlying healthy social change was real to Roszak. And all too many of his colleagues in academia were so smitten with youth, or cowed by it, that they did not make his distinction. If the kids are doing it, there must be something there. An Italian scholar infected with this virus, Massimo Teodori, drafted a convoluted apologia:

Experience with drugs, in itself, is really nothing but a means of accelerating the process of breaking with the past and searching for a genuine "inwardness" which social pressure constantly rejects in favor of a series of models for behavior. Marijuana has been the sign of rebellion, first of all, against the ethic of

> *work and success which requires control, outside*
> *discipline, and double standards . . . the new genera-*
> *tions are . . . looking for a shortcut to the transfor-*
> *mation of personality structure and the building of*
> *"new men!"*

In fact, the Movement and its hangers-on took drugs further than Leary who, after all, until he went to jail, looked on them only as a sacrament, a religion. In the hands of the New Left, drugs and hippie high-jinks became the revolution itself.

DRUGS AS REVOLUTION

Perhaps the first pharmaceutical revolutionary was a young man who will be remembered in the annals only as Teddybear. (The sources for his biography will be difficult.) A drug dealer in the Haight during the summer of love, Teddybear described to a reporter how proper administration could create new human beings. Some members of the Hell's Angels motor-cycle gang had been "burned" (sold phony drugs) by one of Teddybear's competitors. Impulsive lads with a direct, uncomplicated approach to life's little crises, the Angels wanted to kill him. "We got to him first," however, Teddybear related. "We didn't hurt him or nothing. We made him take sixty thousand mikes (micrograms) in the three STP capsules [STP was a kind of improved, that is, more potent LSD], and he doesn't burn anybody anymore."

Why? Because he had been punished? A dose of his own medicine? Hardly. Recall: the pusher's medicine was phony. Teddybear and his brothers and sisters had created Love Generation Man: "He came out of that trip a beautiful human who only sells good shit now. . . . See, that's how we hippie people do it, with love. See, that's where society is all fucked up. If they gave acid to people who committed a crime, we wouldn't need penitentiaries."

It was this insight that lay at the core of the politicization of hippiedom. As Theodore Roszak defined it: "change the prevailing mode of consciousness and you change the world; the use of dope, *ex opere operato,* changes the prevailing mode of consciousness; therefore, universalize the use of dope and you change the world."

A more appealing gospel for New Leftists defeated in their other simplistically defined battles cannot be conceived. Revolution should be fun as a childhood oriented around play had been. But it had not worked out that way. Revolutionary acts should have quick immediate results, spontaneous gratification. Everything the Movement set itself to theretofore had not. Of course, the turn to drugs was in part a fruit of frustration and disappointment. It was also a logical next step for revolutionaries who denied the need for plans before beginning and claimed that through experimentation, through pragmatic "we'll try this and if it works we know what's true," they would construct a new society. All that was needed "to bring about a more human race," one SDSer "modestly" asserted, was LSD. Of course! By their failures all those other campaigns had discredited themselves. Drugs worked!

Peter Berg of the Diggers, a short-lived Movement group—like all of them—provides another link in the evolution of the sixties mind. The Diggers did ERAP-type social work among the hippies, providing free food, a place to "crash" (sleep), and advice regarding medical help and the like, all the time instructing the patronage in the political significance of their lives. Few groups were in a better position to see the human wreckage drugs had created. Berg did know that marijuana and LSD and other drugs were the basis of the Haight and the East Village. "Don't you know that all this is drugs?" he told a visitor to Digger headquarters, pointing toward the sidewalk crowded with hippies. Then he added, "All this is the revolution. Drug consciousness is the key to it."

Berg and his associates were content (for a season) to live entirely amidst the brave new world in the midst of the old: the hell with the straights! The two men who actually organized the hippies into an aggressive, expansive political force were

Jerry Rubin and Abbie Hoffman. They came to the Counterculture along rather different paths.

The first founder of the Youth International Party—the
name was chosen because it conformed to their suggestive
acronym, actually invented first, "Yippie!"—was Jerry Rubin.
After the Free Speech Movement in Berkeley, he had taken to
hanging around with left-wing groups and won some national
notoriety by taking an illegal trip to Cuba. By the mid-sixties,
like most New Leftists, Rubin was devoting all his attentions to
the antiwar protest and he participated, although not prominently, in a number of demonstrations.

In the meantime Rubin discovered the love generation
and its marvelous substances. At one time or another Rubin
invested marijuana and LSD with all the holy and social
attributes that anybody in the Counterculture came up with.
He was a sponge when it came to soaking up inanities.
However, there was always a discordant note of anxiety in his
pronouncements on the subject. Unlike those hippies who
would gobble up anything in pill form (one could sell aspirin
on Haight Street at a dollar a tablet), Jerry distinguished
between "mind drugs" like LSD and marijuana, which were
good and revolutionary, and "body drugs," the barbiturates,
particularly heroin, which were not only bad, but a tool in the
hands of the capitalist enemy. Even Jerry Rubin detected there
was something undesirable in the pathetic dereliction of the
Haight's and the East Village's young addicts.

"The choice is revolution or heroin," Rubin wrote.
"Sisters and brothers have to take care of sisters and brothers
who get trapped into heroin. Heroin is the government's most
powerful counter-revolutionary agent, a form of germ warfare. Since they can't get us back into their system, they try to
destroy us through heroin. We must create a revolutionary
movement and community which will give people an alternative to despair and heroin."

That movement, Jerry concluded by 1967, was to be
based on marijuana and LSD. Indeed, Rubin suggested that

the government crackdown on the insurrectionary drugs was a device of President Nixon and Attorney General John Mitchell to get the flower children buying heroin and speed.

ABBIE AND YIPPIE!

Curiously, Abbie Hoffman made no such fine distinctions between good drugs and bad. That was curious because he was in every way brighter than Jerry. Indeed, Abbie Hoffman of Worchester, Brandeis University, and the SNCC Freedom Summer remains, as he was at the time, the most intriguing and even the most appealing of Movement personalities.

He was born in 1938 and raised in a middle-class family with—it shines on every page he ever wrote—a Jewish identity problem. (The name was Abbott, not Abraham.) Intelligent and quick, too bright and quick for his own good in that whatever came easy to Abbie, which was a lot, soon bored him, he popped in and out of school, hustled pool with, by his own account, some success, amazed employers with money-making schemes he devised and just as quickly chagrined them by losing interest and moving on to something else.

Abbie was athletic and personable with a smile as shiny as a sterling silver coke spoon. Abbie had everything going for him but looks, and those were lacking only in Hollywood's sense of the word. His comically big nose—it could have been the one they used to mold the rubber ones seen about a lot in late October—gave him the appearance of a burlesque clown, especially after, introduced to the future in the mid-sixties, he let his thick curly hair grow long and wild.

It was not long before the Counterculture came to be his lengthened shadow, as beat was personified by Allen Ginsberg. Both men had personalities so compelling as to thrust them to the center of every crowd into which they stepped whether they liked it or not. Both, of course, loved it and they had something else in common. Both were, at the height of their respective tomfooleries, operators, wheeler-dealers, the kind of fellows who could, when they chose, run a complex organization, plan a big affair, make the right phone calls, persuade the right people.

Abbie was one of SNCC's most efficient organization men when he and other whites were told to go home to their own kind. The loss of his kind undoubtedly accounts in part for SNCC's rapid collapse. But the experience also hurt Abbie. In his account of the affair, humble and deferential toward Stokely Carmichael as it was, acquiescent in the correctness of the turn to black exclusionism, it is nevertheless obvious that he was wounded. Hoffman had devoted several years to SNCC, and even after Black Power he continued to run a support organization, Liberty House, in New York City.

It was at this time that Abbie Hoffman met Hippie, and became Him. While still dutifully attending antiwar demonstrations, he adopted the styles of the flower children and was, obviously, as his account of a recruiting session shows, heavily into drugs: "While I was working at Liberty House, a girl came in to volunteer. We got to talking about civil rights, the South, and so on. She asked about drugs. I asked if she had ever taken LSD. When she responded that she hadn't, I threw her a white capsule."

It sure beat "rights" talk and it seems likely that most of Hoffman's political work by 1967 was along these lines. He recalled this particular incident in some detail because, three months after it, he and the new recruit were married, according to the *I Ching*, by a priest who was high on STP.

By this time, Abbie had, with Jerry Rubin and Paul Krassner, the publisher of the iconoclastic *Realist* that was swallowed up by the sixties' dead seriousness, devised the Yippie idea. Like many others, they saw a vast reservoir of energy in the thousands of hippie kids milling about in their ghettos. As a kind of proletariat with no stake in the society, however self-created their alienation was, the kids could be mobilized by making revolution fun. Abbie and Krassner were masters at creating fun. They had devoted their lives to it. And Jerry was the sort to go along with whatever was going on.

Abbie and Krassner had also dealt long enough with the media that they understood how rapidly a message could be spread if they got TV coverage. So, in more or less the Yippies' debut, Abbie forewarned reporters and led a group of East Village longhairs to the New York Stock Exchange for the tour of the gallery the exchange sponsored. When a jittery guard told Hoffman that hippies were not allowed, he responded, "We're not hippies. We're Jews." Once inside, the Yippies sent the floor into an uproar when they showered traders with dollar bills. For a few precious seconds that should live forever in the history of Western capitalism, members of the N.Y.S.E., pillars of Episcopalian churches and Westchester County Reform synagogues, yachtsmen and people who appeared on morning news shows to explain monetary policy to the masses, owners of Lhasa Apsos and Boston terriers scrambled about like so many old bags at a Gimbel's basement clearance, elbowing one another, in a snowstorm of bucks. It was Terry Southern's *Magic Christian* in reverse, the rich and the would-be rich dancing for ragged hippies.

It only lasted a few seconds. The Yippies claimed to have thrown thousands but, of course, their exchequer was limited, and the brokers realized quickly what had been done to them. Their next reaction, however, served Guy Grant–Abbie Hoffman's purposes just as well: they glowered, shouted, and shook their fists at the freaks cheering wildly in the gallery.

A triumph indeed, and thus was born the media cliché that Abbie Hoffman was a "comic genius." Maybe. Definitely, if "genius" is defined and tossed about as they do on television talk shows where every guest is, miraculously, the greatest, sensational, terrific, and so on. That world was Abbie's. The truth is, he was a genius only in the way that, in inflationary times, a cheeseburger is expensive. Among Movement leaders he had as little competition as Burger King's Whopper has at $1.59.

The stock exchange caper was a moment. And Abbie had others as, for example, during the Democratic National

Convention of 1968 when the Youth International Party nominated Pigasus, a pig, as its candidate. Whereas other parties' candidates ate the people, the Yippies said, the people ate the Yippie candidate. As usual—Abbie did know his audience—America helped the gag in its response. Prompted by the SPCA, authorities seized Pigasus and placed him in protective custody before a hickory chip fire could be kindled.

But in the end Abbie's good jokes were few and they were just zingers, the sort of thing harried writers for situation comedies come up with on schedule. Will Rogers once explained why Abbie was no comic genius. "A comedian," he said, "can only last till he either takes himself serious or his audience takes him serious." Abbie took himself seriously. He boasted of the show biz contracts he turned down because of his devotion to the people. Or, when he did not, America did. He was identified in the media as a revolutionary leader, a radical with a difference. America liked him. As Abbie commented in 1980, "I was probably the only professed revolutionary ever described as 'cute.'" But he did not grasp what it meant about his professed revolutionism that merely cute was precisely all he was.

Yippie's brightest moment came at the Democratic National Convention in Chicago in August of 1968. A number of antiwar groups, loosely functioning as the Mobilization to End the War in Vietnam (called the "Mobe"), announced a massive demonstration in the city, calling on protesters to flock into Chicago, and the Yippie leaders took an early and important part in rallying the troops. Abbie and Jerry were valuable to the effort not only as publicists but because Abbie was willing to devote himself to securing permits from City Hall and arranging for the basic needs of the tens of thousands of mostly young people who were expected to respond. (The next summer, he and the Yippies would do the same thing at the famous Woodstock rock concert in upstate New York).

Even more than the seizure of Columbia University by an SDS group in the spring of 1968, Chicago marked the beginning of the end of the fun. The trouble was that Chicago, unlike Columbia, was not governed by the parents of the protesters. Chicago was the fief of Mayor Richard J. Daley's Cook County Democratic organization. This was an alliance along old time machine lines of white ethnic and some black working-class groups. Unlike every other arena in which the Movement had played since retreating from the South, Chicago was firmly in the hands of the class enemy, rude graspers and grafters from the working class who did not like the privileged and mannered upper classes or their privileged, unmannered heirs. In Chicago, the liberal-minded element was powerless. At the most they were able to elect a few district leaders to serve as gadflies whom Daley either humored or quashed with ungrammatical and awkward japes. As for the Republican party, it was in the hands of sterile Gold Coast aristocrats or troglodytic right-wingers and just as impotent. Daley ran Chicago on the principle of rewarding votes with social services.

He liked to boast that Chicago was the only major city that "worked," where the commuter trains ran on time and the city built swimming pools in every neighborhood that knew which way to vote. In 1968, Daley wanted the media attention given his party's convention as a means of showing off his accomplishment. He was getting along in years and may have thought of the occasion as his *pièce-montée*. The Eugene McCarthy supporters within the convention presented no threat, little as Daley must have liked the aloof Senator. But the smartass hippies who were threatening to clutter newly swept streets did.

Daley's functionaries in the bureaus frustrated every attempt by the Mobe to work according to the rules, to get permits for an encampment in Lincoln Park, permission to parade at times and places mutually agreed upon. If Daley's shrewder half had been functioning, he might have realized that this tactic was not going to discourage the protest but only ensure a confrontation. As Saul Alinsky, a much worthier enemy of the mayor, once observed, the most effective way to stymie the Movement was to grant it what it wanted.

But Daley was by no means entirely a smart politician. He was a gut working-class urbanite who hated the hippies, and he conveyed his hostility to the Chicago police. For three days during the convention, the cops first harassed and then attacked—"rioted" in the words of an investigating commission—beating up not only Abbie's Yippies but priests and nuns, orderly demonstrators, delegates to the convention, reporters, cameramen, bystanders. More than one witness reported seeing infuriated policemen smashing lightposts and street signs with their nightsticks when there were no heads immediately available.

In one way Chicago was a moral defeat for Daley. Not in Chicago, however. He would be in the mayor's chair yet but for the inflexible mortality policy of his Irish God; he died in office in 1976. "The people" supported Daley's brutalization of the leaders of the people, but the mayor took his lumps from a federal commission that put the blame for the confrontation on the city. Chicago was "a police riot," the commission said. In one way, at least, Daley's Chicago did not "work."

Nevertheless, Daley's enduring resentment led to the indictment of eight Movement leaders as parties to a conspiracy to cause a disturbance. Among them were Tom Hayden, David Dellinger, Bobby Seale (whose case was later separated), Hoffman, and Rubin. Although at the time "the Great Conspiracy Trial" of the Chicago Seven seemed to be a rallying point, uniting liberals with Movement activists, it was in reality a climax. Hayden's SDS abandoned his measured counsel during the trial, split, and turned to terrorism. David Dellinger's militant pacifist movement virtually disappeared, and he never again commanded an audience. The Yippies either melded into terroristic Weatherman (the rump of SDS), reformed as passive rock fans, or repaired to down-on-the-farm where, in the form of the commune movement, they quietly vanished.

PRIMITIVISM

The Movement had a peculiar relationship with the technology that exploded during the 1960s. On the one hand, the survival of the young militants depended on everything from the immunizations their parents had pumped into their behinds to the media that sustained showmen like Abbie Hoffman. The sophisticated audio-electronics of Movement music has already been noticed. Paul Goodman observed the fatuousness of the Movement's criticisms of technology when he told a hooting group in New York in March 1969, "Don't blame everything on technology. It's too easy. Just the other day I listened to a young fellow sing a very passionate song about how technology is killing us and all that. . . . But before he started, he bent down and plugged his electric guitar into the wall socket."

But this is a book about—in Dr. Johnson's phrase that will, alas, be relevant forever—"unresisting imbecility." The dumb generation and, more important, a good many of their elders, spent a good deal of the late sixties playing Indian.

Beatnik leftover Gary Snyder opined that, with the rise of the occult and revival of fruit and nut diets, society was "experiencing a surfacing (in a peculiarly American incarnation) of the great Subculture which goes back as far perhaps as the late Paleolithic." He was convinced that industrial society was "finished" and crowed that "many of us are, again, hunters and gatherers. Poets, musicians, nomadic engineers and scholars; fact-diggers, searchers and re-searchers scoring in rich foundation territory. . . . A few of us are literally hunters and gatherers, playfully studying the old techniques of acorn flour, seaweed gathering, yucca-fiber, rabbit-snaring and bow hunting."

A generally cool-headed New York journalist thought that the psychedelic rock culture was a reflection of "the same things [that] have happened for eras in primitive rituals and Indian pow-wows." And hangers-on of a dozen stripes claimed to see some primal urge behind the youth rebellion.

They were the intellectual hangers-on who accorded great social import to the primitivism. Some of the primitivists, of course, like a communalist in West Virginia, regarded the return to the natural as "a path from things as they are to things as they should be." But most of those who withdrew to isolated wickiups or caves were doing just that—withdrawing— without apology or explanation. Whether they were ex-activists plunged into despair by the failure of their ideals or simply spoiled middle-class teenagers unable to cope with social pressures, most seem to have wanted only be left alone, especially after Chicago. Most were passive and gentle, some nasty and even vicious. Almost all wanted "out" and thought that a life of acorns and nude bathing was feasible and fulfilling.

It was quite in character with the intellectuals of the sixties, who time after time egged on the immature in their nonsense for their own vicarious thrills, that they left the primitivist wretches less alone than the "rednecks" who were constantly accused of harassment. One after the other, writers and other hangers-on trundled up the steps of slum communes or the slopes of the Santa Cruz hills to annoint the recluses with oil of vanguard. Theodore Roszak returned frequently to the good old days in his thesis that the young represented a counterculture, "If we look beyond the horizon of civilization, we find a condition of life among our neolithic and paleolithic ancestors which, while materially impoverished in comparison to the absurd affluence of middle-class America, was nevertheless plentiful enough to support the vital needs of tribes and villages, and to allow a good deal of time for communal culture."

A sociologist who passed a few months in hippie company came to substantially the same conclusion: "I saw, and to some extent experienced, a kind of extended family life and group sex that was probably practical back in The Beginning. And, on the same scene, I heard the sounds of a highly sophisticated philosophy based on a scholarly study and meditation that could conceivably extricate twentieth-century man from the spiritual ravages of the Great Society, overkill, and the super-mechanical world."

It could be an interesting inquiry to discover the definition of "highly sophisticated" to an auditor who tingled with excitement at his glimpse into "The Beginning." In fact, it seems little worth the effort to treat seriously the swoonings over aboriginal life of immunized and air-conditioned, middle-class academics who should have recognized, at least, that two hundred million people lived and ate in an area that supported "plentifully enough" about a million American Indians who, in fact, had their starving times frequently enough.

This sort of dabbling, of course, has traditionally been the prerogative of decadent, overstuffed scions of the privileged class. Louis XVI and Marie Antoinette cavorted in smocks and shifts as they imagined the happy peasants did on the green of a movie-set village at Versailles. The youth-worshipping dilettantes of the 1960s switched off their symphonies now and then to ponder the sheer happiness of lolling in the grass listening to tom-toms. The temptation from afteryears is to wish that some brawny neolithic had materialized to drub the lot of them with the natural jaw bone of a mastodon. And, in fact, the primitivism fad came pretty much to an end with incidents like the Charles Manson murders and the disturbingly regular discovery of shallow graves on the Big Sur and in the Santa Cruz mountains. The point is that it took such highly predictable (and often predicted) horrors to demonstrate that it was not .45-caliber pistols and napalm that made men capable of brutality. That children should have imagined otherwise is comprehensible. But journalists, historians, sociologists, anthropologists, teachers of philosophy, and others—many of them distinguished and highly respected—subsumed not only their learning but also their common sense and propounded that the answer to the social malaise lay in a return to nature.

The epitome of the primitive movement was in the commune craze which peaked in 1969 and 1970. Whether in cities or, more exciting, in the mountains or New Mexico desert, many of these experiments in alternate life-styles were pounced upon by hangers-on fairly before they were started. A 1970 *New York Times* survey turned up some two thousand communes in some thirty-four states. Most of these were merely urban "extended-families," many of them simple cooperatives of few pretensions.

But primitive rural communes were also numerous, especially in climatically mild areas like New Mexico, and California's coastal mountains. The smaller groups were unstable, and the more ambitious projects proved the most atrocious. Very few lasted more than a season. By the summer of 1971 there were thought to be fewer than five hundred people still back to nature in all of New Mexico. The state police, who had used the primitivist invasion of the state as a pretext for greater appropriations, suggested that an untypically harsh winter in 1970–1971 and the economic recession (which cut off the aborigines' checks from home) had struck fatal blows. Long before the end, celebrated primitivist communes, like folksinger Lou Gottlieb's Morning Star Ranch, had become hells. Lew Yablonsky, who nevertheless continued to prate about the potential in them for twentieth-century man, reported children smeared in their own filth for days, hysterical under the LSD given to pacify them (no "plastic" teething rings for nature's children), terrorization by a Negro hoodlum who knew easy marks, and so on.

Despite the package of immunizations and dental work the young suburbanites fortuitously took into the wilderness, disease was a crushing problem. Venereal infection, pneumonia, influenza, malnutrition, and the unprimitive affliction of hepatitis reached disastrous proportions—all excepting LSD and hepatitis, aspects of life with nature which the promoters of paleolithic ecstasy had forgotten.

The unviability of the rural communes was the unviability of the Counterculture carried to its logical end. The communalists assumed that historical inheritance could be obliterated by an act of will, that, by consciously rejecting their bourgeois mores, comforts, and assumptions, they could thereby escape them. In fact, the animosities, resentments, and "hang-ups" of unconventional society prevailed in the communes without the unprimitive inhibitions on them by which contemporary society barely survives. The communalists thought they could become Indians by playing that they were.

The problem of the irresponsibility of the immature had its effects on the communes as it did on other manifestations of the Movement. Frequently enough, the source of the desperation which produced primitivist fantasies was an inability to cope with the basically psychological problems of survival in advanced modern society. Young suburbanites unable to cope with the minimum of self-dependence suddenly thrust upon them were hardly prepared to set up at Walden, even with Concord nearby, and take care not only of washing the dishes but of the most fundamental necessities of life.

Lew Yablonsky's tour of several communes sometimes reads as if he were touring garbage dumps. Theodore Roszak commented on an underground newspaper's article on how not to catch hepatitis which admonished readers, among other things, to wash their hands after defecation if they planned to prepare food. "You can even afford to get up tight about it, especially if your home is of the tribal kind." Roszak, who nonetheless continued to hope that these infantile barbarians represented a new dawn, put the last word nicely: "My pretribal father used to phrase this piece of folk wisdom as: 'You wash up before you sit down at this table!' But I seem to remember being about five years old at the time."

CHARLEY
The Counterculture was not yet five years old when its message was codified by a Yale law professor named Charles Reich. His book of 1970, *The Greening of America*, posited the triform evolution of modern American history.

Reich's Consciousness I was the entrepreneurial, competitive spirit of nineteenth-century America. Consciousness

II was the corporate world of the twentieth century, the rationalized America created by the New Deal and the business organizers. What was emerging via the Counterculture, Reich said, was a new era, Consciousness III.

The book was astonishingly successful. Its sales allowed Reich to quit his job at Yale. The book was also almost universally condemned by the critics. In putting Counterculture beliefs in declaratory sentences, as opposed to moans of ecstasy and slogans, Reich quite inadvertently showed the intellectuals what they had been rooting on. Nevertheless, the considerable attention paid the book—Philip Nobile was able to collect several dozen essays in a book of his own, *The Con III Controversy*—indicates to what depths the life of the mind in America had sunk by 1970.

For Reich's critique of society centered on such atrocities as the fact that he could not buy real, unhomogenized peanut butter at the supermarket, and that the magazines on airplanes did not please him. His program consisted of smiling, dressing up in groovy duds, lying on the grass, and giggling. Radicalism had come a long way.

THE REBELLION OF THE BOURGEOISIE

Along with Reich, the Movement had become critics of trivialities. When the radicals of the end of the sixties said "bourgeois"—pejoratively, of course—they meant not the people who owned society, but the offensive casual practices of people who were affluent, materialistic, given to nurturing their comforts and indulging their most trivial needs, and accounting their garages full of consumer baubles a fitting statement about their lives. In short, to the Movement, "bourgeois" meant the parents of the young radicals and flower children.

The advantage of defining the enemy by means of style was one that has appeared frequently in these pages: it was easy. It made "bourgeois" a category easy to escape and "revolutionary" an easy one to join. But the saddest irony of the Movement was that in accepting its definition of what bourgeois and radicalism meant, the radicals of the sixties remained bourgeois.

To be more accurate, the liberated youth of the Movement succeeded in transcending only that which was meaningless in their native American culture, while never transcending—in fact, perfectly reflecting—those bourgeois traits that were most venal, dehumanizing, and reprehensible.

Thus, it was accounted a cultural triumph of the first magnitude to leave television and new cars behind. It was regarded as antimaterialistic to drive battered Volkswagen buses instead of "status" automobiles. The Weatherman Manifesto made it clear that it would deign to ally with "working-class youth" because that could be done without "giving up what we have gained." Weatherman would not give "up our old car for a new Dodge."

The whole dirt and sloppiness fetish was made much of; this was reckoned a basic break with the bourgeois ethic connecting cleanliness with godliness. And the vulgar language fixation: to use such *forbidden* words, the pariahs of polite suburban conversation, this was revolution in itself. "When young people start calling those in power 'motherfucker,'" said revolutionary leader Mark Rudd, "you know the structure of authority is breaking down." At the Woodstock Rock Festival in 1969, when the rains threatened to end the affair, according to a political Movement journal, almost everyone "joined in chants of 'Oh Shit' and 'Fuck the Rain.' This was a real sign of the different culture and everyone felt it. Can you imagine 'Fuck the Rain' at Yankee Stadium? Not yet anyway."

This moronism was to be expected of infantile semi-literates. More interesting is an observation of just which American bourgeois traits the Movement rejected and which it continued to reflect. Both New Left in its later stages and Counterculture successfully transcended the American bourgeois's sense of duty and obligation, his acceptance of work, his loyalty and selflessness toward his immediate relatives and voluntary associations, his sense of proportion, his practicality, his acknowledgment at least to descendants of an obligation to the future, his resilience in adversity, his conception of moderation as a virtue, his self-restraint. That the typical American bourgeois is hardly a paragon of all or even very many of these ideals is beside the point. They are bourgeois characteristics and they were rarely to be observed in the Movement.

On the other hand, the intellectual superficiality and smug satisfaction of the American middle classes, the anti-intellectualism, the selfishness and suspicion of larger human relationships—community—the provincial, intolerant, Ptolemaic standards of taste and morality, the petty snobbery, the contempt for the less affluent, for people who worked with their hands, the social irresponsibility, the triteness, banality, and sentimentalism with which the American bourgeois has been identified, these the Movement never transcended. Indeed, the catalog might easily be misread on a synopsis of the critiques of the Movement which began to appear after Charley Reich's inanities and the shocking irresponsibility of the terrorists in 1970 and 1971. And the fact that New Left and Counterculture almost without inconsistency retained the bad and rejected the good is no matter of colossal bad luck in the game of chance. The Movement was simply bourgeois, but it was not commonly decent.

The bourgeois provincialism of Movement people was evident in the earliest days of the Movement in the Buddhalike response with which the earliest New Leftists discovered the brutality, racism, and poverty of American society. Raised in the sheltered affluence of the 1950s which, in effect, did not recognize the conceivability of such contradictions, they were utterly unprepared to cope with simple reality and—touching in a way—were genuinely shocked that the world did not conform to their fairy tale illusions. And the Movement never moved beyond its naiveté. Near the end of the decade, a New Leftist student wrote on the subject of George Kennan's critique of the young radicals that he was "not untypical of many people of his age." To demonstrate his Everymanship he listed his credentials: "I am a senior at Yale University. My father is a judge and I come from a moderate middle-class home in California with family roots firmly buried in the Midwest and in the South." The world was just a bowl of elites.

This parochialism was echoed by Charley Reich. He rattled off his *curriculum vitae* to a *New York Times* interviewer—eastern preparatory school, Ivy League college, Ivy League law school, arranged clerkship with a distinguished Justice of the Supreme Court—"just like everyone else," Reich said. The point of all this is not to reiterate the middle-class origins of Movement people but to indicate that the revolutionaries of the sixties never faced up to the fact that their experience of the world was narrow indeed. The redeeming virtue in the publication *The Greening of America*, wrote one reviewer, is that "Reich's book will help many an elite parent understand the speech of many an elite child." A *Washington Post* writer approached the problem in another way. The "central weakness" of the book, he wrote, is, alas, that "American society is not Yale writ large." That *mot* could be applied to the whole Movement, political and countercultural. The greater number of its leaders and many of its following never grasped the fact that reality was not the suburbs writ large. Writing on the student rebellion, Robert Nisbet noticed that the students failed to understand they were no longer "home."

> *What the student cry for relevance turned out to be was the all-too-familiar middle-class child's cry to be entertained, to be stimulated, above all, to be* listened to, *no matter what or how complex the subject at hand. Having become accustomed in their homes to get attention to whatever was on their*

minds, and of course incessant and lavish praise for
their "brightness," is it not to be expected that when
the children go off to the University the same
attention should be given their *interests and needs?*

When student protesters made suggestions for inno-
vations in the universities, they were never in the direction of
paring down facilities, bureaucracy, expenses. Rather, every
innovation offered actually portended an increase of expendi-
ture. David Riesman detected the consumption-crazed
American bourgeois in this obliviousness to expense. "Many
of the affluent students who often lead the protest movements
at colleges," he wrote, "seem persuaded that the society is fully
abundant and that nothing really costs anything." Indeed, the
ostensible rejection of materialism in the act of "dropping out"
involved little rejection of the implicit belief that society would
not only support the dropout, it would support him rather
well.

The deprivations which the Movement whined about
were fully as trivial as the bourgeois plastics it celebrated
abandoning. Jerry Rubin fancied himself St. Simeon Stylites
because a color television set was his "one possession in
the world." Reich wrung his hands over having to eat
homogenized peanut butter and because American Airlines
deprived him of soulful inflight reading and handed him the
Saturday Evening Post. For all his celebration of spirituality,
Reich periodically lapsed into complaints that might have
appeared in *Consumer Reports*: "Our society produces
products that are unreliable, or unsafe, or that break down and
cannot be readily serviced, or are unusable without another
product that is unavailable (an automobile without parking).
Some products are showing a noticeable deterioration in
quality; others can be frighteningly dangerous in the wrong
hands (an oven cleaner that can damage the eyes)."

It was this sort of thinking that characterized the
profoundest depths of the Movement mind. The Movement

could scream bloody horror so frequently with such conviction because horror, to the young bourgeois, was a pretty bland inconvenience.

Students regarded expulsion from the university as a cruel and inhuman punishment. Andrew Kopkind, a promising journalist whose good sense was shattered by the beauty of the Movement, rose to Aristophanean pathos when he surveyed the miseries of the student left. "Students who would make a revolution are condemned to be judged by their teachers: judged and described, analyzed, categorized. Workers who revolt are merely fired by their bosses; revolutionary peasants are simply driven off the land by their masters. But the intellectual tortures that professors use on their riotous pupils are as maddening as any water-drop or iron maiden."

New Leftists somehow thought that their "individualism," "do your own thing," marked a significant departure from bourgeois life. How neatly this reflected the unwholesome bourgeois trait of "every man to himself" when the rub came, was beyond them. There is an interesting example of this in Jerry Rubin's *Do It!* Like Abbie Hoffman and numerous other of the huckster New Leftists, Rubin was puffed and strident in his use of the pronoun "we" when relating mass actions near to which he happened to be. Thus, it was *we* charged the cops and *we* were beaten pretty badly at times when Rubin might well have in fact been "ballin' some groovy chick" halfway across town. (There is no evidence of Rubin, Hoffman, or any of the Chicago 7 being actually involved in a single violent, i.e., dangerous, confrontation.)

"For in reality, 'hippies are what hippies do,' 'lost bourgeois' who have taken up the highest ideal of the middle class—leisure time," wrote Walter Bowart and Allen Katzman. The Counterculture was a movement which reflected all the gaucheries and vices of the milieu from which it came. The very signals of "liberation" which the Movement waved were in reality bourgeois fantasies carried in some degree to actuality. Robert Jackson observed this in Charles Reich's vilification of a stereotyped young bourgeois couple with their typical bourgeois interests and diversions. How empty and pitiable, Reich shakes his head. "But I am not at all sure," Jackson responded, "that the interests of heightened consciousness that Reich set down one day on his 'yellow pad': delights in trips to the Hebrides, or the lost cities of Crete, desires for 'sexual experiences with many different people,' 'living in harmony with nature,' 'climbing,' 'clothes for fun,'" were all so different from the fantasies of neatnik.

Nor did the Movement manage to establish an acquisitive ethic distinguishable from that of its middle-class progenitors. They called it a "rip off" and fancied that because petty theft was frowned upon in middle-class America that they had made a break. Abbie Hoffman's "Fuck the System" was a handbook along the lines of touring "on $5 a day," differing only in that it cut the budget down to nearly nothing. The pamphlet, later expanded in *Steal This Book*, was a series of tips, many of them long known to young bourgeois anglers, on how to eat, travel, dress, etc., at no expense. Or, rather, at someone else's expense. There was no need to miss the amenities. "Put LP records into pizza boxes." The final irony of his book was that Hoffman was accused of stealing it himself. A young hippie sued him, claiming that Hoffman had written it from notes he foolishly trusted Abbie with. A cash consideration resolved the unpleasantness.

Nor was he the only white-collar criminal among Movement worthies. Stokely Carmichael and Jerry Rubin were involved in decidedly gauche troubles with the Internal Revenue Service. In February, 1971, the IRS filed a claim against Carmichael and his wife Miriam Makeba for $48,193 in unpaid income taxes for 1968 and 1969. These arrears applied principally to the earnings of the popular folksinger, Makeba, but Carmichael did well enough for a people's leader. The next month, in one day, he spoke at three California state colleges at $1,500 a stop. The president of San Jose State College mused that such a salary could tempt him into becoming a "revolutionary."

Rubin's tax problems throw some light on why his only personal property was a color television set: he had given everything else to a foundation. On December 15, 1970, the IRS notified the Social Education Foundation that the government intended to revoke its tax-exempt status. The foundation (it had one trustee, Rubin's wife, Nancy S. Kurshan) was chartered for the purposes of providing "relief of the poor, distressed, and underprivileged . . . lessen the burdens of government . . . defend human civil rights secured by law." Very nice wording for the same sort of corporate tax dodge regularly excoriated by Rubin, among others, in the Movement. Of course the foundation had paid out funds only to Rubin. Between May 1969 and April 1970, it had received $4,468.69 in tax-free royalties from *Do It!* and $9,267.72 in *contributions!* This was a Yippie put-on of the first order. But, like all Yippie put-ons, it was, however unfortunate the phrase, the sleaziness of a bourgeois brat.

According to an informer before a HUAC-type congressional committee, theft *within* the Movement was not so nonexistent as trumpeters of the new culture implied. One Marjorie King, a former SDSer from Chicago, told of how SDS revolutionaries collected bail for comrades from liberal hangers-on:

> *People when they go out and collect money a lot of times they make the calls themselves to these certain people, and then collect it from them themselves. But yet what they sometimes do is that they go, they call more people than they should call, and go and collect more money than they should collect, and keep it for themselves, and turn in the amount they are supposed to turn in yet maybe they have collected three or four times more than they originally should have.*

For all the crowing contempt for bourgeois society, Movement people had an interesting habit of asserting that they could have "made it" had they not been "above it." A New York City

Provo: "We can all play the *Time-Life* game, and make the mass media." Jerry Rubin seems never to have left an acquaintance without dropping the fact that he had been an "ace young reporter" on the *Cincinnati Post and Times Star*. "'Son,' the managing editor said to me, 'someday you're going to be a helluva reporter, maybe the greatest reporter this city's ever seen.'" In fact, numerous studies of New Leftists before about 1967 indicated that they were generally among the brightest of their peers, and successful and respected professionals such as Staughton Lynd and Andrew Kopkind did overthrow successful careers for their diverse notions of revolutions. And profiteers like Abbie Hoffman did well enough by revolution. But there is a small core of evidence that the repetitious protests of great potential in the straight world are significant only in their excess. There is a tentative case to be made for the thesis that the New Left represented the scions of the elite who were raised to be so accustomed to a life of indolence without demands that the fact of work in order to hold it (whether plastic, empty or not) was too much with which to cope. The Movement never gave up its conviction that it had not only support but, indeed, generous support coming to it. What it refused to recognize, in a sense, was that this was other than inherited. Roger Starr, the director of the Citizen's Housing and Planning Council of New York, caught this when he commented on student radicals' refusal to evince any respect for their professors. What they are saying, Starr wrote, is "that rank cannot be attained by achievement, but only by birth and natural endowment."

This, circa 1970, was the Revolution.

CHAPTER
EIGHT

DENOUEMENT

In one of his many shrewd perceptions of the Counterculture, Theodore Roszak commented on the single-mindedness with which hippies fixed on the pharmacopoeia. Scanning the October 1967 issue of the *Oracle*, he sadly listed its contents: an interview with Timothy Leary, an account of an LSD trip with a Bay Area seer, a rock star's true confession about "How I Get High," tips on decorating flower child living quarters so as to convey the ecstasy of drug use, and a health column on avoiding hepatitis infection. The *Oracle*'s literary editor discussed some books about the expansion of consciousness through drugs and, for something a little different, the graphic feature of the week depicted a couple "doing it" beneath psychedelic letters spelling out "L-O-V-E."

"There was a word we have," Roszak wrote, "to describe such fastidious immersion in a single small idea and all its trivial ramifications, such precious efforts to make the marginal part stand for the whole of culture. The word is 'decadence.' And that, unhappily, is the direction in which a substantial part of our youth culture is currently weakening."

Because he insisted on seeing the Counterculture as something more than immersion in drugs, Roszak was able to sustain the hopeful tenor of his book to the last page. Because he wrote his book so early—1969 (and it is remarkable that he was as perceptive as he was at that date)—he did not know how quickly the far-out new world would dissolve, an Atlantis of one season. He did not see that the new way of looking at the world was just another in a series of fads and fashions such as Roszak, and all late-century Americans have seen come and go in their lives as capriciously as housecats.

Fads are an aspect of advanced decadence for they are serial immersions in single small ideas and all their trivial ramifications, no single episode having more than a glancing impact on their participants, like the "graze" wounds heroes sustain with such tedious regularity in cheap western movies.

The least one can say for the decadents everyone recognizes as decadents—the body-builders who shine their arms and legs with olive oil, the kids who develop Frisbee-skimming or their skill at killing monsters from space in electronic games to a fine art—is that they stick to it. Their dubious accomplishments take time. But what is to be said for the flitting fads of the general populace?

Fads are what bind the cultural history of the United States in the 1950s, 1960s, and 1970s together in one historical era. Viewed with some perspective, the sixties marked no break with the ostensibly apathetic fifties, such as the people of the time optimistically thought, nor did a seventies dubbed narcissistic mark a doleful retreat from the preceding altruistic, socially-conscious decade. To name a popular sensation that was talked about, featured in the Sunday supplements, and pompously ruminated over in the "journals of opinion" over those thirty years is to name a fad and to diagnose decadence.

Among those fads were the interests of the Movement, and it is immaterial that, on the face of it, fighting for black equality and protesting against a vicious, wicked war appear to be worthwhile causes compared to mastering the hula hoop, ballin' a lot of chicks, or sitting in a hot tub talking about personal space with bearded men and women smoking comfrey cigarettes. So far as the participants in every one of them were concerned, the social and psychological function was the same: diversion for a little while, amusement, self-gratification, a means of setting up a mirror before which one might cavort and find the sight meet and comely. It no more mattered that the Movement accomplished little of substance in its antipoverty, antiracism, and antiwar campaigns than it matters that, after the first three dozen hearings (and after the first three bars for some), the latest James Taylor release begins to cloy. There will always be other James Taylor songs, and new and exciting James Taylors. As long as the sixties lasted there were always new noble causes, other victims to simper over, other dimensions of one's own victimization to discover and revel in.

Because the agitations and gospels of the sixties were no more than fads of a people decaying culturally, intellectually, psychologically, and morally, it is a pointless exercise to look for logical development within the Movement. Fads do not lead one to the other like premises in a polysyllogism. They do not lead anywhere but to boredom and exhaustion. Fads are discrete episodes that displace one another like bowling pins, the discarded to be forgotten.

Don McNeill looked back on the twelve months of 1967 for the *Village Voice*. Much would be hard to forget, he wrote, "the Be-ins, the Sweep-in, the Smoke-ins, the dealers, the deaths. Others are already forgotten. Chief among the forgotten changes are the valiant attempts at community organization, some of which lasted a week, none of which survive today."

Some are still hard to forget. But what does memorability mean? Frankie Laine is not forgotten. Some remember chlorophyll and lanolin. No one who had what used to be the good fortune of residing on a winding shady suburban street during the 1970s is likely to forget joggers unless spot brain surgery with lasers is refined to such a point that it can be offered as an elective therapy, a kind of nose job of the mind.

To puzzle over the fact that, at the end of the sixties, nearly a million people could be mobilized in the streets to execrate their government while, just a year or two later, no one was available for such revolutionary service, is to make the same mistake that the historian would who wrote: "During the late 1950s, American youth committed themselves to crowding into phone booths and small Volkswagen automobiles as a way of life."

People do not *commit* themselves to fads. They dawdle with them for a little while because they have nothing better to do, nothing better to think about, no reason not to "do it," and the incapability of commitment to such ideas as merit commitment.

The man who should have seen this aspect of the sixties was Kenneth Keniston. On the eve of the troubles, he published a brilliant study of American young people called *The Uncommitted*. Keniston described the youth of 1960 as snared in a "cult of the present." The dizzingly rapid technological and social changes that occurred during their short lifetimes had destroyed any sense of continuity in them (such as their teachers did not convey to them anyway). Lacking a sense of past and future, Keniston's "Uncommitted" functionally disbelieved in the past and the future. "What is left, of course," Keniston continued, "is the present, and all that can be enjoyed therein; 'today' becomes one rock of constancy in a shifting sea of change."

And so, young people "committed" themselves only to "change itself, usually expressed in terms like 'openness,' 'flexibility,' 'responsiveness,' 'sensitivity,' and the absence of 'rigidity,' 'intransigence,' and 'narrowness.'"

It bears repeating that Keniston published this portrait in 1960, before the troubles, because in it he so neatly described Movement activists down to the details of their catchwords and, for that matter, the middle-class Narcissuses of the seventies. And yet, when the troubles began, he did not apply his own insights. In 1968 Keniston wrote another book on contemporary youth, *Young Radicals: Notes on Committed Youth*, and in 1971, *Youth and Dissent: The Rise of a New Opposition*. In these books, one published at the equinox of the Movement, one when it had already set, Keniston defined the youth of the sixties as startlingly different from the subjects of *The Uncommitted*; as, on the contrary, genuinely "committed" and "political," substantial, a real, vital counterforce to conventional (older) Americans, those "unusually two-dimensional, flat, and uninteresting... pasteboard figures upon a painted landscape." (Mercifully, he has not added a sequel on the seventies.) But Keniston was not alone among intellectuals in having his head spun by the young radicals' openness, responsiveness, and sensitivity.

A social psychologist who was not fuddled at the height of the excitement and who helps in understanding the decade was Robert Jay Lifton. His essay, "Protean Man," appeared in the *Partisan Review* in 1968. Like Keniston, he emphasized the forces of historical dislocation that broke "the sense of connection which men have long felt with the vital and nourishing symbols of their cultural tradition."

However, unlike Keniston, and perhaps accounting for why Keniston could become a Movement hanger-on despite his insights, Lifton did not implicitly assume that people could discard their historical inheritance if they chose to do so. They were stuck with fragments clinging to them like foxtails whether they liked it or not.

The people of the Movement did, of course, think they could—that they had—abolished the past through an act of will. Because they did not, Lifton's "protean man" is so accurate a description of them and an explanation of why their "commitments" must be seen as nothing but fads.

In Greek mythology, Proteus was able to change his shape from boar to lion, to dragon, to fire, or to flood at will. Like him, Lifton's protean man was constantly experimenting, exploring, flitting from one shape to another with no particular purpose but the attractions of the moment, with no particular reason to do so but the fact that he could. The only shape of which Proteus of myth was incapable was his own (unless he was chained). Likewise, Lifton's protean man was incapable of constancy. Lacking the chains of learning, of absolute or at least durable standards, of commitment to principles of any kind but change, Movement activists flitted.

A Princeton graduate student who was critical of her contemporaries made the point to George Kennan:

> *Everything about us stresses instantaneousness of gratification of wants. We can travel anywhere in a matter of hours or days. We can communicate instantly, get entertained instantly, etc. . . . Is it any wonder that young people living in this climate want instant spiritual fulfillment, instant physical gratification, instant change in the political and social system? Not only do these people not have the capacity . . . for hard work towards rational goals but they do not even have the patience for the long, hard meditation of the Indian mystic and they take LSD as a seeming short-cut.*

And not only LSD. The young lady's character sketch of her contemporaries also explains why ERAP could be given up so easily; why the principles of the early Free Speech Movement could be perverted within a semester; why when Stokely Carmichael told a movement committed to racial integration that racial separation was actually the way to go that they agreed with a cheer—*vive le neuf!;* why the Movement could scamper from hero to hero more capriciously than adolescents change guitarists they want to marry; why the failure of an antiwar protest to move a powerful government instantaneously could result in a withdrawal to drugs and teepees; why Don McNeill, surveying a mere twelve months in the history of a single New York neighborhood, could discover that half the things he had written about he had already forgotten.

Lifton studiously avoided attaching the concept of protean man exclusively to the young radicals who, at the time he wrote, were making so much noise. He suggested that Americans (and the inhabitants of the developed world generally) conformed to his model. In fact, he suggested that the protean adjustment "may well be one of the functional patterns of our day."

And he was right. Protean radical was not at all very different from protean straight, despite the solemn belief of so many that something new and wonderful was blowing in the wind. Nevertheless, it is the Movement militant who is immediately recognizable in Lifton's observation that protean man responded "with diffuse fear and anger" but could never find "a good cause" or "a consistent target." Protean man cultivated his anger "because he finds it more serviceable than anxiety, because there are plenty of targets of one kind or another beckoning, and because even moving targets are better than none. His difficulty is that focused indignation is as hard for him to sustain as is any single identification or conviction."

Lifton concluded that protean man was consumed with a "strong ideological hunger." Political and religious movements were "likely to experience less difficulty convincing him to alter previous convictions than they do providing him a set of beliefs which can command his allegiance for more than a brief experimental interlude."

In the more playful terms with which this chapter began, the Movement person was a faddist. And with the frustrations that met New Leftists in their antiwar campaign, and the waning of the appeal of the Counterculture, one more fad was on the docket. Like rock and roll, however, the Movement had run out of novel musical variations. Instead, the New Left turned in 1968 to breaking up the instruments and trashing the stage. The best part of the show was that in its final fad, the Movement repudiated the flexibility and rejection of ideology that characterized it since the beginning of the decade. This should not be thought so bizarre. Consider the history of the hemline in the twentieth century.

PL AND SDS

SDS did not cope gracefully with the sudden appearance of the Counterculture. The first reaction of its activism-minded leaders to Timothy Leary and dropping out was jaundiced and critical. However, with no anchorage with which to resist shifting currents, with no inclination to criticize anything young people did and the delights of the Counterculture attracting hundreds of thousands of them, and with its impulse to accept any rebellion against convention as somehow progressive, SDS made its peace with the hippies. By the time of the Chicago police riot, even priggish Tom Hayden had let his hair grow and was nursing a wispy beard. For public appearances he donned a headband and discreet bead choker.

At the same time that SDS was accommodating to the freaks, a group at diametric odds with life-style revolution was insinuating itself into the organization, especially in New York and New England. This was Progressive Labor, or PL, and it represented in caricature the very aspects of the Old Left persuasion against which SDS had rebelled with such distaste. PL was devoted to discipline and an inflexible party line in spades.

The Progressive Labor party dated from 1962. It was a chip off the old Communist party block, a small group of former party members, mostly in New York, who sided with Chairman Mao Zedong in the Sino-Soviet split. Like the Chairman, the PLers claimed to represent the militant revolutionary tradition while the Russian bureaucrats (and the American CP) stood for a cautious, accommodating, perhaps even sinister accommodation with the capitalists.

The PLers were masters of Marxian hairsplitting. Scholars is not too strong a word for them. Their first political actions were fairly conventional, however. PL led a short-lived rent strike in Harlem that was defeated but nevertheless brought the organization some national attention.

Such was the ferment of the sixties that publicity was enough to win recruits among university students. Not only was PL outrageous in its hard-line Marxism-Maoism, but the organization offered its members a badge of identification equivalent to hippie beads, the Little Red Book that the Panthers had peddled in order to buy their arsenal, "Quotations from the Thought of Chairman Mao Tse-tung." That a collection of homilies designed for simple Chinese peasants should provide wisdom enough to satisfy the ideological yearning of the "best and brightest" products of the world's most comprehensive educational system provides another glimpse inside the radicals of the sixties. PLers did not leave home without it.

SDS regulars had nothing against Chinese peasants or the Little Red Book. However, PL's social analysis ran counter to New Left sentiments. Instead of looking for criteria by which they might distinguish themselves from the general population (students as a social class, youth versus adults, black versus white, hippie versus straight, female versus male), instead of looking for grievances some very special groups had against everyone else—"single issue politics"—PL taught that there were, simply, a working class and an exploiting class. The revolutionary's task was to mobilize the former and in the United States of the sixties, plagued with false consciousness as it was, the first step in the long haul was not to alienate working people on the basis of such trivia as life-style rebellion and "adventurist" hell-raising on campuses that, as obviously the mischief of privileged kids, was as disturbing to proletarians as it was to the class enemy. The job, said PL, was to build a working-class base through admittedly dull, plodding, tedious organizational and educational work. This farthest left group in the Old Left was, by the criterion of action, the right wing of the New.

By 1967, PL had carried its message deep into SDS which, through the May 2 Movement, a front group, its members were instructed to join. This was in itself a tacit confession of failure among the working class. While few workers joined PL, its members discovered that, armed with a coherent message and sharply honed apologetical skills, they easily converted impressionistic SDS rank-and-filers to their point of view. In a sense, PL was in the political Movement what the Jesus Freaks and Moonies were in the Counter-culture. They offered a reassuring, absolute, comprehensive prescription for people psychologically conditioned to look for one.

Because they were disciplined as discipline went in the sixties, the PLers soon won some positions of power within SDS. In February 1968, PL elected four of ten members of SDS's New York regional committee, and three of the remaining seven sometimes voted PL's way.

For the first time, SDS meetings, especially in New York, were marked by harsh contention and ill-feeling, real factionalism. Previously, with no program binding the organization together, but only a gossamer web of warm common feelings, internal peace was the normal state of affairs. The atmosphere of SDS meetings until 1967 was typically the atmosphere of a social gathering of good friends. Now, with the PL faction putting forward—pushing—a clear-cut and inflexible program that countered SDS's middle-class prejudices and five-year drift, meetings meant shrill debate and hard feelings.

The SDS regulars had little choice in fighting a faction but to form a faction. In order to combat an ideology (PLers typically showed up at meetings with lengthy documents to support their prepared resolutions), the SDSers had to do the same. Because they were not very good at organization, internally as well as in the outside world, the regular SDS factions inclined to split and splinter themselves, like cancerous cells run amok. Because they had shunned "ideology" for five years, when they turned to program-drafting they devised the most extraordinary absurdities.

Their analysis took on a Marxist cast, but whereas PL offered a simple, traditional class analysis, the SDSers had to resort to their technique of reworking definitions to suit their impulses. Thus, because the anti-Russian PLers were anti-Hanoi (North Vietnam was closely tied to the Soviet Union), as well as critical of other national liberation movements, SDS defined nationalism as a progressive "Marxist" force. Because PL defined students in traditional terms, as, by definition, bourgeois, the SDSers, helped out by academic hangers-on, defined students as "niggers" or "working class" or identified them as a critical segment of society on the basis of some other convoluted sophistry. Because PL disdained racial separatist movements and the growing women's movement as undercutting the absolute importance of social class, SDS devised one explanation or another of why blacks were the vanguard of the revolution and why women had a unique role to play because of their oppression as a sex.

PL's old-time Marxism had the virtue of simplicity. In responding to it, SDS could offer only highly complex and very slippery alternatives: "Third Worldism," for example, which became the basis of SDS's final incarnation; "Weatherman," which taught that all (white) inhabitants of the capitalist and soviet spheres were "bourgeois" exploiters. This "class enemy" included Stanley Kowalski who worked in the steel mills of Pittsburgh and Lee Bill Snopes who farmed a few acres of cotton as a tenant in the Mississippi Delta. Both of them "exploited" all inhabitants of the developing world and all American blacks.

Even the young white militants of the Movement, despite their passionate support of Third World liberation movements and anything any black radical said, enjoyed "white skin privilege," although, after 1968, there was some question as to whether white women were blessed with this armor. After shunning hairsplitting for half a decade, the Movement mastered the craft in record time.

What, then, were white radicals to do? Certainly not to build a base among, of all people, the enemy. Rather, their task was to act, to confront, to cause trouble, to weaken Moloch from within. Mark Rudd of Maplewood, New Jersey, soon to emerge as a national leader of the SDS regulars, was not so burdened with complex thought processes as to hesitate in putting it bluntly. He opposed "organizing and base-building above action and confrontation." In order to demonstrate what he meant, in March 1968 he threw a lemon meringue pie in the face of a military recruiter on an Ivy League campus. This, Rudd explained, was a revolutionary act. It represented the "aggressive approach" as opposed to PL equivocation and cowardice.

CORAGGIO!

People like Rudd and Bernadine Dohrn, a Chicago lawyer of well-to-do antecedents, had a half-baked ideology. Dohrn assumed SDS leadership in 1968 by saying that she considered herself to be "a revolutionary communist." But in reality she and Mark of Maplewood and Mike Gold and Cathy Boudin and other emerging leaders of SDS were merely carrying on the impulse of the Movement from the beginning to equate action with radical political politics, "DO. DO. DO," wrote an emphatic Jerry Rubin. "The Movement gets its unity around tactics. We become a community through collective action." And so as to leave no doubt that he meant any action whatsoever, Rubin continued, "Goals are irrelevant. The tactics, the actions, are critical." Or, as Norman Mailer gently chided, the Movement had reformulated the old cliché as, "I agree with your means but I don't accept your ends."

A short-lived Counterculture group of 1967, the "True Light Beavers," described as "a small band of intergalactic nomads," issued only a single sentence manifesto during its brief visit to Earth: "There are no problems, there are only things to be done." And an un-named Weatherman (the name the anti-PL SDS leaders would eventually assume) was quoted in *Scanlan's Magazine*, a journal of Movement hangers-on: "Perpetual activity is the lifeblood of a revolutionary organization."

If activity, any activity, was revolution, then the boldest actor was the greatest revolutionary. Like operatic sopranos rooting on their tenors in the imminent entry of the basso, the gist of SDS manifestos by 1968 was, *"Coraggio! Coraggio!"* Those who would not act in *any* situation—a category which included PLers—were not revolutionary simply because they were cowards.

Irving Howe noticed this tendency taking shape as early as 1965. The new radicals, he wrote, saw politics as "a

Hemingwayesque contest in courage and rectitude. People are constantly being tested for endurance, bravery, resistance to temptation. . . . Personal endurance thus becomes the substance of, and perhaps even a replacement for, political ideas."

By 1970, Howe's speculation became reality within SDS. According to one of the last Weatherman documents, people were recruited and judged not "on the basis of political principle" or even "on evaluation of their practice." The issue "was whether or not the potential cadre had the 'guts' to carry out armed struggle, to be a *real* revolutionary. Are you revolutionary enough to smash your closest relationships? Are you revolutionary enough to give away your children? This style of 'struggle' came to be known as 'gutcheck.' It was an important form of 'struggle' within the organization on every question."

Mark Rudd, according to writer Kirkpatrick Sale, "continually accused people of cowardice. That was his big word then . . . how you had to get a gun, and stop being afraid, and be a man and all that." Shades of Huey P. Newton and railroad crossings. And in April 1968, Mark got his chance to put his "ideas" into practice and ensure that he would be enshrined in the Movement Hall of Fame alongside the hard-driving Minister of Defense.

RED FLAGS
AMIDST THE IVY

Rudd won his prominence in SDS's New York region, and soon enough in national SDS, by virtue of his chairmanship of the Columbia University chapter. He had joined as a sophomore, and, the next year, he cut classes for five weeks to tour Cuba. The holiday among the *barbudos* instilled in Rudd a yen for revolutionary glory, and upon his return to Columbia he took to assailing the "circumspect" SDS leaders for failing to take aggressive action.

Rudd had no ideas. The son of a retired Army officer who put his pension into New Jersey real estate and prospered, and doubtless thought his Mark might improve himself hobnobbing with Ivy Leaguers, he had the slightly stupid good looks of the athlete-heartthrob whose picture is always autographed in suburban high school yearbooks. Sociologist Daniel Bell described him as "a tall, hulking, slack-faced young man with a prognathic jaw and blue-gray eyes so translucent that his gaze seems hypnotic." In SDS, as at yacht clubs, those were credentials warranting preferment and, by the spring of 1968, Mark was chairman of the chapter.

It did not, of course, matter that Mark had nothing to say. That, when corrected by a sympathetic Roger Kahn or asked to clarify an ambiguity, "the teeth clenched and . . . his rhetoric grows simple. 'Aw, fuck off.'"

Rudd was for action, and so the issues that precipitated the greatest university rebellion since Berkeley do not require detailed analysis. Even Rudd later admitted that they were nothing to him but an excuse for confrontation. One of these was IDA, the Institute for Defense Analysis. Columbia was one of several universities that, under this aegis, researched military matters for the Pentagon. On the question of disaffiliation, SDS had widespread support. In March 1968, some 1,700 Columbia students signed a petition calling for cancelling the IDA contract.

The other issue was a gymnasium. Columbia had plans to construct a multistoried structure in Morningside Park at the foot of the cliffs—Morningside Heights—on which Columbia sits. The city of New York authorized this private use of public land on the condition that Columbia make the facility available to the community that, at the foot of the cliffs, adjoined Morningside Park. That community was Harlem and when Harlem CORE said that projected community access was too limited, Columbia made greater concessions.

After this, very few objections to the gym were heard in Harlem itself. Morningside Park was not exactly a focus of wholesome activities, band concerts, and innocent necking. As historian Irwin Unger wrote, "After dark it was a jungle where no one who had the slightest sense of self-preservation walked." The gymnasium was, conceivably, of benefit in a neighborhood notoriously short in social services.

However, Mark Rudd and the Ivy League revolutionaries knew better what was good for the darkies, teetering on the brink of the revolution as they were, than Sambo himself could be expected to know. They and Columbia's Afro-American Society (AAS), a trendy black separatist group, handpicked and coddled by Columbia as showpieces of the university's social consciousness, demanded the university cancel the project. Tellingly, they did not object so much to the questionable private use of public property. The middle-class white radicals were accustomed to slopping at the public trough, and the black students were looking forward to a career of doing it. They fastened on a meaningless symbol. The Harlemites would use a "back door" to the gymnasium, not the same door on the top of the Heights used by Columbia students.

In one of his frequent foul moods on the subject, Saul Alinsky threw up his hands and said, "Maybe the fastest way to get a revolutionary to start thinking is to give him everything he demands." Had Columbia cancelled the "Jim Crow" entrance to the gymnasium, for example, it would have meant, for would-be Harlemite users, a stiff climb up Morningside Heights so that they could descend, inside, to the basketball courts at Harlem level. In other words, by striking the back door from the blueprints, the Columbia administration would have forced Harlem organizations like CORE to demand its reinstatement and thereby would have mocked SDS and the future bureaucrats of the Afro-American Society. But President Grayson Kirk and Vice-President David Truman were to prove, marvelously enough, less imaginative administrators than the people who ran Berkeley in 1964. It has not been conclusively proven to this day that Kirk, a handsome gray-haired figure, was not in fact a wax statue kept for photographic purposes by a company that prepares glossy stock-holders' reports. Although many claim to have seen him move about, conceivably an illusion triggered by drugs or another testament to the wonders worked with lifelike robots, few remember him ever saying anything. In order to understand the American university, it is necessary to realize that he had proved himself worthy of one of higher education's half dozen most coveted positions. In general, universities are run less competently than a two pump gas station.

Moreover, if Alinsky was correct in implying that New Left "demands" were meaningless or silly, he may have missed the fact that demands were also beside the point, as the events of April 1968 were to show.

Rudd and SDS wanted action, any action. On March 27, about 150 SDSers marched into President Kirk's office and briefly occupied it. When half a dozen, including Rudd, were placed on probation because of the episode, a rally was called at the customary demonstration point at Columbia, "at the sundial" in the middle of the university's principal quadrangle.

The chief subject of the few speeches given was IDA, and Rudd once again led the crowd up the steps of Low Library, where Kirk's office was located. When they found the doors locked and someone shouted that (what the hell!) they should protest the gym instead, the crowd took off across campus. Rudd, momentarily confused, a chronic disability with him, followed fifteen minutes later. (Some said he did not know the way to the site of the intolerable structure.) He found that the crowd had pushed down part of the fence surrounding the construction and one demonstrator had been arrested.

Back at the sundial, someone in the growing crowd shouted that the demonstrators should take a hostage to hold in return for the fallen comrade's release. Within half an hour, the focus had shifted from IDA to the gym to the arrested student. The SDSers and some members of the AAS marched into Hamilton Hall where they announced to Dean Henry Coleman that he was their prisoner. A group of anti-SDS students who had tagged along hooting offered their brawn should Dean Coleman wish to make a break for freedom, but he prudently advised them to disperse.

Having launched the revolution, a decent respect to the opinions of mankind required that the New Leftists declare the causes that impelled them. Their demands were six, but only two dealt with what might be called extra-Columbian issues: the university must cease to support the Vietnamese war by severing its connection with IDA, and the university must immediately suspend construction of the gymnasium. Although the rebels were already aflutter about the possibility of a rising in Harlem, a fantasy in which they were encouraged by the black college boys of AAS, the other four demands were not likely to send waves of fervor rolling down 125th Street: the university would allow indoor revolutionary demonstrations (pleasant as that April was, New York winters could be nasty); all future disciplinary actions against Columbia Lenins and Trotskys would be decided in open hearings according to Anglo-Saxon juridicial tradition; the university would drop charges against the student arrested at the construction site; and the university would grant amnesty to all the revolutionaries then in revolt for all past revolutionary acts and those it might be necessary to commit in the immediate future.

THE OCCUPATION
The events of the next week would be the subject of a dozen books published in 1968, 1969, and 1970. Some of them were quite long. The occupation of four buildings at the alma mater of Lou Gehrig and Allen Ginsberg was widely regarded as a significant revolutionary action worthy of extended and subtle analysis. In part this was due to the fact that, at about the same time, French university students at Nanterre outside Paris and at the Sorbonne also rebelled and very nearly precipitated a real revolution; and, in Germany, Italy, and Japan during 1968, unruly students caused significant social disturbances.

In part, however, the extraordinary scrutiny to which the Columbia rising was exposed was simply another expression

of the foolishness—the stupidity—that had come to character-
ize the social vision of America's literati.

Far from a revolution, the Columbia rising was an
eruption of the most ludicrous revolutionary dilettantism, a
rising of people whose only concern, after a day or two, was
that they not be punished for what they had done. *"Une
révolution que demande que il'on se sacrifice pour elle est une
révolution à la papa."* That was the motto of the French
student rebels—"A revolution that requires sacrifice is
Daddy's kind of revolution"—but it more closely described
the Columbia rising.

The actual events can be related quite briefly. After a few
hours in Hamilton Hall, the Afro-American Society decided
that the principles of black separatism required that the new
world be created by segregated cadres. They ordered out the
SDSers, who, after a little milling about the quad, broke into
Low Library. Within a day, other students occupied two other
buildings.

The New York police, who soon surrounded the revolutionary enclaves and wanted to move in immediately, were
held back by President Kirk. His caution was based partly on
faculty requests that they attempt to mediate the dispute in
order to avoid violence. But Kirk and Truman and the
majority of the Columbia faculty also shared the romantic and
essentially racist delusion of SDS and the Afro-American
Society that Harlem, peopled by congenital revolutionaries as
it was, was on the verge of attacking Columbia University in
order that wintertime demonstrators could enjoy steam heat.

In reality, of course, Harlem could not have cared less. A
few local crazies said to be armed joined the AAS in Hamilton
Hall, but the blacks actually lost their nerve within a few hours.
When it was pointed out to them that the sequestration of
Dean Coleman might be construed as kidnapping, a somewhat
more serious offense in the current criminal code than social
revolution, they let the dean go. Ray Brown of AAS had told
Rudd and the white students, "It's about time you people

stopped talking about revolution and started acting in a manner that is going to bring some meaningful changes." However, by the third day of the rising, the blacks as well as the whites were thinking of only one meaningful change as a condition of their evacuation: amnesty for what they had done. Indeed, abdicating their New Left-annointed role as vanguard, the blacks secretly began negotiations to sell the SDSers out. As faculty attempts to solve the problem did not progress, Kirk had decided, or the people who made decisions for him decided, that if the blacks would settle, they could move in force against the Rudd gang.

On April 30, the blacks settled. Officially there was no amnesty but, tacitly, some guarantees were promised and the AAS filed out of Hamilton Hall in handcuffs. (There was, in fact, no retribution.) Then the cops charged into the white-held buildings. About 700 were arrested and 150, including some policemen, were injured. There is no question that the police took relish in their work, not only knocking heads during the attack but continuing to beat up the revolutionaries after they ceased to resist.

A REVOLUTION
OF DILETTANTES

Much more surprising, the revolutionaries were shocked by the harshness of the white terror. Every student chronicle of the event reflects a sense of speechless shock and outrage that they should be treated so brutally by short-breathed Irishmen. The police themselves were amazed and perhaps deterred from worse behavior by the uncomprehending reaction of the students. Thinking it over, one policeman mused, "the reason the police are such an issue is that you've got a lot of revolutionaries who think they're not supposed to get hurt in a revolution. I can hardly see Lenin complaining about police brutality."

He hit the dilettantism of New Leftism dead center. Just a year before, lecturing at the University of Hawaii shortly after the tragic Newark riots, urban planner Roger Starr met "a young undergraduate whose glistening cheeks and braided hair might have advertised malted milk or Juicy Fruit gum.... Her eyes brimming with what I will swear was philanthropic fervor," she told Starr that he was very fortunate to be living on the mainland and so close to Newark at that. "Weren't the riots just beautiful?" she said.

All very familiar. It was the same romanticism that infused the white SNCC workers who trundled south as if they were stepping through the silver screen into *Song of the South* to set Uncle Remus straight on his constitutional rights. But Starr's friend was, after all, straight off the sands of some Oahu beach, a frame of reference from which seeing the streets of Newark as "beautiful" is not necessarily psychotic. But what is to be said of perhaps a thousand people who seized and vandalized the principal building of an important institution— who were there!—claiming they had fired the first salvo of a nationwide social revolution (their slogan was "One, Two, Many Columbias"), and all the while it was in progress, with ranks of New York's finest shuffling and coughing outside, thought they were in the movies? Whatever the SNCC workers thought before they went south, however curiously they interpreted what they found, they faced up to the fact that they had been mistaken.

An SDS "theoretician" and, appropriately, a sophomore, presented the Low Library rebels with several projections. His "Contingency A" was "fistfights, police violence, similar excitement ... open struggle, perhaps with city cops, will develop." His proposed response: "WE FIGHT!"

The dilettantism of the Columbia revolution is brought into clearest focus by the fact that, by April 30, the only rebel demand was amnesty. The IDA issue was essentially settled: at least Columbia was going to conceal its defense contracting, and no one among the occupiers was still talking about it. Likewise the gym project was functionally dead. While many of the Columbia faculty were unsympathetic to the students, the around-the-clock meetings generally agreed that suspension of construction was in order and, as at Berkeley, the tumult provided faculty with an opportunity to increase its power in making administrative decisions.

Moreover, once they were in the buildings, the rebels lost interest in that issue. The only issue holding up an evacuation of the buildings after about the second day was amnesty. Kirk, of course, could not grant it outright. Some faculty spokesmen did secure confidential agreement to go easy on punishment (as the administration did with the blacks). But the rebels wanted a statement.

The principle at stake, they said, was the "rightness" of their action, its morality. "The seizure of the university," according to the noted anthropologist, Marvin Harris, in *The Nation,* "had been carried out in order to awaken the university community to the ethical blunders of the IDA affiliation and of the gymnasium site. Due to the authoritarian structure of the university, there were available no adequate democratic means of redress. Hence, amnesty rather than punishment was required since people should not be punished for bringing about changes which, as among the faculty, were widely regarded as necessary and just."

Or, as Mark Rudd put it:

> the granting of amnesty by the university was the recognition by the university that what we did had to be done—in other words, that we were right. We didn't think that we were wrong in doing what we had to do, and we didn't think that any change could ever come about within the university until the administration and the trustees realized that what they had been doing was wrong. Why should we be punished for doing what was right? We have not been told and we have been punished.

But surely the crowning touch was administered by Murray Rothbard, a right-winger turned Movement hanger-on. He concluded his thoughts on the incident in *The Libertarian* with, "Besides, Mr. Christian Conservative, what's wrong with mercy?"

This gracelessly put plea for patronization overlooked the fact that the students demanded amnesty *before* they surrendered. The analogy of a jealous husband phoning the judge to get a guarantee of commiseration before he split his wife's head open with a broadaxe is a bit crude, albeit difficult to resist. The New Left's concept of revolution was just as incredible. On the one hand they were red-hot revolutionaries. On the other, they were only doing what was right, and the fascist, racist, imperialistic, war-mongering university administration was expected to hang those epithets about itself. Perhaps Julie Patimkin was with Mark Rudd in the Low Library and helped him devise this principle? She would have been about the right age to be a graduate student in sociology and, like Mark, she hailed from just across the river in Jersey. Julie Patimkin was the little sister in Philip Roth's *Goodbye Columbus* who liked to compete in basketball contests as long as extra free throws were hers for the asking. It was "all nice for Julie" in the Patimkin household and she got used to it.

There was another aspect to the amnesty issue, probably more to the point but hardly more edifying. Stephen Spender thought that the most important reason the rebels refused to give in despite its obvious impossibility was that yielding would mean "casting their most audacious leaders to gnashing authorities." There was, in fact, some sentiment among the rank and file in Low Library for dropping the demand because it "was overshadowing all other issues and obstructing negotiations." But the leadership refused to budge and, shouting *Corragio!,* declared that "where you stood on amnesty defined your whole attitude to the university and the society it serves."

Dwight Macdonald once related an incident he witnessed in a New York Trotskyist cell during the thirties. A fire broke out in a wastebasket and the leaders of the unit rushed panic-striken through the room shouting, "Save the cadres! Save the cadres!" But whereas it took the specter of a fiery death to discredit the doughty Trotskyist devotion to solidarity, the SDSers were worried about their grade point averages. Mark Rudd explained: "We felt that they [the administrators] would use punishment to attempt to stop the political movement that we had built. They would throw the leaders out of school and put the rest on probation."

Building a new world where men and women would live in justice, peace, and love was one thing. But the hell with it if it meant having to sit through Freshman English and Biology I all over again. *Une révolution que demande que il'on se sacrifice....*

Whatever else may be "bugging" New Left rebels, an analyst wrote, "his own social status is high and secure. He presumes that expulsion from one college would involve no more than a transfer to another and a setback of maybe a semester. He presumes his parents will forgive him anything except dropping out altogether; as long as he is working toward a degree, he can call himself a Maoist and proclaim our society rotten, but he's preserving his options and he and his parents know it." Roar, Lion, Roar!

What Robert L. Jackson (a Yale man) wrote of Charles Reich's *Greening* is also appropriate to the so-called political movement and helps to clarify its silliness: "We are in the midst of middle-class utopia. The intermingling of the sensitive and banal is a disturbing feature in Reich's book, as it is in middle class culture.... Have we not really reached the heart of middle class utopia?! Revolution by all means, yes, but without self-sacrifice, without anxiety, without giving up the pleasures of self!"

In the wake of the Columbia occupation, according to the Educational Testing Services, more than three thousand incidents in emulation of it broke out on American campuses. The issues varied from the establishment of black studies programs to demands that deans of women end the war in Vietnam. For all the bloody end of the Columbia incident, spending all night in possession of a university building was fun. Moreover, not wishing to perpetrate a local riot, most university administrators capitulated to rebel demands. This was the year when "Mau-Mauing the Flak-Catchers" was at high tide.

It was also a year when SDS grew from about forty thousand members to as many as a hundred thousand, and when revolutionary dilettantism reached its peak. Abbie Hoffman announced his disillusionment with Cuba because, when he tuned in Radio Havana from his retreat in the Florida keys, he discovered "they play terrible crap music and you wonder why they don't play Country Joe and the Fish or the Beatles. That would be good propaganda."

It was also the year when, as never before and never again, infantile self-indulgent students were encouraged in their sentimentalism. A professor at American University, James H. Weaver, told of reading passages from *Capital* to his class, sections dealing with the living conditions of nineteenth-century English workers: nine- and ten-year-old children working from 3 A.M. until 11 P.M.; potteries in Staffordshire where seven-year-olds worked fifteen hours a day; match factories where children six years of age contracted lockjaw.

Did his lesson teach his students a sense of perspective about their own lives? Hardly. Although "tears were running down the cheeks of the students in the class," one radical lad restored everyone's perceptions to what counted, them and the present, by asking, "Don't the schools play that same role today?"

Did Professor Weaver, as an heir of the university tradition dating back to eleventh-century Bologna, straighten things out? Hardly. "I had to think about it but it seems that he is right—the modern equivalent of the nineteenth-century factory is the schoolroom."

How was such bourgeois sentimentalism confused with social revolution? Do zookeepers confuse gibbons with water buffalo when they make cage assignments? Do airline pilots sometimes absentmindedly climb aboard forklifts and call into the tower for clearance? Did American plumbers, for a decade, connect America's toilet drains with the ice makers in its refrigerators? Then how did so many of America's intellectuals come to the conclusion that the phenomenon that elevated Mark Rudd and Bernadine Dohrn to its leadership represented a revolutionary force in American life?

THE END OF SDS
Charisma.

Charisma was a fashionable word in 1969, and while few admitted liking Mark Rudd and Bernadine Dohrn as, for example, they loved Abbie Hoffman, almost everyone who knew Mark said he exuded an indefinable, compelling power, and Ms. Dohrn had extraordinary legs.

A well-turned leg is universally understood. Vice-President David Truman of Columbia explained what was meant about Rudd several months after the revolution. He was still nervous because Rudd was "totally unscrupulous and morally very dangerous. He is an extremely capable, ruthless, cold-blooded guy. He's a combination of a revolutionary and an adolescent having a temper tantrum.... It makes me uncomfortable to sit in the same room with him."

Roger Kahn saw Rudd's weaknesses: a flaccid "philosophy"; emotional immaturity; an unpleasant speaking voice (he was a whiner); no concept of the future; intellectual shallowness; irresponsibility; ruthless inconsideration for others, including his allies and supporters. But Kahn added that Rudd's "overwhelming strength" was that he knew "how to make his opposition cringe.... Rudd keeps people off-balance. He enjoys rattling them, the way good fighters do."

But Kahn was thinking of people like David Truman and poor Kirk, not the PLers within SDS who were gnashing their teeth not only at the ascendancy of Rudd, Dohrn, Jim Mellen (a rich Chicago boy who helped fund SDS), and other "crazies" within the organization but at the acceleration of student violence in late 1968 and early 1969. While the PLers criticized "adventurism," riots at virtually every major university and hundreds of minor anonymous places fed SDS's following.

In Madison, Wisconsin, SDSers "trashed" State Street, the principal business thoroughfare, apparently because the haberdashers and druggists who owned shops there had done so little to end the war in Vietnam. At Cornell University, in leafy Ithaca, New York, black students presented several demands since lost to history by marching into the administration building armed with rifles and festooned with bandoleros. (The press was, of course, notified in advance so that candid shots might be snapped.) At Berkeley, a battle over the People's Park, a parking lot site transformed into a playground by street people and reclaimed for the cars by force, filled the bracing Bay air with teargas and left a student, William Rector, apparently an innocent onlooker, dead from a police bullet. Hundreds of high schools closed down briefly because of pupil movements emulating SDS. (The SDS regulators countered PL's claim to represent the working class by sending organizers into "working class high schools" which were, of course, mostly middle-class high schools.) And, of course, the summer of 1968 was the summer of the Chicago demonstration.

The tumult was real although not, of course, largely SDS's doing. It was to prompt the new Nixon administration into a repressive campaign that, in the short run won it popularity but, eventually, led to an arrogance and paranoia that ended in the Watergate debacle. Among the SDS regulars, belief that the wave of confrontation signaled the imminent revolution led to a battle with PL that destroyed the organization.

At the meeting of SDS's National Council at Ann Arbor, Michigan, in December 1968, PL and SDS clashed on three issues. On racism, PL succeeded in putting across a resolution that declared racism a device of the ruling class to divide the workers. Racism was to be fought, in other words, because it was an impediment to class organization, not a real social division. The SDS regulars, with no alternative resolution but only the feeling that because white workers were racist they were the enemy, were defeated on the question.

On women's liberation, PL lost. Again, PL insisted that the woman question was a snare, that men and women of the working class should battle against the men and women of the ruling class. This argument was not convincing to the SDS women's caucus, made up of "ruling class" women as it was. They insisted that the war of all women against all men was revolutionary. With the women's movement only beginning (it is properly a subject for a history of the 1970s) and therefore riding the wave of novelty, the regulars won the day.

The third battle came over a document introduced by Mike Klonsky, "Revolutionary Youth Movement." Although opaque, its gist was that *youth* were, as young people, an oppressed group whom SDS should organize. As with the woman and black questions, the RYM proposal contradicted Progressive Labor's class program.

It passed, thereby giving the anti-PL faction a tag, "RYM," but the convention closed on an ominous note. During the closing ceremonies, "traditionally a time of merrymaking and song," according to Carl Davidson, the two factions hurled defiant chants at one another. We-the-People-of-this-Generation had come full circle back to the pep rally mentality that, in this selfsame town of Ann Arbor, Tom Hayden had tried to go beyond. The SDS regulars shouted,

> *Ho, Ho, Ho Chi Minh,*
> *Dare to Struggle, Dare to Win.*

The PLers responded with *"Mao, Mao, Tse-tung"* and *"Defeat SDS's Khruschev,"* waving Little Red Books like amulets stuffed with garlic. When the SDSers sang *"Solidarity Forever,"* the PLers chanted *"Defeat False Unity! Defeat False Unity!"*

THE LAST CONVENTION

In June 1969 SDS met in convention at Chicago's Coliseum. About 1,500 delegates gathered, of whom perhaps a third were PL stalwarts, a third committed to RYM, and a third, new and true SDSers, were committed to neither side. As nearly as can be told, both factions were in a defensive frame of mind at the start. PL feared expulsion and, converting SDSers regularly to its point of view monthly, wanted only to maintain its factional position within SDS. PLers believed history was on their side. The regulars, on the other hand, appear to have had no plans to expel the PLers. They were worried about a PL takeover and were determined merely to hold on to the national office. Mark Rudd, for instance, was planning to stand for election and seems to have been committed to unity and so was befuddled when the convention exploded.

However, two early minor ballots went against the regulars and sowed the seeds of panic in the breast of at least Bernadine Dohrn. First, the convention overruled a decision by the chair to charge a $25 registration fee of all journalists representing the capitalist press. A PL leader moved that such reporters not be admitted at all, and his motion carried. In principle, there was nothing in the decision that should have offended RYM. They, after all, preached the more uncompromising, confrontationalist line toward outsiders. But substance was of less importance by June 1969 than the contest with PL.

Then a PL delegate, Jeff Gordon, proposed that the workshop program be expanded. "Workshops" were the convention's afternoon business, small seminars for the purpose of discussing specific issues such as the woman question, racism, imperialism, and so on. The SDS administration had scheduled fewer than in previous years because it was in such small groups that well-prepared PLers shone, confuting New Leftist sentimentalists and winning converts from among the uncommitted. At Chicago, because the uncommitted third wanted workshops, PL won another victory.

PL narrowly lost a third tactical victory when the convention agreed to hear a speaker on China who had been condemned by Peking as a "deviant." But it was another speaker allied with the SDS faction who caused the final blowup.

Rufus "Chaka" Walls was the Minister of Information for the Illinois Black Panther Party. He never made it as big on the radical chic circuit as some of his brothers, charming white radical and liberal groups by calling them dirty names. But it was not for lack of craft. Chaka had his cordon of macho bodyguards in sunglasses and he knew all the lines. When were whites going to get tough like blacks? When were whites going to show that they were real revolutionaries?

If this made little sense after a year of bitter conflict and violence on whitey's campuses, Chaka soon demonstrated that fickle fashion had left him even farther behind. He had some understanding of the fact that his allies in the convention, RYM, were pro-women's liberation. Unfortunately, he did not know what women's liberation was. Walls announced that the Panthers supported the new wave. By that he meant, "We believe in freedom of love. We believe in pussy power."

The delegates gasped. While the PLers had quietly hissed Chaka's support of nationalist movements, they could not resist this gaffe. Chaka had unknowingly mocked the latest piety of the SDSers. In an ectastic turnaround, the PLers took up the chant the regulars employed when PLers said that sex was subordinate to class:

Fight Male Chauvinism!
Fight Male Chauvinism!

Chaka, of course, was dumbfounded. He muttered something along the lines that "we have some puritans in the crowd" and apparently calculated he could please the RYM cadre even more by saying, "Superman was a punk because he never even tried to fuck Lois Lane."

It is not recorded if Rufus "Chaka" Walls looked toward Bernadine Dohrn for a smile of approval. Nor is it known just how she responded in that historic moment. She should, of course, have mounted the podium immediately and denounced Walls with the invective of which she was a master. But black revolutionaries were still black, i.e., revolutionary, even when they subscribed to counterrevolutionary doctrine. It is a difficult concept perhaps best understood by recalling that the New Left's attitude toward blacks had, throughout the sixties, implicitly viewed them as children, abused children, but children nevertheless. The session ended in shouting matches both at the microphone and on the floor.

If white New Leftists never contradicted black militants, the blacks were not in the habit of confessing they had made a mistake. With no apologies for Chaka's unhappy remarks, the Panthers the next day, "after long study and investigation," called for SDS to repudiate PL's position on separatist movements. Again the convention deteriorated into name-calling and the chanting of slogans. Mark Rudd was on the podium trying to restore order when a livid Dohrn, breaking free of others trying to stop her, seized the microphone and told all who wished to consider the possibility of expelling PL to follow her into an adjoining room.

This caucus decided, after a long and stormy session, to do just that. SDS was dead, although both the caucus and the PL rump claimed, for a few months, to hold possession of the title. In fact, without the parent organization to raid and bicker with, PL soon deteriorated into another little island in the archipelago of American left-wing sects with its cruelest hours ahead (when the nation of revolutionary purity formed its friendship with the United States and built a Coca-Cola plant). Dohrn's SDS, on the other hand, transmogrified into the infamous Weatherman, named after a document that had been submitted to the Chicago convention, "You don't need a weatherman to know which way the wind blows," a line from a pop song of the sixties.

What is most remarkable is how quickly the membership of SDS disappeared. Throughout the sixties, the organization had maintained its position as the single most important organization of the Movement. During the tumult that characterized the universities during the 1968–1969 academic year, it grew to its largest size, one hundred thousand members according to SDS, seventy thousand according to the Associated Press. And yet, by New Year's Day, 1970, there was no SDS. If additional testimony to the Movement's nebulousness is required, this fact should fill the void.

What was left by 1970 was Weatherman, amounting to a couple of dozen well-to-do-kids who held a "War Council" in Flint, Michigan, in December 1969 and disappeared underground to topple the capitalist system through terroristic bombings, and a mood among America's students that was still aroused and angry but without organizational focus.

Weatherman was decimated by its own hands on March 6, 1970, when, in a bomb factory located in a Greenwich Village townhouse adjoining that of actor Dustin Hoffman, three Weatherpeople blew themselves to bits. In June Weatherman bombed police headquarters in New York, and, at the end of July, a branch of the Bank of America. By this time about thirty Weatherpeople, probably the whole organization, were underground under federal indictment for transporting explosives across state lines. On September 15, having communicated to the people that drugs, like dynamite, were revolutionary tools, Weatherman freed Timothy Leary from a minimum security prison in California. From Algeria, Tim announced his complete support of the revolution.

The bombings were exciting and Weatherman had plenty of fans among radicals on university campuses. Like the girl in Honolulu who envisioned the Newark riots as beautiful, like the people who cheer carnage in movies, it was fun to read about a romantic group of revolutionaries who were really doing something. But the mass movement came to an end in May 1970, at Kent State University in Ohio.

KENT STATE

On April 30, 1970, Richard M. Nixon announced that the United States was invading Cambodia, and he confirmed what was rumored but unconfirmed: the U.S. had been bombing Cambodia for over a year.

The reaction was immediate. More than five hundred universities were shut down by protest strikes, discreet administration orders, or both. Violence was common. According to Kirkpatrick Sale, there were 169 bombing incidents in the wake of Nixon's announcement.

On May 2, the ROTC building at Kent State was torched and the governor of Ohio ordered a National Guard unit to the campus. The hundred man detachment was, weirdly, a mirror image of Movement militants. They were dilettantes, weekend soldiers, poorly trained, undisciplined Ohio farmboys who knew what they did not like but little else. They disliked hippies, college kids they viewed as privileged and spoiled.

Shortly after noon on May 4, a small detachment of the Guard suddenly reversed an orderly march away from rock-throwing students, turned around, and fired. A subsequent investigations showed that twenty-eight of them had discharged their weapons.

The incident lasted less than a quarter of a minute. When it was over, four students were dead and nine were wounded. It would be ten years before the books were closed on the incident with the issuance of a statement of regret and the payment of damages to victims and the families of the dead four. In the meantime, novelist James Michener wrote one of several careful studies of the incident that found the action was entirely unnecessary. The soldiers were not threatened in any realistic way. The students were a hundred yards away and farther. There is an undercurrent in all of the books on Kent State, although it is never stated outright, that they were only fooling.

It may as well be said outright. They were fooling. When the news of Kent State reached other campuses, the immediate reaction was a day of mourning during which people apparently looked around and saw that the photographs of the Ohio campus depicted a place not unlike their own cozy greenswards. The lesson was unmistakable. It was no fun fooling around when the other side did not play fair. The lesson made imperfectly at Columbia was all too clear at Kent State. By the second day of the academic year that began in September 1970, professors and students alike were commenting on the entirely different atmosphere. The studied apolitical attitudes of the students were downright fiftyish. People who like to do such things proclaimed an era to be ended.

CHAPTER NINE

LA TRAHISON DES CLERCS

The subject of this book is foolery—the habit of fooling—of acting, as the dictionary has it, with a lack of understanding and reason, of acting in the absence of powers which, when developed, make for wisdom and intelligence. To look back on the troubles of the sixties as something other than this, as a chapter in the history of radical dissent, for instance, or as a struggle for justice and human dignity, is simply to demonstrate that foolery is still the way things are done in this country.

This is not to say that there was nothing "wrong" about the United States of the sixties, no objective realities over which to be angry or against which to rebel. Far from it. There were plenty. Indeed, the perceptions or, rather, the feelings of many of the New Leftists and Counterculture people that something was wrong, that life in the United States—in all highly integrated, modern societies—was often unjust and empty were usually on the mark. But a walk around the block, in 1980 or 1970 or 1960 or 1950, is enough to tell a person that. A cat in a corner knows that. A cat napping knows it.

The point is that the Movement never moved beyond that vague sense of ill-being, never responded to social evils with any more intelligence than a leaping cat. The Movement never seriously asked "what is to be done?"—let alone set about doing it. It merely did anything. The Movement only yowled and leapt.

In a way, along with its consecutive repudiations of ideology, the life of the intellect, and finally reason itself, this was because the Movement also repudiated history and what might be learned from the past. It was a more or less thoughtless philistinism (history was the tool of the establishment), comparable to Henry Ford's pronouncement that "history is bunk." Where Ford thought in terms of a technological progress unhindered by backward glances, the New Left substituted spontaneity and the Counterculture offered mystical intuition in place of historical knowledge. What was different about the sixties was that whereas Ford was vilified by American intellectuals for his blasphemous remark, the Movement militants were cheered on in their own. This is what is troubling about the sixties: not that children, ill-schooled and too numerous and too pampered for anyone's good, should have acted childishly, but that American intellectuals, the "intelligentsia," were in the forefront of the crowd that cheered them on. The kids were true to themselves. The intellectuals were traitors, betraying their social commission to think and to counsel according to reason and understanding.

HISTORY IS BUNK

There was a wall poster popular in the late 1960s which sold as well in the suburbs as in the Counterculture. Its legend, imprinted variously over polychromes of daisies, languid young nudes, and seascapes, read: "Today is the first day of the rest of your life." It is an appealing sentiment—innocent, heartening, and harmless. Firmly within the American traditions of perfectionism and "self-improvement," it reflects the "limited view of history" of young people generally which the Counterculture enhanced into the principle that they (and the world) were totally malleable, subject only to personal will and wish.

This personal perfectionism is most frequently associated with the antipolitical Counterculture. But by the end of the decade, the acts of the avowedly political New Left themselves became little more than "happenings." They were self-justifying, occasions of sensation without reference to serious external cause or to any conceivable consequences. Confrontation was its own reward; the nearest thing to an objective justification was the tenet that such confrontations "radicalized" those who took part in them.

The cross-fertilization of New Left and Counterculture had much to do with this development. From the latter the political Movement was infected with the ideal of self-fulfillment and the belief that "progress" was little more than an ancillary question of will and wish. Thus closely did the "revolutionaries" approach the gospel of Henry Ford. Indeed, inasmuch as the "irresponsibility" that characterized the actions of the 1960s was very much an irresponsibility to history, the Movement exceeded Ford. Nowhere was the automobile manufacturer so cynical as the person who coined the para-Stalinist women's liberation slogan, "We must invent a past adequate to our ambitions."

Still, this was not merely a late random development having its origins in the "Summer of Love." The antihistory of the end of the era was prefigured in the earliest stirrings of the Movement. It can be traced to three related characteristics of the early 1960s: the Movement's rejection of program in favor of an existential activism; the young militants' repudiation of the anticommunism traditional among liberals and radicals; and the attack on "objectivity" in journals like *Studies on the Left*. At the time they were promulgated, all three notions had considerable justification. In retrospect, their lessons grotesquely distorted by the Movement, all three contributed to the unhappy end to which the decade came.

OF PROGRAMS, COMMUNISTS, AND OBJECTIVITY

The New Left must find "premises that are not obsequious in the presence of the ghosts of the eighteenth and nineteenth centuries," leftist historian Gabriel Kolko wrote in 1966. Perhaps his admonishment was already superfluous, for the Movement had by then been acting for nearly five years without reference to radical ghosts or even to much knowledge of them.

The idea for program-through-action eliminated the need for study of past movements—their successes, failures, errors, and insights. Marxist historian Martin Duberman (also writing in 1966) placed the New Left in the anarchist tradition. But, he noted, "to judge from their formal writings, SNCC and SDS seem little aware of their anarchist forebears." Duberman

observed that the militants saw "almost nothing in the past—
and certainly not in the present—admirable enough to preserve." Although himself, like Kolko, a respected and accomplished historian, Duberman interpreted this as making SDS
and SNCC "genuinely revolutionary." Nor were these two
alone among intellectuals who, in their nonpolitical scholar-
ship, practiced the historical method. For a time, historian
Staughton Lynd redefined, tacitly writing off, the value of a
discipline his works had graced and credited.

The phenomenon of the "hangers-on," principally academics who quivered with excitement at the *audace* of their
students and rushed to join them in their vagaries, has been
discussed above. Specifically regarding history, two of the
most dependably truckling of the hangers-on formulated the
cult of the present when they wrote that "the old clichés cannot
be repeated ad infinitum under the rubric of 'history,' . . . new
angles of sight and new vocabularies are necessary if our
visions are to catch up with our realities." The past offered no
insight; it was only another agency of the enemy, "often
invoked in terms of customs, traditions, patriotism, history—
sometimes out of pure innocence and sometimes out of pure
malice by those who want to befog the contemporary scheme."
As if to leave no doubt as to their chic, the two Peter Pans
concluded by deploring "the scruffy spectacles of historians
who have only contempt for the contemporary scene."

This sort of approbation, voiced in conversation a
hundred thousand times by local youth-worshippers for every
time it appeared in print, inevitably had its effect in the New
Left belief that they were a unique generation, entirely free of a
past which was at best "irrelevant" and at worst a snare.
Activist Mark Gerzon, attempting to articulate for his generation, could write without detectable demurrer: "Because young
people are unrelated to the past, they are gaining a freedom of
action and thought that is the root of today's activism." Mario
Savio had told an interviewer in 1964 that the university
bureaucrat was "a historical" because be believed "that noth-

ing new happens." The New Left was to end up far more clearly antihistorical in the assumption that everything that happened (that they did, at any rate) was utterly new. This was a generation, it must be recalled, that believed it discovered sexual intercourse.

New Left antihistoricalism also owes something to its reaction to liberal and social-democratic anticommunism. The early New Left felt none of the disillusion with or bitterness toward Stalinist brutalities or American Communist obeisance to "the party line" that so permeated the noncommunist parts of the old. Paul Jacobs and Saul Landau, Old Leftists with an interest in the New, noted that leftist anticommunism was as "irrelevant" to "young, less-historical, less-educated radicals" as the communist prescriptions themselves. They sensed and (as something of anticommunists) disapproved of the nascent disregard for lessons of the past. The young radicals "think they are being asked to become ten or twenty years older than they are and to take an interest in battles that are still highly personal and carry emotional charges for the older generation but mean very little to them."

It is a confounding logical jump from the particular rejection of social democratic anticommunism to the general rejection of *all* lessons of radical history. Without falling back on the general unintelligence of the Movement, it can only be chronicled and not explained. It is neither more nor less comprehensible than the construction which New Leftists put on the radical commentaries on American historiography formulated in the early 1960s by historians centered around the University of Wisconsin and the radical review, *Studies on the Left*. While some writers like Gabriel Kolko called in effect for a complete break with the past, *Studies* policy more closely followed the attitude of its principal editor, James Weinstein. A committed scholar, Weinstein dedicated his research to examining America's radical history for clues to political success in the present. Looking back on *Studies'* early days, Weinstein and David Eakins characterized the journal's founders as sharing two convictions: "an awareness of the severe failure of the old left, and a commitment to participate in the development of a body of theory to stimulate the creation of a new revolutionary movement in the United States." They hoped to bring together radicals from all disciplines in their stridently cerebral purpose but, as the magazine developed, it became very largely an historical journal that conceived of history as the chief agency for analyzing contemporary society.

The source of Movement's antihistoricalism in this unlikely place lay in *Studies'* grievances against the historical profession. The journal saw historians as cowed by the McCarthyism of the 1950s or effectively befogged and co-opted by corporate liberalism and "the end of ideology." The editors denounced the contemporary historian as "taxonomist... pragmatic... archivist... specialized technician."

The indictment of the establishment historians was best developed by William Appleman Williams. It was he who zeroed in on the term "objectivity" most tellingly in a review of the work of another diplomatic historian, Henry F. May. Williams observed that May preferred the historical methodology of Leopold von Ranke and his refusal to pass judgment on the past to Lord Acton, whom May characterized as "a hanging judge." That is, for May, the task of the historian was to record and explain American foreign policy, not to judge it. The result of this, Williams pointed out, was not judgmental neutrality but, tacitly and implicitly, approbation. "If one is to term Lord Acton a hanging judge," Williams commented, "as May does, then it would seem both more accurate and in line with reporting what happened to call Ranke the acquitting judge."

Williams may be faulted for focusing on the term, "objectivity," but he could not be expected to have anticipated a tumultous movement which could not grasp irony but was perfectly capable of seizing on a single word on a printed page and spinning a fantasy based on its own nuances, rejecting not only the abuse of the term but its essential meaning as well. In fact, Williams and the radical editors of *Studies* were calling, merely, for criticism where it was due. Certainly they were not calling for a purpose-serving rewrite of the past in the manner of Soviet encyclopedists or in tune with the creative aspirations of the women's lib slogan. What they sought was a recognition by historians of the obligation to draw lessons from their research into the past. Paul Goodman frequently criticized the behavioral sciences for the same sort of "objectivity." Their "claim to moral and political neutrality becomes, in effect, a means of diverting attention from glaring social evils, and they are in fact used—or would be if they worked—for warfare and social engineering, manipulation of people for the political and economic purposes of the powers that be." The New Left jumped from this sensible critique of distortion in history for the sake of the *status quo* to the working principle that history was itself a fraud. Ironically, the Movement jumped further and therefore back to a similar employment of history as "a tool," precisely what Williams and Goodman wrote against. In the women's liberation slogan and the propagandist conception of black studies programs in the universities, history (and the behavioral sciences) were imputed value solely insofar as they were "relevant," that is, insofar as they served a "political" purpose.

Paul Goodman neatly characterized this development among his Movement friends when he observed that they "did not believe there was a nature of things." Goodman wrote that "they had learned so well that physical and sociological research is subsidized and conducted for the benefit of the ruling class and that they were doubtful that there was such a thing as simple truth. To be required to know something was a trap by which the young were put down and co-opted."

That a historical sense is vital to a revolutionary politics seems sufficiently rudimentary to warrant no belaboring here. As Kenneth Keniston wrote in his 1960 book, *The Uncommitted,* "the viability of a progressive view of time depends on the ability to maintain a sense of connection with the past and the future.... Without some ... sense of personal relatedness to the personal past, both individual and social history will be experienced as chaotic and disjointed and not progressive." But during the following decade, intellectuals like and including Keniston forgot their own better (and most fundamental) judgments apparently for no better reason than the excitement of it all.

A woeful ignorance of history was a predictable consequence of Movement antihistoricalism, but even here the militants exceeded all expectations. When individual writers did cite a historical analogy, their choice was inevitably absurd. (For example, an occasional writer identified the Movement with the Wobblies, a group with which, as radicals go, the Movement could not have had less in common.) More remarkable, to round out its cult of the moment, the New Left did not even know its own history beyond a day or two of personal past. A women's liberation document written in 1970 stated that "for years SDS had an anti-communist clause in its membership card." Actually, SDS was not a card-carrying membership organization to begin with. And, it came to exist as a substantial movement independent of the League for Industrial Democracy principally because of LID's anti-communism. From the day of its origin SDS was virtually dominated by its "anti-anti-communism," its signal break with the social democracy of the 1950s. Moreover, by 1970 this fact was chronicled not only in SDS documents but in a dozen books and, presumably, ten thousand memories. And yet, the "Bread and Roses Collective," former SDSers, did not know.

THE ANALOGY GAME

If the Movement scorned history and historians, the latter were more than generous in rooting out historical analogies of the Movement. These had very little in common. They wandered through all time and all over the map. But they shared one trait. The historians compared the turmoil of the

1960s to some portentous movements indeed. Charles E. Wyzanski, a federal judge, accounted the 1960s as comparable "only with what happened at the end of the eighteenth century, with the American and French revolutions; what happened in 1848, or nearly happened; what happened in 1917. We are in a great cataclysmic change, one of the most profound in world history, and lucky we are to live in this period."

In times as extravagant as the 1960s, a movement which styled itself "revolutionary" was destined to establish such a pedigree among elders sufficiently articulate to broadcast the idea. Psychologist Rollo May, for instance, delivered a series of lectures in 1970 and 1971 which focused on his time as one when an era was dying and a new one beginning. Unlike Wyzanski, who had an analogy on each fingertip and ended up devaluating them all, May could conceive of nothing so fundamentally significant in Western history since the break between the Middle Ages and the Renaissance. The medieval crisis as interpreted by Ortega y Gasset and Huizinga also appealed to an intelligent graduate student who corresponded with George Kennan. Michael Ticknor saw the decade as "a time of disorientation and extremism," comparable to the crisis of the Hellenistic world or the Middle Ages, a time "characterized by violence, by pessimism, by a breakdown of formerly held concepts of order" with men reacting "by forming mystic cults." The Canadian television figure, Pierre Berton, also looked for a comparable era of crisis, settling on the prewar twentieth century. "What we are watching," he wrote, "is what Barbara Tuchman, dealing with the century's first decade, has called 'the transfer of power.'" Although less cosmic than Wyzanski, May, and Ticknor, Berton joined them in adjudging New Left turbulence as the early stages of an apocalypse.

More cautious historians avoided comparing eras, especially when the exercise augured something like catastrophe. But few could resist setting the Movement beside historical movements that they better understood, the successful, and the merely curious. The Germanic barbarians were popular. The parallels with what are depicted as unwashed, unlettered, but intrinsically vital hordes swooping down on a decadent Rome was, of course, appealing. The recognition of the Counter-culture's debt to the beatniks of the 1950s, whom writer Lawrence Lipton characterized as "holy barbarians," a signal of "a change felt in the rhythm of events," may have played a part. The barbarians were the favorite analogy of Theodore Roszak, a professional historian, who published a book in 1969 that depicted the youths of the Counterculture (not exclusively or even primarily the "politically" active) as, like the barbarians in the ancient world, inchoate creators of a new, necessary, inevitable order.

Roszak's work in this instance is most notable for its sloppiness of analogies. At one point, he moved from the wrong side of the earthworks of Marcus Aurelius to "a stage comparable to the Chartist Phase of trade unionism in Great Britain, when the ideals and spirit of a labor movement had been formulated but had not reached anything like class-wide dimensions." Within three pages, it is backward again, this time to the early Christians:

> But then, all revolutionary changes are unthinkable
> until they happen . . . and then they are understood
> to be inevitable. Who, in Paul's time, could have
> anticipated what would come of the brazen hostility
> of a handful of scruffy malcontents? And what
> would the nascent Christian movement have looked
> like under the merciless floodlights of any then-
> existing mass media? Would it even have survived
> the saturation coverage?

Comparison of the "new revolutionaries" with early Christians was more popular than comparison of them with barbarians among the sympathizers of the Movement, perhaps because the image of renewal and redemption was more congenial to nervous middle-class sentiments than was Lombard rapine.

Roszak's more successful imitator as a book-length celebrator of Counterculture was Charles Reich (who called it Consciousness III). Reich used no historical analogies. His own sense and knowledge of history rivals that of his subjects in the depths of its ignorance. His book, *The Greening of America,* purports to be a history of consciousness but in fact makes negligible reference to historical reality. But Roszak's Christian analogy was widely picked up on by reviewers of Reich's book as well as other writers. Paul Goodman (who would do better), seemed to see the point in 1967 when he wrote using the device of a historian of 1984: "But it was not until the early '70s that humanists began to realize that society had indeed reverted to Byzantine or Late imperial times, and who therefore withdrew to save their souls."

Daniel Patrick Moynihan, never as sympathetic as Goodman was, looked to second-century Rome through spectacles by Gibbon. The analogy was the same. Like hippies and activists, he noted, the Christians were indeed bad citizens, intolerant, disobedient, secular, odd in dress and habits, avoiding service in the military.

The traditional conservative philosopher Russell Kirk was not disposed to accept Gibbon on the Christians or to sully the latter by any positive identification with the rebels of the sixties. But he liked the period. To him, the militants (especially those on college campuses) were Pelagians or, rather, victims of "America's Pelagian Heresy." The student rebels "feel (with reason)," Kirk wrote, "that the typical mass campus has lost its ethical purpose, intellectual relevance, and personal relationships: it has been perverted from its ends." Kirk sympathized with youth's boredom and ennui (if not with its "answers"). Following philosopher Ernest van den Haag, Kirk attributed the New Left to a sort of Pelagian idea that all men will eventually be saved with divine grace because of their essential human goodness. More important, Kirk saw the intimacy of the New Left's relationship to the larger society. "The average American in our century has come to believe that

all can be saved through educationism, without necessity for
thought."

There is a grab bag of miscellaneous, incidental analogies.
Some hostile commentators saw in the Movement's youth
worship, romanticism, pantheism, antirationalism, and (by
the late sixties) bullying, a reminiscence of the Nazis. One
notes, however, derogating the Movement a little more, that
"today's student romantics lack the toughness and insensitivity
to become genuine fascists." And historian Bertram Wyatt-
Brown, drawing in part upon Kenneth Keniston's psychological examinations of New Leftists in 1970, constructed an
interesting comparison of the abolitionists and the 1960s
militants. Wyatt-Brown was interested in personal motivation
and he observes: "'Righteousness fever' seems to strike like a
recurring illness at different times in American history. Two of
the most notable examples, though, are our present situation
and that of the 1830s. Like conditions do not always produce
similar consequences. Yet, one can discern a pattern of events
that link these two periods of moral outrage, alienation, and
romantic extravagance."

The most frequent historical references to the movement
(possibly excepting the early Christians) are Russian. Re-
examining the analogists, it is tempting to attribute the
fascination with the Russian parallel to the fact that, excepting
Kennan, all those who repair to Mother Russia for their
parallels were (1) generally unfriendly to the New Left and (2)
either social democrats or former communists and former
social-democrats with long habits of hostility to Russian
communism and, by extension, with a skepticism of political
things Russian. For that matter, Kennan's long association
with and expertise in Russian affairs left him with similar
attitudes.

Kennan looked further to the right for his precursors, to
the Russian Populists of the 1860s and 1870s. He developed
the well-documented fact of the New Leftists' middle- and
upper-middle-class background, and that they lived lives of

material comfort which they found vapid and unfulfilling. So, Kennan notes, as have others, they look beneath their social positions to find "real" life. "In its involvement with the civil rights movement in the South, and with efforts to relieve the plight of the Negro in the large urban centers, the radical student left is following a course that has strong parallels with that of the young Russian Populists . . ." Kennan observed, "It is not their own plight these people are concerned to alleviate." They "go to the people. *V Narod.*" And, he concluded, perhaps with the emergence of the Black Power movement in mind, they received few thanks from the objects of their attention.

I.F. Stone, Irving Howe, Irving Kristol, and Leo Rosten all pointed to the Russian *Narodniki.* Kristol, for instance, seconded Kennan's observation of the return-to-the-people syndrome and pointed out the terroristic end to which, in their frustration, the *Narodniki* came. Howe added an interesting angle when, for his Narodniks, he focused on the black activists.

> *This kind of young Negro militant, though not of course interested in any kind of individual terrorism, acts out of social motives somewhat like those of the late-nineteenth century Russian terrorists, who also tried to substitute their intransigent will for the sluggishness of history. And the consequences may be similar: the best cadres exhausted in isolation and defeat.*

The queerest of the analogies was the one implicit in the New Left slogans of the late 1960s which depicted the Movement as an anti-Fascist movement. The slogans were "pig fascism," "fascist state," "fascist this," "that," "whatever," and "Amerika." The New Left stands as "the resistance" in this situation, not quite able to grasp that there was no dissent possible, let alone uncountable Gestetner duplicators, in the Nazi world.

Sometimes foolish, sometimes insightful, none of the analogies quite serves the purpose of the device: to understand

something through comparing it with something better understood. The nearest to success—in finding an "equivalent" for
both the movement and the times—seems to be the era of the
Reformation. The educator Peter Marin used the Reformation in a 1969 essay but did little with it. Historian Richard
Hofstadter, writing in a news magazine symposium on the
moral crisis in America, carried it further. But Hofstadter's
error seems to be that, like Wyzanski and others, he saw the
1960s as a revolutionary period, as a time of great change or at
least of active destruction, as something of an apocalypse. Paul
Goodman avoids this unsubstantiated illusion, recognizing
that no Luther of the sixties had nailed anything like ninety-
five theses to a door. Goodman focused on 1510 for his 1970,
not 1517. No revolution had begun, for all the nonsensical
calamity-howling, "but the actual situation... *is* very like
1510, when Luther went to Rome, the eve of the Reformation."
The tumult of the 1960s was not so much a matter of
postrevolutionary Diggers and Levellers, familists and Adamites—it was nothing like it. "Everywhere there is protest,
conflict, disgust with the Establishment." But no revolution
had begun.

Goodman must unhesitatingly be set down as one of the
inspirers of the New Left. And he remained a supporter until
only a few months before the publication of his shattering and
effective (and virtually ignored) attack on the Movement, *The
New Reformation.* In this book, he explained his disillusionment with the Movement and with a great deal of New Left
psychology:

> *In moments of indignation and dissent in writing*
> Growing Up Absurd *and* Jeremy Owen, *during the
> Free Speech Movement and the draft Resistance,
> tax-refusal, and campaigning against the school
> establishment, I have in fact been inspired by
> Wyclif and Hus. I have been sickened by the whore
> of Babylon, and the haunting high horn in Men-
> delssohn's symphony saying* "ein feste burg" *has*

sounded to me like "the faint dawn bugle when the things fall of their own weight." In more sober moments, to be sure, I remember that Luther's and Cromwell's bullies were real bastards.

Goodman's analogy was the single best illumination of the New Left through the method of historical analogy and he drew the lines finely and complexly:

The dissenting seminarians of the Pacific School of Religion or of the Jewish Theological Seminary in New York do not intend to go off to primitive love feasts or back to Father Abraham, but to form their own free seminary; that is, they are Congregational- ists. Shaggy hippies are not nature children, as they claim, but self-conscious Adamites trying to natur- alize Sausalito and the East Village. Heads are Pentecostals. Those who spindle IBM cards and throw the Dean downstrairs are Iconoclasts. The critique of the Organization is strongly Jansenist. Those who want a say in the rules and curriculum mean to deny infant Baptism, like Petrotrusians. Radicals who live among the poor and try to politicize them are certainly intent on social change, but they are also trying to find themselves again, like the young nobles of the Waldenses and Lollards. The support of the black revolt is desperately like Anabaptism, but God grant that we can do better than the Peasants' War. The statement of a Cohn- Bendit . . . that the reason to be a revolutionary is because it is the best way of life at present, is unthinkable from either a political revolutionary or a man imbued with primitive religious faith, but it is hardcore self-conscious Protestantism.

Goodman's analogy is the most engaging because it is so comprehensive. But he achieves this by losing his focus. That is, he stays close to the Reformation period but has to flit to other centuries for his Jansenists and iconoclasts. An improvement retaining the comprehensiveness and his insights seems possible by repairing to another era of religious crisis. Goodman, Hofstadter, and others are correct in seeing the sixties as primarily a time of *religious* turmoil. But the appropriate board for the game is set a millennium before their reformation and five hundred miles south of Central Europe, in North Africa and the era of the young Augustine. To be more precise, the most useful analogical approach to the Movement is to compare the 1960s with the decade 490–500 A.D.

THE MOVEMENT
AND THE MANICHEES

North Africa in the fourth century was a once-prosperous provisioner of the Roman Empire already slipping into bad times. It was directly untouched by the ravages of war which were seen to touch the capital itself, but the province suffered from the inflation, the taxation, the impoverishment of the masses, and the avarice of the wealthy that cursed the whole imperial society. During the years when Augustine grew to maturity, these symptoms of decay were absolutely lost on the people of the time and most of all on the North Africans. Inscriptions on public buildings touted themes like "golden times are everywhere" and "the youthful vigor of the Roman name." A poet wrote that Rome "by living long has learnt to scorn finality." And the emperors, in classicist Peter Brown's fortunate phrase, "were acclaimed, with an enthusiasm that mounted with every disaster, as 'the Ever-Victorious,' 'the Restorers of the World.'"

During the 1950s, it was common for Jeremiahs of a fundamentalist Christian persuasion to compare symptoms of Roman decay (taken from Gibbon) with the munificent self-indulgence and immorality of their own times. It is unfortunate that this sort of thing went out of fashion so dramatically with the social chaos of the 1960s. For, forgetting the rather unworkable criteria of social moral standards, there is a delicious parallel between the American fifties, sixties, and seventies and the Roman North African world in which Augustine spent most of his life.

Just as the slothful fifties gave way to frantic political religiosity in the United States, North Africa in the late fourth century, "a stagnant and affluent backwater" dominated by blind burghers, became the scene for a plethora of religious sects, reacting not only against the deadness of official paganism but against an already highly formalized Christianity. The most important of these sects was that of the Manichees, than whom, according to Peter Brown, there was not "a more extreme group of men." They were "a small sect with a sinister reputation" with all the "aura of a secret society." Brown calls them the Bolsheviks of the fourth century but his brilliant history sometimes reads as if he were writing about the New Left and the Counterculture.

Like the sixties militants, the Manichees were obsessed with the problem of evil. And the first step to redemption was the realization that the individual was "accomplice," that he was himself part of the evil and could not begin to approach "freedom" until he knew his own soul. Of course, to the Manichees, evil resided in the flesh: the body was corrupt along with its sexuality, its passions and emotions. But the fact that the New Leftists and Counter-Cultists of the 1960s sought redemption through the very "half" of their nature that the Manichees abhorred seems rather an incidental reflection of the times than any distinguishing trait. More pertinent is the fact that the people of the Movement envisioned themselves dually, gnostically, and sought to expunge one half—their intellects, their "linear" habits of thought, their bourgeois racist-pig heritage—for what they called the politics of spontaneity, the confrontation of their felt purity with the evil of the system.

The spontaneity and antirationalism of the Manichees was curiously like that of the sixties dissidents. Conversion amounted to a cleansing, unthinking, total rejection "of ideas that cluttered up the religion of the conventional Christian" or, if you will, the conventional "straight." The exegesis and analysis that already characterized the theology of the Christians served at best to obscure a patently *simple* truth. The Manichee needed no study or direction; he could "grasp" the truth; his was a special insight like the insight attributed to "beautiful youth" in the 1960s by so many dozens of awed, jaded intellectuals. "Immediacy was what counted most" with the Manichees; "you don't need a Weatherman to know which way the wind is blowing."

Augustine had himself been a Manichee in his youth. Indeed, like the Movement Manicheanism is, for all its aging Norman O. Browns and William Kunstlers, an approach to the trying problem of evil well designed to appeal to adolescents. It was all very simple. The Manichees

> had claimed to offer absolute certainty, straight-forward and unambiguous to any rational man. The "wisdom" contained in their books described the exact reality of the universe: all a man need do, was to act in conformity with this knowledge. Thus, in supporting the Manichees so fervently, Augustine had been guilty of the crowning temerity described by Cicero: the hot-headed partisanship of a school-boy for a sect.

For Augustine, of course, Manicheanism was to be merely an adolescent "phase." Unlike most of his Manichean friends and most of the ill-educated and unthinking Movement radicals, Augustine was well schooled in the Platonism which demanded certain standards and discipline as a prerequisite to contemplation. When Augustine visited the Manichean guru, Faustus of Milevis, the enthusiastic acolyte came away downcast. "I found at once," he sniffed, "that the man was not learned in any of the liberal studies save literature, and not especially learned in that." To people indifferent to the authority of learning of their gurus, however, searching only for "an example" which amounted to approbation of the wants and whims of the disciples, Faustus remained eminent, and the 1960s produced a gaggle of them.

After Augustine began to drift away from this flaccid mysticism, but before he began the works that effectively demolished it, he retained a certain respect for spontaneous virtue which is reminiscent of the liberals of "radical chic" and the academics and journalists who did so much to encourage the Manichees of the 1960s. A friend, Alypius, recounted to Augustine the stories of the holy hermits of North Africa who had, with no previous indications, abandoned their "bourgeois" lives for retreats in the desert. Augustine sounds like nothing but the pathetic academics of the Charles Reich stripe who, having nothing better to offer, stood agog before the audacity of the youth they had helped to disorient. "I turned upon Alypius. My looks betrayed the commotion of my mind as I exclaimed: 'What is the matter with us? What is the meaning of this story? These men have none of our education, yet they stand up and storm the gates of heaven while we, for all our learning, lie here grovelling in this world of flesh and blood!'"

Fortunately for the future of Western learning (and the analogy of the moment), Augustine did not join St. Anthony in the desert but returned to North Africa and a life of the mind and reason. He soon left the Manichean formulas behind and in epistle, sermon, and disputation, disposed of their pretensions and left them philosophically bankrupt and dying by the time the lumbering establishment moved to suppress them by force. He attacked their simplistic concept of evil, and their *total* condemnation of the world, which doctrine, as Augustine showed, required them to trace it back to God himself, making Him the author of evil. Just as the New Leftists and Counter-Cultists of the 1960s eventually rejected the whole of Western civilization in their simple-minded inability or unwillingness to discriminate and think, the Manichees had ended up with such an untenable proposition. "If we are correct in believing that the present social order is systematically—not just occasionally—unjust, then we should be able to illustrate our belief by simply pointing to the facts of American life," said Mario Savio. If he can be sympathized with as a pioneer standing at the beginning of an epoch, what is to be said of pacifist Mitchell Goodman, writing at the end of the decade?

> *We live in confusion verging on chaos, in the midst of a process of change we barely understand. Only the young (and those who grow with them) begin to understand: they are native to a world in which there is no predictable future, in which governments offer control and terror in place of "the pursuit of happiness." A world in which war criminals are called leaders. They lie, day after day. Masses of men driven by greed and fear swallow the lies of those leaders and hate themselves for it, and turn on one another, seeking the "enemy" on whom they can vent their rage. There is no sense of shared interest, of shared belief. There is no center. The country falls apart. Men who prepare to commit the crimes of nuclear and germ war try to impose "law and order." They fail. The law is suspect and disorder is built into the system. The courts are revealed as agents of control and not justice. Capitalism shows itself as engaged in never-ending social and economic warfare. Profit is a form of theft. War profit is a form of murder. Land, air, water and people's minds are polluted for profit. Police take the law into their own hands, using terror to crush out a spirit that offends their own mechanical lives.*

And having denounced, having accused, having asked, having recognized evil like the Manichees did—the New Left believed it had said something. "This is the problem with which the

Manichees think they can sweep the board," Augustine wrote, "just by posing it—as if posing an awkward question meant knowing anything."

That was all the Movement ever did. Its immediate perceptions were often keen enough. The Movement perceived the corruptions, inequities, dehumanizations, the emptiness of life in the American empire. But the Movement never went beyond these perceptions to the realization that any prescription must be political. Rather, in a panic, they wrote off all. Mitchell Goodman's "insight" into American life, written in 1970, could have been and was written better and more eloquently ten years and more before. It amounted to little more than a recognition of the problem of evil. It marked absolutely no progress beyond what, in an otherwise supersonically moving time, had been described by radical social critics writing in obscure little journals like *Studies on the Left* before SDS was more than an idea. For that reason did the Movement, like Manicheanism, cease to exist so suddenly. Classicist Peter Brown succinctly summarized the denouement of the African sect:

> *The Manichees had avoided the tensions of growth on all levels. Morally, they claimed to do no more than "set free" the good part of themselves, by disassociating themselves from whatever conflicted with the comforting image of a fragment of tarnished perfection lodged within them. The Manichean discipline, therefore, was based on an exceedingly* simpliste *view of the way a man acts ... The complexity of doubt, of ignorance, deep-rooted tensions within the citadel of the will itself, are deliberately ignored in Manicheanism. With all their talk of "setting free," the Manichees had no room, in their religious language, for more subtle processes of growth, for "healing," for "renewal."*

THE TREASON OF
THE INTELLECTUALS

In the end, as in the beginning, it is unremarkable that an extrusion of "youth culture," an "adolescent politics" like the Movement, should evince this sort of flaw. But what does it say of American society that the Movement was indulged and pandered to by large segments of that society, and those segments among its best educated and most articulate?

The Movement never ceased to whine that it was ignored, misrepresented, vilified, and oppressed. The sad ironic fact is that, at its hottest, the Movement received a sympathetic hearing and response in many liberal and especially academic quarters, even as—especially as!—the Movement vilified its supporters. "Oh baby, *épater* me again, harder this time, tell me what a sterile impotent louse I am and how you are so tough and virile, how you're planning to murder me, *épater* me again, baby," Irving Howe had a composite hanger-on react to the Black Panthers. "We need people who are willing to accept our speaking invitations and still have the courage to come and call us fascist pigs to our face," said a composite liberal created by Eugene Genovese. Abbie Hoffman, who possessed the redeeming trait of always knowing pretty much what he was doing, mocked the curious phenomenon from the other side: "That's the nice thing about liberals, though, even though you tell 'em to fuck off, they'll still be around." It was hardly a decade which "neglected" its youth; on the contrary, the intellectuals, and much of the media as well, regarded the antics with amazing indulgence.

The youth worship of the postwar era has been discussed above. The reluctance to inhibit or discourage juvenile creativity and self-expression by criticism, even when criticism was sorely needed, helps to explain how "hanging on" developed. For, when enhanced by the intellectuals' disbelief in their own shibboleths, concern for youth became unqualified and sincere. Early skepticism was forgotten or repressed; the hangers-on were beset by the same demons as the young people and, lacking the latter's "exceedingly *simpliste* view of the way a man acts," retaining some flaccid grasp of "the complexity of doubt," "ignorance," and "deep-rooted tensions within the citadel of the will itself," they wholeheartedly embraced the gospel that youth represented the way, the truth, and the life.

"I can perceive in myself at this moment what I also see in the young," wrote Peter Marin, one of the most honest and seemly of the admirers of youth. "I am reluctant to deal in sequence with my ideas and experience, I am impatient with transition, the habitual ways of getting 'from here to there.' I think restlessly; my mind, like the minds of my students, works in flashes, in sudden perceptions and brief extended clusters of intuition and abstraction . . . There is still in me the ghost of an apocalyptic adolescent, and I am trying to move it a few steps toward the future." Unlike Marin, most hangers-on attempted to do no such thing. If it is true that a society's intellectuals are its dreamers, entrusted with the function of posing challenges for the future, of setting, consciously or unconsciously, social goals, then the cultural bankruptcy of the 1960s is brilliantly illustrated by the fact that society's dreamers deferred to and lionized in great numbers a group entirely incapable of serving that function.

A novel about the New Left, *Two, Three, Many More* by Nicholas von Hoffman, published in 1969, pungently described the older hanger-on of the Movement and the lack of substance that characterized his type. The character was Roysterman, the chaplain at a composite university.

> *He protested against the war, but wanted it to go on forever; he protested radical injustice, and was content to see it perpetuated. He lived not for the triumph of the revolution but for its permanent promulgation, camaraderie, the new man it made of him. He supported any cause that would spread revolt, defiance, disorganization, picked up and spread every possibility of disaster—atomic radia-*

tion, population explosion, famine—prayed that
every proposal for the solution of man's problems,
from vitamins to irrigation, would fail. He hated
computers out of fear they were as good as their
makers said they were. His God was held in being by
contention with evil.

A British journalist observed to administrators of the London
School of Economics that traits of adolescence are under-
standable in adolescents but harder to justify in adults. Even
harder, perhaps, in professional intellectuals. In fact, however,
what Roysterman represented as a type was the same adolescent confusion, negative reference, incapability of positing
concrete proposals, apocalyptic mentality, and impetuousness
which lay at the base of the New Left. Thus, the selfsame group
of educators and counselors whom society charged to preserve
and advance culture were, because of their disbelief in that
society and their bankruptcy of alternatives, the chief rooters
of the Movement.

The famous anthropologist Margaret Mead attempted
the most serious rationale for hanging-on. Her *Culture and
Commitment* was a sad work with which to cap a distinguished
career. In an effort to "get with it," to win approval from what
she remarkably calls "the articulate young rebels," Mead in
effect scrapped and repudiated the implications of much of her
life's work. "Concentration on particulars can only hinder the
search for an explanatory principle," wrote the lifelong student
of a dozen very particular cultures. The anthropologist of New
Guinea wrote that one must "strip the occurrences in each
country of their superficial, national, and immediately temporal aspects." Having thus conveniently whittled away
"superficialities" so that everything will fit the simplistic
schemes of her young idols, Mead was able to lump together
the Czech student movement, the movement for racial equality
in the United States, young Japanese nationalists, religious
hooliganism in Northern Ireland (presumably, youths com-

prising large parts of mobs on both sides, both Protestants and
Catholics), Rhodesian support of the racist regime, and Cuban
excesses. After all, "youthful activism is common to them all."
If one who was perhaps the nation's leading anthropologist
was capable of such nonsense in the cause of "catching up" to
her students, the widespread rush of lesser academic and
journalistic hacks to defer to their charges is less remarkable.

Having shed her personal taste, Mead proceeded to
construct "prefigurative," "co-figurative," and "post-figurative" categories for societies. Whereas in the past, Mead
suggested, there were always some elders who knew more than
any children, change was so rapid in the 1960s that "today
there are none." There are no guides. None, that is, except
among the young. Having exempted the young from the
"simplified linear sequences" on which she, among others, had
sadly wasted her life, Mead came up with a handy
rationalization of the superiority of Mark Rudd's and Bernadine Dohrn's insight into man over Plato's, Jesus's, Augustine's, Aquinas's, Calvin's, Descartes's, Hegel's, Marx's,
Comte's, and other pygmies'. What Mead did was to intel-
lectualize (linearly) the child-centered American society which
reached its zenith in the new middle class of the 1940s and
1950s and from which the scions of the Movement came. She
apparently took great pleasure in the fact that a group of her
nonlinear students told her, "You belong to us," but, being a
humble prefiguratist, replied, alas, no. Mead is the most direct
in calling for hanging-on as a rare privilege. The course for
adults in society, she noted, was to work humbly so that
"enough trust ... be reestablished ... that the elders will be
permitted to work with them [the youth] on the answers."

That American literati were so without a sense of their
own worth can be better understood in terms of the politics
which many thought that youth represented. Their paralysis
during the 1950s hung heavy on them. In 1952, symbolizing the
dilemma of the era, Norman Mailer and Dwight Macdonald
debated the question of "choosing" between the Soviet Union

and the United States. (It is another mark of the liberal paralysis that these two alternatives, defined by the cold war, were thus so easily accepted as exclusive.) Mailer "could not choose." Finding the Soviet Union abhorrent, he was also, he said, painfully cognizant of the "totalitarian fabric of American society." Seeming to disagree, Macdonald chose the West. Whatever its imperfections (which he had aciduously penned for a decade) the United States was preferable to Stalinism. In fact, there was no great difference between the debaters. Unchoosing, Mailer was, by the standards of the time, retiring from politics. But that was also Macdonald's elective. Although "choosing" the West, he abandoned his political interests for literary and film criticism "with the assumption of a negative attitude toward American society, its political machinery, and its intrinsically totalitarian structures."

It is important to note that both Mailer and Macdonald were politically reinvigorated by the Movement. Waspish about it but clearly in support, Mailer literally strung along at various New Left shindigs, joined direct action at the Pentagon in 1967, and wrote a great deal on the subject. Macdonald was less critical. He too participated in various marches and demonstrations and actually kept his peace at fund-raising affairs he sponsored for the Columbia revolutionaries in the company of such illuminati as Mark Rudd. He lauded Charles Reich's *Greening of America,* and he told an interviewer in 1971 that the Movement generation did "have a higher standard of morality and behavior than the old culture does."

The experience of the 1950s could not have better prepared—could not have more thoroughly exhausted—a generation of intellectuals for the abdication of their social role. A decade of suspension of thought (inexcusable, as the suspension of action was not) was too long a layoff to be easily reversed. Benjamin De Mott commented, "What a nine years it has been! What an unholy, inactive lot we were during that time. Bitter, cynical, indifferent, supine; momentous events proceeded without us, life ebbed and flowed in vast movements while we loafed on beaches and in television rooms. How sad for most of us, who rode out our nation's unconnection, remaining unconnected, solitary, alien, complacent."

It is a formidable string of adjectives and anyone with the patience and predilection to pile them up in a self-indictment was unlikely to criticize those who were "doing something," even when that something was "anything." On the contrary, such intellectuals were likely, as they did, to rush to the action and the new leaders in the hope of a smile or gesture, or at least a revision of the not-so-old saw (which was soon forthcoming): "Don't trust anyone over thirty who doesn't swing."

They swung, like longtime teetotalers into their cups at their grandchildren's wedding. Two professors from the City College of New York collected a packet of New Left writings and prefaced it with a three-page introduction which sums up to "Oh, Wow!" A journalist lamented the fact that weekend hippies in the Haight-Ashbury district were "diluting the spirit of the new life style." Warren Hinckle, a wealthy fop who attached himself to one or another New Left cause, coyly refused to condemn terrorism in an issue of his *Scanlan's Magazine,* responding cutely to coeditor Sidney Zion's criticism: "as for guerrillas? Personally, I think those I've met are all right, and I refuse to beat them up." The editor of a collection of absurdist Weatherman documents exulted over the bombing of New York City police headquarters that Weatherman "struck a forceful blow against the enemy and escaped unscathed." The *Saturday Review* was fawning over high school "liberation movements" as late as 1969. The compiler of a book of essays on Charles Reich's *Greening* (which collectively reduced the book to a ludicrous pile) nevertheless urged on his readers that like a scholastic proof for the existence of God, *The Greening of America* may not hold logically in all respects, "but it's nice to believe and it does wonders for the faith." Entrepreneurs like Ralph J. Gleason made a career of latching on to whatever was new and, unhappily in his case, suffered from an incredible string of mistiming, repeatedly grabbing hold of aspects of the Movement on the eve of their debacles and discrediting. Gleason was writing as if there were a monstrous seething New Left as late as December 1970, about eighteen months after it had effectively ceased to exist. *Anything* to share in the imagined vitality of the Movement! Even a critical sophisticated analyst like Benjamin De Mott, perturbed as he was by the phoniness of the tumult, wrote about the Columbia occupation: "But bless them, they did interrupt. Bless them for that. Against the enormous weight of habit, their own included, they set a strong shoulder, and shoved."

The intelligentsia's yearning for "life" surfaced even in *Time* magazine. Robert Hughes wrote an "essay" on "the Myth of the Motorcycle Hog," an initially intelligent little blurb that began by noting that only about three thousand of three million American motorcyslists were Hell's Angels types. He described the social advantages of motorcycles in terms of traffic, air pollution, and so on. But what was the real reason he rode a cycle?

> *Instead of insulating its owner like a car, a bike extends him into the environment, all senses alert. Everything that happens on the road and in the air, the inflections of road surface, the shuttle and weave of traffic, the opening and squeezing of space, the cold and heat, the stinks, perfumes, noises, and silences—the biker flows into it in a state of heightened consciousness that no driver with his windows and heater and radio will ever know. It is this total experience, not the fustian clichés about symbolic penises and deficient father figures that every amateur Freudian trots out when motorcycles are mentioned, that creates bikers.*

It was a long way from Henry Luce just as the academic hangers-on were a long way from former Columbia University president Nicholas Murray Butler. It was not a question of *healthy* social vision. It was a matter of *any* social vision. Luce and Butler were representatives of a value system that, however unjust, was solidly based and confident in itself. The intelligentsia of the sixties which pandered after illiterate political rebels, "groovy" inarticulate mystics, and morally superior motorcyclists and was an intelligentsia which represented a decaying order and which was not at all beyond it. Lacking confidence in their own roles, their heads could be turned by anything that moved. Inasmuch as a great deal moved in the 1960s, their heads spun until the last of their senses were shaken loose.

In 1967, sociologists Christopher Jencks and David Riesman wrote that the danger of the new phenomenon of hangers-on was that "they will... reinforce the incompetent amateurism and the self-indulgent or self-pitying protective cults by which young people so often counteract adult expectations." They prophesied well. At Columbia, students expanded the initial occupations on the counsel of "radical junior faculty members" who thought, not unjustifiably, that "a convincing show of strength at this point would probably be enough to swing the faculty over to supporting amnesty." To peruse a college library copy of worshipful books like Roszak's *Making of a Counter Culture* or Mead's *Culture and Commitment* which a few sixties students have previously checked out is to find sentences like "they are no longer bound by the simplified linear sequences dictated by the printed word" double underlined and marginally notated, "verry importent," as are many justifications, rationalizations, and benign imprimaturs of intellectual sloth or the moral superiority and expansive perspicacity of youth.

"They projected absurd hopes onto the young and then converted these hopes into fact," Nicholas von Hoffman wrote,

> *They wanted a change, immediate and drastic, so*
> *they vested this small band of youth with a prepos-*

terous power it never possessed. Some of the kids believed what they read and, together with the switched-on old folks from the mass media, the boys and girls fantasized they would overthrow one of the most stable societies the world has ever seen, overthrow a government nearly two hundred years old which commands a loyalty from its citizenry that is sometimes frightening and a military power that always is.

It is tragic that a great many children lost the opportunity to be socially useful human beings as a result of the troubled sixties. It is historically unforgivable that a generation of alleged adult intellectuals rooted them on. The phenomenon represented a *trahison des clercs,* an abdication of social responsibility the consequences of which can be known well only by later generations.

Such was the effect of the hangers-on on the Movement. The manifestations among themselves can be amusing. The hangers-on had by their own estimation nothing with which to counter Movement antics. They were, as Robert Brustein phrased it, genuinely "intimidated" by their *avant garde* and "deafened by the clamor of indiscriminate protest." Disbelieving in their own ideals and teachings, they dug for the genuine thought that *must* be in the Movement. We look "for poetry in the lyrics of folk songs and rock music; and for philosophy, we turn to those without the patience to think." The quest was impossible but many stayed tenaciously with it. Arthur Waskow, for instance, conceived of himself as a social *scientist* in the strident sense. His *From Race Riot to Sit In* purported to have delineated scientifically a pattern of behavior in American race relations. But, when faced with the fact that the loosest generosity of analysis could not derive a benefit from the Pentagon March of November 1967 in which he participated, Waskow refused to let go. There must have been something! "I don't know myself, yet, what that meaning was but I feel a need for not throwing away either side of what we did on the Mall."

Better minds than Waskow's refused to believe what good sense told them. Psychologist Kenneth Keniston noted in listening to taped interviews he made with a group of young radicals "a note of apology" in his, the interviewer's, voice: "I realized that I felt considerable admiration and some guilt; admiration of their single-minded dedication to a set of principles in which they firmly believed, guilt because I myself was not similarly involved."

Hangers-on like Keniston frequently made the leap. Unable to offer anything "better" to the Movement; they did not conclude that their own malaise reflected that of the radicals and, together, the decay of a liberal world view of which they both partook. They only flagellated themselves for their inaction, accepted the Movement's pure activism as somehow meaning something, and reserved judgment when they began to recognize the nonsense of it all. Keniston attempted to salvage a piece of salvation for himself by noting relative to his "guilt," that the young radicals did not necessarily "evoke admiration or guilt... avoidance or anger are equally possible reactions to it." Retaining enough sense to stop short of the heaven of the Movement with all the irresponsible behavior the beatific vision required, they invented a kind of purgatory for themselves, painful indeed but relieved by the knowledge that one believed and could expect someday to walk with the saints.

The perceptible result did not look unlike the "bunch of leaping, prancing, palsied, happy-slobber St. Bernards" that Tom Wolfe described. Rare was the personage thinking himself "liberal" or "progressive" who did not have a kind word for a gesture toward what "the kids" had taught them. A blue ribbon committee (the Magrath Committee) investigating student unrest at Brown University wrote in an interesting passage: "In our view, the concept of in loco parentis—if indeed it can be dignified by calling it a concept—is essentially irrelevant to the problems confronting Brown University."

The conclusion is indisputable: the principle of in loco parentis was clearly obsolete as a function of the American university. What bears noting is the aside, "if indeed it can be dignified by calling it a concept." It was totally gratuitous and graceless; a gaggle of distinguished educators and educated men picking up the Movement habit of writing off totally and for all historical time what they found to their distaste. To the Magrath Committee, in loco parentis was not a bad concept, an obsolete concept, a concept once useful and fitting the social mores of another time but disconsonant with the standards of the 1960s. No! It does not deserve consideration or dignity from a group of open-minded men grateful to "the kids" for their help in understanding. There is no history. A member the American Historical Association, writing on the pandering of the organization's leadership to a group of Young Turks who indicted the assemblage as accomplices in American imperialism and racism, characterized that leadership's attitudes acerbically but not inaccurately: The AHA's radicals must, according to the leadership, he wrote, "provide an example to those of us who lack their vision and altruism. Radicals must eschew the evils of our profession and resolutely refuse to join the rest of us as social-climbing, comfortable-living, drinking, seducing coeds, wasting long hours in boring research, and indulging ourselves with good books."

The Movement represented *life*. There was a broad skein of envy when older hangers-on mused on the subject. Hamalian and Karl seemed to say, you have got us, system; our virtue is long lost in a sea of creature comforts and compromise. You will never get them—our leaders. "Spontaneous, creative people cannot be shackled. To hear them speaking in their own unique voices is to hear them at the grass roots, so to speak, of their being. Genuineness is a key quality of the radical vision. Thus, for the radical it is important to allow the matter to acquire its own form if it will, not to superimpose authority on what may be a freely associative interim monologue." In other words, it may *seem* like nonsense but that is *our* fault. It is not surprising that, during the seventies, people like this turned to divorce and remarriage, jogging, a dizzying sequence of self-improvement programs, and a stomach-turning sequence of diets for their fulfillment.

The liberal pandering came just as suddenly as the Movement itself. After the free speech fight at Berkeley, public confession, penance, and worship became a faculty avocation. The director of the Chinese Studies Center confessed to neglecting students. The chairman of the sociology department expressed gratitude on behalf of the faculty for being reminded of the significance of freedom. A professor of English poetry referred to the "beautiful and strong Mario Savio," and an eclectically pious science department chairman concluded that Savio was a reincarnation of Jesus Christ. A professor of English at a New England college, Benjamin De Mott, a few years later aptly summed up what was expected of the academic who would win approval of his students:

> *Success and fame at last. I'm invited to speak at the annual meeting of "my" professional association— the Modern Language Association, membership ca. 28,000—on the subject of English Teaching, How to Improve. Do I know, without being told, what is wanted for this talk? I do indeed. Something about Relevance, assuredly. Something about Involving the Kids and Using the Media. A sample turned-on test question perhaps? (Joseph Andrews was the first Beatle. Discuss.)*

So uneasy were the intellectuals, so without confidence in their own knowledge that they fairly rushed to repudiate it. The sociologist Lewis Yablonsky was unable in several hundred pages to describe "the hippie philosophy," but, seemingly because some of its adherents were congenial and pleasant, he was sure it meant something profound. An unimaginative college administration (of the type clever New

Leftists made short work of) writes on one page how he yearned for an influx of military veteran students who would straighten everything, but on another page "salutes" the hippies "for their incessant efforts to recall a valuable lesson," crying out for "honesty in human relations, daring to attack phoniness, duplicity, and the dollar craze as murderers of friendship." Conservative Russell Kirk, amidst some shrewd criticisms, thanks the student militants for waking "us somewhat from the deep intellectual doze into which plump democracies periodically sink." Kirk had long before found the modern university abhorrent to his traditionalist, elitist concept of learning and had partly left it. He knew well enough that the student movement had no time for his visions either, but he celebrated their act of rebellion.

The rarities in the 1960s were the moss-backed president of Harvard, Nathan Pusey, who modestly suggested that this generation was not unique in human annals, and the small group of genuinely radical academics who frustratingly found themselves almost alone in attacking Movement stupidity while liberals and apolitical functionaries jostled one another in their frantic genuflections.

It could go to amusing extremes. Lewis Yablonsky, presumably a scholar of some sophistication, described a hippie ritual that used to be called, in less complicated days, "copping a feel," as if he were privileged to walk among such blessed souls:

> As we were settling into some discussion, another attractive girl entered the room. Gridley and the girl who had just arrived hugged each other ferociously. (I later observed this most loving greeting take place many times on my trip.) It was much more fervent and effusive than any greeting of affection given in the straight world. It involved a tight encirclement of each other—some swaying—searching smiling looks directly into the partner's eyes, and comments like "too much."

And a physician at Columbia University managed the penultimate leap when he came to the newspeak conclusion that the "straight" students were perverse. "The case could be made that if a male goes through four years of college on many campuses now, without the [marijuana] experience, this abstinence bespeaks a rigidity in his character structure and fear of his impulses that is hardly desirable." Once again the connection between sixties and seventies appears. By the late 1970s, one apologized in certain circles for not jogging, not being a woman, not being homosexual.

THE GREENING OF AMERICA

But the very ultimate leap was represented by Charles Reich's *The Greening of America*. The author was then forty-two years old and a professor at Yale. He was well-born and well educated at an eastern preparatory school, at Yale, and at the Yale School of Law. "Just like everyone else," Reich told an interviewer. A promising lawyer (he was a clerk to Supreme Court Justice William O. Douglas) Reich was a member of a prestigious law firm before he joined the faculty at Yale.

Reich was the tortured young bourgeois *par excellence*, a faddist who grasped at one consumer-society salvation after another, from jogging to food fetishes. In the summer of 1967, Reich lived in Berkeley and underwent the conversion to youth worship, returning to Yale to systematize his impressions of the "love generation" in *The Greening*, published in a well-edited abridgment in the *New Yorker* and, shortly thereafter, in book form.

Reich was tall, spare, and after his shriving, the very stereotype of the aging youth-worshipper, constantly in attendance on undergraduates and apparently comfortable in a new wardrobe of Levi's and bell-bottoms, ballooning mod shirts or slightly anachronistic turtleneck sweaters, love beads, and meticulously untrimmed coif, "coming on," as journalist Karl E. Meyer wrote, "Like the latest trendy Prof," with a "far out" grin midway between a baboon's and Meyer's "hip scoutmaster's."

"It's okay to hang around all the time with students, as Charley does," Yale colleague Robert Brustein said, "but this is the first time that anybody has ever tried to base an ideology on it." That is what Reich's *Greening* amounted to: an indiscriminate idealization and justification of the Counterculture which Reich made into his latest fad. Referring to Reich's consuming interest in haberdashery—like the most callow adolescent, clothing was of pivotal importance to Reich's notions—Gary Wills noted that Reich simultaneously promoted blue jeans (form-fitting, they expressed "the body") and bell-bottomed trousers (the flapping about the ankles symbolized—*was*—freedom) and gibed: "Tight or loose, you can't lose (with Reich) if you are a kid."

The Greening of America was a foolish thing. No society with a shred of substance would have read it as Malcolm Muggeridge implied when he called it "beyond criticism because one cannot criticize unresisting imbecility." Reich himself justified the crack when he refused to reply to three hundred pages of Carthaginian criticism by many of the nation's leading literati (only the ubiquitous Ralph J. Gleason and a semi-interested Dwight Macdonald, in an interview, seemed to approve wholeheartedly) by saying: "My present feeling is that nothing of any distinction has yet been written about my book...the good and thoughtful stuff is yet to come."

The appeal to "thought" was unsporting of one who was the season's top banana as natural man but, in fact, as a Counter-Cultist, Reich's feelings were apparently hurt because George Kennan, Herbert Marcuse, Tom Hayden, et al., did not let the *Greening* by with a mere "groovy." "If what I say in the book isn't so, it should be," Reich told a colleague, petulantly and more in character.

The book is not worth analysis, as Muggeridge said. Reich constructed three "Consciousnesses," I, II, and III, as explaining American development. Respectively, they were the nineteenth-century ethic of unbridled individualism bent on independence and accumulation and disregardful of society; the New Deal corporate ethic of conformism within an organization designed to serve organization ends; and the new consciousness, "Consciousness III," the sensual, liberated consciousness of the youth culture, which promised, from within, to win the society through conversion and create a new humane society.

There was little original in the book. Reich's "Consciousness I" was only a poorly understood presentation of the American liberal tradition. His indictment of "Consciousness II" (personally transcended by Reich only in 1967) was slipshod and impressionistic, little, if at all, familiar with the analyses of American corporate liberalism by scholars such as William A. Williams, Gabriel Kolko, and James Weinstein. And his "Consciousness III" was the articulation by a defter hand of the claims of personal salvation, moral superiority, and arrogance in style that the bourgeois youth among whom Reich plunged had been sporadically talking about through the 1960s. The book is of interest as a document of the times, as something of a *summa* of the pathos of the hanger-on, as an index of the arrogance and the bourgeois character of the Counter-Cultists. And, it is of interest for the attention given it; this silly little book is the illustration *ne plus ultra* of the decadence of American society by the end of the 1960s.

While it was torn to pieces by its reviewers, it was paid a great deal of attention in the process. The *New Yorker* devoted the superior part of an issue to it. The book's sales were rivaled in 1971 only by the novel that also rivals it for banality, Erich Segal's *Love Story*. The *New York Times* could not get off the subject and succeeded in promoting it into a major sensation and money-maker. Virtually every journal of importance solemnly reviewed it. Cocktail parties on New York's East Side and in a hundred provincial cultural centers were built around it. And even its most destructive critics thought it of great moment. Philip Nobile thought the *Greening* merited the labor of compiling its reviews into a book. He wrote, "Whether one likes the situation or not, Charles Reich has written a political/cultural platform with which all parties are forced to reckon."

Karl E. Meyer (a harsh critic) also suspected that "*The Greening of America* will color the thinking of a decade." That was, just as surely, incorrect. Reich's book and what the professor represented stood rather as codas to the phenomenon of "Consciousness III." Unlike John Hersey's *Hiroshima* and James Baldwin's *Fire Next Time,* to which the *New Yorker* thought it had a successor, *The Greening* was the end. George Kennan was closer to the truth than Meyer when he observed: "Could it be that Mr. Reich's teachings, heady as they seem, are six months out of date?"

The depths were profound when intelligent and respected intellectuals were obligated to discuss Reich's preoccupation with homogenized peanut butter as, to quote a critic, "the cruelest imposition of the Corporate State upon the young save premixed peanut-butter-and-jelly." (Reich had listed as sixth on a list of twenty powers of the corporate state "the power to require peanut-butter eaters to choose between homogenized or crunchy peanut butter and to prevent them from buying real peanut butter.") Most of the reviews gallantly neglected to focus on this profundity. Those who did used it for a joke while others, like sociologist Nathan Glazer, rushed to point out that, in point of fact, the corporate elite permitted the Cambridge Tea and Spice shop which he frequented to operate a machine which transformed fresh peanuts into peanut butter ("about as authentic a product as one could get") before the customer's very eyes; and the *New Yorker* editors perspicaciously excised it from their abridgment. The point is that the book rarely transcends this juvenile foolishness. No reviewer dared make a joke of the whole. And the *New Yorker* did not permit its presumed wincing over the passage to inspire any insights into the balance of the manuscript. Reviewers are and were expected to deal with what they are assigned and many of them genuinely saw Reich's prattle as dangerous and warranting serious criticism. The significant fact is that the nation's leading social commentators were reduced by 1971 to haggling over the revolutionary import of peanut butter and bell-bottom trousers. This is what the sixties meant.

Finally, of course, the liberal intellectuals' descent into miasma was arrested. (Reich's infantilia was, after all, almost universally ridiculed.) The promise of the presidential candidacies of Eugene McCarthy and Robert F. Kennedy in 1968 and of George McGovern in 1972, the shock of the massacres at Kent State and Jackson State, the simple exhaustion of directionless frenzy—the same forces that so suddenly extirpated the Movement—caused the intellectuals to back off from their excesses. Indeed, it needs to be remembered that while many were hangers-on, each new incident of Movement inanity sent more thoughtful supporters into criticism and opposition. Perhaps the Movement was dependent upon the rooting on of their elders in a way Margaret Mead's post-figurative doodling did not fathom, dependent in much the same way that the Black Power and Black is Beautiful movements were dependent upon their white auxiliaries? Certainly there is a chronological correlation in the decline of each.

In conclusion it is well to return briefly to the analogy of Augustine and the Manicheans. It is easy enough looking back over fifteen hundred years to recognize the heresy as a symptom of the dissolution of an archaic order. No one mistakes Faustus of Milevus as a voice of the future. Does the analogy tell us something as to the meaning of the troubles of the sixties? It is something of a consolation when reviewing the history of the American intellectuals in that decade that, for a time, even Augustine was taken in. In this, perhaps, the analogy of Manicheanism has a value beyond the shreds of world view it shared with the Movement. The Movement of the 1960s was also a symptom of social disintegration and not the hope of the future.

Paul Goodman was troubled by his Reformation analogy

because, while he could see "lots of troops," there was no Wyclif, Hus, or Luther to lead them. "But being myself an Erasmian skeptic," he added, "I probably wouldn't recognize them anyway." That is where, again, the analogy of Augustine and his times is more useful. No Wyclif, Hus, or Luther, Augustine was an observer and a draftsman during the 390s. Unlike the Reformation era when the turmoil and chaos followed "the beginning," Augustine's age was one when the chaos prefigured the end.

This, it seems, is a more appropriate reflection of the 1960s. From his study in the dusty, isolated little city of Hippo, Augustine witnessed and rejoiced in the disintegration of the old order of pagan, imperial Rome. But all around him he was beset by crazies. (North Africa even had its Weatherman—the Circumcellions, a sect which sanctified as worship their swooping down from the hills, pummeling, robbing, and killing the unshriven.) Augustine disposed of them, and the recantation of the New Left intellectuals in the late 1960s is reassuring in that light. But what Augustine also did was to construct, in *The City of God,* the rationale for a new society which was to provide an order for European civilization for a thousand years.

The 1960s, like the 390s, marked no era of revolution or reconstruction. The turmoil among the young people of the decade represented no incipient revolutionary force or "new culture" within the shell of the old. The Movement—the New Left and the Counterculture—was a symptom of the dissolution and obsolesence of an order as surely as was the ability of a supposedly vital nation to get involved in a destructive war and its inability to get out before it was nearly dead, as surely as was the esconcing in Washington of a crowd of corruptionists as vulgar and crude as any Anaheim used-car dealer. Augustine did not begin to write *The City of God* until 413. With the fantasies of the 1960s and 1970s at a finish, perhaps the next decade will produce something like a new Augustine. At least—and it must be accounted progress—the minions of the Movement are gone. They have shut their mouths for ten years now, either out of breath from jogging, out of fear of being caught, or because they have been too busy enjoying the good life of the American upper classes of which they were always a part.

CHAPTER TEN

WHATEVER HAPPENED TO....?

Fay Abraham was born in 1932, the daughter of a comfortably fixed chemical engineer and a "Jewish mother" so ambitious for her children she could have starred in a bad play. Fay's parents were politically conventional, apolitical in fact. But Fay, intense, intelligent, and erratically rebellious, attached herself to the number of liberal and leftish causes such as could be found with little effort where she grew up— Berkeley.

Fay had all "the advantages." She studied piano (debuting with the San Francisco Symphony Orchestra) and breezed through college and the University of Chicago Law School. At a meeting of the Lawyers Guild, an organization defined by McCarthyites as a "commie front," she met Marvin Stender and later married him.

Fay Stender was much too old to be a New Leftist. She was too smart and too well-educated to fall for Movement silliness. But thanks to a lifelong manic energy, which dazzled her friends, she overcame these handicaps.

Fay never gained the fame of many of the intellectuals of her age who latched onto sixties enthusiasms, but her life with the Movement and after exemplified what happened to many sixties people. With one exception. Fay Stender is not still around, seated in an Eames chair in the Berkeley hills with a book on *cuisine minceur* in her lap, looking back and laughing at those hazy, crazy revolutionary days. She is neither grinning her way superciliously through the 1980s like most of her old friends are nor spouting the banalities *du jour,* the shameless oppression of women, of whales, of gays—name a victim and let's feel great sorrow, publicly—periodically glancing up the street in search of the next guru and self-improvement gospel, and wasting the time of a great many people by telling them what they need to do, read, and think in order to be good persons. Fay would have fit snugly into this world. She would have loved roller skates. But she is dead. Indeed, she was one of the very few Movement luminaries to die a Movement death.

As in the movies, of course, Fay had only a supporting role. In 1960, with two children, Fay Stender went to work for the law firm of a real Movement star, Charles Garry. While still telling her friends and those who would phone her advertized number that breast-feeding was the key to human happiness, Fay rose to be one of Garry's chief research assistants in the case that made him famous, the defense of Black Panther Huey P. Newton. Manias often overlapped in Movement lives but not for long. Fay found something more meaningful than suckling brats. Assigned to interview Newton in jail, and to report on his doings to Garry, she fell in love. The conferences turned into little games of touching hands and knees when the guard yawned (perhaps itself providing an insight into why Movement legal argument was generally so shoddy).

But Fay had not so much fallen in love with the Minister of Defense as with falling in love and make-believe revolution. Through Newton, she heard of another prisoner, George Jackson, a slum-bred thug whose arrest record began with an assault charge when he was fifteen and culminated two years later with an indeterminate sentence for stealing seventy dollars with a gun.

The indeterminate sentence is one of the masterpieces of modern penology, a Chartres Cathedral of social science. When a convict is freed depends, in effect, on how much prison psychologists believe, according to the fad theory of the moment, he or she has become "a good person." Clever prisoners had little trouble divining the follies of unclever but earnest counselors, playing up to them, and often getting release or at least privileges behind bars. Briefly during the early 1970s, Fay specialized in winning the release of prisoners who had found meaning in their lives. "Time after time," her husband recalled, "she would get somebody paroled or moved from maximum security to the main line, and a month later he would be back."

George Jackson did not play the garden variety new-meaning-in-my-life dodge. He was known in California's tough Soledad Prison as "into everything... dope, booze, peddling ass—you name it." But like Eldridge Cleaver a few years before, Jackson discovered revolution. "Marxism is my hustle," he cracked to prison friends. Just as another lady lawyer found a Lenin to love in Eldridge Cleaver, and the girls of the Symbionese Liberation Army found Che Guevara in "Cinque," Fay (in the words of former convict John Irwin) "really had a strong belief that prisoners were going to be in the vanguard of the social revolution."

"Mostly women were doing the organizing," Irwin told Peter Collier and David Horowitz. "They had each picked their favorite Soledad Brother and were kind of oohing and aahing over them. I couldn't believe it." Irwin, a tough, prison-wise con who knew better and preserved a sense of personal dignity, noted that activists like Counselor Stender did not really believe in the existence of criminality. As Paul Goodman saw in his seminar students, there was no nature of things in her world.

Although thirty-eight years old in 1970, Fay Stender was in love again, at the frantic forty-five revolutions per minute of her girlhood. She labored tirelessly to create a vision of Jackson's "sacred victimization" among the remnants of the Movement and Radical Chic, a technique that had worked wonders in the Newton case. Only a person undisturbed by the objections of reason and common sense could have kept it up. But Fay raised a sizable purse for the Soledad Brothers, and her illusions were hardly rattled in August 1970 when Jackson's brother, Jonathan, kidnapped a judge, the district attorney, and three women jurors from a Marin County, California, courtroom. (Within minutes, four, including Jonathan, were dead in a shootout.)

Realities never diverted people like Fay Stender. Only the boredom that follows on all enthusiasms from sexual intercourse to rebirth in the Blood of the Lamb to a revolutionary new hemline one saw downtown could change their minds. During 1970, Fay quarreled with George about the disposition of the Soledad Brothers' fund. George wanted to use it to train a guerrilla army in the Santa Cruz mountains. (The cadres killed one another off before they needed to be suppressed. The issue over which they fought is unknown, but it was not likely a dispute over the implications of Engels' *Anti-Duhring*.) Fay wanted to use the money to continue the politico-legal campaign such as the one that put Huey Newton back on the streets.

A year later it was over. George Jackson got hold of a gun in Soledad. He already had a razor, and he slit the throats of three guards and two convicts before he was cut down by sharpshooters in a break across the yard.

By 1971, of course, the Movement was spent too. Fay was ready for something really new. After a brief factional struggle over a $30,000 grant and some electric typewriters, she discovered feminism and lesbianism. She also took up jogging and other methods of achieving physical and spiritual fullness. As she had said so many times before, during La Leche League days, during Huey P. Newton days, during Soledad Brother days, Fay told her friends, "I feel confident, capable, and happy." She broke up with Marvin Stender and found a red-haired girlfriend.

Fay Stenders are still walking around by the thousands, finding anew their confidence, capability, and happiness every Monday, Wednesday, and Friday, and telling everybody all about it. Fay is not. On May 29, 1979, an ex-convict named Edward Brooks broke into her house, tied up her girlfriend and son, forced her to sign a "confession" that she had betrayed the sainted Jackson, remembered to steal about fifty dollars from the kitchen, and shot her.

Fay was paralyzed and permanently incontinent. (Her principal anxiety, at age forty-seven was her loss of sexual functions.) Trying and failing to effect a reunion with her husband, she testified for the prosecution for the first time in her life in Brooks's trial, sounding for all the world like Leviticus or a Texas Baptist Republican who owned the patent on a disposable electric chair. Like those SDSers who held their convention in a black ghetto and, when they arrived, were scared to death by the sight of all those dusky revolutionaries on the same street, Fay learned that there were such things as criminals, even among oppressed groups, "the hard way."

"The hard way" is, of course, a marvelous teacher. Parents used to be relieved when their children touched the hot stove, "experienced" their burn, and vowed to be more prudent in the future. It used to be believed that the human mind was capable of abstracting from such homely events the application that not everything had to be tried in order to be believed. Either Fay Stender and many other sixties people never did touch that stove or they continued to touch it over and over. Fay was still trying out hot irons at forty-seven.

In May 1980, hiding out in Hong Kong for fear of retaliation by old comrades for her victimization of Brooks, she killed herself.

Fay's biographers, Collier and Horowitz, wrote of her "Tragic Odyssey." No. Tragedy is defined by those who still pause over their definitions as the fall of the great from heights, destroyed by mighty inimical forces because of a flaw in their own characters. Fay Stender was not great. She climbed no heights. To speak of a flaw in her character is absurd. She had no "character" but was only, like so many, an animate bundle of silly sentiments. The appropriate Greek adjective for people like Fay Stender was and remains *pathetic*.

For all the personal suffering and horrors of Fay's final year, her end, like her life, was ludicrous. It seems almost incidental, so similar is her tale to the stories of many

Movement personalities. And they have written up their post-sixties experiences in books with titles like *Growing (Up) at 37* and *Soon to Be a Major Motion Picture.*

The media have, of course, been delighted all around with the way things have turned out. Fay's story made for a tolerable tear-jerker, more chock-full of human interest than Steve McQueen wasting away in a Mexican cancer clinic. Then there were the "happy news" sorts of features such as *Time* magazine's four-column "American Scene" on another bit player of the sixties, Charles C. "Chip" Marshall III in April 1980, headed by a photo of "Chip" with his wife "at home on their houseboat." Chip is neatnik, beaming broadly like, well, a rich man's boy on a boat.

Chip's Movement career began as a teenage liberal at King's March on Washington in 1963. In 1968 he was a student organizer for SDS. At the end of 1969 he left SDS when it was taken over by Weatherman but, in reality, he differed little from the Dohrns and Rudds. Like them his radicalism offered nothing but hell-raising. During the spring of 1970 he led violent demonstrations against the University of Washington because Husky athletic teams competed against Mormon Brigham Young University. Chip called a rampage through eleven university buildings a "Revolution," presumably because on the day the Church of Jesus Christ of the Latter Day Saints elevated a Negro to the Mormon priesthood, all would be well with the world.

After another demonstration in Seattle, protesting the trial of the Chicago Seven, Chip was arrested as one of the "Seattle Eight" and indicted for conspiracy to damage the Federal Building in the City by the Sound. He spent eight months in prison on a contempt of court conviction. Like virtually every other New Leftist brought to trial, he spent no time in prison on other charges.

By 1980 Chip was directing a nine-hundred-acre project for a private housing development company (although he himself lived in "a pleasant houseboat"—none of your silly to-the-people for Chip). *Time* loved it, especially when Chip looked up appealingly from his "Rainier beer" in "Seattle's Red Robin Restaurant" and "firmly" intoned, "Liberal economics just doesn't work.... Self-reliance, productivity and independence are important.... Business interests me." Now there is how a chap named Chip ought to talk! Just like fellows with names like Jerry Rubin.

"Once you are a star actor," Marlon Brando once said, "people start asking you questions about politics, astronomy, archaeology and birth control." Once you have been a New Leftist, *People* magazine never stops doing it, even when you are a functionary in Seattle or a stockbroker on Wall Street.

THE FINANCIER
After Jerry Rubin shook off the numerous indictments and lower court convictions that vexed him during the late sixties, he settled briefly in New York City. In 1972 he moved to San Francisco ("I wanted to free myself from the tyranny of time, but in New York every second counts"). Having toppled one tyrant, Jerry turned on another. He moved back to New York. ("San Franciscans struck me as bland.")

Jerry suffered a series of personal crises. Fortunately, these occurred during the 1970s, a decade dedicated to retreading individuals. Jerry Rubin found a way—many ways—to put his life together. Not wishing to keep the paths of happiness to himself, he listed them: "In five years, from 1971 to 1975, I directly experienced est, Gestalt therapy, bioenergetics, Rolfing, massage, jogging, health foods, tai chi, Esalen, hypnotism, modern dance, meditation, Silva Mind Control, Arica, acupuncture, sex therapy, Reichian therapy, and More House."

Rubin calculated that all this would be of compelling interest to the people so he wrote it up in *Growing (Up) at 37.* But he miscalculated the book market. The middle classes of the seventies loved to talk about their personal experiences, and were a little less avid about sitting through the recitations of others. The books they bought, however, were not confessionals but manuals. With all those experiences to be had, who had time to read about others? The big nonfiction sellers of the decade dealt with happiness through diet, happiness through sex, happiness through one Hindu fakir or another, happiness through transactional analysis, happiness through positive thinking, happiness through ethnic identification, happiness through jogging, happiness through self-assertion, happiness through simply talking about oneself. Unfortunately for Jerry Rubin, the list did not include happiness through idolization of last decade's heroes.

Worse, and doubtless contributing to Rubin's personal crisis, he never really was a hero, a star, but only a sidekick. Poor Jerry Rubin, the eternal *schlemiel.* His whole life people noticed him and said, "What a bright fellow!" and "Isn't he clever!" and "Have you heard what that crazy Jerry has done now?" And every time there was someone to answer, "Yes, but so-and-so is so much brighter, cleverer, funnier. Have you heard what he's done?"

During the sixties, so-and-so was, of course, Abbie Hoffman, and he remained so during the seventies, even *in absentia!* His presence continued to loom over Jerry's head like the raincloud over the Al Capp cartoon character, Joe Bftsplk.

Abbie and Jerry were always described as partners, Hans and Fritz, Stan and Ollie, Bud and Lou, Mutt and Jeff. But Abbie was the one nobody could quite dislike, the cute, funny-looking one with the natural, mischievous smile while Jerry was not very attractive at all. Jerry dressed up in costume. Abbie could not get out of costume short of visiting a plastic surgeon.

"Judge Hoffman equals Adolf Hitler," Rubin shouted portentously at the Chicago Seven trial. "You're a disgrace to the Jews," Abbie quipped at the judge, puncturing half a dozen pieties in half a dozen words and confounding everyone. Abbie had fun. Poor Jerry really believed, and even Judge Hoffman saw the difference. When he handed out contempt citations he gave Abbie eight months and six days for twenty-four counts and Jerry twenty-five months and twenty-three days for fifteen counts. Abbie amused him. He simply did not like Jerry.

And then, in the seventies, while Jerry plodded the university lecture circuit, the one question inevitably asked him was "Where's Abbie Hoffman?" While he peddled books about his personal fulfillment, Abbie fascinated his audiences with burlesque articles from the underground.

Small wonder that, in the summer of 1980, Rubin announced that he was taking a job as a stockbroker on Wall Street. He still believed, of course. Just like his jogging, his new role had profound social import. He would use money to "do good." It must have been gratifying to make such a big splash—half a page in *Time*. But then, not a few months later, Abbie Hoffman resurfaced and got an interview with the television gossip investigator, Barbara Walters.

It is no fun to be a schlemiel in any decade.

THE FUGITIVE

Like Rubin, Abbie Hoffman had just about beaten his political raps when, in 1973, he was arrested in New York trying to peddle $36,000 worth of cocaine. At first, Abbie claimed he had been set up and framed by his enemies, standard operating procedure among children, businessmen, congressmen, and revolutionary persons. Had the evidence consisted of a Baggie full of marijuana, Hoffman might have aroused some sympathy. Not among his Counterculture constituents. Those "unread, unthoughtful, unworldly, pleasure-centered creatures who slithered about like beings in a garden," in Nicholas von Hoffman's phrase, had slithered to new leaves—but among people like von Hoffman, Abbie was the urbane liberals' favorite revolutionary, too. But $36,000 worth of cocaine! And not possession, but pushing!

The cops shrugged and held him six weeks in the Tombs. They had the goods and if there was no frame-up, there was a great deal of satisfaction that the cops' most skillful tormentor had slipped up.

Why was Abbie so stupid? Or was he so consummately the bourgeois that, knowing the police watched his every move, he still could not resist the quick killing of a dope deal? Was he so out of touch with the social realities about which he spoke so much that he failed to see that the fun was over? In his autobiography of 1980, *Soon to Be a Major Motion Picture,* Abbie took the same irrelevant, indignant-kid, moralistic line on the cocaine arrest that had accompanied him from hustling pool in Worcester through Mississippi through Chicago: "Probably everyone reading this book except my mother has snorted coke." Now, in 1980, "my old prosecutor works as a partner with one of my lawyers, defending folks busted for dope. Today in court he argues that coke is harmless."

When, in April 1981, Hoffman appealed for leniency on the charge, he sounded like no one as much as Richard M. Nixon who, when finally pinned down on Watergate, asked to be forgiven because he was truly sorry and promised to do better in the future. Abbie also found a compelling reason he should not be imprisoned: "I didn't have a good time underground." Was the difference between the vapidest Yippie teenager and arguably the most brilliant Movement leader really so small?

Perhaps the judge who sentenced Hoffman to three years in 1981 was unmoved because all evidence says Abbie had a wonderful time underground. He disappeared, went "swimming" in February 1974. He had his nose bobbed, his hair trimmed and dyed, and he grew a beard he cropped closely.

The details of his six-year odyssey are not completely clear, but the highlights are impressive. Even incognito Abbie hobnobbed with celebrities. He steamed frijoles and tortillas for John Erlichman in Santa Fe. He made a gastronomic grand tour of Europe and met Chef Paul Bocuse. He testified before a Senate committee as the spokesman for a citizens' group from upstate New York in opposition to an Army Corps of Engineers project to expand the St. Lawrence Seaway. He was photographed (as "Barry Freed") with Senator Daniel P. Moynihan and commended for his good citizenship by Governor Hugh Carey. He continued to write comical articles from underground under his real name.

By September 1980 Abbie had had enough. Perhaps Jerry's publicity splash irked him? Or the news that other New Left fugitives who came above ground were treated gently may have convinced him that all was forgiven? Or, Abbie had blown his cover to enough people in little Fineview, New York, that he knew it was soon a matter of either moving or setting up anew, no easy thing for a forty-four-year-old man, or the collar?

In any event, he came out of hiding and filed a plea of guilty to the cocaine charge. It was "an act of stupidity and an act of insanity." But Abbie was not yet prepared to admit it was the act of a *petit-bourgeois*. His hat-in-hand humility before the bar was echoed by pleas of fellow celebrities Norman Mailer, actor John Voight, Allen Ginsberg, Ramsey Clark, and Benjamin Spock, to no avail. He got three years although the judge, Brenda Soloff, conscious of being in the presence of the great, had the good taste to whisper her sentence apologetically. The next day, Hoffman announced to the press that he would ask for a pardon. It was Governor Carey's wedding week and Abbie confessed he had a deathly fear of anal rape. Jerry Rubin did not, as he might have, wire Abbie, "Do It!" But he had the last laugh at last. In the period between Hoffman's surrender and sentencing, he made himself available for the lecture circuit Rubin recently abandoned. His agent approached the trendy College of Marin in California and was turned down. "We don't take just anybody," said Sydney Goldstein, the administrator of public events.

There is no tragedy in this. But it would be callous not to pity Abbie Hoffman, a man who thought he was a big shot with the world on a string and discovered it was he who was dangling, society's plaything, something like a hula hoop: cheap, plastic, lots of fun for a while, easily discarded when it bores, and finally obvious for what it was when it is in the dump.

MORE FUGITIVES

Timothy Leary and Eldridge Cleaver also played exile for a time and then returned to show-biz careers. Leary got nowhere. Cleaver seemed to be on the verge of making it big on the Born-Again circuit when he blew everything in a pompous stoned interview with *New West* magazine.

Leary escaped from a minimum security prison with the help of Weatherman in 1970. He surfaced in Algeria where, for some reason, his Tune In, Etc., message failed to move hosts concerned with running a country. Under the kind of pressure which, perhaps, Arab states are best at exerting, he fled for a land more experienced in comforting dilettante expatriates, Switzerland. Although no one back home was particularly interested in hearing from the guru, Leary chafed under the Swiss requirement that refugees keep quiet. After a series of personal quarrels with old comrades-in-LSD, he returned to the United States and straightened out his legal problems. For a time he hosted a talk show for an Orange County radio station. It was a flop. Recently his personal library was auctioned in Los Angeles.

The Algerians were no happier with Cleaver. Like other Europeans, Asians, and Africans, they discovered that American revolutionaries were a lot more appealing when one knew little about them but their victimization. When Huey P. Newton (still very appealing in his remoteness) read Cleaver out of the Black Panther party, and the exile set up a "true" BPP, he lost favor with his hosts. He went to France and, in 1975, he returned to the United States to stand trial for a 1968 shootout with the police.

By this time Cleaver had produced another autobiographical book, *Soul on Fire*. His conversion to Born-Again

Christianity was what people who frequented diners used to call "a beaut." In Paris, holding a pistol to his head, he "looked up at the moon and saw... my former heroes paraded before my eyes.... Fidel Castro, Mao Tse-tung, Karl Marx, Frederick Engels, passing in review—each one appearing for a moment of time, and then dropping out of sight, like fallen heroes. Finally, at the end of the procession, in dazzling, shimmering light, the image of Jesus Christ appeared."

Whether it was because of this edifying transfiguration or as a result of an understanding with the authorities, Cleaver was treated gently in the courts. He was let off for an ambush and wounding of two policemen with five years' probation. He teamed up for a while on the Born-Again circuit with President Nixon's former hatchet man, Charles Colson, but soon alienated the Moral Majority folks either because of a project to market trousers with polyester codpieces or because of contacts with the Reverend Sun Myung Moon. Cleaver's pathetic weakness for playing the big shot sabotaged what might have been a very lucrative career in the Korean sect. While still associated with the Moonies he boasted to writer Kate Coleman that the Moonies "want any kind of zombie they can get." (It was to Coleman that Cleaver also admitted he had in fact ambushed the police in 1968.)

Cleaver no longer considered rape to be revolutionary, a practice that the proto-women's movement found so thrilling. However, unlike Jerry Rubin, he had not gone from one extreme to the other. He still kept his hand in as Coleman learned in 1980 when she asked to interview Cleaver's wife, Kathleen.

"She doesn't want to see you...."

"I don't understand. Why not?

"Her face is messed up."

"What do you mean? What happened?"

"I disciplined her."

In 1981, exploiting the revelation of the President of the Mormon Church's twelve apostles that blacks could become full members after all—enter the priesthood—he conformed to the teachings of Joseph Smith.*

When Bernadine Dohrn came above ground in December 1980, her face was not a bit messed up. She was thirty-eight years old, just a touch matronly as the mom of two children ought to be. But she was still a looker. She had been in hiding for more than ten years after charges of aggravated battery stemming from the "Days of Rage." Most of that time she lived with Bill Ayers, another Weatherman.

Still under indictment, Bernadine refused to speak with reporters, but Bill made a statement:

> *The nature of the system has not changed a bit in 10 years. It is a system built on genocide and slavery and oppression, a system that poisons the earth and cripples future generations for profit, plunders the land and labor of millions, institutionalizes violence against women, takes the world to the brink of nuclear disaster and is in a state of almost perpetual war.*

Ayers did not attribute the system with severely punishing the heirs of the chairmen of Consolidated Edison and their wives for little things like battery, so everything will probably be all right. Keep a close eye on the society pages for the next installment.

Another socialite Weatherwoman, Cathlyn Platt Wilkerson who surrendered to New York authorities in July 1980 to get three years for reckless homicide (the bomb explosion in her father's Greenwich Village townhouse), also got nine months in Illinois for the Days of Rage to be served

---

*In the same year the Mormons announced that blacks who became Latter Day Saints would no longer become "white and seemly" as a consequence of their conversion but "pure and seemly."

concurrently with the New York sentence. Like Dohrn, she is a mom. As of 1981 it was not known if her children will dawdle away her time in prison at the deer park where she grew up.

LAST HURRAHS

Mark Rudd emerged from the shadows at about the same time and was put on two years' probation for his lesser offenses. He took a job teaching at a technical school in Albuquerque. By the summer of 1981, the file on the sixties seemed to be ripe for closing. A few fugitives remained at large, among them Weatherperson Cathy Boudin, daughter of a successful liberal attorney. Some police suspected that, in league with the Black Liberation Army, the remnants of the Movement were responsible for occasional armed robberies in the Northeast. But the consensus was that a handful of ragtags who believed that simple crimes were somehow revolutionary did not appreciably affect the overall statistics with which police deal.

Then, on October 20, 1981, a Brink's armored truck was robbed outside Nyack, New York, with a savagery not usually associated with professional heist men. The thieves simply opened fire on the guards, killing one and wounding others. Two policemen died in a shootout during a botched getaway, but within a short time authorities had several suspects in custody and evidence that led them to hideouts in New York and New Jersey that contained among the furnishings a cache of weapons, explosives, heady revolutionary tracts, and the floor plans of some New York City police stations. Through fingerprints, they discovered that they had captured Ms. Boudin and several other sixties personalities. By the end of the month, among the Movement celebrities, only Marilyn Jean Buck remained at large. Symbolically, Buck was said to be the liaison between the white Weather Underground and the Black Liberation Army, remnants of the two organizations that were at the center of the Movement of the sixties: SDS and the Panthers. As with Dwight Macdonald's Albert Weisbord, the radicalism of the decade was compressed into a bouillon cube.

Writing in *The New York Times*, Tom Wicker asked,
"How much previous criminal activity not identified as terrorist in nature ... might now be traced to radical groups?" The
implication of the question is distressing, as if revolutionary
mutterings in sealed rooms at midnight by a couple of dozen
people change the character of cold-blooded murder and common thievery. The intellectual habits of the sixties die hard.
Unable to see the social inconsequence of the Movement when
it was big—hundreds of thousands of privileged kids making
mischief—Americans continued to delude themselves into
believing that the vicious actions of a few diehard sociopaths
meant something "political," something deserving portentous
analysis where, when a murder is just a murder and robbery
just a robbery, a yawning headline will do.

THE GRAYING OF
THE BLACK PANTHERS
Lest there be any lingering doubt about the truth of the adage
that blondes have more fun, the post-Panther careers of Huey
P. Newton and Bobby Seale pretty well wrap it up. Unlike the
vast majority of their former white allies in the New Left who
went back to the houseboats and comfortable incomes to
which they were destined, Newton reverted to what, in fact, he
always was, a black Pretty Boy Floyd destined to nothing but
trouble.

There were bright moments. When he was sprung from
prison on a technicality, he took up residence in a $600-a-
month apartment in Oakland. The source of the rent was never
disclosed. Some suggested radical chic patrons. Others wondered about rake-offs from the network of government- and
foundation-financed "social programs" the Panthers sponsored—breakfast programs and the like.

But no one ever made any formal accusations, for Huey
was still surrounded by a devoted claque of young toughs who
clung to Panther regalia and that good old sixties scowl.

Another highlight of Newton's career came in the late seventies when the University of California at Santa Cruz awarded him a Ph.D. in "the history of consciousness," a sixtyish discipline if there ever was one. It is difficult to say what Newton learned at UCSC. His dissertation was on the Panthers and he seems to have been in residence at the university rather little. That probably did not matter. It is difficult to say what anyone learned at UCSC during the sixties and seventies. Built in a magnificent mountain glade overlooking the Pacific, Santa Cruz was designed as a place of experiential education and staffed with Harvard and Yale Counterculture hangers-on. It was organized on the English college pattern and students did things such as, in medieval history courses, gamboling about the redwoods beating tambourines and singing madrigals. A Ph.D. from Santa Cruz was not quite the equivalent of those awarded by the Rhineland universities of the nineteenth century. But students had one hell of a parcel of experiences there.

During his student years, Dr. Newton was involved in one ugly legal scrape after another. Had he not been a celebrity, it is safe to say he would have been a long-termer in San Quentin long before May 1981 when, before the Supreme Court, his luck ran out.

On August 16, 1974, Newton was charged with pistol-whipping an Oakland tailor to whom he owed some money. The tailor declined to testify but, before that, police discovered two handguns in Newton's apartment and booked him because, as a convicted fellon, he was not allowed to possess them.

Curiously, Newton had a fair technical case. He argued that as his 1964 conviction had been overturned, he "did not and could not have known that he was an ex-felon." It was the sort of thing that would have worked in the sixties. Indeed, New Leftists beat dozens of raps on far less substantial technicalities. In the seventies, however, Newton was able only to put off the reckoning on appeal. But in October 1980 the California Supreme Court found against him and, in May 1981, the Warren Burger Supreme Court did the same.

Bobby Seale, always more appealing than Newton, more a victim than a victimizer, has had an end with which it is easier to sympathize. He managed to stay out of prison thanks to prosecutors' stupidity and, at the end, technical defenses. In 1972 he helped transform the Panthers into a para-welfare organization in which the worst abuses were about the same as in any bureaucracy: too much money devoted to pay the salaries of the social workers. To a large extent, of course, the Panthers were always a peripheral welfare agency, and Mau-Mauing the people with the grant money had been Bobby's forte. Freed of Newton's inanity, the group's evolution was not surprising.

In 1973 Seale ran for mayor of Oakland on a more-money liberal platform and almost won. The election went into a runoff between Seale and incumbent John Reading. Only then did Seale lose. In 1974 Seale resigned from the Panthers and floated. He tried the book route in 1978, publishing an autobiography, *A Lonely Rage*. But, as Jerry Rubin also discovered, there was no market for that sort of thing in the years of Me.

By 1980, Seale's only contact with old comrades was a personal friendship with Tom Hayden, although he spoke occasionally by phone with Jerry Rubin. Early in 1981 Seale said he was the head of a lobby called Advocates Scene Inc., designed to combat "all the things that Ronald Reagan is trying to do." Early 1981 was not an auspicious season for such lobbies, but Seale had another iron in the fire. He said he was hard at work on a cookbook called "Barbecuing with Bobby."

AND A CAST OF THOUSANDS
If all those thousands who rooted on Bobby Seale buy a copy, he may be fixed. Rennie Davis, Seale's co-conspirator in the Chicago Seven trial, will be able to afford one. He took a job

with the Guru Maharaj Ji, a seventies prophet of self-fulfillment who apparently preached little more than admiration of the Guru Maharaj Ji and made a decent living of it. From time to time, column fillers in the daily press noticed one-time revolutionaries in government jobs. They can afford a cookbook.

Charley Reich can afford one, for old time's sake. He resigned his law professorship and position as faculty moderator of the Yale University wrestling team in 1974. He moved to San Francisco, the scene of his inspiration for *The Greening of America.* What was deliciously *outré* in New Haven, however, turned no heads in Baghdad by the Bay. Reich was reduced to walking into Union Street boutiques and grinning, "Do you know who I am?"

Like Jerry Rubin, the philosopher of the Movement grew up at a most extraordinary time of life. After publishing *The Sorcerer of Bolinas Reef,* a tell-all autobiography that sold less well than Joan Crawford's daughter's, Reich told a reporter for *People* magazine that he had experienced heterosexual sex for the first time at forty-three years of age and wanted everyone to know that he "never had such moments of happiness.... I've so much catching up to do." Perhaps Reich thought that his readers might want to try out his discovery too? This was the man who, in 1970, was said to have given meaning to the Movement. His bed, the interviewer noted, was covered with stuffed animals.

The list could go on and on but must not. Landon Y. Jones has shown how the socially conscious baby boomers of the sixties turned, en masse, into the recreational consumers of the seventies. Whether they will, in the eighties, buy barbecue cookbooks in preference to roller skates and whatever is yet to come is for the future to decide. But let the list end with another of the Movement's saints, singer Joan Baez. Unlike other pacifists such as David Dellinger and Staughton Lynd who realized that having sanctioned Movement violence, they had little moral right to resume preaching pacifism during the seventies and faded into obscurity, Baez emerged regularly from her Carmel dacha to admonish the American people to be good like her and, by the way, to announce a former homosexual episode or something else of cosmic interest that had happened. At Christmastide 1980 she sang outside Notre Dame cathedral in Paris. During the spring of 1981 she was refused the right to offer concerts in several Third World nations. This had more to do with unacceptable political positions than the state of her art. The latter, however, might have served the purpose as well. One of Baez's first lyrics for the year 1981 included a couplet that rhymed Rose with nose, a reference to the film about a famous rock and roll cult figure and the white powder she snorted up the latter.

Cocaine! The revolution of the late 1970s. Yes, indeed. If Abbott Hoffman overstated it, as was his habit, when he named his mother as the only American who had not snorted cocaine as of the year of Our Lord 1980, recreational drug use among the trendy middle class was among the cultural legacies of the revolutionary drug use preached by the Movement. Abbie might also have pleaded for amnesty because he was a pioneer in the revolution that called for promiscuity without second thought and social censure, for that too was the American norm by 1981. Then there was the death of the crewcut. Abbie had a hand in that revolution. What self-respecting defense attorney or corporate executive of 1970 would have sported long hair? And the fact that men were afraid no longer to express their essences through the wearing of brightly-colored clothing and necklaces. Abbie the revolutionary was one of the first.

It was that kind of revolution, the sixties. Indeed, inasmuch as the coke and the joint-after-dinner set of the 1980s handles the coke spoon and roach clip with unself-conscious grace, as they used to handle barbecue forks, it might be said that the Movement's revolution is complete, something not even the Soviets claim to have managed. Movement Man (in the sense of Socialist Man) has become the American middle-class norm. In view of this profound transformation of consciousness, it is of scant importance that the America of the seventies has been compared to that of the fifties in its acquiescence in widespread poverty, racism, militarism, destruction of the environment, and consumer-crazy self-indulgence, that in 1980 American voters elected a president actually unabashed to state that his hero is Calvin Coolidge.

WHAT DID
THE MOVEMENT MEAN?

Are the vulgar narcissism of the seventies and a few new wrinkles in men's fashion all that the Movement accomplished? Pretty much so. In terms of real social change, its consequences were nil. And this should be no cause for so much as a twitch of the eyebrow, for the Movement was an expression of social lassitude and decay, not a radical protest, not radicalism.

Radicalism is not, as the Movement had it, anger, militance, stridency, a willingness to act. Radicalism is, as Daniel Boorstin points out, a movement of "specific content." Radicalism "involves affirmation." The Movement shunned both. "Content"—program—was a snare of the Establishment. So the Movement affirmed nothing but merely negated. The Movement was an ongoing protest, sometimes, especially among university students, against nothing in particular.

The conservative Boorstin is also correct when he states that "radicalism is an affirmation of community"; here, too, the Movement failed to come close. The New Leftists and Counterculture people talked community interminably. It was one of the catchwords of the era. But when they offered alternatives to such sense of community as exists in the United States, most explicitly with the Counterculture, they offered nothing but groups of people doing as they pleased. People "doing their own thing" may be called a community, just as anger may be called radicalism, and a pitchfork called a spade. But that does not make it so.

Likewise, the social movements of the seventies which were heirs of the New Left—women's liberation, gay liberation, ethnic lobbies—were anticommunitarian. They emphasized the divisions between some and others, denied bonds, and demanded of society and the public tough concessions, even privileges, on the grounds that they were not part of a community but interest groups in a marketplace in competition with others.

Boorstin listed a third element in his definition of radicalism: "Radicalism is a search for meaning. . . . When the true radical criticizes society he demands that the society justify itself according to some new measure of meaning." The New Left, as has been seen, never offered a new measure of meaning.

In the end, "radical" still means *root* and here is the crux of the matter. While individuals in the Movement did strive to find root causes, they never transcended the root assumptions on which the American order is based. Their rhetoric was extreme but never radical. The Black Panthers provided the most obvious example of this ambiguity. Bobby Seale spoke smartly of "the jive ass Constitution," but the gist of his complaint was that he was denied some of his rights under it. "Think about the phrase 'All Power to the People,'" a Panther newspaper read. "The founding fathers realized the beauty of the essence of those words and based the Constitution upon them. We must all realize their beauty and live to make them a reality in this country." The Panthers' understanding of constitutional origins aside, this was hardly radical, a demand that the society justify itself according to new principles.

When Jerry Rubin made the mistake of talking politics instead of fun, he was equally foolish. Seale recounted a jail cell conversation with Rubin in which the Yippie *franc tireur* observed "that the system needed an overhauling . . . some sort of socialistic system was going to have to be implemented to really begin to remove the oppressive social obstacles and social evils in the system."

> *Jerry told me he respected Jimmy Hoffa because Hoffa really fought for the workers to have a better life. Hoffa did a lot of things for the workers. I asked him if he thought Jimmy Hoffa was political enough to understand the need for a socialistic system. He said he didn't think that Hoffa was yet, but it would be very good if Hoffa would come around to the side of the masses of people and get the workers to understand that it is necessary to implement some kind of basic socialistic system here in America—for all the workers, both unemployed and employed.*

Alexander Hamilton and Jimmy Hoffa as revolutionary role models!

It bears repeating that this conversation took place in 1969 or 1970, with the decade over, the Movement in full flower, between two people considered by many, including a large contingent of American intellectuals, to be the men who were showing the way.

The early New Left was, of course, explicitly reformist. *Village Voice* editor Jack Newfield summed up the goal of pre-Carmichael SNCC as hoping "to weave the gold of Utopia from the straw of mid-century America." Indeed, SNCC was questing the American Dream, protesting only that blacks had been denied their right to it. Hardly revolutionary, the thrust of SNCC was the profoundest sort of conservatism, a program which called only for the fulfillment of the past. Howard Zinn, the obsequious chronicler of early SNCC, disingenuously provided a major documentation of the movement's non-radicalism not only in his book on the subject but in an essay purporting to demonstrate the Movement's "Marxian" character. The "concerns" of the New Left were, Zinn wrote, "poverty in the midst of wealth, sins committed against the Negro, limitations on free expression by Congressional Committees and public prosecutors, shameful behavior in foreign policy." This is a most remarkable catalog of concerns for a "radical" movement: two matters of moral sensibility, one violation of civil liberties, and one count of naughtiness. This was the sort of analysis which the New Left's gurus offered, helping to reinforce the schizophrenia of calling reformism radical simply because it became louder and louder.

Zinn's essay is also interesting because of his analysis of the Old Left (an analysis generally approved by the New). Developing his rationale for the New Left's rejection of ideology, Zinn notes that "the valuable contributions of the Old Left... came not out of its ideological fetishism but from the organization of the CIO, not from the analyses of Stalin's views on 'the national question' but from the fight for the Scottsboro boys, not from the labored rationales for dictatorship of the proletariat but from the sacrifices of the Abraham Lincoln Battalion." In other words, where the Old Left was right was in building a union within the Gompers tradition, in the defense of civil liberties, and in fighting for the survival of a bourgeois democracy. All were worthwhile, even noble causes. All were also causes in which liberals could and did join. Zinn and the New Left maintained that they were "not arguing against... long range principles" but, in fact, they ignored them and in doing so never escaped the straightest strictures of New Deal reformism.

Studies on the Left pleaded against this essential liberalism of the Movement in 1966 when it pointed out that organization of the poor did not and could not likely go beyond "standard demands of liberal pressure groups." It was a startling prediction of seventies "lib" groups. The peace movement's "repeated demonstrations," James Weinstein and Martin Sklar argued, in effect bolstered the system "by proving that it permits ritualistic dissent" and allowed demonstrators "to believe that they have discharged their responsibilities by publicly taking a stand." Harping on the central theme of *Studies* and its successor, *Socialist Revolution,* the article pointed out the need for "theoretical clarity about revolutionary politics in the United States." Weinstein and Sklar believed that the Movement was potentially radical but, if it continued to thrash around with liberal issues, it was "at, or . . . fast approaching" a severe crisis. It was a prescient piece. By 1966, the Movement's anti-ideological stance had indeed "worn thin" and lacking anything but frustrated liberal aims, it soon plummetted into the vapid fooling of Counterculture and the chaos of confrontation.

The black movement, in both integrationist and Black Power stages, was always *sui generis* within the New Left. The point is that this most patently liberal part of the Movement was not only regarded as radical by both white New Leftist and Establishment energy, the former saw it as the vanguard. Stokely Carmichael, lionized and self-conceived as a revolutionary, ended up the decade strutting about with an automatic pistol and self-designed military uniform on his wife's African estate. But his conception of Black Power at the peak of his notoriety was almost tediously within the American pluralist tradition. It was the press which distorted the slogan, Carmichael said, "Black power seems to be nothing more than black people coming together as a political, economic, and social force and forcing their representatives or electing their representatives to speak to their needs," in other words, interest group politics. And it never amounted to much more. At the universities and colleges the black student groups proved to be so unimaginatively unradical that the most they could think of demanding was, in the crassest terms, a piece of the action, a black studies department, so many black professors, a promotion for this black, tenure for that.

But it was all-pervasive as well in such seedbeds of the New Left as the Free Speech Movement. "We ask only a fair hearing in the open marketplace of ideas," read a document of

SLATE, the precursor of the Berkeley New Left, in 1958. The FSM never went far beyond this unconscious self-parody. The Movement was indeed popularly seen as a radical phenomenon. Paul Jacobs and Saul Landau, however, two of the most perceptive analysts of the early New Left, inadvertently revealed the fallacy of that notion when they wrote: "The FSM revolt against bureaucracy was a revolt against liberalism, against the rhetoric of freedom and democracy." They were correct on the second count; the focus of the attack was the *rhetoric* of liberalism, not its ideals. "Civil liberties and political freedoms which are constitutionally protected off campus must be equally protected on campus for all persons," ran a typical FSM document. And Mario Savio, in his eloquent "An End to History" speech, explicitly stated that the Movement's demands were firmly within conventional ideals.

> *The things we are asking for in our civil-rights protests have a deceptively quaint ring. We are asking for the due process of law. We are asking for our actions to be judged by committees of our peers. We are asking that regulations ought to be considered as arrived at legitimately only from the consensus of the governed. These phrases are all pretty old, but they are not being taken seriously in America today, nor are they being taken seriously on the Berkeley campus.*

Even when the *student* movement came in the late 1960s to demand restructuring of the universities so that students at least shared in their operations, the salient point seems to be not the absurdity of students deciding how they should be taught what they did not know but, rather, that their understanding of historic American political principles was sound enough. They wanted to apply these even to an institution which by its nature could not accommodate them.

The fact is that the New Left never transcended the liberal tradition. Eugene Genovese called the Movement people "liberals turned inside out," a movement based on "the ideology of the marketplace in violent caricature." One of the queerest commentaries on the New Left is that one of its best statements of principles was written by a group within the "ultra rightist" Young Americans for Freedom, a kind of coven of marketplace freaks. Karl Hess, a speechwriter for Senator Barry Goldwater, found little support within YAF for his ideas and subsequently emphasized his kinship with "the Movement." The point is that his philosophy was an outgrowth of his right-wing, classical liberal thought and that he ended up on the New Left. Murray Rothbard is another example of this. "Twenty years ago," Rothbard wrote in 1968:

> I was an extreme right-wing Republican, a young and lone "neanderthal" (as the liberals used to call us) who believed, as one friend pungently put it, that "Senator Taft had sold out to the socialists." Today, I am most likely to be called an extreme leftist.... And, yet, my basic political views have not changed by a single iota in these two decades.

It is an honest and, by implication, correct assessment of New Left philosophy. Rothbard was a classical liberal. This put him at hostile odds with Old Left collectivists and corporate liberal statists. For, essentially, the same reasons for which the Movement was to react: these were two among the many world views which prevented one from doing "his own thing."

> Our motto could be "Live and let live" [a New Leftist wrote] for among us no one tells anyone else how to live, or how to be accepted, or how to become a success; everyone is left on their own, to develop their own ideas of life and love.... After a long struggle with my fears, after facing up to myself, I am coming to understand that I have no one else to answer to for my life, that I can live as I want to, as a unique individual.

Or, as Jacobs and Landau observed of SDS, the organization "has several partially developed ideologies, but they converge around the importance of the individual and his ability to make meaningful decisions."

It is not a reprehensible ethic. It has been one of the glories of Western humanistic development for centuries. That is the point. In no significant way did the Movement offer a new, a radical version of human society, even in the sullied sense that the communists did.

Expressing mainstream ideals, the Movement was also the antithesis of social revolution in that it was the expression of an elite. The historian Genovese put this to the well-heeled conservative readers of the *National Review* when, at the end of 1970, the magazine invited him to comment on the dying phenomenon:

> *As for the hippies, the freaks, the Mother Fuckers and the several other exponents of "cultural revolution," these are the natural-born legitimate honest-to-goodness children of the pseudoconservative suburbanites of the 1950s. They are the problem children of the solid bourgeoisie and constitute a problem for the Left only because their antics are confused with left-wing politics by the working class and lower middle class of Middle America. Beyond that, they constitute an essentially apolitical excrescence of the world of indebted affluence—a collective withdrawal of that part of the middle class (and especially the upper middle class) which is superfluous to the task of preserving a middle-class social and economic order. One suspects that relatively they form no larger a percentage of bourgeois youth than criminals, lumpens and tragically broken souls have traditionally formed of working-class or poor-rural youth without anyone's bothering to notice. But these are the children of the people*

> *who own the country, and they do have the power to*
> *burn down a campus or two: they will therefore be*
> *noticed and even pampered—at least until the*
> *gentlemen of the ruling class are forced by con-*
> *sciousness of the responsibilities attendant upon*
> *their ownership of property and of the state to deal*
> *harshly with their own children.*

And nothing better illustrates the non radical character of the Movement than the fact that "the gentlemen of the ruling class" granted their children much of what they wanted and generously indulged them in all that they did until the activists of the confrontation period went, in parental words, "too far," and committed not political crimes but offenses against society such as no constructive radical or revolutionary could countenance.

Regimes uneasy about the preservation of the *status quo* (not to mention fascist pigs) do not indulge, let alone embrace, radical challenges. The governments of the United States during the 1880s, 1910s, and 1950s did not tolerate the anarchist, socialist, and communist movements of those periods even though they never managed a serious threat to established authority. The people who ran the country during those eras of red scare recognized that, in principle, potentially, they were faced with real enemies.

Not so during the sixties. The Movement was not suppressed as the Old Left was. The activists of the sixties were either accommodated because what they demanded required no radical change, or they were shrugged off with a chuckle and a patronizing pat on the head, as the 1880s shrugged off whole-grain food faddists; the 1910s, mah-jongg; and the 1950s, Bill Haley and the Comets. It is in a category with those trivia that the Movement belongs, not in the radical tradition.

The civil rights movement succeeded in overturning legal discrimination on the basis of race because integration represented no threat to the corporate system but, instead, the modification of an archaic, embarrassing, and—thanks to the civil rights movement—troublesome institution. HUAC was shushed at the beginning of the sixties and quietly let go before the seventies were fairly under way because it was no longer necessary and, again, troublesome. The Berkeley Free Speechers got their way, not William Knowland. The student movement generally was a glorious success. At the behest of students in search of relevance, courses in English composition and higher mathematics were dropped at hundreds of universities or, at least, made optional. What did they matter in an age when the computer and television made literacy in the work force unnecessary and even dangerous? If "the kids" chose to put some profound, self-serving construction on educational reforms that strengthened the established order, well, God bless them. Students at all but a few small private colleges accessible only to the monied were in effect told that they could define their course of study and take a degree in sitar stringing or vaginal self-examination for women if they chose to do so. To the extent that public higher education was a means of keeping unnecessary labor off the market and bureaucrats in well-paying jobs, it mattered little. The few crank professors who bemoaned the destruction of higher learning could be accommodated in the elite's private colleges or bought off with comfortable Great Society salaries.

To slough over into the seventies, it made no difference to the men who ran the corporations and bureaus whether they addressed their secretaries as Mrs., Miss, Ms., Toots, Babe, Kiddo, or, for that matter, should the radical feminists of the eighties find it appealing, Grand Duchperson. Indeed, it mattered not a whit that women, blacks, Chicanos, even homosexuals—not singly, as tokens, but in any numbers whatsoever—sat on every board of directors in the *Fortune* five hundred.

Father Marx observed somewhere that the Church of England would happily scrap thirty-eight of its thirty-nine Articles of Faith before it would consider parting with a thirty-ninth of its property. The Movement of the sixties never questioned Articles of Faith. It was content with assailing Articles of Style, and it called it a revolution. It was not. It was only troubles, easily ridden out. As Murray Kempton observed of faculty acquiescence in student-run black studies programs in American universities, people do not part easily with those things they value. That America fell over itself accommodating Movement demands tells the tale. Did Negroes (Stokely Carmichael, anyway) demand that they be called blacks? So be it. Would Mexican-Americans prefer to be Chicanos? Done. Women to be called Ms? Sho' enuff. The point is that the Movement made such frivolities not only the core of their programs but defined the same in terms for human dignity and radical social change. Small wonder the seventies lost sight of what small dignity there is in humanity.

Of course, not every New Left demand was met. The Black Power yokels who demanded Alabama, Mississippi, and Georgia for the purpose of establishing a separatist republic based on *limpieza de sangre* were not indulged. The antiwar protesters did not end the bloodletting in Vietnam; the antiwar movement was long dead when it finally ceased. The Panthers and Progressive Laborites and Weathermen said many nasty things about capitalism but the *Fortune* five hundred were not wrapped up and turned over to them.

But excepting the demand to end the war, no one, least of all the activists, took these protests seriously. The most indulgent parents eventually draw a line. Few American children are given horses for Christmas (although the proportion of child equestrians among the New Leftists was probably higher than the national average). Even at that, it was not on the basis of scrawling "palomino named Randy" on their Christmas lists that, in 1970, the Movement was ended in a bang of repression. The gentlemen of the ruling class dealt harshly with their children only when, with the horse not forthcoming, they set fire to the tree. And when they were punished for that, the reasonable demand for ending the war was heard no more.

To speak of the legal trials of Movement personalities and the police actions at Chicago and Columbia in 1968, and at Kent State in 1970 as political repression is not convincing. If most revolutions are violent, only a tiny proportion of all acts of violence are revolutionary and the Movement's actions are among the majority.

One way of looking at them is to ask what would have been different if Richard Daley's cops had not brutalized the antiwar demonstrators at the Democratic convention? At the most, another demonstration. And Daley got that anyway with the Days of Rage.

Surely it is not incumbent on a human being of rationalistic pretensions to consider the seizure of a few buildings at an Ivy League university, and the subsequent reclamation of them, to be an aborted—ruthlessly suppressed—social revolution. At the time, the Columbia incident was compared to the French student riots of 1968 that nearly toppled Charles de Gaulle's Fifth Republic. But those who did so were forced to overlook the fact that, in France, what shook de Gaulle, and then only momentarily, was not the Rudd-like ravings of Danny the Red Cohn-Bendit, but the simultaneous strike by tens of thousands of industrial workers. During the Columbia seizure, of course, not even the university custodial staff had a good word for the students.

It was a Christmas tree burning by children unable to comprehend that sixteen-hand thoroughbreds do not thrive on quarter-acre lots, that one of the ingredients of a revolution is the understanding of what one is fighting for—of having something to fight for. Ditto Kent State. The only difference in that sad incident was the fact that Mom and Dad got really ugly.

No New Leftist went to jail during the 1960s for unambiguously political reasons. In every one of the few arrests for which Movement leaders did more than a few weeks' time, they were found guilty of acts that would violate the criminal codes of Utopia and Erewhon. This in a country with a spotty record for justice in trying political dissidents.

The list of social radicals imprisoned and even executed in the United States for trumped-up crimes is a long one. The prosecution did not even try to connect the Haymarket anarchists with the bombing murder of policemen for which, ostensibly, they were tried. Everyone understood that the purpose of the prosecution was the disposal of anarchists. The evidence connecting Joe Hill and Sacco and Vanzetti with the crimes for which they were executed was at best faulty. The chronicle of framed American radicals is a long one. During the sixties, however, rather than suffering from judicial railroading, Movement personalities over and over escaped through loopholes generally thought to be stitched for the benefit of bankers and oilmen.

This was not repression such as revolution invites. It was indulgence of mischief which was, at most, troublesome to those who are in charge of the country. Indeed, for every Movement militant who did time for rioting, bombing, or peddling cocaine, a dozen, including many of the convicts, were lionized and richly rewarded for their hell-raising. The Watergate people were not the first to discover that disgrace was profitable. The New Leftists were. Except for pathetic Fay Stender and the alleged robbers of Brink's, from the Weather Underground, it is not easy to think of a single Movement personality who is not, at least potentially, better off in 1981 than he or she would have been had Dwight D. Eisenhower contrived to live to age ninety-five, repealed the Twenty-Second Amendment, and been reelected and reelected, carrying the world of the 1950s along with him, until the present hour.

Would Jerry Rubin have parlayed an M.A. in sociology into a nice Wall Street office? Would Eldridge Cleaver likely be out of prison? Would Abbie have a surefire show-biz career ahead of him? Would Bobby Seale be able to sell a cookbook to his uncle?

This is not to overlook the anonymous thousands of social and psychological wrecks from among the Movement rank-and-file, the ones at whom Landon Y. Jones was pointing

when he described the high suicide rate and other derange-
ments among the baby boomers. But Jones provides persuasive evidence that that generation's problems (of which
their Movement participation was one) owe more to their
numbers, the demographic trick played on them, than to
sixties mischief. Indeed, the blissful hedonism of seventies
America indicates that the "idealism" of the previous decade
left few jagged scars.

Nor is this to argue, as some have done, that the American
order that was so generous to its troublemakers is *ipso facto*
benign. It is to say, merely, that the Movement could be
indulged because it never mounted a challenge to the foundations of American society. It has been the genius of the ladies
and gentlemen of the ruling class that they have known what
counts even when their children and retainers do not.

THE END OF THE RADICALS
The Movement destroyed American radical dissent in several
ways. First of all, it associated the concept of "radical" with, in
the American mind, mere militance, hell-raising, long hair,
chanting "Om," marijuana, and other trivia. The activists liked
to fault the mass media for distorting their message, but it is
difficult to see it that way. Industrious reporters merely took
protesters at their word. If, during the seventies, "radical" and
"left" came to refer to where one stood on the correct form of
address for females, attitudes toward homosexuals, smoking
in public places, carnivorous diet, and the apportionment of
jobs according to sexual and racial criteria, that was because
no radical voices were raised in objection. Americans ceased to
know what "radical" meant. In 1980, the author of a textbook
history of the United States received a critique from a
respected academic who described it as conservative in its
interpretations.... The author is constantly hammering on
social class and property and downplays sex, sexual orientation, and life-styles.

The traditional Left that looked to social class and
property as the keys to understanding society was indeed

conservative by 1980, and not only conservative, but weaker than the Old Left had been in 1960. What happened to all those old stalwarts? Many of them, as has been seen, leapt fish-eyed and slavering into the Movement's train. They suspended their better judgment because "the kids" were doing "something." For fear that any criticism would isolate them from the young protesters (as indeed it would have), social critics of the Left who knew better kept their mouths shut, or even compromised their principles in the wan hope that, in time, the young militants would "grow up." For example, in 1969, with *Studies on the Left* in ruins (thanks largely to including New Leftists on the editorial board), James Weinstein founded a new journal, *Socialist Revolution*. It was designed to be the organ of a preparty organization, that is, the journal of groups of people determined to hammer out a program for future political action that would attract, so they assumed, the radically conscious young militants.

As in his *Studies* days, Weinstein, a historian of the old Socialist party of America, was committed to the policy of building a genuine political organization based on socialist principles. But he and the other serious radicals associated with *Socialist Revolution* failed to see, or refused to see, that if and when the New Leftists "grew up," they would not grow into radicalism but into some other therapeutic, self-fulfilling fad such as the seventies manufactured in profusion. Within three or four issues of its founding, *Socialist Revolution* was devoted overwhelmingly to pained reports of how difficult women were having it in Seattle and homosexuals in Butte. To read the journal was, understandably, to believe that socialism in the United States would arrive shortly after everyone felt more kindly about gays.

By 1980 American radicalism was weaker than it had been at any time during its history. Early in 1981 another journal, *Marxist Quarterly*, a serious scholarly publication, announced it was shutting down after publishing fewer than half a dozen numbers. *MQ* had no preparty ambitions, nor did it seek a mass audience. It was designed as a medium through which serious radical scholars could exchange the findings of their often abstruse research. In a way, *Marxist Quarterly* was designed to serve the purpose which, until it came to terms with the New Left, *Studies* had done. But in 1981 there were not enough people in the universities—in the universities, the citadel of the New Left, in the universities where, all agreed, the "radical" Movement triumphed!—to support . . . a little magazine. It is tough to read in a hot tub.

THE SOLE SURVIVING SON
So was there nothing there at all?

There was something. There was the perception that "something was wrong." The *Port Huron Statement*, practically the sole forward-looking, potentially revolutionary document of the decade which the Movement did pay homage to (if it did not read it), recognized that change must be based on some kind of program and a great deal of work. In the 1980s, ironically, its author, the Movement's founding father, Tom Hayden, qualifies as the Movement's sole surviving son. Let it pass, with this book, that in 1982 he is just about where he should have been in 1963, a year after Port Huron.

Like the others, Hayden lost his senses during the sixties. He supported the silly Panthers and, in 1968, convinced himself that Mark Rudd and the Columbia heirs and heiresses were involved in significant political action.

But there is a background hum in his Movement career, like one of those high-voltage buzzes that are audible at night in the countryside, that is absent in the doings of the Hoffmans, Rubins, Newtons, and Seales, the hint that he never quite believed.

By the summer of 1969, at least, as the Chicago Eight began to plan for their conspiracy trial, Hayden realized that the New Left had gone nowhere. Dozens of intellectuals were still preparing their glowing accounts of the Movement's future. Hayden's fellow defendants thought that their case might be the catalyst that precipitated the final days.

But Hayden did not. Although the eight, later seven, defendants maintained a public front of fraternal solidarity, rumors wafted out of their conferences that they were split. To Hoffman, Rubin, and generally a majority of the group, egged on by attorney Kunstler, the trial was a milestone in the history of revolution. The object was to stir up their circus-loving followers with a show of shows.

Hoffman and Rubin chronically thought that way, of course, and they were encouraged by Weatherman's Days of Rage. Hayden, on the other hand, had had enough of theater. He had begun the decade thinking the task was to build a political movement and he understood that none existed. As he saw it, the trial should be gotten over with. The government's case was legalistically weak. If Judge Julius Hoffman's decisions were predictable, the idea was to fight the indictments on technicalities and get back to real work ... to get to work that had been suspended since ERAP collapsed.

In the end, the Chicago Seven were sprung on just such legal technicalities as Hayden insisted on exploiting. However, by the time Tom Hayden was cleared of all criminal charges, the Movement was gone. There was no reservoir from which to draw political workers.

For a while, it looked as if Hayden was going the way of Cleaver and Leary. He married film actress Jane Fonda, to all appearances nothing but a show biz trendy, and settled on her southern California ranch. However, the Council of Economic Democracy (CED) the two founded was no pair of trousers with codpiece but a well-organized social-democratic machine within the California Democratic party. The CED organized where issues like nuclear power, environmental pollution, and California's traditionally rapacious real estate developers had stirred up substantial local protests. When the council won local victories, sometimes in alliance with conservation groups, sometimes as a political alliance, in the cities of Santa Monica, Berkeley, and Chico, Hayden won patronage and tacit support from the ambitious governor, Edmund G. Brown, Jr.

Hayden and Fonda remained capable of irrlevant frivolities on the woman and homosexual questions. Their opponents generally fastened on that and on Fonda as something on the scarlet side of the Whore of Babylon, in the ugly battles that characterized the CED's rise to prominence. But unlike during the late sixties, Hayden tried to stick to issues of substance. He is, in 1982, pretty much where he was in 1963, a wan believer in the possibility, desirability, and even the urgency of changing America. The sole surviving son may well wonder if the mischief of all of his old brothers and sisters has not made that impossible.

BIBLIOGRAPHY

I hope no readers take this for a complete or even "comprehensive" bibliography of the subject. The publishing industry was booming during the late sixties and early seventies and editors were no less infected with enthusiasm for the Movement than the academics who wrote for them with such abandon. When the complete bibliography is compiled, and it should be done, it will be book-length in itself. Below will be found the titles of only those books I found most illuminating in preparing *The Troubles*.

Albert, Michael. *What Is to Be Undone: A Modern Revolutionary Discussion of Classical Left Ideologies*. Boston: Sargent, 1974.

Ali, Tariq, ed. *The New Revolutionaries*. New York: Morrow, 1969.

Alinsky, Saul. *Reveille for Radicals*. New York: Vintage, 1969.

Altbach, Philip G. *Student Politics in America*. New York: McGraw-Hill, 1974.

————, and Robert S. Laufer, eds. *The New Pilgrims*. New York: McKay, 1972.

Anthony, Earl, *Picking Up the Gun: A Report on the Black Panthers*. New York: Dial, 1970.

Aptheker, Bettina. The Academic Rebellion in the United States. Secaucus, New Jersey: Citadel, 1972.

Aron, Raymond. *The Elusive Revolution: Anatomy of a Student Revolt*. New York: Praeger, 1969.

Avorn, Jerry L., and members of the staff of the Columbia *Daily Spectator*. *Up Against the Ivy Wall: A History of the Columbia Crisis*. New York: Atheneum, 1968.

Aya, Roderick, and Norman Miller, eds. *The New American Revolution*. New York: Free Press, 1971.

Bacciocco, Edward J., Jr. *The New Left in America: Reform to Revolution, 1956-1970.* Stanford, California: Hoover Institution Press, Stanford University, 1974.

Barbour, Floyd, ed. *Black Power Revolt.* Boston: Sargent, 1968.

Bell, Daniel, *The End of Ideology: On the Exhaustion of Political Ideas in the Fifties.* New York: Free Press, 1966.

Berger, Bennett M. *Looking for America: Essays on Youth, Suburbia, and Other American Obsessions,* Englewood Cliffs, N.J.: Prentice Hall, 1971.

Berger, Peter L. and Richard J. Newhaus, eds. *Movement and Revolution.* New York: Doubleday, 1970.

Berman, Ronald, *America in the Sixties,* New York: Free Press, 1968.

Boskin, Joseph and Robert Rosenstone, eds. *Seasons of Rebellion: Protest and Radicalism in Recent America.* New York: Holt, Rinehart and Winston, 1972.

Boyle, Kay. *The Long Walk at San Francisco State.* New York: Grove, 1970.

Breines, Paul, et al., eds. *Critical Interruptions: New Left Perspectives on Herbert Marcuse.* New York: Herder & Herder, 1970.

Brisbane, Robert H. *Black Activism: Racial Revolution in the United States, 1954-1970.* Valley Forge, Pennsylvania: Judson Press, 1974.

Brown, Peter. *Augustine of Hippo.* Berkeley: University of California Press, 1967.

Brustein, Robert. *Revolution as Theater: Notes on the New Radical Style.* New York: Liveright, 1971.

Canfield, Roger B. *Black Ghetto Riots and Campus Disorders: A Subcultural and Philosophical Study of Democratic Legitimacy and American Political Violence, 1964-1970.* San Francisco, California: R. & E. Research Associates, 1973.

Cantor, Milton. *The Divided Left: American Radicalism, 1900-1925.* New York: Hill and Wang, 1978.

Carden, Maren Lockwood. *The New Feminist Movement.* New York: Russell Sage, 1974.

Carmichael, Stokely. *Stokely Speaks.* New York: Random House, 1971.

————, *Testimony of Stokely Carmichael.* Committee on the Judiciary, U.S. Senate Subcommittee to Investigate the Administration of the Internal Security Act. Washington, D.C.: U.S. Government Printing Office, 1970.

————, and Charles V. Hamilton. *Black Power: The Politics of Liberation in America.* New York: Vintage, 1967.

Chester, Lewis, Godfrey Hodgson and Bruce Page. *An American Melodrama: The Presidential Campaign of 1968.* New York: Viking, 1969.

Cleaver, Eldridge. *Soul on Ice.* New York: Dell, 1969.

————, with Lee Lockwood. *Conversation with Eldridge Cleaver: Algiers.* New York: McGraw-Hill, 1970.

————, *Soul on Fire.* Waco, Texas: Word Books, 1978.

Clecak, Peter. *Radical Paradoxes, Dilemmas of the American Left: 1945-1970.* New York: Harper & Row, 1973.

Cohen, Jerry, and William S. Murphy. *Burn, Baby, Burn!* New York: Dutton, 1966.

Cohen, Michael, and Dennis Hale, eds. *The New Student Left.* Boston: Beacon Press, 1966.

Cohn-Bendit, Daniel, and Gabriel Cohn-Bendit. *Obsolete Communism: The Left-Wing Alternative.* New York: McGraw-Hill, 1968.

Conant, Ralph W. *The Prospects for Revolution: A Study of Riots, Civil Disobedience, and Insurrection in Contemporary America.* New York: Harper's Magazine Press in association with Harper & Row, 1971.

Conlin, Joseph R. *American Antiwar Movements.* Beverly Hills: Glencoe Press, 1968.

Cook, Bruce. *The Beat Generation.* New York: Scribners, 1971.

Cranston, Maurice, ed. *The New Left.* Freeport, New York: Liberty Press, 1971.

Davies, Peter. *The Truth About Kent State.* New York: Farrar, Straus & Giroux, 1973.

Dellinger, Dave. *More Power Than We Know: The People's Movement Toward Democracy.* New York: Doubleday, 1975.

Dickstein, Morris. *Gates of Eden: American Culture in the Sixties.* New York: Basic Books, 1977.

Divale, William Tulio. *I Lived Inside the Campus Revolution.* New York: Cowles, 1970.

Draper, Hal. *Berkeley: The New Student Revolt.* New York: Grove, 1965.

Draper, Theodore. *The Rediscovery of Black Nationalism.* New York: Viking, 1970.

Ehrlich, John, and Susan Ehrlich, eds. *Student Power, Participation and Revolution.* New York: Association Press, 1970.

Eichel, Lawrence E., *et al. The Harvard Strike.* Boston: Houghton Mifflin, 1970.

Eisen, Jonathan, ed. *The Age of Rock.* New York: Random House, 1969.

Epstein, Jason, *The Great Conspiracy Trial.* New York: Random House, 1970.

Ericson, Edward E., Jr. *Radicals in the University.* Stanford, California: Hoover Institution Press, 1975

Fager, Charles E. *Selma, 1965.* New York: Scribners, 1974.
————. *Uncertain Resurrection: The Poor People's Washington Campaign.* Grand Rapids: Eerdmans, 1969.

Fanon, Frantz. *The Wretched of the Earth.* New York: Grove, 1966.

Ferber, Michael, and Staughton Lynd. *The Resistance.* Boston: Beacon, 1971.

Feuer, Lewis, S. *The Conflict of Generations: The Character and Significance of Student Movements.* New York: Basic Books, 1969.

Fischer, George, ed. *The Revival of American Socialism: Selected Papers of the Socialist Scholars Conference.* New York: Oxford University Press, 1971.

Flacks, Richard. *Youth and Social Change.* Chicago: Markham, 1972.

Foner, Philip S., ed. *The Black Panthers Speak.* Philadelphia: Lippincott, 1970.

Forman, James. *The Making of Black Revolutionaries.* New York: Macmillan, 1972

Foster, Julian, and Durward Long. *Protest! Student Activism in America.* New York: Morrow, 1970.

Franklin, Howard Bruce. *From the Movement Toward Revolution.* New York: Van Nostrand-Reinhold, 1971.

Freeman, Jo. *The Politics of Women's Liberation.* New York: McKay, 1975.

Friedenberg, Edgar Z. *Coming of Age in America.* New York: Vintage, 1965.

————. *The Dignity of Youth and Other Atavisms.* New York: Vintage, 1965.

Garrow, David J. *Protest at Selma.* New Haven, Connecticut: Yale University Press, 1978.

Gerzon, Mark. *The Whole World Is Watching: A Young Man Looks at Youth's Dissent.* New York: The Viking Press, 1969.

Geschwender, James A., ed. *The Black Revolt.* Englewood Cliffs, New Jersey: Prentice-hall, 1971.

Ginsberg, Allen, *Howl and Other Poems.* San Francisco: City Lights, 1956.

Goldman, Arthur, *Freakshow.* New York: Atheneum, 1971.

Goldman, Eric. *The Tragedy of Lyndon Johnson.* New York: Knopf, 1968.

Good, Paul. *The Trouble I've Seen.* Washington, D.C.: Howard University Press, 1975.

Goodman, Mitchell. *The Movement Toward a New America: The Beginnings of a Long Revolution.* New York: Knopf, 1970.

Goodman, Paul. *Growing Up Absurd.* New York: Random House, 1956.

_____. *The New Reformation: Notes of a Neolithic Conservative.* New York: Random House, 1970.

_____. *Seeds of Liberation.* New York: Braziller, 1964.

_____. *Utopian Essays and Practical Proposals.* New York: Random House, 1964

Gornick, Vivian. *The Romance of American Communism.* New York: Basic Books, 1978.

Grant, Joanne. *Black Protest: History, Documents and Analysis.* New York: Fawcett, 1968.

Grier, William H., and Price M. Cobbs. *Black Rage.* New York: Basic Books, 1968.

Guerrilla Warfare Advocates in the United States. Report by the Committee on Un-American Activities, House of Representatives, Ninetieth Congress, Second Session. House Report No. 1351. Washington, D.C.: U.S. Government Printing Office, May 6, 1968.

Hamalian, Leo, and Frederick R. Karl, eds. *The Radical Vision: Essays for the Seventies.* New York: Crowell, 1970.

Hamilton, Charles V. *The Black Experience in American Politics.* New York: Putnam, 1973.

Harrington, Michael. *The Other America: Poverty in the United States.* New York: Macmillan, 1962.

_____. *Toward a Democratic Left: A Radical Program for a New Majority.* New York: Macmillan, 1968.

Hayden, Tom. *The American Future.* Berkeley: South End Press, 1980.

_____. *Rebellion and Repression.* Cleveland: World, 1969.

_____. *Trial.* New York: Holt, Rinehart and Winston, 1970.

Heath, Louis, ed. *The Black Panther Leaders Speak.* Metuchen: Scarecrow Press, 1976.

Hechinger, Grace and Fred. *Growing Up in America.* New York: McGraw-Hill, 1975.

Heirich, Max. *The Beginning: Berkeley 1964.* Columbia University Press, 1968.

Hodgson, Godfrey. *America in Our Time.* Garden City: Doubleday, 1976.

Hoffman, Abbie, *Revolution for the Hell of It.* New York: Dial, 1968.

————. *Soon to Be a Major Motion Picture.* New York: Putnam, 1980.

————. *Steal This Book.* New York: Pirate Editions, 1971.

————. *Woodstock Nation: a Talk-Rock Album.* New York: Vintage, 1969.

Hole, Judith, and Ellen Levine. *Rebirth of Feminism.* New York: Quadrangle, 1971.

Holt, Len. *The Summer That Didn't End.* New York: Morrow, 1965.

Horowitz, David. *Student.* New York: Ballantine, 1962.

Horowitz, Irving Louis. *Radicalism and the Revolt Against Reason.* 2nd edition. Carbondale: Southern Illinois University Press, 1968.

————. *The Struggle Is the Message: The Organization and Ideology of the Anti-War Movement.* Berkeley: The Glendessary Press, 1970.

Howe, Irving, ed. *Beyond the New Left.* New York: McCall, 1970.

————. *The Radical Papers,* Garden City, New York: Doubleday, 1966.

————, and Lewis Coser. *The American Communist Party: A Critical History.* Boston: Beacon, 1957.

Huie, William Bradford. *3 Lives for Mississippi.* New York: New American Library, 1968.

Jacobs, Harold, ed. *Weathermen.* Berkeley: Ramparts Press, 1970.

Jacobs, Paul. *Prelude to Riot.* New York: Random House, 1967.

————, and Saul Landau, eds. *The New Radicals,* New York: Vintage, 1966.

Johnson, Chalmers. *Revolutionary Change.* Boston: Little, Brown, 1967.

Jones, Landon Y. *Great Expectations: America and the Baby Boom Generation.* New York: Coward McCann, 1980.

Kahn, Roger. *The Battle for Morningside Heights.* New York: Morrow, 1970.

Katope, Christopher G., and Paul G. Zolbrod. *Beyond Berkeley.* Cleveland: World, 1966.

Kaufman, Arnold S. *The Radical Liberal: The New Politics, Theory and Practice.* New York: Simon & Schuster, 1970.

Kelman, Steven. *Push Comes to Shove: The Escalation of Student Protest.* Boston: Houghton Mifflin, 1970.

Keniston, Kenneth. *The Uncommitted: Alienated Youth in American Society.* New York: Harcourt, 1965.

_____. *Young Radicals: Notes on Committed Youth.* New York: Harcourt, 1968.

_____. *Youth and Dissent: The Rise of a New Opposition.* New York: Harcourt, 1971.

Kennan, George F. *Democracy and the Student Left.* Boston: Atlantic Monthly Press, 1968.

Kerr, Clark. *The Uses of the University.* Cambridge, Massachusetts: Harvard University Press, 1964.

Killian, Lewis M. *The Impossible Revolution.* New York: Random House, 1968.

King, Martin Luther, Jr. *Stride Toward Freedom.* New York: Harper & Row, 1958.

_____. *Where Do We Go From Here? Chaos or Community.* New York: Harper & Row, 1967.

_____. *Why We Can't Wait.* New York: Harper & Row, 1963.

Klein, Alexander. *Natural Enemies.* Philadelphia: Lippincott, 1969.

Kopind, Andrew, ed. *Thoughts of Young Radicals,* Washington, D.C.: The New Republic, 1966.

————, and James Ridgeway. *Decade of Crisis: America in the 1960s.* New York: World, 1972.

Kunen, James Simon. *The Strawberry Statement.* New York: Random House, 1968.

Lader, Lawrence. *Power on the Left: American Radical Movements Since 1946.* New York: W.W. Norton, 1979.

Lasch, Christopher. *The Agony of the American Left.* New York: Knopf, 1969.

————. *The New Radicalism in America.* New York: Knopf, 1965.

Lauter, Paul, and Florence Howe. *The Conspiracy of the Young.* Cleveland: World, 1970.

Leamer, Laurence. *The Paper Revolutionaries.* New York: Simon & Shuster, 1972.

Lens, Sidney. *Radicalism in America.* New York: Crowell, 1969.

Lerner, Michael P. *The New Socialist Revolution: An Introduction to Its Theory and Strategy.* New York: Dell, 1973.

Levine, Maryl, and John Naisbitt. *Right On!* New York: Bantam, 1970.

Levitan, Sar A., William B. Johnston, and Robert Taggart. *Still a Dream: The Changing Status of Blacks Since 1960.* Cambridge, Massachusetts: Harvard University Press, 1975.

Lincoln, C. Eric. *The Black Muslims in America.* Boston: Beacon, 1961.

Lipset, Seymour Martin, and Philip G. Altbach, eds. *Students in Revolt.* Boston: Houghton Mifflin, 1969.

Lipset, Seymour Martin, and Gerald M. Schaflander. *Passion and Politics: Student Activism in America.* Boston: Little, Brown, 1971.

Lipset, Seymour Martin, and Sheldon S. Wolin, eds. *The Berkeley Student Revolt: Facts and Interpretations.* New York : Doubleday, 1965.

————. *Student Politics.* New York: Basic Books, 1967.

Lothstein, Arthur, ed. *All We Are Saying: The Philosophy of the New Left*. New York: Capricorn, 1970.

Lowi, Theodore. *The End of Liberalism*. New York: W. W. Norton, 1970.

Luce, Phillip A. *The New Left*. New York: McKay, 1966.

_____. *Road to Revolution: Communist Guerrilla Warfare in the USA*. San Diego: Viewpoint Books, 1967.

Lukas, J. Anthony. *Don't Shoot—We Are Your Children!* New York: Random House, 1971.

Lynd, Alice, ed. *We Won't Go: Personal Accounts of War Objectors*. Boston: Beacon, 1968.

Lynd, Staughton, *Intellectual Origins of American Radicalism*. New York: Pantheon, 1968.

_____, and Tom Hayden. *The Other side*. New York: New American Library, 1966.

McCarthy, Eugene, *The Year of the people*. New York: Doubleday, 1969.

McEvoy, James, and Abraham Miller, eds. *Black Power and Student Rebellion*. Belmont, California: Wadsworth, 1969.

McNeill, Don. *Moving Through Here*. New York: Knopf, 1970.

Mailer, Norman. *The Armies of the Night*. New York: New American Library, 1968.

Mairowitz, David Zane. *The Radical Soap Opera*. London: *Wildwood House,* 1974.

Malcolm X. *The Autobiography of Malcolm X*. New York: Grove, 1965.

Marcuse, Herbert. *One Dimensional Man: Studies in the Ideology of Advanced Industrial Society*. Boston: Beacon, 1964.

Meier, August, and Elliott Rudwick. *CORE: A Study in the Civil Rights Movement*. New York: Oxford University Press, 1973.

Menashe, Louis, and Ronald Radosh, eds. *Teach-Ins: USA*. New York: Praeger, 1967.

Michener, James A. *Kent State: What Happened and Why.*
New York: Random House, 1971.

Miller, Michael V., and Susan Gilmore, eds. *Revolution at Berkeley.* New York: Dial, 1965.

Mills, C. Wright. *The Power Elite.* New York: Oxford, 1959.

Mitford, Jessica. *The Trial of Dr. Spock.* New York: Knopf, 1969.

Moynihan, Daniel P. *Maximum Feasible Misunderstanding.* New York: The Free Press, 1969.

Mungo, Raymond. *Mungobus.* New York: Discus Books, 1979.

Myerson, Michael. *These are the Good Old Days: Coming of Age as a Radical in America's Late, Late Years.* New York: Grossman, 1970.

Navasky, Victor, *Kennedy Justice.* New York: Atheneum, 1971.

Newfield, Jack. *A Prophetic Minority.* New York: New American Library, 1966.

————. *Robert Kennedy: A Memoir.* New York: Dutton, 1969.

Nobile, Philip. *The Con III Controversy: The Critics Look at the Greening of America.* New York: Dutton, 1969.

Obst, Lynda R., ed. *The Sixties.* New York: Rolling Stone Press, 1976.

Oglesby, Carl, ed. *The New Left Reader.* New York: Grove, 1969.

Oppenheimer, Martin, and George Lakey. *A Manual for Direct Action.* Chicago: Quadrangle, 1964.

Osanka, Franklin Mark, ed. *Modern Guerrilla Warfare.* Glencoe, Illinois: Free Press, 1962.

Osborne, John. *Look Back in Anger.* New York: Criterion, 1967.

Peterson, Richard E., and John A. Bilorusky. *May 1970: The Campus Aftermath of Cambodia and Kent State.* Berkeley: The Carnegie Commission on Higher Education, 1971.

Powell, William. *The Anarchist Cookbook.* New York: Lyle Stuart, 1971.

Powers, Thomas. *Diana: The Making of a Terrorist.* Boston: Houghton Mifflin, 1971.

———. *The War at Home: Viet Nam and the American People, 1964-1968.* New York: Grossman, 1973.

Powledge, Fred. *Black Power, White Resistance: Notes on the New Civil War.* New York: Simon & Schuster, 1971.

Rader, Dotson, *Definance: A Radical Review #1.* New York: Paperback Library, 1970.

———. *I Ain't Marchin' Anymore.* New York: McKay, 1969.

Rapoport, Roger, and Laurence J. Kirshbaum. *Is the Library Burning?* New York: Random House, 1969.

Reich, Charles. *The Greening of America.* New York: Random House, 1970.

———. *The Sorcerer of Bolinas Reef.* New York: Random House, 1976.

Rembar, Charles. *The End of Obscenity.* New York: Random House, 1968.

Report of the National Advisory Commission on Civil Disorders. New York: Bantam, 1968.

The Report of the President's Commission on Campus Unrest. New York: Arno Press, 1970.

Rights in Conflict: The Violent Confrontation of Demonstrators and Police in the Parks and Streets of Chicago During the Week of the Democratic National Convention (The Walker Report), New York: Bantam, 1968.

Roszak, Theodore. *The Making of a Counter Culure.* New York: Doubleday, 1969.

Royko, Mike. *Boss: Richard J. Daley of Chicago.* New York: Dutton, 1971.

Rubenstein, Richard E. *Rebels in Eden: Mass Political Violence in the United States.* Boston: Little, Brown, 1970.

Rubin, Jerry. *Do It! Scenarios of the Revolution.* New York: Ballantine, 1970.

————. *Growing (Up) at 37.* New York: Warner, 1976.

————. *We Are Everywhere.* New York: Harper & Row, 1971.

Sale, Kirkpatrick. *SDS.* New York: Random House, 1973.

Saunders, Doris E., ed. *The Day They Marched.* Chicago: Johnson, 1963.

Schlesinger, Arthur, Jr. *Crisis of Confidence: Ideas, Power and Violence. in America.* Boston: Houghton Mifflin, 1969.

————. *A Thousand Days.* Boston: Houghton Mifflin, 1965.

————. *Violence: America in the Sixties.* New York: Signet, 1968.

Schultz, John. *Motion Will Be Denied: A New Report on the Chicago Seven.* New York: Morrow, 1972.

Schwartz, Edward. *Will the Revolution Succeed? Rebirth of the Radical Democrat.* New York: Criterion, 1972.

Seale, Bobby. *Seize the Time: The Story of the Black Panther Party and Huey P. Newton.* New York: Random House, 1970.

Shulberg, Budd. *From the Ashes: Voices of Watts.* Cleveland: Meridian, 1969.

Skolnick, Jerome H. *The Politics of Protest.* New York: Simon & Schuster, 1969.

Sobel, Lester A., ed. *Civil Rights, 1960-1963.* New York: Facts on File, 1964.

Spender, Stephen. *The Year of the Young Rebels.* New York: Random House, 1969.

Stern, Susan. *With the Weathermen.* Garden City, New York: Doubleday, 1975.

Stevenson, Janet. *The Montgomery Bus Boycott.* New York: Watts, 1971.

Stone, I.F. *The Killings at Kent State.* New York: New York Review, 1971.

Strout, Cushing, and David I. Grossvogel, eds. *Divided We Stand: Reflections on the Crisis at Cornell.* New York: Doubleday, 1970.

Sutherland, Elizabeth. *Letters From Mississippi*. New York: McGraw-Hill, 1965.

Teodori, Massimo, ed. *The New Left: A Documentary History*. Indianapolis: Bobbs-Merrill, 1969.

Trilling, Diana. *We Must March, My Darlings*. New York: Harcourt, 1977.

Tytell, John. *Naked Angels: The Lives and Literature of the Beat Generation*. New York: McGraw-Hill, 1976.

Unger, Irwin. *The Movement: A History of the American New Left, 1959--1972*. New York: Dodd Mead, 1974.

Viorst, Milton. *Fire in the Streets: America in the 1960s*. New York: Simon & Schuster, 1979.

Von Hoffman, Nicholas. *We Are the People Our Parents Warned Us Against*. Chicago: Quadrangle, 1968.

Wagstaff, Thomas. *Black Power: The Radical Response to White America*. Beverly Hills: Glencoe Press, 1968.

Wallerstein, Immanuel, and Paul Starr, eds. *The University Crisis Reader,* 2 vols. New York: Random House, 1971.

Warren, Robert Penn. *Who Speaks for the Negro?* New York: Random House, 1965.

Waskow, Arthur I. *From Race Riot to Sit-In: 1919 and the 1960s*. Garden City, New York: Doubleday, 1966.

Weinstein, James, and David W. Eakins, eds. *For a New America: Essays in History and Politics From 'Studies on the Left' 1959-1967*. New York: Random House, 1970.

Westby, David L. *The Clouded Vision: The Student Movement in the United States in the 1960s*. Lewisberg, Pennsylvania: Bucknell University Press, 1976.

Westin, Alan F. *Freedom Now: The Civil Rights Movement in America*. New York: Basic Books, 1964.

White, Theodore H. *The Making of the President: 1960*. New York: Atheneum, 1961.

———. *The Making of the President: 1964*. New York: Atheneum, 1965.

———. *The Making of the President: 1968*. New York: Atheneum, 1969.

Wilhoit, Frances M. *The Politics of Massive Resistance.* New York: Braziller, 1973.

Wolfe, Tom. *Radical Chic and Mau-Mauing the Flak Catchers.* New York: Farrar Straus, 1970.

Wolin, Sheldon S., and John H. Schaar. *The Berkeley Rebellion and Beyond.* New York: New York Review, 1970.

Yablonsky, Lewis. *The Hippie Trip.* New York: Pegasus, 1968.

Zinn, Howard. *SNCC: The New Abolitionists.* Boston: Beacon, 1964.

INDEX

Student involvement in civil
rights movement, 108–111,
115, 126, 143, 173, 193
Student League for Industrial
Democracy (SLID), 90–91,
92
Student Non-Violent Co-
ordinating Committee
(SNCC),
  civil rights movement
  and, 62, 63, 64, 66, 94,
  99, 171–172, 373–374
  leaders of, 79
  role in black power
  movement of,
  149–150, 156,
  173–174, 178
  white support of, 95,
  109–111, 126, 173
*SNCC: The New Abolition-
ists* (Zinn), 174
Students for a Democratic
Society (SDS),
  confrontation tactics and
  amnesty demands of,
  282–295
  counterculture and,
  277–278
  decline of, 295–303
  early history of, 66,
  88–99, 267, 314
  ERAP, 108–111
  leaders of, 79
  Port Huron statement
  of, 99–104, 386

PL and, 278–282,
295–300
See also Weatherman
Studies on the Left, journal,
129, 139, 195–196, 311–313,
374–375, 385
Sweezy, Paul, 177

Taylor, James, 272
Teach-ins, antiwar, 211–215
Teller, Edward, 209
Teodori, Massimo, 245–246
Terrorism and violence,
  fear of, 185–186
  incidents of Brinks
  armored-truck
  robbery, 81, 365–366;
  freeing of Timothy
  Leary, 301;
  Greenwich Village
  townhouse explosion,
  301, 364;
  Soledad Brothers,
  353–355
  Weatherman policy of,
  80–81, 174–176, 178,
  179, 220–222, 254, 301
Theft and the counterculture,
234, 266–267
Thomas, J. Parnell, 23, 24, 25
Thomas, Norman, 89
Thoreau, Henry David, 210
Ticknor, Michael, 315
Time, magazine, 334, 356–357
Towles, Katherine, 119–120